Case Theory in Business and Management

Sara Miller McCune founded SAGE Publishing in 1965 to support the dissemination of usable knowledge and educate a global community. SAGE publishes more than 1000 journals and over 800 new books each year, spanning a wide range of subject areas. Our growing selection of library products includes archives, data, case studies and video. SAGE remains majority owned by our founder and after her lifetime will become owned by a charitable trust that secures the company's continued independence.

Los Angeles | London | New Delhi | Singapore | Washington DC | Melbourne

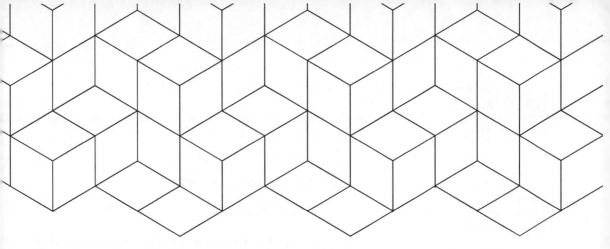

Evert Gummesson

Case Theory in Business and Management

Reinventing Case Study Research

Los Angeles | London | New Delhi
Singapore | Washington DC | Melbourne

Los Angeles | London | New Delhi
Singapore | Washington DC | Melbourne

SAGE Publications Ltd
1 Oliver's Yard
55 City Road
London EC1Y 1SP

SAGE Publications Inc.
2455 Teller Road
Thousand Oaks, California 91320

SAGE Publications India Pvt Ltd
B 1/I 1 Mohan Cooperative Industrial Area
Mathura Road
New Delhi 110 044

SAGE Publications Asia-Pacific Pte Ltd
3 Church Street
#10-04 Samsung Hub
Singapore 049483

Editor: Delia Martinez-Alfonso
Assistant editor: Lyndsay Aitken
Production editor: Sarah Cooke
Marketing manager: Alison Borg
Cover design: Shaun Mercier
Typeset by: C&M Digitals (P) Ltd, Chennai, India
Printed by CPI Group (UK) Ltd, Croydon, CR0 4YY

Library of Congress Control Number: 2016947048

British Library Cataloguing in Publication data

A catalogue record for this book is available from
the British Library

ISBN 978-1-44621-061-1
ISBN 978-1-44621-062-8 (pbk)

At SAGE we take sustainability seriously. Most of our products are printed in the UK using FSC papers and boards.
When we print overseas we ensure sustainable papers are used as measured by the PREPS grading system.
We undertake an annual audit to monitor our sustainability.

*To our granddaughters Sophie and Louise, born during
the writing of this book and who added a perspective
on how human beings learn and thus indirectly
helped me write this book.*

PRAISE FOR *CASE THEORY IN BUSINESS AND MANAGEMENT*

'I trust ... brilliant practitioners of market and management research who have based their cumulative theories as much on proprietary data as on published data ... I trust the management theories of Peter Drucker ... and the market theories of Evert Gummesson ... which are based on both kinds of data.'

Hans L. Zetterberg, Professor Emeritus in Sociology; former owner of Sifo AB, Sweden's leading institute for political polls and market and social research; past President of the World Association for Public Opinion Research. (Source: Zetterberg, 2013, p. 77).

'This meticulous book submits research and the research process to deep scrutiny. It debunks the unhelpful dichotomy between quantitative and qualitative research and highlights the great value of multi-method and interactive research, approaches that have greatly deepened our thinking. Evert Gummesson combines many decades of experience in research as both a renowned scholar and a reflective practitioner effectively bridging the divide of theory and practice. This is the best book on case theory and case study research in decades.'

Professor Adrian Payne, University of New South Wales, Australia and Professor Pennie Frow, University of Sydney, Australia.

'As theory informs practice, so can methodology advance both. More than ever, practitioners and researchers alike need better methodology for data-driven decision making. Gummesson's new book provides the roadmap and the springboard to reinvigorate our methodologies for the 21st century.'

Jim Spohrer, PhD (computer science and artificial intelligence), Director, Understanding Cognitive Systems, IBM, and one of the 100 Innovation Champions of IBM.

CONTENTS

LISTS OF BOXES, FIGURES AND TABLES

Boxes

Figures

Tables

ABOUT THE AUTHOR

Evert Gummesson is Emeritus Professor of the Stockholm Business School at Stockholm University, Sweden. He graduated from the Stockholm School of Economics and received his PhD from Stockholm University. In Finland he is Honorary Doctor of Hanken School of Economics and a fellow of the University of Tampere.

He has written or contributed to over 50 books and published numerous articles and reports – altogether around 400 publications. His earlier book by Sage, *Qualitative Methods in Management Research*, passed 4,500 citations in 2017. His articles have appeared in the *European Journal of Marketing, Journal of the Academy of Marketing Science, Journal of Service Research, Journal of Marketing Management, Service Industry Management* and many others. He is a present or former member of some 25 editorial boards for journals and publishers.

His research embraces service management, relationship marketing and networks and he takes particular interest in the theory of science and how research methodology is practised by academic researchers and consultants. He is a co-founder of the Service Research Center (CTF), Karlstad University, Sweden, and its first professor; the QUIS (Service Excellence Symposium) conference series; the International Colloquium of Relationship Marketing (ICRM); and the Naples Forum on Service. He is an elected fellow of the World Academy of Productivity Science and a former member of the Scientific Advisory Board of the Swedish Institute for Quality (SIQ).

Dr Gummesson has received awards from the American Marketing Association, and The Chartered Institute of Marketing, in the UK, has listed him as one of the 50 most important contributors to the development of marketing. He became the first recipient of the S-D Logic Award (established by Professors Robert Lusch and Stephen Vargo) for 'Pioneering and Continuing Achievement' and of the Grönroos Service Research Award, established by Hanken for 'excellent achievements in service research challenging common understanding and demonstrating significant originality'.

He is a frequent speaker around the world and has over 20 years of experience in business as a marketing manager and a senior consultant and director in one of the largest consultancies in Europe. His former clients include Ericsson, Mastercard, IBM, the Swedish Cooperative Union, Swedish Railroads, Swedish Telecom and the UN.

FOREWORD

By John Van Maanen, Erwin Schell Professor
of Organization Studies, MIT Sloan School of
Management, Cambridge, MA, USA

It is a distinct pleasure to write the Foreword for Evert Gummesson's timely new book spelling out and indeed celebrating the importance, charm, eloquence, beauty and learning potential of the well-done case study. It is a form of social research that is again on the upswing partly as a response to the turbulence and change that mark the 21st century. Yet, case studies, and their affinity for narrative, particularity, context and, yes, uncertainty and ambiguity that the writers of the best of them display, may make some readers nervous for their embrace of anti-foundational precepts and suspicion for all types of essentialism. This is a misunderstanding that *Case Theory in Business and Management* is out to correct.

Understanding cases first means being clear as to what we take them to be. As Professor Gummesson suggests, this can be a troublesome matter because definitions of case studies differ and sometimes differ spectacularly. What they represent and how such representations contribute to our learning is of central interest here. One generic but abbreviated definition holds that cases are simply investigations of some particular social setting with a focus on the events that occur in and over that time setting. The more strictly bounded yet broadly and comparatively located the setting, the closer the writer to the events that occur in that domain, the more detailed and linked the elements of the descriptive work, the higher the quality of the case.

Creating the high-quality case is however no easy matter. Most cases are not well done. A typical business school case, for instance, falls at the low end of the scale since it often rests on a flying visit of short duration by a case-writing team to a self-selected organization to interview a small smattering of managers as to their handling of a particular problematic matter. Most cases in business school libraries – and perhaps most cases of all sorts – are quickly forgotten and shelved as superficial if not fictive versions of events chronicled for no apparent reason. It is their ad hoc and careless character, their lack of analytic bite or interest, their want of an identifiable perspective, their failure to properly situate the case – by similarity or difference – in broader matters, their disguised character, their formulaic language and format that make them so intellectually vapid, dispensable and easy to satirize (e.g. 'Leaning back from his cluttered desk and rubbing his temples, Richard Preston, head of Acme's New Product Development department, closed his eyes and wondered what he had done to get himself in this mess').

Moving up in quality are the various sorts of case studies produced by business and management researchers – and some journalists as well – where the authors, by intention, seek to extend a reader's acquaintance with the particular setting the activities take place in. The aim and function of such work is basic: to familiarize readers with the complex cases of the world. This writing is rarely comparative or theoretical but it is precise, explicitly located, and takes readers where they have not been before. Such cases constitute travel over a field of study, and students of business and management who have never been in a military unit, a biological research lab, a police department, a Japanese assembly or a Swedish civil service agency have presumably missed something, such that whatever generalizations they are apt to make of organizational life will be based on too restricted a field. Cases that provide readers with a broader view of their respective areas of interest help prompt reflection and curb conceits.

But of most interest in this text are those case studies that are rich in detail, history, member perspectives, scholarly musings and set on solid temporal and spatial groundings. The writing displays apt analogies and comparative moorings with conclusions of a narrative sort not easily detachable or decontextualized from the story told. Whether it is the strange being made familiar or the familiar being made strange, new ways of seeing the world are put forth. These are cases that lead long lives and thus anchor the high end of the case study trade. And how such work is imagined and produced in the business and management milieu – along with the epistemic and methodological assumptions on which such work rests – is Professor Gummesson's overriding concern.

Just why case studies seem to have recaptured our attention these days requires commentary. I have 3 intertwined accounts in mind, all of which are fleshed out in far greater depth in the pages to follow. First, consider the sorry state of unifying theories. Across the social sciences, from psychology to economics, the very idea of discovering and validating highly general covering laws – akin to the laws of physics or chemistry – is slip-sliding away (and fast). Postmodernism (and all the post-toasty variants such as post-structuralism, post-positivism, post-Marxism, post-colonialism and so forth) has put grand narratives on the run. Modernism stresses coherence and order, postmodernism emphasizes competing perspectives, contests of meaning, contextual modifiers, and the always uncertain processes of signification. Increasingly, narrow paradigms are out and variation and difference are in. Thus, it will do us well to make sure the cases we do have are good ones, composed with patience and skill. Case studies of a careful and trustworthy sort in the business and management sphere must today treat theory with gentle hands and make few (and usually tentative) claims to generality. Conceptual imperialism is (justifiably) out of fashion these days, making Professor Gummesson's restraint and modesty quite appealing.

Second, fragmentation and disorder are more than a characterization of our scholarly worlds. They attach to contemporary life. We live everywhere in unsettled times. To wit, communication and transportation technologies cut into the social and cultural singularity of societies. Human migrations change the character of villages, cities, regions and nations. Multinational organizations cross borders with impunity, seeking new markets and remaking, sometimes obliterating, old ones. Global contrasts are omnipresent as people become increasingly aware of how things are done elsewhere. In changing times, previously unquestioned cultural understandings and traditions unravel. Stories conveyed by cases are therefore vital – perhaps all we have in an uncharted world.

Third, the promise of case studies probably rests in part on some old-fashioned pragmatism and a little preaching or beseeching. There are many good things to say for the practicality of case studies. The ease, comfort, relatively low cost and timeliness in which such studies can be conducted have much to recommend them in these times of rapid change, scarce resources and pinched research budgets. Case studies are typically small, flexible and nimble endeavours. To my mind, they are rather attractive counterparts to the elaborately designed, big budget, statistically governed and over-controlled studies where the findings are sometimes obsolete before they reach print. Equally important is that the case study remains something of a solo act and thus the work and results are filtered through 1 head rather than many and hired-hand problems are not a concern. A consistent point of view, a sense of moral and ethical responsibility that comes from personal identification and interest, and a set of craft-like norms are more likely to be in place and respected when a study is conducted by a single scholar.

All this is to say that I believe case studies are important, and perhaps more important than ever. The goals of this work are to expand our horizons, to reflect seriously and intimately on the events that surround us here, there and everywhere, and to increase the range of human possibilities for both thought and action. By learning how and sometimes why real people, in real places, at real time act as they do, these aims can be advanced. In short, the case for case theory – as argued, presented and illustrated by Evert Gummesson – is a compelling and formidable one.

PREFACE AND ACKNOWLEDGEMENTS

A privilege when writing about the methodology and philosophy of scientific research is that I can hobnob with the greatest of the past and of today. I have a daily dialogue with Albert Einstein, Winston Churchill, Aristotle and Leonardo da Vinci, just to mention a few, and of course with colleagues in my international network. I have been to conferences, universities and business firms all over the world and learnt good things and bad things. Meeting the people in person and making friends is a seminal part of my development as a scholar. When the Internet was introduced, the hype said that online contact would take over and physical meetings would be redundant. It was dead wrong. There have never been so many conferences as there are today! Networking is both high-touch physical interaction and high-tech computer-mediated contact. High tech or high touch, these meetings with you have all taught me something. I am not listing you here but many of you will find your publications in the references and citations. I thank you all!

Very early on, I was puzzled by science and research methodology. Sometimes it felt far beyond my comprehension but sometimes it felt shallow and in conflict with my experience and judgement. Working both in industry and academia, I soon lost my faith in surveys, except as a technique to be used in very special instances. Since then surveys have grown enormously in quantity and technical sophistication. They fit academic career plans. But my conclusion is that they contribute very little to scientific development. I lost interest in quantitative techniques and case study research especially became a priority. Glaser and Strauss, Patton, Van Maanen, Yin and many others put me on a new track. I wanted to expand on these sources and let my own experience from business, academic research and as a consumer and citizen come out. I did so in *Qualitative Methods in Management Research*, first written in 1983, then published in Swedish in 1985 and in English in 1990 by Sage. It has been revised and reprinted several times. After 30 years it is more cited than ever. When asked by Sage to make yet another revision, I found there was nothing I wanted to change.

John Van Maanen of MIT who had come out as an early supporter asked me to write a book on case study research. This inspired me and I started working on it in the 1990s. The book was postponed and postponed and postponed.

I wasn't ready and the time was not ripe. I now feel ready and consider the time ripe. But it has been a hard struggle. How I survived the hardships of those years travelling in Methodologyland I don't know. It is ever so impenetrable and wild as a jungle. The writing became a passion. It was felt in my whole body; it was more than an intellectual adventure and led to the discovery of case theory.

Special thanks to my editor Delia Alfonso. Without her kind and patient enthusiasm, this book would never have become reality. Many thanks also to Lyndsay Aitken, Alison Borg and Sarah Cooke.

Evert Gummesson
Djursholm, Sweden

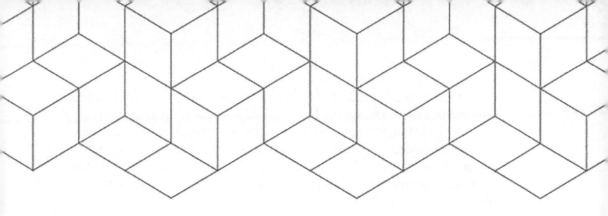

PART I

THINK RIGHT

We can only do useful research in business and management if we think right.

The philosophy and theory of science offer guidance.

This book started out as a methods book on case study research in business and management. During the long journey of writing, my conviction grew stronger and stronger that cases are much more powerful than their reputation says. It ended up with the discovery of *case theory*. Analogous to network theory, systems theory and grounded theory among others, 'theory' then includes both the methodology of doing research and the types of results that come out of it.

There are philosophical as well as technical and practical aspects of doing research, and we need them all. Most methodology in the social sciences is in practice technique-oriented, assuming that if we follow a set of prescribed steps the outcome is by default valid and useful. This is not so.

By convention and less by reflection, research is divided into *quantitative* and *qualitative*, and case study research is classified as qualitative. Quantitative research presents itself as royalty and treats qualitative research as the underdog. I consider the quantitative/qualitative divide misleading. Quantitative and qualitative are only 2 of many characteristics of a research approach and they do not earn the status of overriding categories. The increasingly used concept of *mixed methods research* allows each specific research project to draw on the most suitable and combined methodologies.

When academic texts are the object of a *critical review*, the reviewer is usually looking for faults and deficiencies. Please, *look for strengths and improvements* in the first place! This book keeps an *open code*, which means that constructive ideas on how to improve case theory and its applications are welcomed.

Part I introduces my perception of research and science. It is an effort to encourage you to THINK RIGHT. Although philosophy may sound impractical to many in business and management, its original meaning was 'love of wisdom'. It was the only discipline at university. Today's philosophy of science deals with the fundamental principles of acquiring knowledge and making our existence more liveable and meaningful. Part II is about transforming case theory into research practice. It is hands-on and technical: DO RIGHT.

> 'Nothing can stop the man with the right mental attitude from achieving his goal; nothing on earth can help the man with the wrong mental attitude.' (Thomas Jefferson, US president, 1801–1809)

1

FROM CASE STUDY RESEARCH
TO CASE THEORY

This chapter is an introduction to my efforts to give case study research a proper place in science, explaining how, when and where it can be used and doing away with misconceptions, condescending characterizations and sloppy applications. Above all, I stress its capacity to address business and management complexity, and offer better solutions to a particular problem as well as to develop better general theory for decision-making and action.

Science and research are about understanding the riddles of life. Even with the riddles unsolved, human beings have a genetic drive to survive and sometimes to develop themselves. For lack of complete knowledge, we 'muddle through' as best we can. One of the ways to muddle smarter is to apply scientific methodology.

My scientific credo has developed over many decades. An important milestone was my book *Qualitative Methods in Management Research*, first written in the early 1980s and then published and revised several times, the last time in 2000. It is my most cited publication. My credo is further reflected in several articles on methodology and theory from the 2000s.[1] This book is yet another stop on my journey through Methodologyland. It is also about how I experience today's research and education in business and management and what I would like to change. Going through methodology books and reflecting on my own research experience, I get the weird feeling that we are drowning in a whirlpool of methodologies, techniques and advice in our efforts to discover true knowledge and be accepted as 'scientific'.

For decades I have experienced quantitative research as being highly overrated and inefficient. Yet it is given priority in most business schools and journals. Qualitative research is equally underrated, not least case study research. In writing this book I found it urgent to explain how cases could be more

---

[1]Among them Gummesson 2001, 2002b, 2003, 2006, 2007.

productively used in research. Gradually I realized that the 2 taken-for-granted categories – quantitative and qualitative – are delusive. They are focused on language – numbers versus words – and the ritual of doing research, not on the results and their usefulness. That it took me so long to acquire this insight shows how indoctrinated I was and how naively I had accepted received categories.

Throughout the book I strive to be outspoken rather than opportunistic and diplomatic. I have long asked myself whether researchers and practitioners are addressing real and consequential issues or if they are creating a pseudo-reality. And are they using research methods that really help them understand today's business and management? This book is an effort to come closer to the real world.

The book is meant for all those doing research in business and management. A book is mass-produced but readers can customize it to fit their individual needs and interests; a book is also what the reader perceives it to be. You read it differently if you are an undergraduate student, a master's student or a PhD student, and faculty reads it from the perspective of researchers and educators. Those who do research for organizations – in-house researchers, external research institutes and management consultants – have more practical reasons for reading it. The business press and investigative reporters can have a plethora of drives and address wide audiences. And consumers of research – those who read scientific journal articles, research reports, business and management books, the business press and consultant reports – could learn to better assess what they are exposed to.

A goal was to write a book of 250 pages, thus making it reasonably accessible to the reader. To a degree it is possible to condense a message without reducing its actual content. This is also educational for the author: Do I express myself distinctly? Am I repeating myself or using too many words – academics swim in a verbal ocean! Or is it too brief to be clear? I managed to cut out 200 pages but the book still came out much bigger than planned – and I could not find a way to reduce it more!

You can read the book in several ways:

- The whole book, if it is part of a course and you have to take a test. It is commendable that you read the whole book anyway but time pressure often provides a hindrance.

- If you are impatient, read this chapter and then go to Part II where the theory and philosophy of Part I transcend into research practice. You can look up concepts and philosophy in the earlier chapters during your research if you feel it called for.

- As an encyclopaedia – the index is extensive so you can easily find an issue.

After you have read the book, you should be able to start doing case studies for research purposes. But it takes time to become a seasoned 'case chef' and the best way of learning is to start practising. You have to cook the food, serve it and let others taste it: 'The proof of the pudding is in the eating.' If I can get you on track, I have done my job. Then it is up to you. If you are lucky, you are also supported by mentors and colleagues.

We have already met the word *research* several times. But what is it? It is a systematic process of acquiring knowledge and learning about life and society. The word comes from the Latin *circare*, meaning to 'go about, wander', and it is related to both circle and circus. The original meaning goes very well with my perception of research as a never-ending and *iterative* process of search, re-search and re-search, meaning search, search again and again and again.

Science is another word that will appear frequently in the book. It originates from the Latin *scientia*, which meant knowledge in a generic sense but later became synonymous with the *natural sciences*. Even today many just say science when they mean natural sciences, especially physics, which leads to misunderstandings. It indicates that physics is superior to other types of science and that the social sciences and the humanities should imitate them. This issue will be brought up later. *Scientific research* is primarily associated with academic institutions but is also carried out by business firms and other organizations as well as by individuals. Scientific research should fulfil certain criteria but what these are is not necessarily evident.

A third word associated with research and science is *theory*. In a very general sense, theory strives to get fragments of knowledge together to see connections and patterns. In this way we can better overview the world and what we are doing.

What research, science and theory are and should be will be scrutinized throughout the book. The central theme of the book is how I consider that cases should be used in research. It is a condensation of my methodology-in-use and philosophical issues that have influenced me. The ambition is to take the case study beyond the current mainstream and to boost its scientific status.

Time and again I find that researchers hesitate to benefit from their everyday and personal experiences. Most writings on methodology make reference to iconic philosophers of science and designers of established research methods, techniques and strategies, but also to scientists and philosophers in vogue – yes, there is not only fashion in clothes but also in science. Although studies of what others have said and comparisons between them are essential, the goal here is not to discuss the differences between what Foucault said and how that agrees or disagrees with what Wittgenstein said. That is another discourse.

It is mandatory in academic publications to give ample *references*. With the swiftly growing number of publications, long rows of references increasingly interrupt the flow of the reading. I am more restrictive. Germane references are given in the text, in footnotes and in the reference list. For articles and books, it is redundant to load a text with sources that can easily be found in electronic databases and on Google and similar sites. Note, however, that Internet sources such as Wikipedia have to be double-checked to make sure the information is correct and up to date.[2] Complete references can be found at the end of the book followed by an index.

What Does 'Case' Mean?

In business and management disciplines, cases are used in different ways and for different purposes:

- *Case study research* is the traditional name of a methodology for studying the complexity of the 'real' world. It can include any issue which the researcher finds worth studying, for example the efficiency of an organization, the behaviour of financial markets or the success or failure of a merger. It can also be about a single consumer or citizen or a community of consumers and citizens. Case study research can lead to extensive descriptions but the real contribution appears when data is analysed and interpreted as the ground for conceptualization and theory generation, conclusions, reporting and practical application. *Case theory* is a broadened version of case study research and the topic of this book.

Cases are also used for other purposes – as:

- *Examples and illustrations* – to make abstract concepts, models and theories easier to grasp. By relating to everyday events such as shopping, it is easier to understand theories of consumer behaviour. Throughout this book there will be plenty of examples of applications of methods and excerpts from actual cases.

- *Practitioner cases* – presented by CEOs and others at conferences, in the media or in books to offer the audience accounts of how, for example, a company makes decisions, encourages innovation and plans for the future. This can be inspirational both to academics and practitioners. The presentations are often part of public relations and may be hyped and seductive; they are usually success stories, even 'feel-good anecdotes'. The cases are rarely about failures, although these should be equally interesting. Practitioner cases do not qualify as the sole source for research but can provide elements of useful input.

- *Educational tools* – Harvard Business School introduced cases in classrooms to give students with little or no business and management experience a taste of the real world. Students were asked to analyse cases, compare them to what theory said, comment on what happened in the cases and make recommendations. This use of cases is common in business and management training today. Such cases are often, but not always, based on research and have been edited for teaching rather than for scientific purposes. Topical cases reported in the media can also be used in classroom discussions.

---

[2]The evaluation of sources is treated in Chapter 9.

Cases are often dismissed by orthodox researchers as 'anecdotal evidence' and not generalizable. A case cannot be both anecdotal and evidence at the same time, so the expression is an oxymoron. Do not use it and if people do, demand that they explain what they mean – with scientific rigour of course and not just as convention, opinion and advocacy. A couple of times I have listened to former McKinsey consultant Tom Peters, co-author of *In Search of Excellence*,[3] the most widely sold business book ever. When he spoke he gave example after example after example: 'Thomas Watson of IBM said ... At Federal Express Fred Smith did ... The taxi driver from Kennedy Airport told me...'. He made his ideas come alive to the audience which is a feat in itself; it is communication and especially appealing to practitioners. But the people he referred to have expressed nothing about the scientific value of their ideas; they just related their practical experience. It is called *exampling* and is not meant as general evidence – you can probably find an example to support whatever absurd idea you have.[4] But examples can trigger thoughts for researchers and managers when they compare them with their own experience and needs.

The Discovery of Case Theory

Many authors make sincere efforts to give brief, yet complete definitions of case study research. They embark on mission impossible. The method has many characteristics that you will run into as you read this book. Yin's[5] definition is the best known but does not entirely coincide with my personal research experience and case theory. One reason for this could be that Yin's background is psychology in a wide sense, but the context of this book is business and management and to some extent economics. It is often claimed that research methodology is generally applicable, but my conclusion is that each methodology has both general and specific properties. Each application requires minor or major adaptation to the context.

Case theory here is an expanded version of case study research but it is hard to give a precise definition. Although we strive for precision in research, reality rarely allows it. In terms of modern mathematics, reality consists of *fuzzy sets*. This means that each definition, concept and category have a core that overlaps with other definitions and categories and the core gradually fades away. Unambiguously defined sets, *crisp sets*, are the exception. Accepting that cases

---

[3]Peters and Waterman, 1982.

[4]Glaser and Strauss, 1967, p. 5.

[5]Yin, 2014, pp. 16–17.

are fuzzy sets, I will not attempt to give a brief and distinct definition but instead start with a description followed by the basic purposes of case theory:

> Case theory is an overriding methodological approach to address both a particular case and to generalize to a broader area. Cases come in numerous forms and no one has found a universally valid classification. Cases allow us to address complexity by studying numerous factors and their links and interactions in dynamic contexts. Researchers are only restricted by their access to the focal issue, time and other resources, and the ability to keep it all together. Cases are extensively used in business and management research in Northern Europe and the majority of PhD and masters theses at its business schools are based on cases. In the USA, by contrast, they are not.

The basic purposes of case theory are *particularization* and *generalization*:

- *Particularization* is about the study of a single case with the main purpose of understanding a specific situation and sometimes recommending decisions and actions. The car manufacturer SAAB got into acute difficulties in 2011 after many years of fading profits. Efforts had been made by SAAB as part of daily operations to solve internal problems, find a stable financial base, develop its markets and customer relationships, and so on. If the situation is critical and management is aware of it, as was the case with SAAB – it could also be that management does not see the problem or hopes it will solve itself – the search continues for a strategic and long-term solution. The research questions could be: What is happening? What is causing our problem? What action should we take? What might the future be? The research attacks a problem that has to find a solution for SAAB and its network of stakeholders: employees, shareholders, retailers and others. It is, further, a worry for society in general and for governments that may be confronting unemployment and other social consequences if a company fails. Consultants are often hired to assist in such cases. Addressing a single case is *applied* research but it is also of interest to *basic* research; it is an opportunity to look into the reality of running a business or other organization. Increasingly, business schools offer consultancy as an income source and cooperate with companies and other organizations to develop solutions. This is also a way for academia to share research and theoretical knowledge with practitioners, and in return get close access to real-world events. Research funds sometimes stimulate such cooperation where, for example, a fund puts in half of the money and the organization the other half. In such instances, research results must be published and made available to anyone (perhaps with the exception of particularly sensitive information), whereas a report by a hired consulting firm is for the client's eyes only.

- *Generalization*: while a specific case is not directly meant to be generalized, it can offer *substantive theory* to be used in other cases of the same kind, but not beyond that. It can however be the start of a row of cases and generalization to *mid-range theory* expressed as checklists and models, and eventually to *grand theory*. This process is known as *theory generation*. It is both about *incremental improvements* of extant theory and the *discovery* of new theory. All this refers to new knowledge – *innovation* – which is currently at the centre of attention for business and management research. Theory generation is usually presented as the opposite of *theory testing* but case theory includes both, as will be shown later.

So we are talking about case theory as useful both for particularization and generalization, noting that the purposes form *both/and* categories; they should not be treated as opposites, i.e. *either/or*. Even if particular cases can have the original purpose of staying single, they may be compared to other cases and general lessons may be learned.

The methods literature recommends that you write *thick* and *rich descriptions* – *narratives* – of an organization, an event, a process, etc., free from analysis, interpretation and value judgements.[6] Note two things, though. First, a thick narrative becomes rich if the data has relevance for your research questions. Hence, thick and rich is not about a maximum but about an optimum or, in practice, about what we can accept as satisficing. Second, we cannot make an objective description even if we want to. Any description requires us to make choices about what to include and to decide what words, numbers, diagrams, etc., to use. Certain data can be noted as facts to remember in *field notes*, but researcher *memos* include the start of analysis and interpretation.

A case can include any issue which a researcher finds worth studying, for example the efficiency of an organization, the behaviour of financial markets or the success or failure of mergers. It can also be about single consumers or citizens or communities of them. The real scientific contribution of case theory is the *conceptualization* of cases as the ground for theory generation, conclusions, reporting and practical application. Furthermore, there should be a desire to learn from one study to another to understand the underlying, general dimensions of an issue. So a case account is not just any narrative and will later be referred to as a *scientific narrative*.

If you want to ground your conclusions properly, you need to study a phenomenon in depth. For example, the fierce competition between the major global players in the passenger aircraft market, Boeing (America) and Airbus (Europe), may be called a case but, more correctly, it is a network of cases, each big and complex in itself. For practical reasons, we have to limit a study but then, as Murray Gell-Mann, Nobel Prize winner in Physics in 1969, said: 'It is vitally important that we supplement our specialized studies with serious attempts to take a crude look at the whole.'[7]

Cases are usually classified as *single, multiple* or *embedded (nested)*. To me this is not important. A single case is often followed by more cases unless the purpose is limited to a particular case. Multiple cases can be anything from 2 to 100s or even 1,000s and there is no standard rule for the number; it is always contingent on what you are studying and why. In light of the *complexity*

---

[6]See also Czarniawska, 2004.

[7]When I refer to Nobel Prize winners, and I will on several occasions, you can find the source and extensive information at www.nobelprize.org.

paradigm and *network theory, systems theory, fuzzy set theory* and *chaos theory*, all cases are embedded. What else could cases be? Standalones with no connection to the rest of world? 'No man is an island, entire of itself', as the English poet, priest and lawyer John Donne wrote 400 years ago. A companion to complexity is *simplicity*. In business and management practice, quick decisions and actions are called for. A purpose in understanding the complexity and 'boiling it down' to its core, is to find well-grounded mid-range theory that offers checklists and rules-of-thumb.

Case study research can concern *ongoing processes* (the present), be *reconstructive* (the past) or be *predictive* (the future). The time dimensions are interlinked but all offer specific challenges and all are afflicted by uncertainty. Being part of an ongoing process is sometimes straightforward but often we cannot grasp its complexity. We may think we can find out what happened in the past but in the complex social settings of companies, governments and markets, it is difficult to sort out the essentials and get access to pertinent data. The past and the present connect with tomorrow and we start making predictions. Although there is a classic requirement that theory should have predictive capacity, predictions remain guesses unless there is a stable, repetitive pattern, such as the number of kids born in a year determining the need for schools some years later. If the future is affected by discontinuities, like the new infrastructure offered by the Internet, mobile communication and social media, there is no established pattern.

I was once asked to make a classification of cases as they are used in research. I thought it reasonable and tried – but failed. Why? The reason was simply that case theory can take so many forms. Literature, films and TV are filled with criminal cases, all the way from news reports and documentaries to various degrees of fiction. For example, since the 1990s over 100 cases of the UK TV series *Midsomer Murders* have been aired worldwide. Great detectives are researchers and we can learn from them.

In business and management, cases can be the study of a single company or other organization (see Box 9.3 on Enron); 2 organizations compared (Box 4.2 on Norwegian Oil and Swedish Methanol); a large number of cases compared in order to generate grand theory (Box 6.4 on Nordic School contributions to service management and IMP contributions to business-to-business, B2B, marketing and management); a product (Box 10.2 on the launching of Absolut Vodka); a sector (Box 7.3 on complex networks in healthcare); an event (Box 2.1 about the Nobel Prize in Economic Sciences); how retrospective action research including 100s of cases on shady business practices is used to generate grand theory on competitive markets (Box 9.7); the testing of a strategic planning model through management action research (Box 6.7); and people and the persona factor (Box 2.2).

Case theory is an overriding methodology within which numerous other methods and techniques can be hosted; it is a *mixed methods approach*.[8] You can, for example, use a statistical survey or time series analysis to acquire certain empirical input to a case. Furthermore, most of what is presented as sophisticated quantitative research is no more than a limited case. All methodologies and research techniques have strong and weak sides; there is no perfect way to understand reality. We therefore have to stay humble in our search for knowledge. When in this book I present and conceptualize my experience of research, the intention is not to push it on you. The ambition is to encourage researchers to address complexity and use an extended case methodology.

Let me first pose a basic question and explain why case study research needs to reinvent itself: *Is the quality of case study research in business and management disciplines higher today than 50 years ago?* The question can be divided into sub-questions:

- Has case study methodology improved through incremental polishing and/or quantum leaps?

- Has education in case study research improved?

- Have researchers and authors of scientific papers become more skilled in applying the methodology and have supervisors of term papers all the way to PhD theses become better coaches?

- Have editors of scientific journals, reviewers of journal articles, book scripts and conference papers, and members of examination, promotion, grants and certification committees adequate knowledge of case study research?

- Have those who design bibliometric indexes, rankings and impact factors adequate knowledge of case study research?

My general answer to all these questions is: No, not in any major way! There are more books and articles now but they mainly come from sociology, education, ethnography and psychology. There are only a few written by people from business and management and I have not found any in economics. As has been pointed out earlier, claiming that a methodology is valid in all contexts is overgeneralizing; certain customization is necessary.

The minds of the majority of the reigning academic power elite in the social sciences are formatted by an unconsummated love affair with *classic physics* and *positivism* or *empiricism*[9] from the Scientific Revolution 400 years ago; paraphrasing Freud it is referred to as 'physics envy'. Einstein presented his General

---

[8]See also comments on *triangulation* in Chapter 5.

[9]To avoid an overload of terms, I will consistently use positivism.

Theory of Relativity in 1915 and opened up a new type of physics – *modern physics*. It has largely gone unnoticed by social scientists. Before I proceed, it should be pointed out that there is also considerable opposition in the social sciences to the positivist paradigm, and alternatives have been launched.

An empirical study concluded that qualitative research was often assessed by the wrong criteria ('inappropriate procedural correctness') and inconsistent use of criteria.[10] It further disclosed that business school courses are biased in favour of quantitative approaches. Another indicator of inadequate knowledge and training is that Bent Flyvbjerg, Professor of Management at Oxford University, finds it called for to explain 5 misunderstandings about the basics of case study research.[11] Should not these misunderstandings have been cleared up long ago? In Chapter 12, you will find answers to be used when case theory is misunderstood or under fire.

My contention is that case study research has been floating around in pretty much the same water for several decades. Every single article or thesis I read or get to review, and where cases have been used, refers to Yin. He has written the most widespread book on the topic, first published in 1984 with a 5th revised edition in 2014. The number 1 article reference is Eisenhardt (1989) on the use of cases for theory generation.[12] The citations in 2016 were well over 100,000 for Yin's book and over 30,000 for Eisenhardt's article – and the citations keep growing.[13] This is hard to beat; any author who gets 1,000 citations for a book or an article can feel very pleased.

Their publications are in many ways excellent – but has nothing happened in the past few decades? One development is more texts on the intricate issue of analysing and interpreting qualitative data, together with advice on how to do so. There is also wider acceptance of using mixed methods. Computer software for qualitative data has kept developing and it helps to code, organize, retrieve and link data, and thus facilitate thinking, writing and the designing of diagrams. The software has become progressively more flexible, relieving you of the time-consuming paper-and-pencil job of sorting data – but it cannot take over analysis and interpretation.

I still get article scripts to review which refer to Yin's 1st edition from 1984 instead of his latest edition which includes new developments. A journal article or even a PhD thesis often just refers to Yin and Eisenhardt in general terms. It is sometimes obvious that the authors have read the publications poorly but

---

[10]Cassell, Symon, Buering & Johnson, 2006.

[11]You'll find them in Chapter 12. See Flyvbjerg, 2006; they are further elaborated on in Flyvbjerg, 2011.

[12]See also Eisenhardt & Graebner, 2007.

[13]According to the Publish or Perish evaluation (see www.harzing.com).

have been advised that they are 'must-use' references. Even in so-called top journals, a general and routine reference to Yin seems to be accepted without question. In this way, references are reduced to celebrity name-dropping, and efforts from others to improve the understanding of case study research go unnoticed. It shows that it is high time for educators, researchers and authors, thesis advisors, journal editors, reviewers, examiners and bibliometrics designers to study case theory.

Case theory is guided by the *complexity paradigm*, which acknowledges that businesses, governments, society and life in general are complex phenomena. Human properties, behaviour and interactive relationships play a central role. One of the axioms of the complexity paradigm is therefore the emphasis on *interactive research*. This means that close interaction between the researcher and the object of study, its data, the people involved, etc., is necessary. By understanding complexity and its interactive properties, it is possible to generate better theory and arrive at the *simplicity* needed in practical work:

> Out of intense complexities intense simplicities emerge. (One of the numerous quotes tagged to the speeches of Winston Churchill (1874–1965), the man who saved Europe in World War II, statesman, historian and Nobel Prize winner in Literature)

My knowledge concept includes two partially interdependent types: *explicit knowledge*, which can be communicated to others through words, numbers, graphs and software; and *tacit knowledge*, which cannot be openly communicated and is learnt though participation and practice. Tacit knowledge includes common sense, experience, intuition, insights, wisdom, instinct, hunches, gut feeling and more. It exists in scholarly and practitioner work as well as in our private lives and shows as *judgement calls*. Common sense and suchlike is rejected in mainstream science but is present whether you like it or not. It is true that common sense can be wrong – but so can explicit knowledge. Genuine knowledge grows from iterative and interactive procedures involving both explicit and tacit knowledge. As a researcher, you should be true to yourself and the world, trying to look at the world both from your outside – *extrospection* – and your inside – *introspection*. You need to be a *reflective researcher* and not just an administrator of research techniques.[14]

Theory in business and management needs to open up to practical application. The words *pragmatic* and *practical* have the same roots, both referring to getting things done. I use the concept *pragmatic wisdom* for what can be transformed into decisions, actions and results. In my view, this is the most developed

---

[14]Within the same spririt, Shah et al. (2012), introduce the 'Insight IQ' which represents an employee's ability to balance judgement and formal analysis.

form of knowledge. Pragmatism has its philosophical roots in facts as well as in intentions and ideals.[15] It is *pluralistic*, recognizing that the reality we face is varied and can be mastered in many ways. It is *instrumental* as it uses concepts, categories and models – theory in a wide sense – as guiding maps, or a GPS in the lingo of today's digital world.

The Reflective Researcher and the Great Philosophers

My knowledge of research in business and management disciplines is inferred from a wide range of roles: being an around-the-clock consumer in today's commerce-centric society; doing scholarly research and studying that of others; doing research for companies as a consultant; being a buyer of market research and advice from consultants; using research data as input to decisions and action; designing and implementing corporate strategy and business models; and having hands-on experience of how research enters management processes, often as part of internal politics rather than rational decision-making, planning, action and control of the outcome.

Each of us has the opportunity to discover important research areas in our daily lives. What may seem trifling details and useless knowledge may come alive when we challenge it. We live with it and have to take the consequences. Our experience and understanding of the shortage of unpolluted water and air, how human relationships and interaction work in commercial settings, or seeing our savings disappear into thin air after following our bank's 'expert advice' to buy an Icelandic Kaupthing fund, are real and only partially understood by science.

I used to envy colleagues who had studied classic philosophers like Aristotle, Socrates and Plato from the years 400–300 BC up to contemporary ones like Russell, Wittgenstein, Habermas, Foucault and Bourdieu. I felt an urge to do so too, but I would be dead before I get through half of them and in the process be so impressed and confused that I could not develop a single thought of my own. The way I bring up philosophy here is guided by its ability to facilitate our work as researchers in the applied field of management and business; it is pragmatic.

Western values are implanted in the business school culture. It is intellectual and verbal and very much controlled by the idea that the world is mechanistic and rational. But there are professors and business schools with a more philosophical and humanistic approach. Traditional Eastern philosophy is different by emphasizing that you can only understand through practice and experience and in interaction with those who have come further than you (the Masters).

---

[15]See also Fendt et al., 2008.

You then need to mature. There are exceptions and – especially in new areas such as the Internet where the Masters have no experience – young people can contribute and a few get world-renowned in no time.

The Chinese philosopher Confucius, who lived 2,500 years ago, said: 'I hear and I forget. I see and I remember. I do and I understand.' To understand case theory you have to do it. Another of Confucius' sayings is: 'By three methods we may learn wisdom: First, by reflection, which is noblest; second, by imitation, which is easiest; and third, by experience, which is the bitterest.' In modern times, American psychiatrist William Glasser (1965) refers to his work as 'reality therapy'. He claims that we learn 10% of what we read, 20% of what we hear, 30% of what we see, 50% of what we see and hear, 70% of what we discuss, 80% of what we experience, and 95% of what we teach others. This rings very true. It aligns with the idea that personal experience, interactive research and involvement are essential parts of science. But conventional research methodology is preoccupied with the low end of the scale: what we read, hear and see.

Science, knowledge development and innovation have a theoretical side but the importance of personal experience has not only been spelt out by Confucius and others but also in our time. Göran Schildt, a famed Finnish-Swedish author and philosopher, said that he 'only accepted such material that he could integrate with his living existence'.[16] Very few natural and social scientists admit that personal experiences are a source for their research. However, physics professor John Hagelin[17] says that learning must be experiential as well as intellectual and that we must reach 'direct experiential familiarity'; and in a recent book – *Our Mathematical Universe* – physicist Max Tegmark (2014) advocates that the world functions in accordance with mathematical logic but also says that he draws on his own experience as a scientist, father and citizen. This is commendable; all knowledge is related to our persona but strict positivist scientists pretend detachment and objectivity.

We can see that scientific development is not just an issue of the past few hundred years but dates back to ancient cultures. However, just as today's science, ancient science had its strengths and weaknesses. In all instances, it is a matter of weeding out the irrelevant and cultivating the relevant. Many times I have asked myself if my personal experience of research can add something to the impressive history of science. Or am I just conceited? Obviously I decided I could contribute, not least encouraged by Confucius' claim that gaining wisdom by experience is the bitterest.

In contrast to most of my colleagues in academia, I have been both a practitioner and a university professor. Very early on, I became preoccupied with

---

[16]Schildt, 1995, pp. 200–201.

[17]Hagelin, 1998, pp. 36–38.

the gap between what textbooks and research offered and my personal practical experience. When these did not match, who was to be trusted? I decided that I had to stay in the present and the future rather than in the past, to reflect and have a dialogue with others – but to trust myself more. That is how my research started out. To close the gap became my priority and after many decades it still is.

To avoid misunderstandings: we cannot experience everything ourselves so we also have to listen and read. I do consult the literature and get both inspired and discouraged; without it I could not do my own thing. I am also in continuous interaction with others through email, conferences and invitations to give seminars at universities, businesses and other organizations.

Note that whatever I say on methodology – or anyone else says – can be argued. All methodologies have strengths and weaknesses as our 'knowledge of knowledge' is incomplete and may be so forever. Karl Popper (1902–1994), Professor at the London School of Economics and one of the renowned philosophers of science, went far and once said that all we know is but 'a woven web of guesses'.

My contribution here is to explain how I think case theory can be reinvented and used more efficiently. I especially draw the attention to implicit, taken-for-granted paradigms and assumptions, and to mainstream research techniques that are accepted at face value. Their strengths are blown up and their weaknesses are stowed away. I want to offer a reasonable way of doing research that can lead to continuous and incremental improvements and, at times, also to major innovations. A lot of what I say can be found in other books and articles but a lot cannot.

This book offers both philosophical aspects and hands-on, technical advice. A dose of the philosophy of science is indispensible. If it is not there, the researcher becomes a *technician* instead of a *scholar*. Technicians are skilled at using one or two research techniques but lack the ability to see these in the broader context of outcome and usefulness. All too often they lack awareness of the paradigm and the limiting assumptions on which their techniques are founded and just follow the old saying, 'For he who has a hammer, every problem is a nail.' To expand the metaphor, an architect is needed to conceive the idea of the whole building, the plumbing system needs a specialist to design it, and it takes plumbers, carpenters, masons and other technically skilled people to erect the building.

To be successful in research and make a contribution to a single client or to theory generation and innovation, you must understand what is behind the techniques. Only then can you choose between the hammer, the screwdriver and the saw. You should also be familiar with the topic and the context you research. This is the reason why this book keeps referring to applications in business and management.

Ticket to Methodologyland

One can easily drown in principles and advice and find them difficult to apply. Reading and analysing published cases is a recommended way to learn how researchers have handled their confrontation with a complex and ambiguous reality.

There is no such thing as the perfect, complete case that you can just imitate. Cases are different because the reality they reflect is different. We want to learn something, either for a particular case or because it contributes to generalization and moves us closer to grand theory and better mid-range theory. When you read cases by others, do it in a constructive way and focus on their strengths. Avoid cliché comments like 'the purpose is not precise' (can a purpose ever be precise?) More likely it is adequate and guides the researcher reasonably well; avoid demanding more references, more theory, more empirical data, more advanced testing, and so on. Ask for more only if you are convinced it is reasonable and needed. We are always restricted to staying within our purpose and our resources.

Journal articles are important but as they are limited in size it is also wise to read masters and PhD theses and reports and books where a study can be more fully explained. There are also great books written by consultants and business-people. Genuine investigative journalists often go further than academic researchers and they usually write in a more engaging way. Be careful, however, and evaluate your sources and their credibility. Journalists today are also spin-doctors who work for lobbying and PR firms and their clients who want a certain message to reach out. Under the pretence of investigative reporting and documentaries, and hidden behind the profession or reporter, authors or filmmakers can spin any story they find called for.

Setting out to write this book, my motto was to improve case study research and make it better used by researchers in the academic world, in consulting firms and in organizations. I soon found that my text grew into more than that. It took me places where I had not been, although I had long experience of cases. How should I communicate my revelations? Finally, the book is here after a long, intellectually and emotionally demanding journey. My motto has changed and case study research became case theory, which is a general scientific approach that harbours multiple methods and techniques. Cases are underrated and underused in academia, misunderstood in most business schools, and by default seen as inferior to quantitative research, especially to surveys and hypothesis testing. But quantitative research is too crude and too restricted to address real-world complexity, and in business and management we are surrounded by complexity. Research should help us make decisions, implement them and achieve results. Implementation requires simplification and pragmatic wisdom.

I had partially lived under an *illusion* and the journey took me out of it; it became a *delusion* – which changed into a *vision* and a *passion*. This book is a ticket to a journey through my *Methodologyland*. It is a country of discovery, magic and surprises, just like Alice's *Wonderland*. It may be felt as a paradox that Lewis Carroll, who wrote *Alice's Adventures in Wonderland* in 1865 and *Through the Looking Glass* in 1872, was both a reverend, a lecturer in mathematics and a prolific author of learned mathematical treatises as well as of stories and nonsense poems. Obviously this pluralism in professions and activities did not conflict but were supportive. Perhaps the message is: be pragmatic and use all roads available to gain knowledge! Alice ventured out on a journey that did not follow any of the regulated paths of mainstream inquiry. She met with the unexpected, she asked the unexpected and the answers were unexpected. Alice was the Harry Potter of her day and she lives on. In today's business and management language, Alice and Harry were innovators and entrepreneurs, just like those who right now bring about new and unexpected uses of information technology (IT).

Part I will proceed by discussing the most commonly used terms and concepts in the social sciences and show that many of them represent mythology and rhetoric. In order to get something done in our private and work lives, we have to enrich our pragmatic wisdom.

By convention, case study research is classified as a qualitative method to be used as a crutch when you cannot put numbers on what you do and show them in tables, indexes and equations. Apart from anecdotal, it is referred to as exploratory, conceptual or pilot research, but also as journalism and story-telling. It is accused of lacking rigour and reliability and that the results cannot be generalized. It is simply second rate. Quantitative research, on the other hand, is presented as the epitome of great science. There is, of course, sloppy case study research but there is equally sloppy quantitative research.

Initially I mentioned that I consider that the quantitative/qualitative categorization should be abandoned. It only represents one of several ways of characterizing research; it does not qualify as overriding. It only leads to meaningless discussions and claims. Abandoning the divide is also necessary in order to challenge the megalomania that quantitative research exposes when it claims it can do everything through mathematical, statistical and computer-based models. As the quantitative language keeps promising what it cannot fulfil and claiming it is number 1, the crown of science and the gold standard, I have to argue against it. But books on qualitative and interpretive methodology seem to avoid challenging them, and quantitative researchers are reluctant to expose their weaknesses. It could be even worse; they do not realize the weaknesses and unwarily suppress them. I would like to hand over the burden of proof to them, to urge them to voluntarily try to define their proper role. If they do not, we should force them to, using whatever means we can conceive of.

2

THE BUSINESS AND MANAGEMENT CONTEXT

Research methodology in the social sciences is mostly presented as generally applicable. My experience is that even if a research method has a generally valid core it has to be adapted to each specific context in which it is applied. This chapter will therefore outline the properties of business and management contexts. Further, research is performed by people, which means that their persona affects the result.

University students usually have limited personal experience of business and management and this chapter therefore offers an account of its overriding characteristics. Even those with work experience may profit from it; practitioners are stressed by ongoing events and rarely have the time to reflect on what they are doing and why.

In a broad sense, business and management disciplines embrace suppliers which can be business firms, government organizations or non-government organizations (NGOs). Among the sub-disciplines are accounting, costing, finance, marketing, operations management, leadership, organization and human resource management. They also embrace the users which are households where the members are both citizens and consumers.[1] This is studied at universities, business schools, schools of management and institutes of technology.

It is important that the unique features are taken into account when a methodology is chosen for a specific study. If not, we risk methodologies taking over that are ill-suited to uncovering the essential properties of our object of study and risk the study being evaluated from the ability to use a certain research technique and not for the value of the outcome of the study. In the numerous books and articles on methodology, I can hardly find the basic conditions of business and

---

[1]Considering the large number of visitors and immigrants today who are not citizens, it would be more appropriate to talk about *residents*. To avoid too many terms, citizen will be used to include all residents and to stress the difference to the role of consumer.

management reality noted at all.[2] The literature on qualitative methods (where case study research is traditionally placed) refers to the social sciences in general. Although social science disciplines overlap – for example, in the study of organizational decision-making, consumer attitudes and employee motivation – there are also topics and perspectives that keep them apart. Some years ago I came across a PhD dissertation in sociology dealing with service and it had no mention of the extensive service research that had been done in business schools from the 1970s onwards, and that had produced thousands of publications. The sociologists were not aware of it because they did not search outside the boundaries of their discipline.

Institutional factors that characterize the object of the research have an influence on the choice of methodology and how data is accessed, generated and interpreted and how conclusions can be drawn and implemented. For example, the basic elements of statistical surveys – sampling, statistical processing, response rate, etc. – may be similar but applying them to voters' political preferences during an election campaign is different from applying them to customer satisfaction with cars or bank service.

Among the more obvious contextual influences are national and cultural dimensions. For example, many Northern European companies are more transparent than Chinese and US companies. This affects the information that can be generated in interviews with managers and employees as well as the access to documents.[3]

More than half a century ago, business and management disciplines began to distance themselves from economics. It was not noticed at first and even today conventional economists have not noticed it. The gap has grown and today you hardly ever find a reference to economists in a textbook on marketing or accounting and you never find references to business and management research in economics textbooks.

Theory in business and management disciplines is developing continually, not least because of the dynamics of markets. For example, the breakthrough of IT in the 1990s has changed communication, and the relaxing of planned economies in favour of deregulation and privatization has led to profound changes in the behaviour of organizations and households. We still have to learn to handle the new situation and traditional economics has shown little ability to address it.

The abundance of literature on methodology in the social sciences gives me an uncanny feeling of being exposed to Harry Potter-like witchcraft and wizardry beyond my intellectual comprehension. For example, I study a handbook on

---

[2]Three quite different books specifically approach case research in a business and management context: Woodside, 2010, Baker and Foy, 2012 and Saunders et al., 2012; and they all show differences and similarities to case theory.

[3]See Box 9.4 on interviewing in Chinese guanxies.

qualitative research (over 1,000 pages) and it is a goldmine in many respects. But gold does not come in pure form; it is embedded in rock and the trick is to extract the gold grains and occasional nuggets. Of the 59 authors of the handbook, 21 come from pedagogics, 17 from sociology, 10 from anthropology, 8 from communications and 3 from other areas. One chapter explains that economics, sociology and political science receive the bulk of social science research money and dominate social science publications.[4] However, economics and political science are not in the book, and psychology and business and management are marginally mentioned. In reviewing the Second International Congress of Qualitative Inquiry, Lee (2006) noted that out of about 200 sessions, only 1 was dedicated to qualitative research in management disciplines. He concludes that this is the qualtative researchers' own fault rather than unwillingness by the of the congresss hosts to accept presentations based on qualitative research. Flyvbjerg (2001) claims that every discipline that does not make systematic case research is ineffective.

The following sections elaborate on the distinctive features of today's business and management reality. They are my personal perception and interpretation based on my experience as a practitioner, a university professor, a consumer and a citizen. So feel free to add an additional or differing experience of your own. The chapter ends with human behaviour aspects referred to as persona and researchscapes.

Business Firms and Financial Organizations

Business firms are the key players in free (capitalist) economies as opposed to planned socialist economies where production and sales are part of government. Within its business mission, a firm must set up goals and generate a certain profit adequate to get the firm going, surviving and sometimes also growing. The revenue must be big enough to pay the daily costs and to allow investment in product and market development, new equipment and replacements. Costs must be under control, especially as businesses and markets are exposed to ups and downs. Businesses should live on what they produce and sell and on how well this adds value to owners, customers, employees and citizens. The trend of business and management being about maximizing profit and management bonuses is getting so pushy that it jeopardizes economies and societies.

In corporate strategy we used to talk about a *business mission* as the raison d'être of a firm. It should be what it says – a mission. That means a desire to do something that adds value to customers, citizens and others, and from that earn

---

[4]Greenwood & Levin, 2005, p. 53.

a living. There is reason to recall the philosophy of the great industrialist Henry Ford. He is remembered as the man who redesigned the car to fit the wallet of ordinary Americans. His focus was on how to solve this technically. He was proud of being in the automobile business; it was a lifestyle. To do so he introduced mass manufacturing and the assembly line, known as 'fordism'.

Ford's memoirs offer a wealth of wisdom, for example: 'greed blocks the delivery of true service' and a well-conducted business 'cannot fail to re-turn a profit, but profit must and inevitably will come as a re-ward for good service. It cannot be the basis – it must be the result of service.'[5]

In the professions, people were originally driven by a *calling*. Being a medical doctor or a lawyer was a calling to help others. The strongest driving force in healthcare today is not to cure patients but to make pharma companies rich; and the legal profession and chartered accountancy seem to have maximum fees as their 'mission'. The mission of creating a just society and stopping fraud and crime is upheld by a minority of true professionals.

In recent decades, investors, financial analysts and the media have become increasingly aggressive in demanding continuous growth of shareholder value. The short term has taken over and investment in long-term industrial projects has become difficult in the West; it is discouraged by the financial market. If the share price was a rational issue based on revenue minus cost, it would be easy. But it is largely psychological and influenced by expectations about the future, media hype, public relations campaigns, brand management, rumours and intentional manipulation by financial actors such as banks and brokers.

When companies start they are very much linked to the owner. Ford and Ericsson are examples where the family name remains even after they were listed on several stock exchanges. The modern corporation with limited liability (with Inc., Ltd or Pty after the name) and ownership and responsibility separated from a private economy made it possible to start companies with few or no funds of your own. In came the hired chief executive officer, the CEO, 'the professional manager', to run the company. Ordinary people could become small owners through stock exchanges but they do not know from day to day who has power over the company.

Gradually, ownership in the old sense has become rarer. A business is largely anonymously controlled by the price of its stock on exchanges and those who speculate in a stock going up or down. Since international deregulation, trade goes on 24/7. With computers and sophisticated algorithms, *high-frequency trade* has been introduced, characterized by short-term investment, high speed, high turnover, high volumes and high cancellation rates, thus creating a highly volatile market.

The business mission has got lost and faceless owners only look at the bottom line of their stock portfolio. But there are exceptions. Small, local companies often have family ownership and are known. Founders of major

---

[5]Ford, 1922/2008, pp. 10–11. See also Bejou (2011) on 'compassionate business'.

companies can become strong brands, for example Richard Branson (the airline Virgin Atlantic), Warren Buffet (the world's most successful investor) and Ingvar Kamprad (IKEA). Sometimes a hired CEO is turned into a celebrity to give a human face to a company, although he/she is not a dominating owner (e.g. Jack Welsh, General Electric).

In capitalist economies, the ideal market is described as 'free'.[6] The economic philosopher Adam Smith is best known for the concept of *the invisible hand*. It refers to the interaction between limitless numbers of suppliers and customers whose self-interest in getting the best deal sets a market price where supply and demand meet. This is explained in microeconomics but its assumptions are not viable today. Despite this, the free market idea with all its limitations, but supplemented by regulations, has worked better than the alternative – a socialistic economy planned and controlled by government. The economist Milton Friedman has been a passionate crusader for free markets. The economist Milton Friedman has been a passionate crusader for free markets and says that it is the only way to get people collaborate voluntarily. The world runs on self interest and therefore individual freedom has to be preserved. He does not claim this to be the most desired state but it does the least harm.[7]

Completely free and completely planned are extremes that in real life are no more than exceptions. The extremes do not represent real-world complexity. Markets are an amalgamation of free forces, plans, efforts to control, trickery to exploit ignorance, diversion from the important, practices, and so on. However, cherry-picking quotations can become misleading. If you really read Ford, Smith and Friedman, you will find that their knowledge was deeper than the popular quotations disclose.

In a free economy the idea is that businesses should be in competition. This increasingly stretches out on a global basis through the European Union (EU), the World Trade Organization (WTO) and other alliances. Competition is a self-regulatory mechanism that can counteract complacency and force companies to adapt to changed conditions and strive for improvements and innovation. There are also monopolies and there may be weak competition if the industry members are traditional and passive or markets have been divided between cartels. The increasingly fierce global competition, especially from Asia, has alerted US and European industries and is a driving force for Western economies. All industries, however, are regulated in certain aspects to curb the sale of dangerous and unhealthy products and other types of misconduct, but this is only partially successful.

---

[6]For a recent analysis of free markets and capitalism, see Kotler, 2015.

[7]See further Friedman & Friedman, 1980. Friedman has stated this in many debates and interviews, see Youtube.

As with anonymous ownership, the 'free' economy has run out of control and opened up for major scams referred to as 'creative bookkeeping' where complexity is used to conceal irregularities.[8]

There are countless *business models.* As consumers we are mostly in contact with retailing models when we go shopping, for example at a Tesco supermarket. Internet sales now dominate some retailing markets like Amazon for books. In franchising, an independent company may use an established firm's business model and get support from the franchisor, for example Hilton Hotels & Resorts. In air travel we find full-service airlines like Lufthansa and 'no-frills' airlines like Ryanair that compete on price in the first place. Every company's business model is unique in a major or minor way but it is not unique forever. It can become dysfunctional because of market changes or get disrupted by new technology and new systems solutions. The threat often comes gradually and it has turned out that, especially if the change is major, many established companies will have great difficulty in adapting to the new situation even if they are aware of the threat. Kodak, the leader in everything in photography, is an example; new electronics made their knowledge and products obsolete.

Financial organizations are brought up here as they exert so much power on the economy, both for good and bad reasons. The serious side of financial organizations is that they let people deposit money, save money and make cash transactions; lend money to people against an interest rate; offer insurance against damages, accidents and ill health; and offer retirement plans. Companies need to borrow money to expand or solve a temporary deficit or may need to deposit a surplus and get paid an interest but still have easy access to their money. Financial organizations also assist with mergers and acquisitions and introductions on stock exchanges.

Money is only a representation of value; it has no value in itself – it is just intended to facilitate transactions between sellers and buyers. First, humans were self-sufficient, eating what nature offered by picking berries, hunting and fishing. Then they started to cultivate land, grow vegetables and other plants and keep animals. The next step was to swap things with neighbours, for example getting potatoes in exchange for carrots.

An anomaly in the market economy is that 'money', once introduced to represent value and facilitate exchange, has become a product in itself. There is a 'money market', in more fancy language called the 'financial market', just like there are markets for rice, clothes and tattoos. Even more anomalous is the fact that those who trade money have power over customers and have figured out ways to mislead and milk them.

The original idea of finance has largely got lost. It is less supportive of actual value creation than it should be. Speculating to get rich quickly – filthy rich – without

---

[8]See the Enron case in Box 9.3.

working for it is probably part of human nature and the financial sector is exploiting it. *Financial instruments* have been introduced which are sold to consumers who have little ability to understand the risks. *Shadow banking* (banking outside a regulated system) has increased. There are financial institutions that embezzle people's savings by recommending investment in funds from which only the seller can make money while the buyer takes the whole risk. Especially in the USA but also in new market economies like Russia, the business firm's perception of its goal is simple: *the maximization of short-term profit and shareholder value*. It is odd that an individual is expected to be a responsible citizen, while a group of people – a business firm – is not.

The deregulation and globalization of financial markets have opened up the possibility for banks to risk the money of whole nations, its citizens and taxpayers. Iceland and the USA are recent examples. The financial crisis that started in 2008 and was still in bloom in 2016 would most likely not have occurred on such a grand scale if markets were regulated. On the other hand, deregulation may have made other financial markets more efficient. All this is little known to science and to get anywhere research has to address the complexity of economic life – which is the purpose of case theory and will be further explained in later chapters.

It is especially critical in financial firms where, for example, you buy savings funds for your retirement. Who manages your money and who owns the financial firms? The money may be in a tax haven and the biggest owner may be a Russian oligarch.

When this book was being written, an article, 'American capitalism's great crisis' by Rana Foroohar, appeared in *Time*. Foroohar has also written a bestselling book, *Makers and Takers: The rise of finance and the fall of American business*.[9] One of her findings is that *the financial sector takes 25% of all corporate profits but only represents 7% of the economy and 4% of all jobs!*

In summary: business is complex and consequently the research methodology-in-use must be able to handle that. Today, the methodological mainstream cannot.

Government Organizations and NGOs

National, regional and local governments – referred to as the government or public sector – are essentially non-commercial organizations. Non-government organizations (NGOs) are also primarily non-commercial but are operated on private or group initiatives.

---

[9]Foroohar's book (2016a) and article (2016b). See also Brown, 2007, 2013, and the Public Banking Institute, CA, USA.

Their goal is not profit but basic service to society and its citizens. Governments get their primary funding from taxpayers (citizens and companies); NGOs get it from governments and donors. But the commercial versus non-commercial categorization is seductively simplified, which shows the need to study the complexity of organizational structures and processes. The democratic system elects presidents and political parties to power for a period based on promises in political campaigns. It is easy to see how vulnerable and often dysfunctional this system is. While consumers in developed countries have many individual choices in competitive markets, democratic means either/or for everybody. For example, when there was a referendum in Norway about membership in the EU, 52% voted against. In Finland it was the other way around – 57% voted for. So Norway did not become a member but Finland did. After that, citizens and organizations have no choice but to comply. However, membership of the EU is not a crisp set; it is fuzzy and each membership therefore has to be treated as a specific case.

To increase the efficiency of public organizations, certain concepts have been taken over from the private sector. This is referred to as *new public management*. It was especially promoted by the UK Prime Minister Margaret Thatcher, who saw the necessity to get her nation more value-creating by being more competitive, more cost-effective, more service-minded and more citizen-oriented.

Decentralization, outsourcing and privatization were made possible through deregulation, a key strategy worldwide. Unfortunately, the strategy has often run amok. There is always a trade-off between regulations and the free market, and between what private business does best and what needs to be handled through government organizations, NGOs or the citizens individually. The mission of hospitals was once to help patients, of schools to educate young people, of lawyers to uphold justice and of universities to appoint professors who were free to do the research they found important and to be higher-level educators. Today, finance has expanded its influence over the health sector, research, education and legal matters. Most of the time of university professors goes to raising research money, managing departments and reporting their doings, to be 'evaluated' by politicians, bureaucrats, students, accountants and bibliometric systems. A high trust and high ethics society based on values has been replaced by a formal control society. The opposite to the new public management is equally detrimental, as we have seen from the live experiments with regulated, planned and tightly controlled societies such as the former Soviet Union and currently existing dictatorships.

The mission of the government sector was once primarily to keep people down and give unchallenged power to presidents and their governments. This is still so in many countries but progressively the government sector has become a service sector to render value to citizens. New public management challenged the efficiency of the public sector as a service and value-creating sector. It is still not in many ways, one reason being that too much influence comes from people trained at law school, who turn law into an internal parlour game without any sense of their service role.

NGOs are basically non-profit organizations. They are closely related to *cooperatives*, which are owned by the users. They are commercial but as the owners and the customers are the same people the surplus stays with them. The cooperative movement was highly successful in local retailing, housing, savings banks and mutual life insurance. As the physical proximity and close interaction between those involved was reduced, cooperatives lost their true content. Most of them have become like any other large business, but there is growing interest in re-establishing the originals. One example is Skandia Liv, a leading pension fund in Northern Europe, which, in 2014, was reconstructed from a commercial business into a mutual fund. The Internet, its social media and the focus on interactive relationships that are not dependent on physical proximity have also given birth to a new type of global customer community.

Traditionally NGOs have picked up the 'leftovers' from businesses and governments. Leftovers are not the same as insignificant; on the contrary, the issues may be highly urgent to solve but they are not rooted in official institutions. NGOs may grow and become institutions in themselves, like the Salvation Army and the Red Cross which were founded 150 years ago, the scout movement 100 years ago and the environmental and consumer interest groups that have emerged in recent years. Such issues are constantly being taken up through the initiatives of citizens but the lead time can be long; for example, equal rights for women have been on the agenda for more than a century. The causes are operated both by voluntary citizens and hired executives and employees. They can be commercial in some respects, but their mission is to serve citizens and the welfare of society in areas where business and government fail; it's not to make a profit. Political scientist Elinor Ostrom (a Nobel Prize winner in 2009) has studied *the commons* and how ordinary people take charge of local services that are not adequately handled. Examples are child and elder care, security in the streets, pure water supplies and garbage disposal. It is close to an NGO but it is less formal and can rather be described as a network of relationships between likeminded citizens who feel they have a responsibility.

Hybrid Organizations and Networks

In very rough terms, small and medium-sized companies (SMEs) constitute 95% of the number of companies in a country and account for half of business revenue and employment. The division of big companies and SMEs is reminiscent of the past, and big company and SME are unfortunately used in official statistics as overriding categories, thus distorting our image of what business firms are. They are networks which compete with networks. Statisticians should rethink this but they don't want to. It would force them to use new procedures – but would make their work more exciting and useful.

A business has a formal core. As a legal entity, it is expected to follow laws concerning accounting, taxation, etc., but *operationally* a company is far from well defined. Percy Barnevik, former chairman of the electrical giant ABB with 200,000 employees, described his company as a network of 5,000 small enterprises of local and domestic character. To that we can add part-owned companies, alliances with competitors and customers, joint ventures with governments and other forms of resource integration and collaboration.

In reality, our economies consist of numerous hybrid organizations that are embedded in vast networks. It is necessary to recognize this complexity. Today, it is often difficult to discern which organization is commercial and which is not. In some countries, the national government controls major industries; an example is the North Sea oil operations in Norway. In Japan, business and government are highly intertwined, not least through personal and social networks. The USA claims that it is a free market economy but government contracts on building and construction, war equipment and other products are also offered on political grounds to support industries which, in return, employ more people and give election campaign contributions. Government agencies also start their own incorporated subsidiaries. These fall under the laws of business enterprises which, apart from working for their parent company, may compete on the open market. So government gets involved in commercial activity. Work that was once performed by in-house units is increasingly outsourced to private companies. Deregulation and privatization have led to companies taking over hospitals, schools, local transportation, water supplies, part of the military defence and other basic services that in many countries are seen as a citizen's right. For example, the NGO 'Ashoka: Innovator for the Public' combines social entrepreneurship with business thinking and collaboration with business firms in developing innovative solutions to social problems.

The discussion shows that categories like business, government, NGO, supplier and customer are too simplistic to function as platforms for research. The specific conditions of each case must be considered. The categories are fuzzy and thus overlapping, leading to ungrounded generalizations. If categories are too loosely defined with high intra-variation, they do not serve as tools to understand reality. Not only are apples mixed with pears, but also with raspberries, potatoes and what have you. This simplicity is damaging to the validity of research.[10]

---

[10]Categorization is further discussed in Chapter 5.

Households: Organizations of Citizens and Consumers

The organizations mentioned so far are conventionally categorized as suppliers while households are categorized as consumers. A household can consist of a single person but often includes mother, father and children, and in some cultures several generations. They are the smallest organizational units but they are powerful as there are so many of them. Simply put: households are half of an economy as you cannot supply more than is consumed.

Customer orientation is held up as a key strategy in competitive markets. You have to understand customer needs and wants, how to establish relationships with customers and how to retain them. Although basic, the customer-in-focus strategy is not well understood by many businesses, who often treat customers with inertia, rigidity and insensitivity. To improve their operations, companies both observe and discuss with customers. Some firms are sensitive to signals in the market while others are not. Companies also engage in formal marketing research but the value of the information is highly dependent on the choice of research method. The most popular techniques to try and learn about customers are satisfaction surveys, personal interviews and focus groups. They may offer data that can be transformed into decisions and action but only after reflection and interpretation.

The taken-for-granted categorization of suppliers and customers used in mainstream research does not reflect reality. A more realistic alternative is offered by Service-Dominant (S-D) Logic, where all stakeholders are co-creators of value and resource integrators.[11]

Both consumers and organizations have to look in their purse and see what they can afford or buy on credit. The business mission of IKEA was to make furniture cheap and available for ordinary consumers. Consumers take over part of the work by travelling to IKEA stores, collecting the furniture in flat packages from the shelves, carrying heavy objects to their car, getting them into the car and driving home. Then they carry and assemble the pieces, and finally get rid of the packaging material. As the cost of transportation and assembly is high, the price can be kept substantially low in this way. The customer becomes a co-creator of value. IKEA also sells office furniture and small firms especially constitute an important customer segment.

We should note that businesses, governments and NGOs are not only suppliers but major customers as well; they constitute the *B2B* market. They need to buy to be able to produce. Further, *customer-to-customer interaction* (C2C)

---

[11]See Lusch & Vargo, 2014; Gummesson, Kuusela & Närvänen, 2014; and Box 6.5 on S-D logic in theory generation.

has become an increasingly important concept in business. It has always been around, sometimes as *word-of-mouth* (WOM) where customers inform each other about what to buy and what to avoid. C2C is broader and has gained further ground through the Internet with social media and online consumer communities.

Ethics, Crime and Corruption[12]

Ethics is rarely one of the heavy subjects at business schools. Crime and corruption are not on the curriculum at all, despite the fact that they are omnipresent and rapidly growing. By not actively opposing this unfortunate development we support it; once established it is difficult to get rid of. It is a sad fact but there is crime and corruption in any market and any organization. They should have a place in business and management research and education. They do not disappear just because we pretend they do not exist.

The official US definition of organized crime embraces (1) the illegal monopolization of markets and business deals; (2) the use of planned corruption; and (3) the use of threat, force and violence. Today, advanced organized crime is operated like a business and is often extremely efficient. Its top 'executives' do not look like crooks; they may have graduated from the best business schools. Criminal organizations act as both competitors and collaborators within market networks, trying to control network nodes, links and hubs.

Crime is global but largely invisible. It includes drug trafficking, the illegal weapons trade, prostitution, extortion, etc., and one of its latest 'products' is immigration to the EU. In my country, Sweden, the politicians and most of the inhabitants do not understand it. Mafia organizations organize travel, teach their 'customers' how to exploit social security in Sweden and that the police and other authorities do not have the knowledge or capacity to be a threat. The immigrants and their families are mafia customers, yes, because the mafia charges high fees to get them going.

Laundered money increasingly ends up as 'white' when crime syndicates buy stock in legitimate companies, mostly without the companies knowing who the buyers are. As their financial muscle is strong, these crime syndicates can exert considerable influence. According to our research, crime is the fastest growing economic sector. Four major changes in market conditions are unintentionally stimulating the growth of crime: the Internet and mobile communication, the EU, the high-speed economy and the global financial crisis. Crime offers new opportunities as regulations and institutions lag behind, not just for months but

---

[12]This section is mainly based on Bagelius & Gummesson, 2013.

for years and decades. In this time of unemployment, organized crime has 'scouts' looking for young people on the streets who display suitable talent, and offering them jobs and social belonging.

If shop and restaurant owners are forced to pay a percentage of their income for 'protection' or to buy pirate copies from organized crime, the market and competition become dysfunctional. Bribes and kickbacks are common in the building and construction business. If the buyer is a government organization this is particularly grave. The cost is raised for consumers and taxpayers and quality is reduced.

Unfortunately, we have taken a step back to the time when robber barons ruled. Today, there are huge corporations as well as small businesses and banks that run a cowboy economy. The extreme focus on profit has given birth to the concepts of *corporate social responsibility (CSR)* and *corporate citizen*. In practice, this is too often ignored or handled by public relations departments through white-washing and green-washing of corporate activities, often decorated with charity. There are seriously meant exceptions though. Warren Buffet, the long-term investor who has gone against Wall Street's short-term speculation and become one of the world's richest men, considers it his mission to support society and be a good citizen. He uses his power to encourage others to follow suit.

There has always been crime and the police, courts and other law enforcement institutions are assigned to hold it back. These institutions have an impossible task today when it comes to truly organized crime. People have gained their image of organized crime from TV and film where crime is thrilling and romanticized by celebrity actors and elevated to culture and art status, for example *The Godfather* trilogy of films and *The Sopranos* TV series. However, TV and film are sometimes far ahead of business schools in explaining how business reality works.

Corruption exists in government sectors and is a necessary condition for organized crime. It is often invisible to the public and to those who work in an organization and if people suspect foul play they get frightened. *Whistleblowers*, those who report irregularities, too often get in trouble. It may give rise to the idea that a nation is free from corruption, a naive conclusion. Organized crime cannot exist without the support of people in key positions in national, regional and local governments, as well as politicians and specialists like lawyers, bankers, accountants, brokers and medical doctors. It needs loyal 'friends' in the legal system. It leads to a widespread but covert corruption.

When presenting our research on crime, we have sometimes got comments from academics that this has nothing to do with business and management; it is handled by the legal profession and criminologists. We object to these reactions. Crime does not seek publicity and takes measures to cover up its activities. Its actual size is not known – there is a 'dark number' – but estimates are continuously made. One of our efforts to bring together the data of economic crime landed at an estimate of US$2–3 trillion (1 trillion corresponds to 1,000,000 million) for 2012. It equals the GDP of France (US$2.8 trillion) or the collected GDPs of Greece, the Netherlands, New Zealand, Spain and Switzerland.

The ugly face of organized crime has been accounted for by many serious authors. Among the most noted in the past few years is Roberto Saviano's[13] books based on in situ observations of organized crime environments from childhood and his dedicated and reflecting research. It has its price; he is on the death list and cannot stay alive without high security. When I interviewed him, he was accompanied by heavily armed police officers.

From a large number of cases, sociologist Paul Blumberg (1989) concludes that competition in the market economy has a built-in weakness: it forces companies to cheat to be able to survive. Based on his personal experience, Perkins (2004) explains how governments use 'economic hit men' to force other countries to cooperate. A hit man is a killer-for-hire but the economic hit man does not use physical force. For example, he/she offers governments seemingly favourable loans to build roads and other infrastructure which after some years are found to be debt traps.

Corporate crime is committed by a company or other organization by its owners, management and others in control for the benefit of the company or organization. Occupational crime occurs when people misuse the trust of the employer to acquire personal gains. Recent cases of corporate and occupational crime are Elf-Aquitaine (France, oil), Enron (USA, energy), Parmalat (Italy, food), Systembolaget (Sweden, alcoholic beverages) and Yukos (Russia, oil). In 2013 the largest bank in the USA, JP Morgan Chase, was fined $13 billion because of its subprime loans for housing that were a major cause of the 2008 global financial crisis. Wrongdoings can go on for a long time without being detected. A question in a business paper about Enron's profitability triggered the disclosure process. Warnings had already come from business partners and a whistleblower inside Enron but these were ignored. A warning from Bank of America revealed the irregularities in Parmalat.

Although there are criminology and emerging institutions to detect and punish organized crime, they have very limited resources. Organized crime is quick to act, can be extremely efficient and immediately punishes disobedience.[14]

---

[13]Saviano, 2006, 2015. See also *Gomorrah*, a movie based on his first book and a recent TV series with the same title. They show the ugly reality of organized crime.

[14]For further information, follow the financial press and read books by judges and others who have seen crime and corruption from the inside. *Transparency International* is an NGO that watches over corruption and takes measures. However, I find their rankings partially superficial, not observing the more subtle ways of corruption.

Economic Sciences

This section broadens the business and management context to the *economic sciences*. These embrace several disciplines but economics is still perceived by most people as the leading discipline. Economists dominate the public debate and dominate as advisors to governments and political parties. Professors of business and management are less visible. Many think that economists represent the core of the economic sciences and can answer all types of questions where economic issues are involved. They seem to think that themselves. The Nobel Committee thinks so. But it is not true.

Economics has its core in overriding macro issues and is by no means a unified science. In the 19th century it was named 'the dismal science' by the historian Thomas Carlyle, as opposed to the skill of writing poetry which was named the 'gay science' ('gay' then still meant 'merry' in a general sense). In my perception, macroeconomics addresses one of the most complex issues of social life. It has to deal with a series of 'dismal' issues: inflation, depression, poverty, taxation, unemployment, financial crisis, etc. It has got stuck in fragmented theory and old mathematics but should learn from modern physics, the humanities, case theory, action research and the many business and management disciplines.

Business and management now form the largest and fastest growing area not only in the economic sciences but in all the social sciences. On a worldwide basis, business and management as a whole is at least 10 times as big as economics. Other economic sciences include economic history and economic elements in law, sociology, psychology, political science and statistics.

The word 'economy' originally stood for 'household management' and 'thrift'. It was about how to survive on scarce resources and make the best of what we have. Economic philosophers, who were not economists in today's sense, took an interest in the wealth of nations, the world market price of rice, the role of manufacturing versus services, and a number of other topics, both conceptually and as practical issues. For example, Anders Berch (1711–1774), the first Professor of Economics in Sweden, did a longitudinal study of how to design the most efficient plough. At that time, agriculture was the dominating economic sector. He not only tried different solutions in theoretical terms but he had the ploughs made and literally did field tests of their functionality.

In books on economics, there is ample reference to people who have developed philosophies and practical ways of controlling economic issues. Economics was first a part of social philosophy and developed into macro- and microeconomics. Although called *microeconomics* it rarely went deeper than 'industry' or 'sector'. It did not deal with the real micro issues, such as the behaviour of people inside an organization, the role of leadership, how consumers behave in markets, etc. This micro-micro behaviour, which should constitute the substantive data and input to the micro and macro levels, was neglected. Microeconomics became *pure theory* and if the value of a single variable was changed, the *ceteris paribus* principle was applied, meaning that all other variables were kept constant. But a complex context like the economy never stays the same. Microeconomics is also called *price theory* which is what it really is.

For decades a large number of economists and others have tried to infuse realism into microeconomics and the pure theory has become a heavily *patched theory*. *Managerial economics*, based on microeconomics, was an antecedent to business and management. It was an effort to apply economic theory to decision-making in organizations, but not to how decisions were implemented and led to results. Then it became *the theory of the firm, the behavioural theory of the firm* and, today, *behavioural economics*. Microeconomics hangs on to outdated roots and is stuck in the positivist paradigm which puts quantification – the numbers language – in the centre, instead of the issue as such. If an existing theory is continually amended, it loses its uniqueness. Still, scientists are reluctant to abandon such theory.

One of the many who have tried to turn microeconomics into viable theory is Ronald Coase. He introduced *transactions costs* and *social costs* in two short articles, one from 1937 and one from 1960.[15] Although he won the Nobel Prize in Economic Sciences in 1991, clearly displays pragmatic wisdom and is heavily cited, his impact on management and business seems low. In 'developing' behavioural economics, economists seek help from psychology without knowing that their 'discoveries' have long been found in the marketing literature, even in undergraduate textbooks. Despite this, behavioural economics is heavily promoted as an innovation. In 2012 the prominent marketing professor Philip Kotler sent me the following email:

> The irony is that the marketing field has been doing behavioural economics for 100 years without calling it behavioral economics. We discovered that producers, middlemen and consumers make decisions that are influenced by a mix of rational and emotional factors and have spelled out how the economy and competition work on this basis. Ever since marketing has become customer-oriented and introduced segmentation theory, the field has been delivering behavioral economics in every way but in name. The economists would do well to acknowledge marketing as the core economic activity of all institutions in adapting to a changing marketplace and as actually altering the marketplace through its strong branding and innovation activities.[16]

---

[15]For a synthesis and overview, see Coase & Wang, 2011. It is also a reflection on whether microeconomics can be applied to the growing Asian economies, especially China, and the conclusion is in line with the complexity paradigm: it has to be treated inductively and the theory has to grow from the real world and not be deductively forced into received Western economics.

[16]See also Kotler 2016.

Box 2.1 on the Noble Prize in Economic Sciences provides a case supporting this quote. I also checked some of the most common economics textbooks from the 1960s and up to 2016 and the concept of marketing is not even mentioned. It shows how far apart even seemingly close disciplines are and that the much acclaimed interdisciplinary research is difficult to implement.[17]

Box 2.1   The 2010 Nobel Prize in Economic Sciences

Same procedure as last year: the Prize was again given to economists although it is a Prize in Economic Sciences. In 2010 it was shared between 3 professors of economics 'for their analyses of markets with search frictions'. Being educated in microeconomics, where price regulates everything automatically towards an equilibrium and buyers and sellers find each other instantly, they 'discovered' – in the 1970s – that there were frictions and search costs in the market.

I sat in at their official prize lectures in Stockholm. One of the laureates began by answering the question 'What are search frictions?':

> Perhaps the best way to answer the 'what' question is by example. Two years ago my wife and I decided that it was time to move from our home of 35 years to a more comfortable and convenient condo. The apartment had to be relatively large and on one floor, with a view of Lake Michigan. With these features in mind, we consulted several agents to generate a list of possibilities. We then spent considerable time searching for the right one, at least one which could meet our needs and fit our budget. Finally, a year ago we bought the apartment, which has since been remodelled. So, now we need to sell the house. How do we find a buyer willing to pay the price we are asking? All of the time and effort spent by both sides of such a transaction represents search and matching frictions.

This has been taught in business schools for ages and has always been a daily reality for practitioners: How do sellers find customers and how do customers find sellers? It is treated in any textbook on marketing, sales and purchasing. As the earlier quote said, marketing theory and education have been concerned with this for 100 years.

Friction and search in markets is what marketing is about. Unfortunately, this was unknown to the Nobel Committee which in 2010 reinvents the wheel by awarding the 'inventors' with the Nobel Prize for their 'discovery'. If you are critical you could say that the awarded 'discovery of search frictions in markets' is unashamed plagiarism. But the truth is more likely ignorance stained by an arrogant attitude towards business and management disciplines as not being scientific. Microeconomics claims it is science despite the fact that it only defines an exception and cannot

(Continued)

---

[17]The Nobel Prize as a potential quality model for scientific research in business and management is further discussed in Chapter 11.

be generalized. But it is rigorous and mathematical – 'pure theory' – meaning that it has taken out most of the disturbing complexity of reality in order to make it fit the language of mathematics.

A benevolent conclusion is that the laureates have applied their 'discovery' to the labour market and its specific context. Based on empirical data – I suspect it is mainly macro statistics and not case study research and other 'softer' data – they have designed a model for politicians and governments to use for labour policy planning and activities that reduce labour market frictions. I have not evaluated their model in the labour policy application and its predictive and planning qualities. If the model works in practice I do not know. But that is not what they got it for, according to the Prize motivation. The Prize could certainly not be justified by discovering a general dimension of markets that has been lived by practitioners for 1,000s of years and has been in the core of marketing practice and research for ages and can be read about in any undergraduate textbook on marketing.

I felt frustrated and left the lecture.

It so happened that I wrote this section on 10 December 2015, the very day the 2015 laureates received their Prizes. The one for Economic Sciences went to Scot Angus Deaton 'for his analysis of consumption, poverty, and welfare'. He found that the macro picture of consumers was too simplistic as based on traditional microeconomic assumptions. Instead, it was necessary to have empirical data on the actual behaviour of consumers. From that he built a new theory of consumers. I have not had time to investigate his work in depth but after some checks I find that although he has written in *The Journal of Consumer Behavior*, the leading journal in the field, he does not seem to be noted in the comprehensive research on consumers emanating from marketing, nor to have any references to it. And I do not find him in textbooks on consumer behaviour. I suspect that he collected his data primarily from surveys, panels and statistics, and not cases. Deaton has taken a step forward but it shows the big gap between several researchers, depending on what discipline they belong to and the way their researchscape encapsulates them, thus keeping down the productivity of science.

Persona Factors and Researchscapes

So far we have dealt with the conceptual and institutional features of business and management in impersonal terms. But this is not enough if we want to understand how knowledge emerges and is used. A business strategy is selected and implemented by people whose personalities and idiosyncrasies affect its content and outcome. It's the same in academic research. After having completed my PhD in 1977, I made the following note: 'Doing scientific research is 50% intellectual and 50% social.'

The persona of a researcher can be anything from too modest to be noticed to megalomaniac. In that sense scientists are no different from other people. The best-known professors are not necessarily the best contributors to knowledge enhancement. If you think you have made a contribution you have to market it and make it visible or it will not get noticed. Some go for the big speaker's fees and get hailed and highly ranked. I meet all of these types in academic research.

The term *persona factor* will be used for *individual* personalities and their behaviour but also includes the context in which a person functions, the *group persona* of an organization with its atmosphere, culture and values. A term from psychology is *group think* which is a nicer term for 'gang mentality'. Vedic philosophy talks about *collective consciousness* which is different from *individual consciousness*. If the collective consciousness is not mature enough to receive new knowledge – such as when it was proposed that the earth is round and not flat – the individual risks being harassed. *System* is another concept. We live in political and social systems which we cannot change as individuals, at least not in the short run, and to do it over a longer period we must be strong, smart, daring and persistent. We know as individuals that something is not right but if we don't comply we get punished. It is a sensitive issue in research; it's even taboo. On a political level, people eventually start revolutions against dictatorships and we get informed about them through the news every day.

There are numerous theories and guidelines about leadership; someone found over 1,500! Cases of successful leaders are presented in the business press and some such leaders are held up as role models. But leadership is contextual. One type of leader may fit an entrepreneurial growth stage, another a consolidation stage. We can learn from quantum physics that you can't know, measure or use anything unless you address it within its context. At one stage a skilled engineer may be needed, at another stage a skilled marketer, and in a third stage a financial wizard. A leader may not find a working chemistry with one organization while in another he/she fits in beautifully. Innovative and entrepreneurial leaders constantly have to go against the mainstream which raises stress and there is no wonder that many of them are difficult to work with; they are often unpleasant and offensive. Some employees can work constructively with them but many cannot.

These were examples to show that everything occurs in a context, in a specific environment and under specific circumstances. A general concept like strategy cannot be understood unless you know in what context the strategy is designed and meant to work. It is dangerous to reduce academic research to knowledge that is strictly conceptual and methodological – 'scientific' – and to overgeneralize it. We can't disregard the specifics of the situation at hand, which becomes blatantly obvious when we go to the next step: implementation of knowledge.

In *Absolut: Biography of a bottle*, Carl Hamilton (2000) tells the story of the launch of the brand Absolut Vodka (Box 2.2). His interest in people and relationships, to a large extent, explains why certain ideas emerged, why certain decisions were taken and how implementation took place. The persona factor adds to complexity but also to the validity and relevance of research.

Box 2.2 Absolut Persona

When the Swedish advertising wizard Gunnar Broman arrived at Madison Avenue, New York, to negotiate with a potential US partner agency for the launch of Absolut Vodka, he was first introduced to the people in the meeting room (Hamilton, 2000, p. 20):

> Broman burst into hearty laughter. He laughed with joy. He laughed his way through the creative process.
>
> – I come from the land of the thirsty, he solemnly declared.
>
> And then he laughed and the Americans laughed, too. It always started with the laugh. Broman laughed, and soon everybody was laughing together. The laughter meant that they were picking up the message.

I have worked with Broman. When I read this I said to myself: This is Gunnar in a nutshell. That's the way he was. The author also characterizes other people, not always in flattering terms but most likely correctly. For example, when Lars Lindmark, an impatient, high-ranking civil servant who was appointed Director General of the Swedish Liquor Monopoly, arrived at his new office his reaction is described as follows (p. 84):

> Lindmark could not believe it. It was as stuffy as an English gentlemen's club ... He threw the three directors off the board. He just didn't like them. The administrative director was mean, the technical director hostile, and he thought the financial director was just plain stupid.

This may be perceived as fiction, but it isn't. Not unexpectedly the Liquor Monopoly did not like the description. Was the author too open? Had he embarrassed people? If he had withheld unpleasant information in the consideration of people, would the case still have validity? Is he unethical? He praises some of the actors in the case for their talents but he also shows their weaknesses and idiosyncrasies. It is an effort to be frank both about the good and the bad. This is the way life is, we all know that.

At the time the book was published, Hamilton was a PhD student and faculty member of the Stockholm School of Economics. The Liquor Monopoly complained to the president of the school and the author was expelled. This may not be encouraging for an academic in his/her career but it is a risk you take if you go beyond convention. For your consolation, Hamilton has been doing very well since his dismissal.

The excerpts from the Absolut case concern the persona of a business setting as studied by an academic researcher. The persona factor is also a driver of how research is done and what comes out of it. Many researchers are true scholars dedicated to science and if they are lucky they meet likeminded colleagues and form a productive group persona. I refer to the group persona of a research environment as the *researchscape*. The Latin word persona originally meant 'mask', a role that a person is expected to play which may be different from the way he/she really is. In business we don't talk about a mask but of image and brand, which refer to how you are perceived by others. If you comply with the values and behaviour of the group persona, you become a *persona grata*, an acceptable person; if you deviate you can become an outlaw, a *persona non grata*.

But behind a scientific front, real life offers a spectrum of human virtues and frailties. Academic intrigues and the bullying of colleagues are as alive today as they have always been; ask anyone who has been through a university career. The demand on scholars to advance science creates an atmosphere of competition and some of those who are less successful get stuck in frustrated behaviour. Strong commitment to a cause can give rise to conflict which could be a constructive driver but can also become a destructive blockage to progress. Having worked both in business and academia, I know that a dark side of the persona can exist everywhere, but I have found it more frequently in academic institutions. This was the reason why I stayed in both business and academia and for a long time rejected offers for a full chair.

Although an intellectual achievement is closely knit to the persona of the researcher, one must never evaluate a contribution based on the perceived persona image, but on the knowledge-enhancing content. For a researcher to become known it is rarely enough to make useful contributions; it is also necessary to build a scientific persona brand. There is an old saying that 'a good product sells itself' but it is not as simple as that. In science and research it works the same way as the branding of soda drinks and perfumes. If a researchscape is prestigious, its brand spills over to the individual researcher, and a single professor with a high profile lends fame to the whole researchscape.

I am amazed to see how much some researchscapes put into defending and promoting their research even when it is outdated. They consciously do not cite the new, they repeat their old references forever and they sometimes seem to do this in alliance with journal editors, even those of top journals. These people have lost their scholarly mind but they may very well uphold an image of being scholars.

It is always important not to confuse an intellectual achievement with the person behind it. Einstein is probably the premier brand in science; he is even a household name although few of us understand his theory of relativity. Business and management also have their premier brands. The problem with a brand image is that sometimes it is true and corresponds to the content, sometimes the brand is high but the content is low and sometimes the brand is low but the content is high. A 'top university' or 'top journal' should of course mean top in content but that is not necessarily so. Brands are marketed and reputations sometimes earned at one time, but the content may since have deteriorated though the image is retained. This creates a dilemma for the serious scholar: to get known and get a message and discovery spread, he/she may have to make a compromise between profiting from the image and still sticking to the content – but it is easy to start to believe in one's image and lose sight of the true content.

Researchers are taught to be critical of whatever new thing they encounter. By many researchers, and sometimes reflecting the general spirit in research-scapes, this is perceived as judging everything new negatively, with the purpose of faultfinding. It fosters *destructive criticism*, finding joy in killing off every-thing that deviates from the mainstream, even being sarcastic and arrogant. You can frequently see this in anonymous reviews where the critic does not have to face the 'accused'. It's risk-free and non-committing. Criticism can be a blow to the one exposed to it, even if it is unjustified, because it can lead to a loss of motivation and a constant feeling of inferiority. True scholarly criticism is *constructive* and directed at encouraging the 'victim' to make improvements. It then works as an impetus.

Despite the 'calling' to devote their life to knowledge development, educa-tion and high ethical standards, scientists are probably no more or less moral and dedicated than any other human beings. They, too, are affected by the 7 deadly sins and the counteracting 7 virtues (in brackets): hubris/overbearing pride (humility), envy (satisfaction), wrath (patience), indifference/laziness (diligence), greed (generosity), gluttony (abstinence) and lust (chastity). We can apply the both/and rather than either/or mode to each of these 'opposites' and recognize that it is the tension between them that makes life vibrate. For example, a dash of greed is necessary to make a profit but coupled with generosity it gives balance to life, and too much humility can be just as counterproductive as too much pride.

Accepting that the alleged objectivity of scientific research is influenced by the persona factor widens the understanding of the reality of science. Methods books promote the *scientific man*, the ideal scientist and scholar who is solely dedicated to science. In economics there is the archetype of the *economic man* and in management the *administrative man*, both representing absolute rationality. These extremes exist but they are rare and may even stand out as human parodies.

To understand how research works in practice and the influence of the per-sona factor, we can benefit from a branch of research called *the sociology of science*.[18] Its topic is the behaviour of scientists in real life and how this behaviour

---

[18]See Merton, 1979.

may affect the productivity and quality of research. It is rarely mentioned in methodology books.

Improving established theory is one of the tasks of science. It is too often misunderstood and you can become accused of hubris and disrespect. It is therefore extremely important to distinguish between the person and the value of that person's theory. If an idea is found to be wrong or invalid, it does not by default imply disrespect for its originator or those who use it. They may have done a great job and provided a platform for future researchers. 'A diamond is forever' has been voted the most successful advertising slogan of the past 100 years but few theories are diamonds; most have a short life unless they are coupled to a heart–lung machine.

Great engineers, great doctors, great chefs and great fashion designers have *passion*. So do great researchers, be they in business and management, cosmology or mathematics. Sadly enough most academics are mainstream followers, doing and saying the 'right' thing, using the 'right' research techniques and publishing in the 'right' journals. Although innovation is the buzzword of the 2000s, they don't challenge the establishment for the risk of being called unscientific and blow their chances of promotion. They play along and become *bureaucratic researchers* – but we need *entrepreneurial researchers* who are the true scholars.

Aristotle talked about *ethos, pathos* and *logos* as the qualities of excellent argumentation. Logos – logical study – is rational and taught to researchers. Ethos – being ethical and credible – is more problematic; the ethics of science is less understood. Finally, pathos – being passionate – is rare. You don't find passion in the methods literature but you can find it in biographies, novels and movies. I have only found one book written by scholars that relates passion to research: *Passionate Sociology*.[19] They say that scientific knowledge is presented as 'a product of the mind rather than the heart, body or soul ... [a] desire to rise above the partiality of the knower's embodied form, preferring to experience the world as a set of fixed and external objects', and continue: 'Despite the common use of the term "reflexive", sociology normally refuses to analyse its own practices sociologically. It is happier to view itself in terms of the history of ideas.' But just like business and management, sociology is concerned with everyday practices. And how can a discipline describe and interpret life and reality when it steps out of life and reality?

They further say that 'Sociology, history and anthropology have all been traditionally motivated by horror of disorder ... Although analyses promising a complete order are often prized, they are a megalomaniac's fantasy ... It is not that the former have *found* a complete or objective point of view, it is that they hide their ignorance and the specificity of their knowing.'

---

[19]Game & Metcalf, 1996; quotations from pp. 4, 38, 85 and 86.

We seem to be possessed by finding security in a world that is inherently insecure and look for:

> enlightened knowledge that explains (away) wonder, that demystifies the dark space of myth, that replaces emotion with intellect ... [but] ... Scientific rigour cannot offer direct access to the real or eliminate the distance between self and other, but it can help us understand how we create what we feel we know.

The more I have experienced the academic and research world, the more the persona factor and the culture of researchscapes have stood out in influencing the scientific aspects. I see how journals and conferences are besieged by certain cliques. Their agenda is to defend the past and their own contributions. Elaborate diplomatic tricks are used to avoid confrontation and infiltrate and dilute the new discoveries. There is little confrontation in articles – silence is the most used weapon. You simply avoid citing someone. I don't know how many times I have heard completely meaningless presentations at conferences but not said anything. Why not? Mainly because the presenters may not be able to take it and may start defending themselves; you do not want to confront the presenter in front of an audience and you risk getting hostility back from others.

Journals and books set up priority research lists based on several co-authors and citations from others; sometimes others have also been interviewed. But if you know the field you can see how biased it can be. I am not sure the editor-in-chief always understands what he/she is doing. A rather recent trick is to say that 'we are one global community'. We are not – if we want to advance research. We are *networks of numerous* communities and today we can more easily build our own global networks. New discoveries rarely pop up in organized groups. They come from individuals or a few close buddies who gradually gather a core group and a critical mass around them. It is not democratic; it can't be decided by voting among peers.

> Be still when you have nothing to say; when genuine passion moves you, say what you've got to say, and say it hot. (D.H. Lawrence (1985–1930), novelist, best known as the author of *Lady Chatterley's Lover*)

3

THE COMPLEXITY PARADIGM

Case theory is an effort to better address the complexity of business and management and the need to transform research and theory into simplicity, thus facilitating decision-making and action and reaching meaningful results. Case theory rests on the complexity paradigm; it is the paradigm-in-use.

A paradigm consists of *axioms (postulates, absolutes, basic assumptions)* which are chosen to constitute a firm ground on which a piece of research can rest. For example, free competition and free enterprise form the foundation of most Western markets; in socialist states the foundation is central government planning. The two paradigms lead to different types of research.

But it is a concocted ground; its firmness includes objective and factual elements as well as values and intentions, all turned into axioms. This often remains implicit, one reason being that the researchers lack awareness as they have been gradually socialized into a certain way of thinking through education or professional work. So the basic tenets of a paradigm are *absolutes by appointment*. In periods of *normal science*, every thought and activity is derived from the reigning paradigm, *the mainstream*. A paradigm can be challenged and this opens up for a *paradigm shift*.

A paradigm also connects with the persona factor as it must be represented by someone or it does not exist; each of us is a *2-legged paradigm*. The mainstream persona is a *centipede paradigm*; all feet are joined together and march in the same direction and all stop when told to do so – like a military parade.

In order to advance science, the awareness and choice of paradigm are critical. Thomas Kuhn, who launched the paradigm concept, has shown how paradigms control the minds and acts of scientists.[1] Popper has pointed out that we take so much for granted in research, and according to mathematician and philosopher Kurt Gödel (1906–1978) the axioms we use in our paradigm cannot

---

[1]Kuhn, 1962/1970.

be objectively proven. Kuhn's idea grew out of the natural sciences but the paradigm concept is universal, although it has to be adapted to the context in which it is used.

There is a true story about Ingemar Stenmark, the winner of more international competitions than any other alpine skier in history. In the finals of a World Cup, he beat the no. 2 by a few hundredths of a second. Reporters pushed microphones in his face and asked: 'Ingemar, how do you feel?' Exhausted from the run, how could he verbalize the flood of emotions and thoughts that criss-crossed his mind? He is a man of action and results but of few words. He was quiet for a minute and then said: 'That you can't explain for those who don't understand anything.'

Understanding is a keyword in the complexity paradigm. It is the outcome of successful research and tacit knowledge. It is preceded by *preunderstanding*, a concept with close affinity to paradigm but less general and more persona and situation specific.[2] It includes the researchers' knowledge of methods, the type of problem they select for study, intellectual and social skills, attitudes, emotions and professional as well as private experience. It is your personal starting capital in research. Paradigm, axiom, postulates, absolutes, assumption, understanding, preunderstanding, and even more, are closely related fuzzy sets.

Paradigms and preunderstanding work as a *basis* or a *bias*. Combined with an open mind and sensitivity, they form the basis for better and quicker under-standing. Combined with rigidity and prejudice, they work as a bias; you believe your theories and methods are superior and your perception is so selective that nothing novel can enter. The insecure and rigid researcher will use preunder-standing as a limiting force, while the secure and reflective researcher will respond to anomalies and conflicting evidence with curiosity and excitement.

Understanding and preunderstanding can develop via one's *own research and experience – access at first hand* – or via *intermediaries – access at second hand, third hand, etc*. The further the distance from an actual research object or event, the higher the risk of misunderstanding, insensitivity and premature generalization. This creates a major hurdle when governments use politicians, social scientists and lawyers to investigate a problem and come up with policies and legislation. They easily overgeneralize and are inconsiderate of variety and diversity. This leads to conflict and dissatisfaction in society. Many of the laws, regulations and procedures that officials force on people are thought-pieces from the armchair with insufficient rooting in actual life.

When we use certain research approaches continuously, we take them for granted and consider them forever valid. We cease to reconsider our paradigm and its relevance as a scientific foundation. Our methodology – techniques for data generation, analyses, interpretations, terms, concepts and categories, and

---

[2]Understanding and preunderstanding are discussed in Gummesson, 2000a

mid-range and grand theories – has taken much sweat to master and becomes the *truth-in-use*. We can get inspiration and support from the researchscape to which we belong, but we also risk getting victimized and retaining repositories of insulated theories that live their own lives outside of the business and management reality.

The Mainstream and Paradigm Shifts

There are many reasons to reconsider the reigning paradigm, the mainstream. In business and management we have met with *discontinuities* and *quantum leaps*, such as when the engine replaced manual work and when we moved from an agricultural to an industrial society. Some of the social sciences offer similar concepts, among them *transformative learning, perspective transformation* and *critical realism*. To keep down the many concepts and terms, I will stick to paradigm shift for major changes. Innovation is *the* buzzword of today, presented as the saviour of our economies. Innovation can be incremental and evolutionary or revolutionary and cause paradigm shifts. Both types can offer true development and improvements – but often they just offer something different without any actual progress.

Kuhn says that a new paradigm is there when it has been accepted by the mainstream. In my disciplines I see two stages: an *initial paradigm* which is only understood by a single person or a minority of innovators and their closest followers; and the *established paradigm*, when it has become mainstream.

The best-known paradigm shift in science is probably when we went from perceiving the earth as flat and the centre of the universe to it being round and one of a myriad of planets. The idea of a spherical earth officially dates back to ancient Greece and the 6th century BC. But we do not really know; it could have been there much, much earlier. It was only at the end of the Middle Ages, about 400 years ago, that it became generally accepted. So the shift was in progress for at least a millennium! In the 17th century, the reigning paradigm based on Aristotle's philosophy and Christian theology was replaced by what has become known as the *Classic Scientific Revolution*. Among the prominent scientists from that time are Bacon, Copernicus, Descartes, Galileo, Lavoisier and Newton.

The new period was focused on the natural sciences and characterized by *reductionism* and a *rationalistic* and *mechanistic* view of the world. Experiences that could be quantified and measured were in the centre, while emotions, quality, ethics, values, consciousness and soul went down the drain. Life became a physical machine. It was postulated that complex phenomena could be broken down into small parts. The parts were studied and the results added and from that the whole would spring out. Mechanical physics became the paradigm of science. It still underpins many areas of the economic sciences.

People used to be harassed, jailed and hanged for new ideas. In the free part of the world today, scientists who propose a paradigm shift may very well be socially harassed, jailed and hanged by being blocked from research funds and promotions and seeing their article scripts rejected. So the vast majority of researchers keep silent out of fear of losing their job and income. By introducing *bibliometrics* (*scientometrics, altmetrics*) as quality indicators on an international scale and the basis for promotion and funding, these new restrictions have become institutionalized and are politically and bureaucratically controlled.[3] Even if a group of pioneers is strong and persistent, major breakthroughs can be delayed for decades or may never be implemented even if they are viable. Paradigmatic tenets are too little analysed and discussed in business and management. This is a shortcoming of the majority of today's researchscapes and a loss for science and society.

A new paradigm can retain elements of the old but the paradigm as a unified entity is different from its predecessor. When later I talk about designing grand theory based on a new paradigm, I do not mean that there is necessarily just a single paradigm and theory that can be of use; its viability depends on the context and the situation. The usefulness of parallel paradigms has been noted in business studies.[4] In physics, Stephen Hawking, Professor at the University of Cambridge, UK, and described as the most brilliant British scientist of his generation, says that there may be several paradigms within which the universe can be understood.[5]

A puzzling observation is that many researchers remain with one foot in the old paradigm while they put one foot in the new. This is an oxymoron. You cannot say that the earth is flat but maybe a little rounded and that it is the centre of the universe but perhaps not entirely. Paradigms are also contextually dependent. We look for a flat space to build our house on because our individual 'universe' is the immediate environment and we can disregard the fact that the earth is round and travelling in space. Many paradigms also co-exist during transition periods because of inertia and old paradigms can remain functional for certain people and contexts.

A paradigm shift in technology and equipment can be obtrusive and forceful, while a paradigm based on mental and emotional change within existing technology and infrastructure develops more slowly. Take the breakthrough of mobile communication which was almost instant in the 1990s when the technology had matured, and compare this with the slow progress of gender equality

---

[3]See further Chapter 11.

[4]Saren & Pels, 2008.

[5]Hawking, 1996, p. x.

which has been on the agenda for over a century but has not been pushed by uncompromising technology. There are also research paradigms that do not support the study of reality and lead us astray. When simplification and generalization are prematurely promoted to stardom and backed by iconic professors, both science and society suffer. This is not uncommon.

Genuine researchers are looking for some kind of truth and results that can be trusted and used.

An airplane can only crash once; the feedback is clear and immediate. A model in the economic sciences can crash repeatedly as its quality is not clearly measurable. It is open to many interpretations and the effects may be long term, making it difficult, even impossible, to establish causality.

The Positivist Paradigm

The term *positivism* signifies a conventional view of science based on the natural sciences, mainly physics from the Scientific Revolution. The positivist paradigm still largely rules the minds of ordinary men and the media – and of too many scientists! In the economic sciences, positivism promotes the quantitative and searches for unambiguous causal relationships between independent and dependent variables. It is deductive and reductionist; relies on social constructs and the operationalization of variables; engages in technically sophisticated hypothesis testing; uses statistical random samples; and offers probabilities and distributions rather than conclusive results.

The more approximations we introduce in a study, the more errors we accumulate. We need not introduce many categories, averages and random distributions before their synergy effects turn the phenomenon we are looking for into a child that not even its mother would recognize and love. Validity has gone to blazes but our equations look neat and palatable; they are 'pure'.

Positivists characterize themselves as rigorous and objective and able to make generalizations. Reliability is a key quality, meaning that a study should give similar results if replicated by others. There are also indexes for the validity and generalizability of results. When positivists say 'go empirical' they mean 'go quantitative'. Positivist research is useful in specific instances, but it is not universally applicable and should not be presented as the benchmark for science.

There are ongoing controversies about what results are truly scientific and what the best scientific methods are. The advocates on either side come in many forms but can often be characterized by an extreme rigidity ritualism of the same potency as religious and political fundamentalism. My standpoint is as follows: *What counts is if a chosen scientific method works or not. Its capacity to reach results is paramount, not the properties of the procedure.*

Table 3.1 What you do in scientific research according to a positivistic top journal editor

1. Read the literature.
2. Define the expected contributions of your research.
3. Select precisely defined constructs.
4. Define specific research hypotheses and make the theoretical arguments underlying the hypotheses convincing.
5. Ensure correspondence between the conceptual definitions of the constructs and their operational measures.
6. Enhance the internal and external validity of experiments.
7. Build meaningful mathematical models.

An essay[6] discussing why practitioners do not read scientific journal articles points out that practically all articles, especially those in the so-called 'top journals', are positivistic and rarely contribute usable knowledge. How rooted this is stood out at an international conference in 2012 when the editor-in-chief of a business journal, classified as a 'top journal', presented his view of what you do in scientific research (Table 3.1). The table is based on the notes of one of the conference participants.

The instructions in the table look logical and neat. *My objection is that they are presented as the role model of high-class science.* This is *one* – but only *one* – way of doing research and it is based on the positivist paradigm. Unfortunately, many business schools teach this one-sided view. It means that crucial problems cannot be addressed as the approach does not allow for the study of complexity and is rooted in the past rather than in the present and the future. Had the presentation taken place in 1612 during the Scientific Revolution, it would have provided a challenge. But 400 years have passed and something has been learnt in the meantime. Although some of what was thrown out during the Scientific Revolution is back – emotions in business disciplines and later in behavioural economics, quality in management, value in marketing, and ethics in organizational culture – the 'physics envy' stays put among positivist social scientists. During the past 100 years, paradigm shifts have occurred in the natural sciences and others are in the making. Today, classical physics is a special case. Innovation in business and management should connect to the *modern natural sciences* which have added the theory of relativity, quantum physics and many others.

The social sciences in their present form established themselves in the mid-1900s as a spinoff from the humanities. Although consisting of many diverse disciplines, they have given rise to new methodologies and new applications of, for example, statistics. The positivist paradigm has been preceded by a series of paradigms, among them postpositivist, critical theorist, postmodernist and

---

[6]Tapp, 2005.

constructivist. I am not going to go into comparisons between the paradigms unless they come up naturally when explaining the complexity paradigm.[7]

In the either/or spirit, the positivist paradigm is usually set up against the *interpretivist paradigm*. The first is thought of as quantitative and the second as qualitative. I have chosen to compare positivism with the *complexity paradigm*. It will be explicated in the next section.

The Complexity Paradigm

The word complexity has already appeared several times. If something is complex, this means that it is difficult to grasp and handle. What this means in science has already partially been explained but it will haunt us all the way through the book. At the other end of the scale is simplicity. Following the both/and idea, the two are not opposites but complementary. When something is difficult, we need to transform it into something simpler to make it manageable.

The positivist paradigm with its emphasis on certain elements – rational, rigorous, objective, etc. – was a necessary stepping stone and some of it remains in the complexity paradigm. But I strongly resent the fact that the majority of social scientists, when speaking of the natural sciences, fall back on old physics and have missed the developments of the past century and the modern natural sciences.

The complexity paradigm states that business and management are characterized by numerous factors and interrelations, that these are hard to identify and that their behaviour is hard to predict. As complexity is not a major element of mainstream research and education in the economic sciences, its meaning and importance will be explained. I consider complexity to be the overriding characteristic of traditional case study research but this has not been properly highlighted. Network theory, systems theory, fuzzy set theory and chaos theory will help us move from case study research to case theory, and better address complexity and accommodate multiple dimensions of reality.

Our research methodology must be responsive to complexity, or research in management will make a contribution neither to theory nor to practice. In an article, the authors address the elusiveness of the fuzzy concept of strategy.[8] Conventional and rationalistic simplifications are challenged through multiparadigm inquiry (Box 3.1).

---

[7]Accounts of different paradigms can be found in e.g. Brown, 1993; Guba & Lincoln, 2005; Lee & Lings, 2008; Alvesson & Sköldberg, 2009; and Easterby-Smith, Thorpe & Jackson, 2015, pp. 56–77.

[8]Bakir & Bakir, 2006; quotation from p. 167.

Complexity has started a natural science family known as *complexity theory*. Its
supporters embrace complexity instead of shunning it. They strive to find grand
theory by condensing the core of a phenomenon and making it manageable.
Among the complexity theory members are Einstein's theory of relativity, quantum mechanics, autopoeisis (self-organizing systems), fractal geometry, network
theory, systems theory, fuzzy set theory and chaos theory. Case theory especially
considers the last 4 theories.[10]

The global financial 'system' of today is huge but the economic sciences only
offer fragments, some loosely linked, some not linked at all. They are preoccupied with pure theory to fit the format of the mathematical and statistical

---

[9]GT is further explained in Chapter 10.

[10]See Chapter 7.

languages, instead of focusing on the actual outcome and its validity and relevance. We do not face it the way science should demand. That there are billions of stars, no, billions of galaxies, is a challenge to astronomers. They face it. Why do we not face complexity in the economic sciences? In the summer of 2015 there was a huge controversy among the 19 members of the EU who use a common currency, the euro. One of them, Greece, was facing bankruptcy and the question was if and how the others should help or if Greece should exit the euro zone. Economists and politicians had great difficulty in establishing which would be the best solution. They referred to some known fragments of theory but most of it, even among established economists, was endless rhetoric based on opinion and experience of the past – an example of mega-babble. There was no grand theory to help the politicians in their decision-making.

Not many efforts are made to introduce complexity from the natural sciences in the research and training of business and management. Starting from organization and strategy, one of the exceptions is UK professor Ralph Stacey who has written several books on the topic.[11] Fritjof Capra is another boundary-transcending scientist active at Schumacher College, UK, a college inspired by E.F. Schumacher and his seminal book *Small Is Beautiful* (1973). Together with Plymouth University, it offers degrees in holistic science and transformative learning for sustainable living. Capra urges Western science to abandon the linear and *mechanistic* heritage of the Scientific Revolution. Modern physics has done so but it is still highly influential in the social sciences. Critiquing the *reductionist* view that everything can be broken down into parts, Capra encourages everyone to take a *holistic* approach. He focuses on the systemic information generated by the relationships among all the parts, thus emphasizing interconnectedness and a network structure of all systems.

Complexity issues in business and management and the social sciences in general are getting increased attention but have not yet reached the critical mass of researchers that is necessary to have a major impact. This is not the place to make an inventory of the conferences, books and articles that keep appearing; you can search for them on the Internet.

I know from long experience that a fundamental change in scientific attitude, such as the one I suggest – from the currently fragmented view with few variables and links to complexity – is a giant leap. To paraphrase the words uttered by Neil Armstrong in 1969, the first astronaut to walk on the moon: 'That's one small step for mankind, but a giant leap for business and management research' (he originally said: 'That's one small step for a man, one giant leap for mankind').

When complexity comes up on the research agenda, it is taken for granted that it is about advanced quantitative modelling, artificial intelligence and big

---

[11]Stacey, 2009, 2010; see also Stacey et al., 2002; and an article by Sokal, 1996.

data. This is unfortunate as the spotlight is put on methodological technicalities rather than on the issue under investigation. *Computer simulation* can be used for *scientific modelling* of human systems in order to gain insight into their functioning. Key issues in simulation are data generation and the selection of key characteristics, behaviours, approximations and simplifying assumptions, and an assessment of the reliability, validity and relevance of the outcome. Mathematicians might find elegant formulas and present pure theory. It should be a condensed (not a reduced) formula that uses a minimum of variables to express something important. Sometimes it just looks elegant because so many limiting assumptions have been introduced and so many troublemaking variables have been excluded or been treated with cosmetic surgery and Botox injections.

Changing mindsets in the academic researchscape is not only intellectual, it also activates the persona features: emotions, frustrations, power, and so on. It does not take years but decades. Do we have the time? No, we have to learn to speed it up. That requires moving from techniques within the positivist paradigm to research methodologies within the complexity paradigm. It needs theory generation based on inductive research and case theory.

Case theory traditionally uses verbal language, while network theory uses a nodes-and-links language, and systems theory speaks of open systems, subsystems, components, the environment and their links, together forming a coherent whole. They open up for the use of graphs, mathematics and computer simulations in addition to the verbal. If these fit business and management issues, they can elevate traditional research to new heights. As I wrote in an article, 'case study research, network theory and systems theory are birds of a feather and as such they should flock together – but so far they don't'.[12]

Complexity is usually non-linear but the reduced traditional model in business, management and other social sciences is linear. In Figure 3.1 a straight highway serves as a metaphor for *linearity*. The highway allows motor vehicles only and they can just drive in 2 directions. It is a fair illustration of pure theory where the variables, the cars, can be identified and the links between them follow simple rules. The highway is a technical solution for simplifying car traffic and making it more efficient. Apart from the physical design of the road, regulations like speed limits, no stopping etc. secure a certain pattern of behaviour.

Even so, the highway is not 100% linear. There are human beings in the cars but we cannot see them. We do not know who they are, why they are there at this point in time and what they are thinking or talking about. Each car is a black box but the black boxes interact based on a driver's input – primarily what the other cars are doing – and the output – a driver's reaction to the input. Getting from one place to another requires 'special instruments' (cars) and a technical infrastructure of roads that make fast driving possible. In this way,

---

[12]Gummesson, 2007.

simplicity-in-use for drivers has been introduced. The simplicity is the outcome of condensing a complex transportation system into something manageable.

As an example of *non-linearity*, Figure 3.2 shows a densely populated village street in Bangladesh. It includes lots of people walking, some being transported in small bicycle-type vehicles, lots of stores, and so on. The street is a complex system. As an outsider, my understanding is superficial. Had I grown up there I would have been socialized into its essentials both through explicit and tacit knowledge. If you want to turn it into a model to help understand it, research questions include: What variables and what links between them should be included? What should be excluded? What could be made linear without losing critical data and information? Within the complexity paradigm, the first activity will be to try to understand the complexity and later condense it and find the underpinning principles. If you exclude 'disturbing' variables because they are difficult to grasp or subjectively judge them as 'insignificant', you reduce the complexity and lose validity. Your model will neither be useful for theory generation nor for practical guidance. It depicts a pseudo-world – but it is referred to as rigorous and thus scientific. I do not get it together.

Figure 3.1 A linear environment; a straight highway illustrating complexity condensed into a few variables to arrive at simplicity (© the Author)

Figure 3.2   A non-linear environment illustrating substantial complexity that embraces numerous variables and relationships (© the Author)

As a young hitch-hiker in postwar Germany, I learnt an old saying: 'Why make it simple when it can be made so beautifully complicated?' It was a joke about snobbish academics and their lofty language and theories. For scientists, it should be the other way around: to find the soul of a phenomenon and, even if complex, turn it into something manageable. Complex should not, by default, be kept complicated.

Complexity and *simplicity* are interdependent in the both/and spirit. Understanding business and management means to attack complexity, sort it out, condense it and find the simplicity behind it. Only then can your research be made useful. Simplicity comes from the Latin *simplex*, 'characterized by a single part', and *simplicitatem*, 'the state of being simple'. Herbert Simon, one of the very few winners of the Nobel Prize in Economic Sciences with a contribution to business and management, says in his reflective autobiography that 'The whole purpose of science is to find meaningful simplicity in the midst of disorderly complexity'.[13]

In the turmoil of our professional and private lives, we are looking for simplicity. Some things are simple and can be learnt quickly by experience; they do not need scientific research. But the road to simplicity often goes through complexity. The business and management disciplines stay in the lower zone or mid-range theory and show as concepts, categories, models, frameworks, heuristics

---

[13]Simon, 1957, p. 2.

and checklists. They are tools that facilitate practice. But many of them which fill scientific journals and textbooks never get any further than being published. We must therefore strive towards more general and inclusive theory, grand theory. Then we can also see the basic patterns of a phenomenon – and it becomes simpler. This will later be shown in Figure 6.1 where 3 issues in particular are emphasized:

- better grounding of theory in real-world, substantive data
- more effort to conceptualize data and generate theory, moving in the direction of grand theory
- giving back to mid-range theory condensed complexity in the form of simplicity that facilitates action.

Named after an English medieval philosopher, *Occam's razor* – also known as the *Law of Parsimony* – states that simpler explanations are generally better than more complex ones. In quality management it is known that the fewer parts you need to make an engine, the fewer can disconnect or break down and the more reliable the engine. And when James Bond was facing an attacker, he acted 'with an economy of movement'.

We drown in an overwhelming mass of data in which we do not discern themes and patterns. I know both practitioners and scholars who are good at detail and get suffocated by it. There are also those who jump at conclusions and drive a hard sell of their opinion. But there are also the good ones, those who practice what GT calls *theoretical sensitivity*, the ability to keep an open mind for data and combine them into something whole.[14]

Henry Ford, the founder of the Ford Motor Company, introduced the assembly line and repetitive work in his factories. In his book *My Life and Work*, Ford says that his effort is in the direction of simplicity.[15] He tried to make things simpler, both to cost less and be more functional. Ford understood this from experience and was able to turn it into action. This was over 100 years ago. He made judgement calls that combined explicit and tacit knowledge, simplified it and standardized work.

But this standardization also forced workers to do tedious and unhealthy work. With Taylorism,[16] also called time studies or scientific management, standardization went to extremes. It broke down each little moment of work, timed it in seconds, identified the quickest way of performing it, and taught all workers to apply this 'best' way of doing things. It was rigorous and positivist. It could

---

[14]See Glaser, 1978.

[15]First published in 1922, republished in 2008.

[16]Invented by Frederick Taylor (1856–1915).

increase productivity but it could also backfire. Taylor did not consider the persona factor – that workers are individuals – and although they could be taught to improve their work, they could only be standardized to a degree; there had to be some leeway for individualism. The way of working was later modified and what can be clearly standardized has been taken over by machines and robots.

Unfortunately, simplicity has got lost in the complexity of huge corporations, not to talk about the huge government organizations on national, regional and local level. They have been conquered by bureaucracy, legal technicalities, incoherent systems and stylized quantitative metrics.

Some of Ford's original strategies were given a major boost in *total quality management* (TQM) in the 1980s. Toyota has kept revamping quality and productivity by combining explicit and tacit knowledge and consistently developing simplicity through the strategies of continuous improvement, just-in-time and lean production.[17]

> Simple can be harder than complex: You have to work hard to get your thinking clean to make it simple … once you get there, you can move mountains. (Steve Jobs (1955–2011), innovator, co-founder and CEO of Apple)[18]

Explicit and Tacit Knowledge

The British philosopher Bertrand Russell (1872–1970) had a major impact on modern science. One contribution was his distinction between *knowledge by description* and *knowledge by acquaintance*.[19] The distinction has affinity to *explicit knowledge* and *tacit knowledge*.[20] Both pairs are interdependent; they are both/and. For the sake of simplicity I will stick to explicit/tacit knowledge. They form a central part of case theory and its complexity paradigm. They were introduced in Chapter 1 but will be more fully explained throughout the book.

A commonly held opinion is that the difference between *data from everyday life* and *scientific data* is that the latter is derived by means of an approved methodology. It is however my contention that there is method and systematic treatment of data in tacit knowledge as well, even if it is tied to the persona factor.

In accordance with an academic and positivist tradition, methods books in business and management focus on explicit knowledge. Tacit knowledge is

---

[17]See further Chapters 4 and 11.

[18]Reindhart, 1998

[19]Russell, 1914/1993.

[20]The concept of tacit knowledge is ascribed to Polanyi, 1966.

rarely mentioned and I will therefore bring some of its key elements and concepts to the fore. These phenomena exist but are considered unreliable, whimsical folklore without reliability and validity. In the complexity paradigm they have their place.

I propose that knowledge grows from iterative and interactive processes which involve both the explicit and the tacit and the two types are given equal status. In conventional Western science – at least officially – only explicit knowledge counts, meaning that my approach is controversial. As luck would have it, I am not alone in giving tacit knowledge prominent status. Cohen (1998) notes that the Japanese focus on tacit knowledge nurtures 'knowledge communities', whereas in the USA the focus is on explicit knowledge through research projects, plans and measurement. Nonaka and Takeuchi (1995) show how Japanese companies systematically make tacit employee and customer knowledge explicit. Linestone and Zhu (2000) claim that the combined perspectives of the East and the West are necessary to address the variety and complexity of systems such as corporations or markets. By not only merging Western science with Western common sense, but also with Eastern philosophy, we can arrive at a higher understanding of what knowledge is. Einstein's theory of relativity started as a hunch; it was intuitive understanding. He praises innovative thinking as the most important in research.

The one-sided focus on the explicit is counterproductive to innovation, entrepreneurship and paradigm shifts at the same time as these are hailed as the drivers of economic development. Making tacit knowledge explicit may require years of work and is not necessarily successful. Speeding up the explicit-making process requires judgement calls, as tacit knowledge can be quite subtle and, if rushed, its genuine content may get distorted.

Daniel Kahneman shared the Nobel Prize in Economic Sciences in 2002 'for having integrated insights from psychological research into economic sciences, especially concerning human judgement and decision-making under uncertainty'. His book *Thinking Fast and Slow* from 2011 has become a bestseller. As a basic categorization of decisions, he suggests the *intuitive and automatic (system 1)* and the *systematic and intellectual analysis (system 2)*. It has affinity with the division in tacit and explicit knowledge. There is also an affinity with *rapid reconnaissance*[21] used in science for the need to quickly assess a problem without going into systematic analysis; practitioners constantly live with this demand.

Kahneman separates *clinical prediction* from *statistical prediction*.[22] When we face a decision we can do an in-depth case study embracing a complex set of variables and links. But Kahneman claims that a statistical prediction based on

---

[21]Patton, 1990, p. 134.

[22]Kahneman based this on Meehl, 1986.

a simple checklist works better than the more advanced clinical effort. He later explains how checklists, algorithms and heuristics ('rules-of-thumb') work. I will not go further into arguments with him but we should remember that there are always exceptions and that heuristics are temporary and contextual. We all use heuristics in our professional and private lives.

Kahneman applies the research tradition of psychology to behavioural economics. Although psychology as a social science partially overlaps with business and management, the context differs and requires a partially different outlook. I have already pointed to the naivety of behavioural economics in thinking that it has discovered that the economic man is not a good image of a consumer, that emotions are drivers (they were eradicated in the Scientific Revolution), that people are individuals and that statistics may create a non-realistic model of man.

The following sections will comment on some tacit knowledge types: experience, common sense, intuition, ethics, truths and untruths, pragmatic wisdom and judgement calls.

Experience. As babies we start learning through practical experience. In a business meeting I heard a person say: 'I have 20 years of experience of this. So do not tell me what to do!' The other person retorted: 'You just have 1 year of experience repeated 20 times!' How do we avoid experience becoming stale and not renewing itself as much as it should? It is very individual. Some keep up with changes and stay curious, while others do not. In my experience, the ability to develop and be creative is – contrary to folklore – not age-related. I meet rigid people and those who are open-minded and creative in all age groups. The problem is sometimes that younger people re-invent the wheel. I hear them at conferences, for example a PhD student writing a thesis explaining something that was topical in the 1960s with nothing to add to it.

Common sense is often used as the motive for a conclusion. It is a perception of the world developed over the years through experience. But it can also be a blockage and make you blind to changes. In *Brewer's Dictionary of Phrase & Fable* from 1870, the word 'common' is given an alternative meaning: 'Common sense does not mean that good sense which is common ... but the point where all five senses meet ... where it judges what is presented by the senses and decides the mode of action.' It is a synthesis. We can go further and claim that we should not only use our 5 conventional senses – sight, hearing, touch, smell and taste – but all our faculties including emotions (now also called 'emotional intelligence'), social skills, masculine and feminine instincts, and our preunderstanding of the research context. What is beyond our 5 senses is called extra-sensory perception or, in some languages, the sixth sense. Positivists dismiss it as paranormal and supernatural mysticism. I disapprove of this because there are senses which we have not cultivated or discovered. There is nothing mystical about it. We are constantly criss-crossed by waves and signals but we need a TV set or a mobile phone to receive them. We need a medium, be it an instrument or a human being. Physicists cannot see the atoms or molecules and science uses instruments and models that mediate the phenomenon and the observer. And most of us have met people who can sense more than others and we know that animals use other senses. Dogs are trained to trace animals at hunts and narcotics at airports.

Common sense resting on experience needs revising if conditions change. For example, what is common sense when business relationships are primarily personal and exist in physical proximity may not be common sense if they are carried out online.

Common sense may be wrong but so may statistical calculations. It is no secret that even intelligent and well-educated people often draw the wrong conclusions.[23] Consciously or unconsciously, scientists can design a study to 'prove' almost anything with numbers. The outcome depends on the scientist's paradigm, choice of research techniques and definition of categories and variables. So explicit and tacit knowledge are both needed to surround a complex phenomenon and capture its meaning.

Intuition. There is a considerable literature about intuition but I rarely see it referenced in the case methods publications. Intuition is the condensation and synthesis of knowledge and its merger with our persona. In a split second, intuition can combine an unlimited number of data. How does this compare to artificial intelligence and big data?[24] How can it be developed? For example, it has been found that a person in balance, with coherent brainwaves, will make better intuitive assessments of situations than an unbalanced person. Meditation is a way of creating coherence in our brainwaves and improving understanding and intuition, but even though hundreds of studies have been conducted in accordance with the positivist causality, mainstream brain specialists refuse to accept them. What happened to rationality, not to talk about ethics?

> Never ignore a gut feeling, but never believe that it's enough. (Robert Heller, 1932–2012, best-selling author of business books)[25]

Wisdom will be used here as the highest level of knowledge. I especially stress *pragmatic wisdom*, which is the wisdom that can be transformed into decisions,

---

[23]See Kahneman, 2011.

[24]This is further treated in Chapter 4.

[25]Heller, 1984, p. 87

actions and results. The words *pragmatic* and *practical* have the same roots, both referring to getting things done. The concept *phronesis*,[26] used by Aristotle 2,400 years ago, refers to the same thing. It also says that young people may be good thinkers but lack experience and understanding of the particulars of a situation, the context. They lack the network of contacts that may be necessary to build up knowledge by merging many sources. This needs time to grow and mature before they can act with pragmatic wisdom.

Phronesis also puts emphasis on *truth, honesty, ethics* and *trust*. These used to be ideals for a civilization as compared to a savage society. Truth and untruth are fuzzy and composite concepts. I have already stressed that science should be a quest for the truth. In his book *On the Good Life*, Roman philosopher and statesman Cicero[27] wrote about contentment and moral virtue as intertwined. He said that life is about 'the ability to distinguish truth from falsity, and to understand the relationship between one phenomenon and another and the causes and consequences of each one'. My text has endorsed Cicero's statement but I like to expand it to 'the need to understand the interconnectedness and interdependency between the parts of complex phenomena and how they merge into a whole'. We then go beyond the simple one cause/one effect construct. I feel confident that Cicero endorses this wherever his spirit is located at this very moment.

Today, we are surrounded by so much data that it is impossible for us to sort out what is true or not. The media and top decision-makers in democracies as well as in dictatorships cannot be trusted. Politicians make promises to get elected but they seldom fulfil those promises. The financial sector sells retirement funds and makes promises to ordinary customers who have limited or no understanding of the intricacies of finance. It is pragmatic – but it is not true wisdom; it is *corrupt wisdom*.

The methods literature is about explicit knowledge and its alleged rigour and reliability (replicability). The focus is on the research procedure rather than the outcome of research where validity and relevance are in the centre. Business and management are applied sciences and their goal is to be useful for something in the end. But in the end all sciences are meant to be useful, even if it can take time. That is so in physics and medical science, for example. Quality evaluation of research is mainly geared to the research process and statistical technicalities and little to the relevance of the outcome. It is based on the subjective assumption that if the research process is 'rigorous' the outcome will be superior.

---

[26]See Flyvbjerg's, 2001, adaptation into *phronetic social science*.

[27]Cicero lived from 106 to 53, BC, His book is reprinted in 1971.

When positivist researchers find that their results are not precise, they add a host of indexes, decimals, new concepts and indicators to 'explain' it. In a mechanistic mode, they break everything down into smaller and smaller boxes. This is not a viable approach as the logic of tacit knowledge is different from the logic of explicit knowledge. Again, science and research shall not deal with forcing. Tacit knowledge can be taught to a limited extent but it requires experience and introspection. The outcome should be pragmatic wisdom.

Today, there are thousands of methods books and articles devoted to explicit knowledge; tomorrow there should be thousands devoted to tacit knowledge and to the interaction and interdependence between the two. I would like to inspire academics and scientists to study tacit knowledge and to do it on its own terms – not trying to squeeze it into the explicit knowledge format.

Untruths – or to be more blunt: lies – come in many degrees and for many purposes. Researchers are very much unaware of the frequently low quality of data. Statistical surveys, personal interviews and observations have to be interpreted and evaluated before they can be used in research. It is imperative that researchers evaluate the credibility of sources.[28]

Distortion of the truth has always existed but today it is becoming openly professionalized. It is practised by lawyers, journalists, advertising people, lobbyists and public relations consultants.[29] These professions are among the fastest growing 'industries', perhaps only outranked by the IT industry and organized crime. You never know when you can trust them. There are contrived stories disguised as documentaries. There are PR 'professionals' who take on campaigns to smear a person's reputation ('dark PR'). If they do not find a skeleton in the closet, they invent one and spread rumours. This is not dystopia; it is today's reality. There is a title for 'professionals' who have distortions of reality in the centre of their business mission: *spin doctors*. They get paid for promoting anything, good or bad. It could be for a good cause but equally for a business run by organized crime or a dictator and warlord. The decision variable for these 'professionals' is just one: do we get well paid for it? I advise researchers in business and management to take a look at the Internet on the subject of spin doctors, lobbying and public relations. There you will find spin strategies listed that clearly show how fuzzy and fluid 'truth' is and how it can be systematically manipulated.[30]

---

[28]See further Chapter 9.

[29]Stebbing, 1939/1961, offers a discourse of fallacies in argumentation that we should watch for.

[30]See e.g. 'spin (public relations)' on Wikipedia; an article by Cave & Rowell in *The Guardian*, 14 March 2014; and ALTER-EU reports.

You increasingly find this among researchers and scientists. One of the major reasons is that the real content of scientific research has been set aside for financial goals and compliance with political and bureaucratic demands. To get research money you have to adhere to the regulations of funds, governments, private companies and others. This is part of your researchscape. If you need the money to support your family and pay the mortgage on your house, your survival instincts take over. So you comply – or leave academic life.

In the Western university world, there are still areas with considerable freedom to follow your own calling but it requires integrity and stamina. There are also those who comply simply because they are not aware of the situation. Their education has brainwashed and socialized them into what they are. For the moment we have to live with this and we can only hope it will reach a tipping point.

In business and management research, it is what true knowledge can do for us that should count. Theory can help sort things out and make us act more cleverly. Good theory has a constructive kinship to practice, just like friends that you trust are supportive.

It is also about attitude. Salespeople are taught that the market offers both problems and opportunities and that they should set their mind on opportunities and solutions, not on problems and difficulties. There is a saying that a glass can be half full or half empty; the denotation is the same but the connotation is far apart. Half full sends signals about opportunities; half empty about failure. The true apparatchiks – government officials and other bureaucrats – proudly point out difficulties. They look for regulations that may be used as an excuse not to act. If they do not do anything they cannot be accused of making mistakes. There are also bureaucrats who take risks but at the same time have to cover up what they are actually doing. The bureaucratic culture can be more or less permissive, flexible and pragmatic – but unfortunately also corrupt.

The complexity of today's organizations, new technology and the growing mass of laws and regulations lead us into a maze of data without a lucid context. Companies grow, merge, downsize, and change their procedures, and employees cannot overview the meaning of their job. They need pragmatic wisdom to survive – and so do researchers who attempt to understand the companies. Close access through presence in both practice and science are essential. *Management by walking around* – leadership through presence where and when the action is – gives you firsthand knowledge of what is happening. This was once common but has been replaced mostly by written reports, metrics, online interaction and a meeting-room 'culture'. It means going from firsthand understanding to understanding through intermediaries and with each intermediary between you and the objects of study you lose information and enhance the risk of distortion. *Science by walking around* should have much to teach the scholar. It has an affinity with *management action research* which is based on close involvement and participation in decision-making and activity processes, thus getting privileged access and the possibility to deploy all your senses.[31]

A note of warning: the word *culture* is highly misused. It goes back to the Latin *cultura*, meaning 'growing and cultivating land to get harvests'. Fukuyama's (1995) extensive treatise on trust identifies *high-trust* and *low-trust* cultures. In high-trust cultures, you can be quite informal as there is no need to waste time on checking foul play. If you talk about the drug culture among teenagers, the culture of a mafia organization, or review films about crime and killing under a section called 'Culture' in a newspaper, it is misleading; they are destructive actions and not about culture. Instead, you should use the more neutral environment or context.

Besides the methodology texts, we have books written in more popular but still consistent form about complexity, prediction, networks, tipping points, the doubtful consistency of statistical analysis, and so on. The authors are from the social sciences and the natural sciences as well as from investigative journalism. Many of these books are to my liking as they align well with my practical and scientific experience.

Both/and, Either/or

High tech/high touch states that when technology increases so does the need for human contact. The conventional idea is that tech takes over. Instead, tech and touch grow hand in hand; they have a both/and relationship instead of the assumed either/or relationship. There are several either/or variants, for example *online/offline* and *virtual/physical*. *Digilogue*[32] – *digital minds/analogue hearts* – with an affinity to *left brain* (language and calculation)/*right brain* (creativity) is close to high tech/high touch; it is both/and. Technology has opened up new platforms for social contact. But nothing is sacred; *social media* are just as much the new *commercial media*. Advertising is thrown in our faces just like on TV, and those who develop social media, online newsletters and blogs for free, earn their money by letting in commercial messages.

One reason why forecasts turn out wrong – almost always *very* wrong – is that they do not pay attention to the complex *high tech/high touch* balance. It is one of the few both/and concepts that seems to be accepted in research. It was introduced in John Naisbitt's book *Megatrends* (1982). I had difficulty in grasping it at first; I was either/or programmed. This was before the personal computer, before email, before the Internet, before the cellphone, before social media, even before

---

[31]Management action research is further explained in Chapter 9.

[32]Sörman-Nilsson, 2013.

the fax. I find it even more true today.[33] High tech/high touch is based on the notion of 'balanc[ing] the material wonders of technology with the spiritual demands of our human nature' and Naisbitt's conclusion was: 'The more high technology around us, the more the need for human touch.'

It shows in many ways. The more comfortable our lives become with the assistance of technology, the more people indulge in adventure travel or withdraw to a summer cottage where they grow vegetables and have physical contact with nature. Television technology does not only give us an opportunity to watch sports 24/7, but it raises our interest to try the marathon and even the triathlon. At the same time as Internet trade was launched, huge supermarkets and malls began to grow, offering experiences with theme parks, cinemas, hotels and even churches. Another example is that the Internet can technically replace conferences so you don't have to travel and meet physically. But since the breakthrough of the Internet in this millennium, the number of physical conferences has grown steadily. In 2011 I checked which conferences were planned in the world where delegates meet physically. In October alone, the list was topped by 29 international medical conferences. With the same frequency throughout the year, a new medical conference begins every day. In accounting 15 international conferences were listed, 1 in Las Vegas, which in my mind conflicts with the credibility of accountancy – or perhaps reflects its status in today's casino economy of 'creative' book-keeping.

Why – in the name of economic rationality – do not the delegates convene in Internet conferences? They need not leave their homes or offices or pay for air travel and hotels. But online relationships and swift global communication stimulate the desire for offline contact. High tech can also add human dimensions that are in short supply in the physical world; it is IT-mediated high touch. The computer becomes an extension of mental abilities and can satisfy needs and wants. The Internet and email open up for chats and conversation dealing with the quality of goods, services and suppliers. It can help us search for medical information to be better prepared for a high-touch meeting with a doctor. It can offer social interaction between communities with common lifestyles, which previously required physical presence.

Although high tech may seem less personal, high touch is not automatically warm and human. For example, there is often a lack of knowledge and social skills in front-line personnel interactions with customers. It gives rise to discontent and not everyone wanting to have contact with others but rather preferring the impersonal and anonymous.

The either/or preoccupation in Western thinking encourages conflict and competition between categories. This is counterproductive, leading researchers, politicians and others to spend resources on 'solving' the wrong problems. We will later deal with the terrorism of obsolete theory and its concepts and categories.

---

[33]See Naisbitt's follow-up book, 1999.

The positivist paradigm tells us that definitions and categories should be clear-cut and not overlapping – but reality does not comply. What occurs in business and management is more often ambiguous, contradictory and fuzzy. A set is a collection of something that forms a category. *Set theory* from 1874 and even earlier defines a set as binary, either/or. A set corresponds to a category – a box – where either you are a member or you are not; such sets are called *crisp sets*. *Fuzzy set theory* has been the object of mathematical development for 50 years – but this is hardly noted in the economic sciences. Fuzzy sets allow for a both/and approach and therefore fit well in the complexity paradigm. It is a generalization of set theory on a higher level to come to grips with the ambiguity and imprecision of the real world. Even if we do not go into the mathematical intricacies of fuzzy sets, when approaching reality our minds are supported by it. When are quantitative researchers in the social sciences going to start using fuzzy set theory? They have to deal with modern mathematics and its ambiguous sets without fixed boundaries and have a core that fades out and overlaps with other sets.

From left to right, Figure 3.3 shows the clearly delineated boxes of the ideal concept, category or definition as *crisp sets*. Next are more realistic images where each concept, category or definition has a unique core (black in the figure) which fades away, becomes increasingly greyish and gradually merges with other sets; they become *fuzzy sets*. Try, for example, to define the most frequent word in the economic sciences: money. What is money? Where does it come from? Is it true that banks 'make' money digitally through their computers? How much money is in circulation? Most of us just have a fuzzy perception of what money is in its generic sense – we may even wonder if there is a generic sense. Or does anyone really know? If the specialists knew, would we then have a global financial crisis?[34] Other fuzzy everyday business terms are company, leadership, customer and quality. Daily life revolves around relationships, friendship, love and health. The categories are both/and; they need each other. We encounter them in the complexity paradigm, for example big *and* small factors; parts *and* the whole; structure *and* processes; and tech *and* human aspects.

Despite their fuzziness, these words represent phenomena that have a core which differentiates them from each other and we seem to need the words. Scientific understanding rarely becomes clear-cut for the very simple reason that reality is not clear-cut. For example, the village street in Bangladesh from Figure 3.2 is chaotic to me but not to those who live there. There is order in chaos when we have learnt to understand how something works.

Finally, the far right of Figure 3.3 illustrates the Procrustean bed, named after a robber who generously offered visitors a bed for the night. The catch was that

---

[34]See Krugman, 2012.

Figure 3.3 Types of set definitions: 2 unambiguously defined crisp sets (left); fuzzy sets (middle); and the Procrustean bed before and after the 'correction' (right) (© the Author)

he got furious if they did not fit the bed perfectly. If too big, he cut off their feet; if too small he stretched them to fill up the bed. The visitors became sick or died. Such torture is ongoing practice in the economic sciences.

The use of *term* and *concept* is often mixed up. A concept is an idea about something, its content and meaning. A term is the name or label you give the concept to facilitate communication. By mixing them up we risk creating a pseudo world. For example, it is often claimed that relationship marketing stems from the 1980s: the term, yes, the concept, no. Businesspeople have always known that relationships, and the more complex ones that form networks, are the core of successful business practice.[35]

The term/concept issue raises a number of dilemmas. A term often has several meanings, and sometimes several terms are used to represent the same concept. Sometimes a concept is given a new name to make it stand out as fresh but the content is the same as before. For example, genetically manipulated food has a bad ring to it. A new label, gene-modified organism (GMO), was launched by the industry with the hope that it would sound friendly, even hide its true content to consumers. In science we will later meet the current hard sell of evidence-based research and life science.[36]

A known term may change its meaning over time but still be kept. If there is a critical change in an idea, should the old name be kept or should a new name be given to it? Currently, the concept of 'service', traditionally used in the expression 'goods and services' and telling us that these two are fundamentally different categories, is undergoing a transition. In new theory, service (in the singular) includes everything that renders value to customers and other stakeholders.[37] This is causing confusion as international and national statistics keep up the old terms (although their definitions are highly arbitrary and fuzzy).

---

[35]For the origins of relationship marketing and current developments, see Christopher et al., 2002; Gummesson, 2017.

[36]See Chapter 5.

[37]See further Box 6.5 on S-D logic.

The Research Edifice

The research edifice (Figure 3.4) offers an exhibition of phenomena that exist in all types of research, be it called quantitative or qualitative. It shows that the positivist paradigm is not as rational, rigorous and pure as its proponents claim.

We enter through the *basement* where we find that the researcher's paradigm and preunderstanding are composed of a mix of factors that lead to an interpretation of the world which is both objective and subjective, both explicit and tacit, and both emanating from extrospection and introspection. It is a judgement call that is only as advanced as our current level of pragmatic wisdom.

Walking upstairs to the *middle floor*, we are confronted with data generation and analysis/interpretation. Even if we choose the numbers track in the belief that one can be entirely objective and rigorous, we still have to make a series of

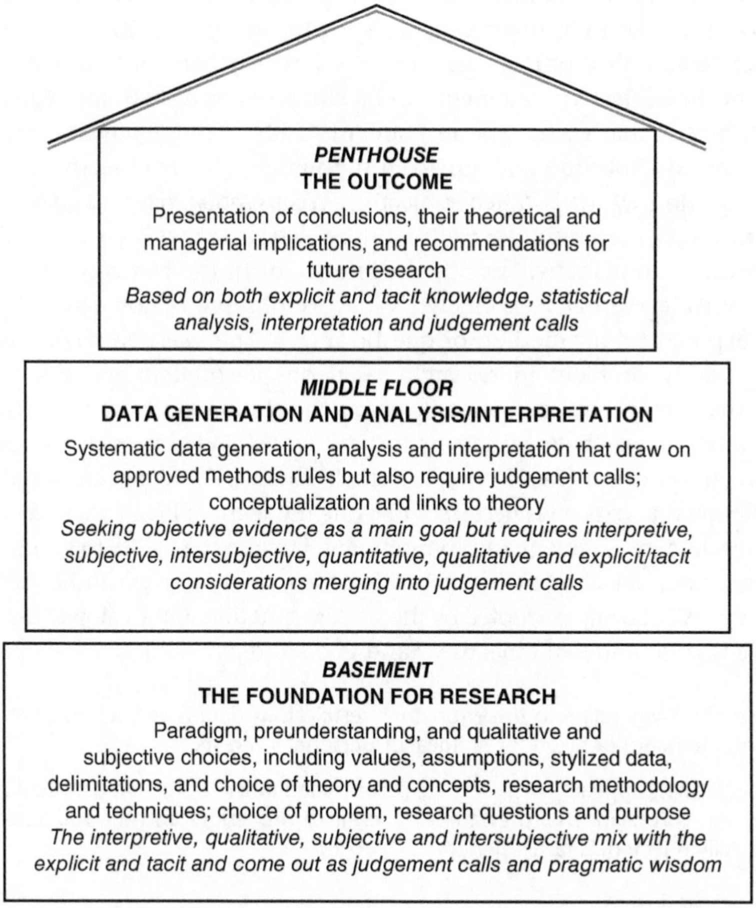

PENTHOUSE
THE OUTCOME

Presentation of conclusions, their theoretical and managerial implications, and recommendations for future research
Based on both explicit and tacit knowledge, statistical analysis, interpretation and judgement calls

MIDDLE FLOOR
DATA GENERATION AND ANALYSIS/INTERPRETATION

Systematic data generation, analysis and interpretation that draw on approved methods rules but also require judgement calls; conceptualization and links to theory
Seeking objective evidence as a main goal but requires interpretive, subjective, intersubjective, quantitative, qualitative and explicit/tacit considerations merging into judgement calls

BASEMENT
THE FOUNDATION FOR RESEARCH

Paradigm, preunderstanding, and qualitative and subjective choices, including values, assumptions, stylized data, delimitations, and choice of theory and concepts, research methodology and techniques; choice of problem, research questions and purpose
The interpretive, qualitative, subjective and intersubjective mix with the explicit and tacit and come out as judgement calls and pragmatic wisdom

Figure 3.4 The research edifice. Revised from Gummesson, 2003 (© the Author)

judgement calls. Data must also be conceptualized and compared to extant theory and other research.

We finally reach the top floor, the *penthouse*. Here results and conclusions are presented in written and oral form. If the purpose of the research is action, the researcher could make recommendations while those concerned have to make and execute decisions, monitor the outcome and make amendments. Whether the research is aimed at academic theory generation and testing, or is consulting on or part of operative work to solve a particular problem, judgement calls and interpretation are required.

The research edifice shows that the completely systematic, rigorous and objective pursuit of the truth is scientific mythology. Interpretive, subjective, intersubjective, qualitative and tacit elements are found on every floor. This leads us to two highly misused concepts. One is *objective* research, which is usually only objective in part. Even in the laboratory and medical research based on double-blind tests, randomization and attempted control over nuisance factors, you have to make judgement calls in the end, using your pragmatic wisdom. Whether you admit it or not, elements of *subjectivity* come into it. For example, we accept the subjective statements and feelings of consumers and register them as hard facts – 'that's what the respondents said!' – and aggregate them. They come from extrospection and are given the status of being objective as opposed to introspection which is called subjective. We *operationalize* and *stylize* an issue to fit our research techniques; we treat fuzzy sets as if they were crisp. The chosen process of knowing will decide the known, or in the words of physicist and Nobel Laureate Werner Heisenberg: 'What we observe is not nature itself, but nature exposed to our method of questioning.'[38] The *interviewer effect* is a well-known quality problem in research based on personal interviews. It is well known that the interviewer persona affects the respondent's way of answering.

Role-model researchers are taught to be *detached* and *dispassionate*, not letting emotions and engagement affect their work. In Chapter 2, we met passionate sociology, claiming that passion is necessary to ignite the spark of life in scientific research. It requires close involvement and commitment, but also the ability to swing between that and distant detachment. The more detached, the less access and closeness and the less the risk of being corrupted by the studied situation, but the lower the validity.

There is good and evil objectivity and good and evil subjectivity:

- *Good objectivity* refers to the effort to ascertain that data is correct and not opinion, wishful thinking or faked for political or personal interests.
- *Evil objectivity* appears when science is controlled in the bureaucratic, ritualistic sense and non-compliance with established research procedure and the rulebook is automatically rejected as false science.

---

[38]Quoted from Capra, 1997, p. 40.

- *Good subjectivity* recognizes the value of persona factors and other aspects than just the explicit and logical that intellect offers. Tacit knowledge from experience, intuition and insights is equally pertinent; it is part of pragmatic wisdom. To become a top mathematician, you must demonstrate extreme intuition and an instant understanding of mathematics at a very early age. What is not in your persona cannot be compensated for through hard studies of maths later in life. The selection of a problem, its variables, and the design and purpose of a research programme are based on an amalgamation of subjective and objective elements.

- *Evil subjectivity* is when persona factors and destructive researchscapes take over and science becomes a social, bureaucratic and political power game driven by special interests.

Those who advocate objectivity usually – and perhaps unknowingly – mean *intersubjectivity*, referring to what has become the approved standard by an academic jetset through peer review, power or image. Intersubjectivity can be a temporary stepping stone to facilitate a dialogue but wrongly applied it becomes an obstacle. *Truth is not a democratic voting issue.* The majority vote is not the same as objectivity, quality or progress.

Although the processing of numbers may be objective to some extent, the interpretation of statistical tables is partially subjective and the decisions to act on the data become subjective as well as the acts themselves. Even if positivist researchers point out the weaknesses and limitations of their studies (sometimes in an appendix which few read), the seductively precise numbers and indexes give the impression of rock-solid evidence and absolute truths. Many managers, especially those who are insecure but have to make difficult decisions and choices, do not want the 'on the one hand it is like this, but on the other hand it could be like that' reasoning. They like a yes or no answer – even when there is no such answer. Business and management are about getting the right things done, not necessarily in the optimal way, but in a satisficing way reaching acceptable results; they are pragmatic. We have to make compromises and trade-offs and develop conventions. The danger is when conventions become permanent and a forcing element of the paradigm. Both the social sciences and universities must therefore re-think their direction and mode of operation:

> [O]ne can only be amazed by the emphasis that so many conventional social scientists still place on the claim that being 'scientific' requires researchers to sever all relations with the observed. Though epistemologically and methodologically indefensible, this view is largely dominant in social science practice ... This positivistic credo obviously is wrong and it leads away from producing reliable information, meaningful interpretations, and social actions ... [and] has been subjected to generations of critique, even from within conventional social sciences. Yet it persists.[39]

---

[39]Greenwood & Levin, 2005, p. 53.

The Scientific Narrative

The traditional foundation of case study research is a verbal narrative, often referred to as an essay or worse: anecdotal, storytelling or journalism. It is treated as a pilot study, an exploratory and conceptual prelude that you have to get over with quickly so you can call in the kalashnikovs and combat drones: quantitative methodologies and hypothesis testing.

It is important to realize that you do not leapfrog from verbal narratives to rigorous mathematical and computer applications that offer absolute truths. Efforts to address complexity in economic life have been made but have mainly added better defined fragments. We are far from understanding the systems on which our economies rest. We have not had the same breakthroughs as in some parts of the natural sciences. Medical science, though, is now seeking a refuge in evidenced-based medicine which leaves most of the understanding of an individual's health unanswered.

By merging explicit and tacit knowledge and adding network, systems, fuzzy set and chaos theory, steps are taken to open up to better addressing complexity. These theories offer languages that can be used in discussions and in hand-drawn graphical sketches, in mathematical and statistical applications as well as in computer simulations. *Network theory* is traditionally referred to as the study of *structures* but it equally embraces *processes*. *Hierarchy* is often set up as an opposite to the network but networks include hierarchies as well.

Such theories offer better opportunities for mixed methods studies. I call them *scientific narratives*. They are not the final answer to addressing complexity but they offer a manageable step forward.

Narrative research is concerned with the ways 'in which social actors produce, represent and contextualise experiences'.[40] There are warnings: 'the *narrative fallacy* or the *distorted narrative* ... is associated with our vulnerability to overinterpretation and our predilection for compact stories ... [which] ... increases our *impression* of understanding'.[41] Finally, a reminder from communications theory: 'A story that is told is never the same story that is heard.'[42]

A case is a story, yes, but so is an interview, whether it is structured in a questionnaire and scaled for statistical analysis, or a qualitative in-depth interview. And the presentation of statistical results and the ensuing discussion and conclusions in a journal article are also exposed to the narrative fallacy. Sigmund Freud, the neurologist who introduced psychoanalysis through a set of cases, is known to have 'upgraded' the cases to make them more convincing. This led some to call him

---

[40]Coffey & Atkinson, 1996, p. 54.

[41]Taleb, 2007 pp. 63–64.

[42]Denzin, 1989, p. 74.

'Freud the Fraud'. But perhaps he appeared under the wrong label – medical doctor presenting scientific research instead of novelist with a seminal idea. He was creative and insightful and after 100 years his ideas are still alive. He has inspired others to develop numerous alternative treatments of mental disturbances, some of these successful and some catastrophic. Psychological and mental health problems have only partially found satisfactory solutions. The search goes on.

A narrative is basically *linear* – 'story*line*' indicates linearity. A love story traditionally starts with boy meets girl, tells how their relationship develops; they get married and have kids, the kids grow up and they marry, grandchildren arrive, and the couple dies in the end. The chronology creates an illusion of the physical and mental world as orderly. Henry Mintzberg has pointed out that 'linearity is what makes writing so difficult'.[43] But to some extent the storyteller can jump between youth and old age, between the time before a couple had children to the time when the children are grown up. But the complexity of life requires a lot more non-linearity. Novelists and filmmakers have tried to introduce parallel themes interwoven into a complex web. But it is difficult to squeeze them into the book or film format and the audience may get confused. In his film *Inland Empire* from 2006, director David Lynch, known for his trendsetting TV series *Twin Peaks*, presents the simultaneity, interdependency and unpredictability of human relationships accompanied by multiple interpretations. His stories follow the principles of quantum physics rather than those of the mechanical physics of the Scientific Revolution. He is a seeker, inspired as much by today's Western civilization as by ancient Vedic philosophy from India (*veda* means 'knowledge'), and mixes extrospection with introspection. But how does he turn this into a narrative that the audience can follow? I have tried to watch *Inland Empire* 3 times, but I lose track. However, the film has received several awards of excellence, so there must be those who can perceive the message. Some years ago I had an opportunity to talk with Lynch, a gentle person who patiently explained to me the meaning of his films. It was inspiring; the non-linear narrative came alive – and yet is so hard to keep together.

In scientific texts, you refer to past pages and coming pages, to previous work by others and yourself, provide an index to list all pages where certain concepts or authors appear, and so on. It becomes a *hypertext* but it is still a long way from the complexity of real life. How about conceptualizing the storyline, condensing it and turning it into grand theory, and in a pragmatic way sending it back in a simplified version? Good authors probably do just that. Poets go even further, but very few of us understand and enjoy advanced poetry. By presenting research as a narrative, we avoid the fragmentation that is inevitable when we break down networks of events into abstract and stylized concepts, categories and numbers.

---

[43]Mintzberg, 1979, p. xi. He is especially known for innovative research in organization and strategy. See also Mintzberg 1983, 2007.

Methods books recommend that case narratives should provide *thick* and *rich descriptions*. This can be intuitively understood to mean comprehensive descriptions presenting complete and detailed data. But the word description is easily misunderstood. Sometimes I hear the remark 'This is just a description', indicating that it is a listing of raw objective data. But there is a catch. The tenets of the researcher's paradigm, preunderstanding and perception of reality affect what is described and how to describe it. Story, novel, narrative, account or verbal does not say whether it is journalism, fiction, entertainment or science.

In a case study of a company, it is quite common to present the company history, its size stated as revenue and number of employees, its organizational structure, what it produces and which its markets are. It is sometimes recommended that the 'milestones' of the company history are listed and an effort is made to find a logical storyline that leads up to the present situation. As was pointed out earlier, history is not an open book; it may be just as difficult to explain what happened as to predict the future. Of course, there are links between the past, the present and the future. The past may stand out as firm ground but in reality it is more like a slippery stepping stone and it is easy to slide off, simply because we do not understand it enough and it may have no relevance at all for the future. An obvious case is when new technology comes in and a company is well established in the old technology, both with products, manufacturing plants, culture and distribution channels. Changing this is sometimes possible only if 'creative destruction' comes in. It may be better to start a new company with no history.

The characteristics of the scientific narrative are summarized in Table 3.2.[44]

Table 3.2 The characteristics of the scientific narrative

- It embraces the complexity paradigm and interactive research where tacit knowledge and introspection are just as pivotal as explicit knowledge and extrospection.
- It strives to be as systematic, logical and rational as the topic allows it to be – but no more.
- It is focused on certain themes related to a problem, a purpose and research questions.
- It is conceptual and factual but on select occasions it can include illustrations, metaphors or fictional elements to facilitate readability and understanding.
- No narrative can be just descriptive as the author has to make choices of what to include and how to present it. In this way analysis and interpretation are present from the very start.
- Even if the narrative strives to be descriptive, its most important contribution is to start conceptualizing data into something that offers meaning.
- A narrative stimulates inductive research addressing complexity; a verbal text is not restricted by extant theories and formats (such as 2×2 matrices) or by mathematical and statistical language.
- Going beyond the verbal language by adding network, systems, fuzzy set and chaos theory, the conventional narrative can benefit from the additional languages of graphical representation, mathematics, statistics and computer simulation.

---

[44]See also Van Maanen, 2011.

Condensation – Not Reduction

One of the recommendations in the literature is *data reduction*, that data should be reduced to manageable concepts and categories and eventually theories. Having access to an overwhelming richness of data is positive per se, but difficult when it comes to analysis and interpretation. The term is unfortunate as it may lure us to look for the average or the typical, thus hiding variety and anomalies. In reducing data, you land in a situation where you:

- avoid or get rid of disturbing, non-linear data, thus taking out complexity to make data easier to manage for the researcher, at the same time mutilating the character of the phenomenon under study
- define conceptual constructs and operationalize them, which includes the Procrustean strategy of cutting and stretching
- get obsessed with averages, the 'normal' and the 'typical' and shun individual variety and diversity
- accumulate approximations, stylized and operationalized data and probabilities, thus multiplying errors
- build on previous and accumulated research without clearly scrutinizing the paradigm and assumptions on which it rests.

The reduction approach is what Habermas in critical theory refers to as 'the objectivist illusion' and the 'illusion of pure theory', and the necessity of challenging the foundation of research and the societal consequences of its practice.[45]

Instead, it is about *condensation* of data, making data *denser* without losing in content. That requires syntheses and theory of a higher level of abstraction. You find it in the colloquial saying 'What it boils down to is…'. Consider what Albert Einstein and Hans Christian Andersen have in common. Both offer narratives but they use different languages and both present a condensed version of a slice of reality; Einstein in the extremely dense mathematical formula $E = mc^2$ (energy equals mass multiplied by the speed of light squared); and Andersen in tales like *The Emperor's New Clothes*, from which you cannot deduct or add a single word. They have turned complex phenomena into grand theory and simplicity without losing any of their core content.

> A sentence should contain no unnecessary words, a paragraph no unnecessary sentences, for the same reason that a drawing should have no unnecessary lines and a machine no unnecessary parts. This requires not that the writer make all his sentences short, or that he avoid all detail and treat his subject only in outline, but that every word tells. (William Strunk & E.B. White in *The Elements of Style*, first published in 1918, later revised and still in print; named by *Time* magazine as one of the 100 most influential non-fiction books – and it is only 105 pages long)

---

[45]See further the discussion in Packer, 2011, p. 291.

Context, Parts and the Whole

The words *holistic* and *holism* refer to evolution as 'a process of unification of separate parts'. It is known as *holism theory* which says that whole entities are fundamentally different from the sum of their parts. A common objection is that if we try to grasp the whole we get lost; we have to settle for the parts and work our way up. In my view, it is a matter of iterations, swinging between the whole and the parts, and of having a least a rudimentary perception of where in the whole a part belongs. To use a metaphor, if you watch a football match at a stadium you can see the whole big field and all the players at the same time. But you can also focus on a single player or one of the teams and follow their moves, and you can change your attention from one to the other. To score a goal, a player is dependent on the interaction with their fellow team mates (collaboration) and with members of the other team (competition). In the end it is the outcome of the whole that counts.

Pick factors from a context and isolate them and you regress to the mechanical idea that if you study all the details you can screw them together like parts of an engine – and there is the whole! The Humpty Dumpty syndrome, derived from the nursery rhyme in which Humpty Dumpty fell off a shelf and went to pieces, shows that specialization

> resembles all the king's horses and all the king's men tackling the puzzle created by the fragments of Humpty Dumpty's broken body ... Despite the fragmentation in professional specialties, professionals and managers are expected to somehow put their – and only their – pieces of Humpty Dumpty back together again. Further, they are to accomplish this task without really understanding what Humpty Dumpty looked like in the first place, or what the other professions can do to make him whole again.[46]

The fact that Humpty Dumpty was an egg, and assuming that it was raw and not hard-boiled, makes the dilemma even more obvious. How do you put a broken egg together? It is an organic, live phenomenon whose elements mix and merge after a crash and quickly degenerate – much like an organization or a market.

Chaos Theory: Change, Risk, Uncertainty and Tipping Points

This is reflected in the VUCA acronym which emerged in military strategy in the 1990s. It stands for volatility, uncertainty, complexity and ambiguity, a realistic alternative to the conventional idea of predictions. Volatility means fast

---

[46]Waddock & Spangler, 2000, p. 2011.

and unpredictable change, often used to characterize the stock market where predictions remain guesses and/or efforts to manipulate the market. Ambiguity is not liked by positivists.

The Swedish prime minister solemnly informed his nation that 'we live in a time of change'. A former boss of mine, the founder of a major international management consultancy, went on a study tour to America. In his report to his consultants, he wrote how impressed he was: 'I talked to US executives who emphasized that everything changes so fast these days that it is hard to keep up.' And Bob Dylan got famous for the song *The Times They Are a-Changin'*.

Yes, it all happened in the early 1960s, half a century ago, but I still hear the same rapid-change story. If change has been speeding up all this time, the future must certainly be here before the past these days. The change story is of course not true unless its context is considered. Change has always been there in real life: sometimes slow, sometimes fast, sometimes sudden, sometimes planned, sometimes unexpected, sometimes beneficial, sometimes disastrous. The Second World War years probably represent the fastest period of change in modern history. Apart from the human disaster, technology and natural science developed at a higher pace than ever, driven by the need to win the war. Nuclear power, new aircraft, submarines, roads, radar, radio communication, weapons and new materials came out of the war. Very much of this has peaceful and civilian applications which we benefit from today.

I get journal articles to review that start by telling me that everything changes faster and faster today; we now live in a world where all business is global, communication is instant, the service sector is expanding at a rapid pace and the manufacturing and agricultural sectors are in decline; we live in a post-industrial society and a service economy; and all new jobs come from services. The authors have at least openly exposed their paradigm. I reject such articles; they should have been desk rejected by the editor in the first place. The authors list hyped clichés without evidence and nuances. The truth is that change is of a different kind now, that global contact is different and that the divisions in the service, manufacturing and agricultural sectors represent statistical categorizations without correspondence to the real world of today.

Some do not say that everything is *changing* faster and faster and faster but that everything is *developing* faster and faster and faster. 'Developing' has the connotation of 'good', meaning that everything is *improving* faster and faster and faster. It's time that someone says that it is not – with some exceptions. Many things may be changing faster and faster and faster but not getting better and better and better, just becoming different. There is also the 'dark strategy' in business known as *planned obsolescence*. An old example is the light bulb which can last for a very long time, but manufacturers build in a weakness to make it burn out earlier. Today, the most obvious example of planned obsolescence is computer programs which are substituted to force you to buy new hardware and software.

The renowned quality expert J.M. Juran used to talk about 'the vital few and the trivial many' and introduced the idea of *Pareto optimality*: a few factors cause the major share of the outcome. It is also known as the 80/20 rule: 80% of the outcome is caused by 20% of the factors. It may be a pragmatic guideline in specific cases but it also has its limitations. It is especially dangerous in trying to design grand theory. An increasingly popular concept is the *tipping point*: 'the straw that broke the camel's back' is a well-known adage in the English language; 'the drop that made the cup run over' is a variant in other languages. Even if you have driven your car for 90 minutes and spent 40 minutes parking, checking in, getting through security and walking to the gate, you need only be a fraction of a second late to miss your flight.[47]

Chaos theory recognizes the importance of the small factor and the long and seemingly insignificant cause-and-effect chain, popularized by the 'butterfly effect': when a butterfly flaps its wings in one part of the world, it can start a hurricane in another part.

In making assumptions in research and in selecting the variables and links to include in an equation, it is customary to exclude small factors. It is a technical necessity because the mathematical language only accepts a limited number of factors and links. If the scientist puts rigour over relevance and validity, which is the practice in quantitative modelling, this modus operandi is rational. But can we accept that a research technique is used which cannot harbour the complexity of an issue just by making the assumption that small factors do not matter? This is being done all the time – technique over outcome is a conventional research strategy in the economic sciences.

Ideally, change should be positive, which is the meaning of development and innovation. But undesirable things happen. For example, getting through airports is slower today because of the increased security against terrorism and sabotage. Although you can check in from your computer or mobile phone and do not have to physically wait in a slow line for manual check-in, you now have to wait for security control, have your computer inspected, not carry liquids over 100ml, and both you and your belongings are scanned. In addition, congestion over airports and in air corridors slows down takeoff and landing. Passenger airplanes do not travel faster today than they did after the jetliner started to replace the propeller aircraft around 1960. The effort to increase the speed of passenger air travel came and died with the Concorde (1976–2003), a supersonic jet that cut travel time between continents in half. I travelled on it once from New York to London and loved the short journey: 3 hours and 15 minutes.

Business as well as government organizations and NGOs today can be in a state of constant flux, can be stable or grow steadily for long periods, then slow

---

[47]See Gladwell's, 2000, treatise on tipping points,

down and even reach a sudden death. The future is only partially predictable. Research methods therefore must allow for the study of change processes. A snapshot of one point in time (statics) may be totally inadequate and a series of discrete snapshots (comparative statics) may be better but not enough to satisfy the non-linearity and dynamics of business and management reality. The classic independent/dependent variable causality is just a special case. We can take out a single dyad and allocate a single type of behaviour to its parties if we have everything else under control. It is a special case and in practical life it exists, but only temporarily. We may have been able to condense the complexity of, for example, an event, find its inner core and provide actionable simplicity; this is pragmatism. But we cannot, just for convenience and the drive to use mathematics, assume that variables behave a certain way without having gone through the whole complexity.

Summary

With the complexity paradigm as the base, we can develop case theory. Table 3.3 provides a summary of complexity paradigm tenets followed by specific case theory characteristics. Some of them have been briefly explained already, while others will be explained in later chapters. They will all accompany us on our continued journey in Methodologyland.

Table 3.3 Case theory in summary

Tenets of The Complexity Paradigm

- We must recognize and address *complexity* to understand an issue. We then search to *condense* a complex reality into *simplicity* to make it manageable. Complexity and simplicity are not *either/or* concepts but *both/and*. The predominant either/or thinking in Western social sciences stressing opposites and differences is secondary to both/and, indicating simultaneity, interdependence and interaction. It exists in the *dialectic* approach and in Eastern philosophy as *yin and yang*. Among such pairs that we meet in society today are *high tech/high touch, online/offline, virtual/physical* and *digital/analogue*.

- *Explicit* and *tacit knowledge* are interdependent and both exist in all kinds of human activity, and in quantitative as well as qualitative research, which was shown by the research edifice. *Pragmatic wisdom* is the highest level of knowledge. It connects understanding with decision-making, action and results.

(Continued)

(Continued)

- Data, concepts, categories and definitions are *fuzzy sets*; they have a core but it fades out and overlaps with other sets.

- The *scientific narrative* strives for conceptualization and is an expansion of the conventional *verbal narrative* used in case study research by including all sorts of languages – verbal, numbers and observational, and adding the support of *network, systems, fuzzy set* and *chaos theories*. A narrative is usually referred to as a description but the scientific narrative is an intentional *conceptualization* of the content. It begins *inductively* – researchers should not start by forcing received theory on to reality – and proceeds both through induction and *deduction* in what is sometimes called an *abductive* relationship.

- Research is not just a *conceptual* battle. Case theory applications must be put in the *context* of business and management, and must consider that everything is enacted by people whose *individual and group persona* exerts influence.

- *Interactive research* and *management action research* are central to achieving better access to the object of study; their central strategy is *involvement* of the researcher to allow *close access*.

- In business and management as well as in other social sciences, *change* takes place and has to be considered: 'the only constant is change'. Some factors influencing an issue may be big and others small; excluding a small factor is risky as it may be the *tipping point* determining the outcome. *Chaos theory* shows our limited ability to foresee the future.

Additional Case Theory Characteristics

- The traditional *overriding categories* in research – quantitative/qualitative and natural sciences/social sciences/the humanities – impair validity and relevance. They have given some characteristics an overriding status, while they are only a few among numerous others. The *research edifice* shows that both qualitative and quantitative research are dependent on the subjective and the objective, on judgement calls and pragmatic wisdom.

- Data should be the object of *condensation*, meaning that its content remains in denser form, while the *reduction* of data means loss of content.

- A *mixed methods approach* is usually desirable as no method is a crisp set, and each methodology may have a generally valid core but each application has to be adapted to the *context* of study.

- There can be numerous changing and multidirectional *causal relationships* between variables and just studying an independent and a dependent variable is rarely adequate; further, *covariation* between variables is no proof of causality.

- *Analysis* and *interpretation* are both necessary in drawing conclusions from research.

- *Theory generation* is a major tool; it travels through fuzzy zones, from the *substantive* and particular to a *mid-range theory* zone in the direction of general and abstract *grand theory*, and can eventually give back better and simplified mid-range theory for use in practice.

- *Theory testing* is made through constant comparison between extant theory and new theory; the repeated requirement of quantitative hypothesis testing of case theory can only contribute in special cases.

- In case theory, the number of cases is small, but the number of variables and relationships is large, while in positivist and quantitative research the number of observations is large, but the number of variables and relationships is small. Randomization is not used in the statistical sense; it is a matter of reaching data saturation. It can mean a single case or multiple cases, and mostly 5, 10 or 20 cases will suffice. For more complex issues, like the global financial system or the healthcare system, 100s or even 1,000s of cases are needed. We need all these cases to see the similarities and differences in the patterns of the substantive evidence derived from our object of study. Only then can we cross the mid-range theory threshold and move in the direction of grand theory and see the essential, generalize and gradually find true simplicity.

4

KNOWLEDGE – OR NOLEDGE?

The mission of research and science is to generate knowledge. To do so, we need basic insights into what knowledge is, how it relates to business and management, and the role of theory. Knowledge should further be pragmatic and pragmatic wisdom has already been launched as a designation for useful knowledge.

The conventional view holds that knowledge expands and, as a consequence, ignorance is reduced (Figure 4.1). But the relationship between knowledge and ignorance is more complex than this; it may even be perceived as a paradox. In primary school our schoolmaster used to give us some quite good commonsense advice: 'The more you learn, the more you realize that the more there is to learn.' We thought it funny and laughed. How could it be? We lived under the impression that when we leave school we know all there is to know. Much later, physics professor Johan Hagelin echoed my schoolmaster's observation: 'The intellectual approach to knowledge, by itself, is only partially satisfying. [What is] open to scientific investigation is essentially limitless [and] as one grows in knowledge, an even larger horizon of the unknown awaits one. *One senses ignorance growing faster than knowledge*' (italics added).[1] So knowledge is a moving target (Figure 4.2).

The line representing knowledge in Figure 4.1 shows a long-term trend of continuous growth. If more detailed, it would both show incremental and linear knowledge accumulation and sudden quantum leaps and discontinuities. But instead of closing in on ignorance we find a widening gap. The outcome is that in *absolute terms* we know more but in *relative terms* we know less.

Every discipline drowns in journal articles, books and conference presentations and no one can keep up with them. That top-ranked journals with their editors and reviewers screen the market for the very best is no guarantee. I follow several journals in my areas of study, both those with high and low impact

---

[1]Hagelin, 1998, p. 34.

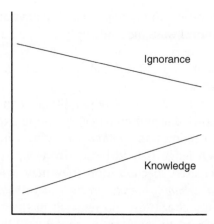

Figure 4.1 The conventional view: knowledge expands and ignorance decreases (© the Author)

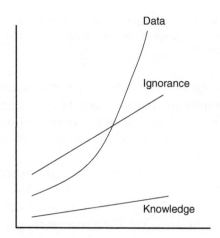

Figure 4.2 The realistic view: the amount of data is soaring, and knowledge grows but at a slower rate than ignorance (© the Author)

factors, old journals as well as new ones, and I have taken part in numerous conferences. I have learnt how fragile the system is. For example, it still primarily represents elements from the positivist paradigm. It does not combine explicit and tacit knowledge, and the persona factors of journal editors seem to be ignored.

We refer to the *knowledge society* populated by *knowledge workers*, where we develop knowledge and make sure that we can benefit from it. But there are many hurdles under way. It easily becomes systematically and rigorously derived non-knowledge – henceforth referred to as *noledge* – posing as hard-core, rigorous knowledge.

Knowledge and innovation and entrepreneurship have also become buzzwords which are used in rhetorical ways, not only by academia but also by CEOs, politicians, the media and others. A commonly held view is the modern wizard's formula of 'more research and money' and – whoops! – knowledge materializes and ignorance evaporates.

What have we got instead? Increasingly politicians and the media promote opinion more than knowledge and prefer celebrities to experts and people with pragmatic wisdom. It becomes an *opinionated society* where popular advocacy rules and genuine knowledge is held back. However, experts are not always preferable as with increased specialization they may lose pragmatic wisdom. We have entered into a *babble society*, even a *mega-babble society*, of words, words, words. University education and research in the economic sciences are unfortunately more geared to mainstream theory, methods rigour and numbers, and the intricacies of actual decision-making, implementation and outcome are left dangling.

> We are skating on pretty thin ice. (Perry Mason, fictional lawyer and detective, who had hunches – but surprise, surprise: in the last minute of the trial he always came up with hard evidence)

Yes, Perry Mason was right! As researchers we skate on thin ice. We sometimes break through and fall into the cold water but we mostly get up again. The more research I do and the more I read what others have published, the more humble I feel. How far can we get? What we call knowledge about 'life' and 'reality' – 'the truth' – is only partially understood.

We need knowledge to manage our lives and jobs better. What knowledge is in a generic and final sense has been an issue for philosophers for millennia – and still is. My methodology-in-use is focused on finding knowledge that is applicable in business and management contexts. It is a pragmatic view of what we can know and cannot know, and how we arrive at knowledge or have to do without it. By realizing what it is in a broader philosophical sense we can enhance our *resilience*, which is our capacity to adapt to new data and new situations.

Knowledge is a smart fugitive who is sometimes caught, sometimes not. We increase our knowledge in certain areas but most of what we do in social life remains ambiguous, uncertain and fuzzy. Knowledge is surrounded by mythology and has multiple meanings. I have gradually understood that the most important parts of life are fuzzy – and they have to be treated as such. Locking them up in statistical boxes explaining deviations with averages, distributions, approximations, etc., only locks us deeper into the boxes. I come back to fuzzy sets theory where a complex and important concept has a core and the concept then fades away and overlaps with other concepts. We have already met the dilemma of either/or and both/and dichotomies. There is a desire to find crisp sets in the social sciences even when they don't exist, and Western thinking likes to set up categories against each other and create a civil war of noledge.

Resources were once defined as natural resources like land, forests, water and minerals, but Drucker says that knowledge is the unique resource of an individual and an organization. Do we live up to the claim that the true capital is human knowledge? We place trust in technology replacing human beings by assuming that machines are more reliable and productive. We require that scientists follow a certain established methodology and confess to a certain paradigm. We behave as if everything outside the subject is objective; what is inside is subjective and of doubtful value. We are taught that objectivity represents a reliable truth and subjectivity does not. There is considerable contradiction and confusion in these established 'truths'.

I warn against cocksure researchers, executives, politicians and others who claim they know what knowledge, science and research are, and keep pushing their view on each and everyone. But is that not what I am doing in this book? No, I want to *share my truth* with you, in the hope that it will help you *find your truth*.

As I cannot solve the existential questions that the above approaches to life offer, I have to stay *pragmatic*: How can I survive, live well and at best enjoy life under uncertainty, contradictions, imperfections, fuzziness and chaos? As practitioners, we collect experiences of what has worked in the past and we try – with an open mind of course – to see what currently works and what might work in the future.

Suppose our experience tells us that dramatically reduced prices (input) during a sales campaign – 50% off! – lead to increased profits (output). This is supported by microeconomic theory that tells us that sales go up when price goes down and vice versa. But we may not really know *why* people buy and there are numerous individual reasons. The desire to save money may be one. It is not certain that we save money because we may buy more than we had planned and the cost of travelling to the store and the time we spend have not been counted. We also get emotionally excited by bargains, or the price reduction may be a reminder to buy something we have long wanted. There are many other reasons in idiosyncratic and complex combinations.

We can design a strategy for launching a new car model and we can control the input but we can only make predictions about the output in the market, the sales. We know that predictions of that kind are uncertain, even after research. It is worse if we launch a genuine innovation. The customers may not understand it; they may say they will buy it but when it is on the market they don't. Expressed attitudes and intentions in consumer surveys are unreliable in predicting actual future behaviour.

It is accepted research practice to look at the input/output relationship and this is often justified. Do we need to know what is in the consumer's mind, the *black box*? It could be that if we knew, we would be able to organize our operations and sales better. But big data claims that the computer will solve this. Will it?

Research should strive to go further and find out what is inside the black box. By not doing so, we risk creating a sustained pseudo-world of noledge, based on 'armchair deductions' and 'conventional wisdom'. Within the complexity paradigm this is not to be accepted. Research requires curiosity and a constant drive to understand. It is demanding to enter the black box and researcher convenience keeps us back. If we do not access the substantive area of the customer's mind, we do not stand on solid empirical ground.

A well-known case is that of Dr Semmelweis in Austria who, 150 years ago, noted that childbed fever among mothers, which had a very high mortality rate, could be avoided if staff and mothers properly washed their hands before entering the maternity ward. He spread the word among colleagues but they were affronted by the idea that they needed to hand wash; they asked for scientific evidence. Dr Semmelweis did not know why, just that there was a connection. He lost his position and was confined to a mental hospital where he died at the age of 47. His advice was only accepted after his death when Louis Pasteur demonstrated the existence of germs. The input–output observation was not accepted as long as the doctors could not see what was in the black box. I was told this at a lecture by a medical professor who used it to show how much science had advanced. When I asked him how many Semmelweises we have today, he looked at me like I was crazy. He meant that this could not happen today. My observations tell me otherwise. It is always risky to go against the mainstream and conventional truth.

The black box model is summed up in Figure 4.3.

The chapter proceeds to explain a series of basic issues of special relevance to case theory.

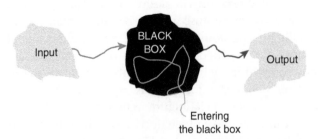

Figure 4.3   The black box input–output model as fuzzy sets (© the Author)

Causality and Covariation

Establishing cause and effect, *causality*, and *explaining* something is the dream of the social scientist. It remains a dream that seldom comes true because social reality is too complex. Figure 4.4 lists two types of variables and their links. First is the classic requisite that you identify an *independent variable* (the cause) and a *dependent variable* (the effect) (a). However, the relationship can vary with the context and time. In a dynamic environment such as an organization or a market, variables may change roles and the independent variable may turn dependent (b). Further, the variables can become interdependent; they can become the cause and effect of each other, for example in the interaction between suppliers and consumers, where they are co-creators of service (c). The question 'Which came first: the chicken or the egg?' has never been answered. Finally, the connection between the variables may cease to exist and they may both become independent (d).

But reality does not consist of dyads; it consists of complex networks of nodes and links. The roles of these networks can be stable for a long or short period and they can keep changing in numerous patterns. The new mathematics looks for *causality patterns* rather than simple causality (e).

Tyler Vigen (2014) shows in a book that with big data it is easy to find correlations. Many of them are *spurious*, meaning that they are not showing causality but only covariation between phenomena. For example, US expenses on science have a 99.79% correlation with the number of suicides, and the per capita cheese consumption has a 94.71% correlation with the number of people who die by being entangled in their bed sheets. Common sense and experience make these examples easy to doubt but in other cases tacit knowledge may not help. For example, if a scientific study finds a correlation between fat intake and

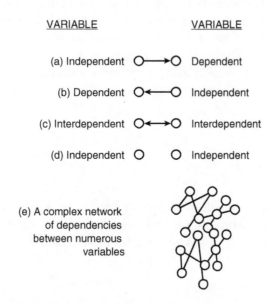

Figure 4.4 Relationships between variables (© the Author)

heart failure, we have to go deeper into the research to assess whether this is spurious or genuine causality. However, both research teams and the media are eager to present results as 'research indicates that...'. Indicates, yes, but that is all. Unfortunately, people read this as if it were a scientifically proven result, and the more it is repeated the more it stands out as true.

We have already encountered the Law of Parsimony, about the need to search for true simplicity. The risk is of course that we take refuge in explanations that are superficial and convenient but not true. On the other hand, we should avoid heavy and fancy vocabulary just to impress others.

> The most important lesson in the writing trade is that any manuscript is improved if you cut away the fat. (Robert Heinlein (1907–1988), often called the dean of science fiction writers)

To establish causality, the cause must precede the effect and there must be a clear link between the two. 'Co-variance' just means that two or more variables vary in a similar way but does not say they have anything to do with each other. 'Co-relation' says that there is a relationship between the two. For example, there is a relationship between price and sales volume. This is sometimes easy but also sometimes difficult to identify. In ongoing processes like the economy with unemployment, economic growth, inflation, house prices, etc., it is often impossible to pinpoint what preceded what; it is a complex causality pattern.

Understanding has been mentioned as a key aspect of knowledge and part of the complexity paradigm. Finnish philosopher Henrik von Wright concluded that explanation is primarily intellectual and cognitive, whereas understanding has a broader humanistic content, including such phenomena as empathy and intentionality.[2] Other words that appear together with knowledge are *skills* and *competence*. The word 'skill' originally referred to 'separation' but has also come to mean 'to understand' or 'to make a difference'. Competence has the same roots as competition and today refers to 'sufficiency to deal with what is at hand'.

Stylized Data

At times, when we get stuck in complexity and cannot move forward we need to make simplifying assumptions. I will use *stylized data*[3] for data that has been manipulated in the process of squeezing it into quantitative languages. It offers

---

[2]von Wright, 1971, p. 6.

[3]A term coined by Kaldor, 1957.

generalizations of complex statistical calculations and simplified presentations of empirical data, claimed to be facts. It means that details are excluded or not even noted and the grounding in the real world is inadequate. Such facilitation should only be temporary and be abandoned as soon as we have taken a step forward. If it is upheld by celebrity professors and the mainstream, we get used to it and forget its shortcomings.

Scientific research has elaborate ways of giving uncertain and ambiguous 'knowledge' a pseudo-precise identity. Examples are the operationalization of variables, averages, probabilities and normal distributions, where there are 'exact' indices and numbers to account for deviations. It is an impressive way of saying 'precisely perhaps' and 'exactly approximate'. It claims to be rigorous and systematically arrived at, despite the fact that the 'rigorous' process includes assumptions, judgement calls and an unknown number of errors.

Several well-meant efforts have been made to plant law and order in complex and ambiguous decision-making and turn the messiest of all business disciplines, marketing, into a rigorous and objective science. They have used numbers, stylized data and correlations.

In the early 1960s, the Profit Impact of Marketing Strategy (PIMS) project claimed that by building a huge quantitative database it could discern patterns of general application and guidance. Closer scrutiny showed that covariation between variables could be observed but not causality, and that operational and other definitions severely limited the generality of the results. From meetings with PIMS representatives and their clients and from reading their publications, I began to doubt the approach. Companies using PIMS consultants explained that it was extremely demanding and costly but could have certain effects in challenging taken-for-granted procedures. In very specific cases, PIMS applications could give useful guidance, but the results could not even be generalized from one profit centre to another in the same company. After 50 years of efforts, PIMS clearly shows its weaknesses. Despite this, every 10 years or so, there is an outburst of demands for more elaborate *metrics* to measure the financial consequences of marketing, now called *marketing accountability*. One of the recent variants is *customer relationship management* (CRM). Making it work is demanding but through a cross-functional system, data warehouses and algorithms for data mining, a company should be able to know considerably more about its customers and keep track of changes.[4]

In the early 1970s, *operations research* (*management science*) was promoted as the ultimate solution to business and management problems. It promised to revolutionize business firms by making decisions scientific and not leaving them to people with all their whims and idiosyncrasies; tacit knowledge is not taken seriously. It was another hyped idea of finding law and order by using

---

[4]Payne & Frow, 2013.

mathematics, statistics and the new (and at that time ridiculously overrated) computer capacity. It happened at the same time as the idea of the paperless office was launched and all a CEO would have to do was ask the computer for the optimal decision – no tedious meetings and paper-and-pencil exercises needed. I then worked for an international management consulting company that sensed a new opportunity for consulting and made an inventory of existing management science models. Approximately 1,500 were found – but only 12 seemed to have practical applicability and just a handful of huge multinationals were judged to be sophisticated enough to benefit from them.

The *balanced scorecard* and *intellectual capital*, to better measure the factors that in the long term affect profits, were found by most companies not to work so well in practice. But as business in the past 10–20 years has increasingly become a short-term money-making machine for anonymous shareholders and management, and value-in-use and value to society have been set aside, the long-term aspect has lost much of its flavour.

Those who promote more and more numbers and appoint them to facts despite them being stylized, sometimes very heavily, have no understanding of the reality of business and management; they lack pragmatic wisdom. They even seem to think that the mission of a company is measurement instead of value creation through production and sales.

Some academics got helplessly drunk on these alleged panaceas. They had not considered the complexities, ambiguities and data imperfections of decision-making and implementation in social settings. The efforts made some specific contributions but they offered no general methods or theories.

Box 4.1 is a thought-piece on measurement.

Box 4.1   Marketing Metrics: Generating True or Illusory Knowledge?[5]

It may be unnerving to learn that the word 'measurement' (derived from Sanskrit 'maya') means witchcraft, illusion, or image. Numbers are often used both as witchcraft and illusion, being pretentious and claiming that they represent – or even are – hard facts. Obsession with measurement can mean handing over the future of a company to an 'accounting tribe', abolishing vision and leadership. Many executives never become leaders, just grossly overpaid accountants. It is easier to quantify short-term profits than to quantify profits lost because of mismanagement of long-term relationships. We have to avoid *reification* where the indicator is not the phenomenon as such, but should offer the validity of a fair image of the phenomenon we are trying

---

[5]Quoted from Gummesson, 2004a, p. 140.

to understand. When indicators image certain phenomena with reasonable accuracy and validity, there is no problem. But when they do not, management will make flawed decisions and employees might go for the indicators that promote their careers and not for the real thing. Measurement becomes self-deception even if the full-colour, 3-dimensional and animated PowerPoint images look persuasive.

Certain phenomena can and should be measured in terms of money; others should never be allowed to come near a number.

'There is nothing more frightful than ignorance in action'. (Goethe (1749–1832), German author, natural philosopher, diplomat and civil servant; best known for Faust, a scholar who gets bored with his life and sells his soul to the Devil)

The real growth is in stored *data*. The word *information* originally meant 'to give form to the mind' and to denote 'the essence of something'. When I watch the TV news, most of what they announce is not relevant to me and some I do not understand. For example, they love to 'inform' me that the Nasdaq Stock Exchange dropped 1.2% during the day. It does not make sense to me; it is not information, just *noise*. I use data as the generic word, and reserve information for data that has meaning and relevance to my research or practice. We wrongly talk about 'information overload' when we mean 'data overload'.

Human Intelligence

In his book *Here Be Dragons: Science, technology and the future of humanity*, Olle Häggström reflects on the constantly promoted slogan that science and technology will take care of everything: 'Scientific progress has the potential both to cause humanity great harm and to bring great benefit.'[6] For example, nuclear bombs can kill millions of people but nuclear power plants can produce energy for heating houses (although the technology is not risk-free); and mobile phones and portable computers facilitate communication but without them global terrorism could not exist. Who is responsible? Scientists? Politicians? Everybody? Häggström's plea is for us to act with foresight and use pragmatic wisdom. But is this possible, or will the 'dragons' that science lets loose take over and even make us extinct? The level of the collective consciousness with morals and ethics is too low.

---

[6]Häggström, 2016, quotation from p. 5. He is Professor of Mathematical Statistics, Chalmers University of Technology, Sweden.

The prevailing belief is that science will guide us into the future through cognitive intelligence (in its narrow sense). Darwinism and atheism are preferable to a belief in something deeper than science can deliver, call it God, consciousness or whatever. We also see that religion can be just as belligerent and destructive as politics and we cannot control the forces. Better controlled systems and more legislation only take us so far.

When today artificial intelligence is extended and it and big data are brought up as the saviours of this and that, we have to think twice. Artificial intelligence so far is able to solve certain problems better and more quickly. Within the complexity paradigm: Does it consider the dependency between explicit knowledge and tacit knowledge, sound judgement and the importance of consciousness? This is where *general, human intelligence* comes in. If it can be replicated by machines and develop *machine intelligence*, in what direction will it go?

When we hear the word *intelligence*, we usually think of smart people with a high intelligence quota (IQ). An IQ of 100 is 'normal'; if you get above 130 you qualify as a Mensa member and are recognized among the top 2% of the most intelligent. The person with the highest IQ today is mathematician Terrence Tao with 230; Stephen Hawking has 160 and so had Einstein. However, this is not the same as becoming rich and successful. Ingvar Kamprad, founder and owner of IKEA, is dyslexic, with an IQ of 98, but is one of the most successful and richest businessmen in the world. Dyslexia – not being able to get letters and numbers together coherently – can largely be cured today, but many dyslexic people are highly successful, finding their own way to do things.

The IQ is an operational definition: 'Intelligence is what you measure with an intelligence test.' This may be practical in select situations but it does not hit the core of intelligence. As always, making a definition operational and rigorous means loss of validity. Intelligence is a rich and demanding concept and we may have an intuitive feeling for what it is. Going back to its origin, the Latin *intelligere* means 'the ability to understand' or 'to pick out' what is important. It seems to be everything we can understand and do, and some understand and do it better – they are more intelligent.

The IQ offers seductive preciseness, a number. It may measure the ability to think in logical sequences but not the ability to 'think outside the box', and does not include emotional, social and ethical intelligence. It does not include tacit knowing. Even with extensive testing, it is not uncommon for psychopaths to become leaders. They often have a high IQ, can be extremely charming at times as well as hard-working but lack empathy, and are compulsive liars, aggressive and conflict-prone.

A simple yet informative definition links success in life to a combination of analytical, creative and practical intelligence.[7] *Analytical intelligence* is the favourite

---

[7]Sternberg, 1985.

of mainstream science. But innovation is increasingly considered the driver of our economies and this points to *creative intelligence*. Einstein is a role model of the dual capacity of analytic and creative intelligence but he stressed that creativity is what makes the difference. *Practical intelligence* is the ability to get things done and achieve results; this is where entrepreneurs come in. The question is whether it goes beyond buzzwords and is no more than an effort to lock it into the law-and-order box. For a long time, emotions were kept aside but now we also talk about *emotional intelligence* – the ability to handle our feelings for ourselves and others. Intelligence has an affinity to *cognition* which has broadened its meaning from primarily referring to intellectual and orderly analysis to greater dimensions of understanding including tacit knowledge.

Richard Dawkins[8] is hung up on the categories of religion and science, in an either/or approach. Being called a category should include phenomena which have one or several variables in common. These variables should be of special interest to us in understanding or explaining something. Religion is labelled a belief system and is therefore just ludicrous to Dawkins. But is science the truth, the reality, something that can be 'rationally' proven? And are politics and atheism 'rational' ways of building a good society? Most people cannot, if asked, explain what they mean by science but they use the word all the same. Are religion, politics and science not just variants of *belief systems*?

Knowledge cannot be locked up in a box and unambiguously defined without being crippled or even killed in the process. That this was felt long ago is illustrated in the folk tales of many cultures. *Aladdin and the Genie of the Lamp* from the *Arabian Nights* tales is about a spirit who Aladdin lets out of an oil lamp. To show his gratitude, he makes Aladdin rich and powerful. Such tales and metaphors give inspiration to novels, movies and videogames. Some of them also offer condensed wisdom which is valid in daily life as well as in research. Is big data today's Genie who will prove theories, make exciting discoveries and make researchers respected and even rich some day?

This brings us to espionage. The Central Intelligence Agency (CIA) in the USA has become the symbol for advanced spying. There is also *business intelligence*, an umbrella term for everything that has to do with data and information for business purposes. There is considerable *industrial espionage* in the business world. The revelations of Wikileaks and whistleblowers making confidential data public have become a hot issue as the Internet opens up for new possibilities. Very much triggered by the fear of terrorism, it has been shown that governments hack personal databases, secretly film people's private lives and track their whereabouts.

From the day a child is conceived but yet unborn, he/she begins to receive and understand what is happening within the mother and her environment. It is tacit

---

[8]See further on Dawkins in Chapter 5.

knowledge; it is wordless and because of that we think children do not understand. It is the start of a 20–25-year process until a person is fully developed.

The brain consists of nerve cells (neurons) and links between them (synapses) forming neural networks. The total number of brain cells is, on average, 86 billion (a billion is 10^9) and the number of synapses for a 3-year-old is about 1 quadrillion (10^{15}). The total number of cells in the human body is estimated at 37 trillion (10^{12}). It is through this 'human software' that data is processed and a combination of explicit and tacit knowledge arises.

Can our experience, intuition and wisdom handle more or less than big data can manage? We do not know, but my best guess is that tacit knowledge can handle more. It is quite strange that in our private lives we can keep thousands of things going like driving fast in heavy traffic and interacting with hundreds of other cars. In the role of researcher, the very same people are taught to deal with just a few variables at a time and do it rigorously – no complexity, little interaction. I do not get this: How come you are so much smarter as a car driver than you are as a scientist? Even those with a low IQ can learn to drive a car and to recognize friends from a long distance. What evidence do they have? How long would it take to rigorously establish that they are their friends by using operational definitions and constructs and end up with a 'friends probability index'? Before this, the friends are long gone, and they have failed in terms of scientific precision.

Although businesspeople want 'hard facts' (too often meaning numbers), the good ones are cleverer than that. In their practice, they look for creative solutions; they know that decisions are often based on tacit knowledge; that some people see difficulties where others see opportunities; that statistics can easily be twisted; and that friendship, good vibrations, charm and charisma can be decisive in establishing relationships and networks that form the grounds for success.

This leads us on to the current interest in big data which is made possible with computers.

Most people use research much as a drunkard uses a lamppost – more for support than illumination. (David Ogilvy (1911–1999), legendary American advertising man)

Artificial Intelligence and Data Big and Small

While human intelligence is referred to as limited, *artificial intelligence* – created by machines and software – is thought to be unlimited. Herbert Simon is reputed to have said: 'By 1985 machines will be capable of doing any work Man can do.' This prediction is repeated today with the provision that it will take longer than

Simon suggested. New books are written about the possibility but also about the risk that we may become slaves to computers. What would be the goal of this 'superintelligence'? Will it be arbitrary and just make Bill Gates richer or would it also benefit mankind?

My view is that the computer brain will keep developing but the human mind will be of equal importance. The risk is that we lean on high tech for everything and fall into a brain coma; when the brain is not used synapses disappear. High tech and high touch offer a both/and win/win relationship; they are not in either/or win/lose competition.

A lot of hope is currently invested in *big data*. Its enthusiasts promise complete knowledge of everything and prophesize a new era of scientific research. We have met similar predictions time and again but none has proven true except for limited applications. Still, we need enthusiasts and compassionate entrepreneurs in science; they have a drive that can move mountains. In the future, we will see whether big data means a paradigm shift that forms the core of knowledge, if it will be dropped or given a place alongside a row of aspects of knowledge.

However, the big data idea is stuck in the positivist paradigm and its religious reverence to big numbers. The complexity paradigm acknowledges all kinds of data, big and small. We have met chaos theory and the tipping point, indicating that it is not the size that determines the outcome. It also depends on the context, and it is not possible to predict what will happen. Positivism has also had an influence on democracy, where the majority counts and 51% is taken as representative of 100%. The minority – 49%! – is allowed to be neglected. This is of course against common sense and pragmatic wisdom.

A Google executive explained to me the amazing size with which 'information' expands these days. In the year 2011 alone, a volume of 1.8 zettabytes of data was added. I had never heard of zettabytes; gigabytes were as far as I had come. But a gigabyte is a measly 10^9 data volume, while a zettabyte is a whopping 10^{21}. A newspaper reports that the volume of 'knowledge' (probably meaning 'data') doubles every 4 years, or otherwise expressed: in 4 years we develop as much data as in the previous 150,000 years. How this is calculated is beyond me. We have an enormous capacity to register, transmit and store data. The problem is in finding the data that makes usable information that can be transformed into knowledge.

Combining the power of modern computers with the ever-increasing abundance of data is predicted to solve any problem through number crunching and statistical correlations.[9] Big data may detect correlations that are otherwise missed but there is no telling if a correlation is meaningful or spurious. Human

---

[9]This section is inspired by an article by Marcus & Davis, 2014, p. 23, in the *New York Times*.

analysis and interpretation are always needed based on tacit knowledge and introspection. Much of big data is stylized to fit equations and computer software, which means that it only partially represents what it claims to represent. Once someone learns how to manipulate the data and the software to their advantage, they will misuse the system. It may be impossible to detect, for example, by a journal article reviewer or reader. Today, we have so much ambiguous data, on, for instance, unemployment, so when the party in government says that it has brought unemployment down by 9.2% and the opposition says that it has gone up by 6.9% they may both claim that they are right – they both use stylized evidence.

Big data further claims that it will revolutionize our ability to predict the future – perhaps at times, but the future is not just a variant of the past and the claim is in conflict with chaos theory. The future is also the outcome of discontinuities, new phenomena and unexpected events. The basis for the number crunching is data that was generated through some method and source. Much of big data comes from the web and is therefore itself a product of big data. Errors can multiply and vicious circles appear. Much measurement sounds very scientific on the surface while its validity is low. Bibliometrics do not identify the best scientists and educators. An overreliance on the explicit and a shunning of tacit knowledge do not lead to pragmatic wisdom.

Hype comes and goes; we want sensations. The medical-industrial complex has its many PR officers announce that the riddle of cancer is being solved – almost every week! And the media publish it. In a magazine from 1916 I found an article by an MD who said that cancer research was advancing. He was more humble than they are today and said that the advancement is long term and slow, using, essentially, surgery, radiation and medication. This was 100 years ago. Have there been major breakthroughs since then except in some specific areas? It is hard to tell as cancer has also changed character.

In their book *Big Data: A revolution that will transform how we live, work and think*, the authors[10] see a next step when data will be complete and omnipotent. Big data will make it possible to trace trends and patterns, and new grand theory is promised to emerge. Waiting for this to come true, a pragmatic approach is to stick to what we know and rely on our tacit knowledge. The purpose of theory generation is to turn data into meaningful information and knowledge. We do this in two ways: (1) access data pertinent to our research needs; and (2) select and organize the data into patterns, into theories. It is like finding a couple of sand grains in the big data desert. The other grains may be nourishing manure for someone else's research but only smelly dirt for others.

When, according to the Bible, the Great Flood was going to hit Earth, God asked Noah to save all living species by building an Ark and bringing couples

---

[10]Mayer-Schönberger & Cukier, 2013.

of each onboard – *big and small* – and to keep them there until the water had receded.[11] So he did. In the same spirit, Martin Lindstrom (2016), in his book *Small Data: The tiny clues that uncover huge trends*, presents his most recent research. It fulfils the demands of the complexity paradigm and case theory. Data is taken from close access to families and their homes; he spent hundreds of days visiting 2,000 consumers' homes in 77 countries, discussing, observing and acting. He combines explicit and tacit knowledge, extrospection and introspection, merging it all into pragmatic wisdom. He is a truly exceptional explorer of human behaviour related to marketing and consumption. His approach is both/and: high tech/high touch, online/offline and big data/small data.

Lindstrom concludes that big data is insensitive to diversity, is based on certain sources while not searching others, and cannot create insights. Further, innovation comes from juxtaposition, where 2 separate things combine and are brought side by side for comparison or contrast. The more physically distant we are, the less empathy we have. For example, laptop-to-laptop communciation, social media which are also partially anonymous, or being in a car surrounded by hundreds of others in cars, does not stimulate empathy. My conclusion is that big data is living in the positivist paradigm.

We further have to separate *facts* from data. A fact is something that can be proven true – but only within a certain context. We must keep in mind that scientific paradigms contain both fact and opinion. One of the world's most requested speakers is Hans Rosling, Professor of International Health. He says: 'I use facts.' No, he does not. He uses statistics and statistics are only 'facts-by-appointment'. They can be manipulated in all sorts of directions. They can represent facts but they are almost always 'stylized facts', approximate or distorted images of reality. They are deliberately skewed to favour special interests. He is a great presenter and showman and he engages his audiences in the same way as Mick Jagger and Bruce Springsteen by giving them a 'statistical rock concert', 'proving' among other things that it is getting better in the world at a time when everyone worries about war, epidemics without a cure, uncontrolled migration and growing organized crime. I do not say that his conclusions are wrong – I have not studied them in depth and I hope he is right – only that he still has to prove himself.

In 2012 President Obama announced the Big Data Research and Development Initiative to explore how big data could help solve government problems. Amazon, Wal-Mart and Facebook are working with big data solutions to process the masses of data they register every day. It is expected to improve decision-making in employment, economic productivity, and so on. It is further claimed that big data will give accurate predictions.

---

[11]Genesis 5:32–10:1.

In another book, *Unchartered: Big data as a lens on human culture*,[12] the human aspect is considered. The book does not criticize the humanities for not trying to copy old physics but says that research is driven by curiosity, the unexpected and serendipity, rather than preconceived hypotheses and controlled experiments.

Big data is focused on *What?* rather than *Why?* In connection with the black box model in Figure 4.3, we noted that knowing what happened outside the box was useful but, if possible, we would like to know what happened inside the box as well.

Google makes masses of data available for anyone to process. Wikileaks and others hack computers, retrieve confidential data and makes it public. This is of course unfortunate if the information could start a war and terrorist actions. But when a government has lied to citizens on important matters, does not the public have a right to know? At the same time, the intrusion by national security agencies into the private lives of people can be motivated by the prevention of terrorism – a price we have to pay for security. Espionage has taken new forms.

For many decades, artificial intelligence has been predicted to beat the human brain. It works better than human intelligence for explicit step-by-step deductive and logical issues. The tacit knowledge part, which is sneered at by positivists like Dawkins, is seen as a challenge and it is not rejected. It would be meaningless to reject it for two reasons. First, every decision is based on both explicit and tacit knowledge even if this is not admitted. Second, the human brain has a huge number of cells and synapses. Add to this how persona properties such as greed, hatred and extremist ideologies conquer the world – a large portion of leaders on all levels are psychopaths – and outrank the human and rational.

We can go on endlessly in search of data, information, facts, evidence, etc. Every new term and concept we contrive seems to lean on another that cannot be unambiguously defined. We get a network of words and we behave like the puppy that tries to bite its own tail, which of course moves away with the same speed as the puppy turns around. When we try to define the fuzzy concept of quality, we are sent to the fuzzy concept of excellence and to the fuzzy concept of customer satisfaction, which leads to the fuzzy concepts of needs and wants which lead to the fuzzy concept of promises and then back to the fuzzy concept of quality. The circle is closed and we may have discovered many facets of the issues during the bumpy voyage, but has it led to understanding and an improved ability to take action?

One of the most important strategies for researchers designing grand theory is to do what can be done but accept that the outcome is usually tentative, can be further improved and in the future even totally changed. In mainstream research, methodological rigour is favoured over relevance. In practical work and

---

[12]Aiden & Michel, 2013.

applied science, it must be the other way around. Most of what we do in social life is not scientifically supported. The same is true in psychology, medicine and many other disciplines.

We rarely arrive at the final truth because reality is complex and business and management keep changing. There will always be a residue in research that may look small but can be the tipping point; the recently found Higgs particle is such an example.[13] By recognizing complexity and ambiguity and that our knowledge is more often tentative than final, we improve our ability to manoeuvre our way through life.

We have seen that artificial intelligence can beat human intelligence in the deductive processing of data based on rational thinking, which is primarily contained in explicit knowledge. But where does tacit knowledge come in? Is big data a solution? Many doubt it, but we will see. We can of course also ask why machines should take over the human being, some promising that then people will have so little to do that they can do whatever they like. But what will that be?

Innovation and Entrepreneurship

Innovation refers to new knowledge and entrepreneurship to the implementation of new knowledge or a variant of extant knowledge. Innovation and entrepreneurship can be perceived in different ways. Box 4.2 is a narrative of two cases compared. They are condensed here because of the limited space and to qualify as scientific narratives they need to be expanded.

Box 4.2 Norwegian Oil and Swedish Methanol: Two cases Compared

This is a brief comparative study of two cases, focused on a single aspect: how innovation and entrepreneurship in the energy sector are approached in two countries, Sweden and Norway. Being neighbours in Northern Europe, they have several commonalities but also differences. Their economic structures are very different. Particularly relevant for this case is the fact that half of Sweden's exports are manufactured products, while gas and oil account for over 60% of Norway's exports. Sweden has to import all oil and its stock of oil lasts only 2 months.

In the 1970s Norway began exploiting the North Sea for oil, a totally new industry for the nation. Today, 40 years later, Norway is one of the richest countries in the

(Continued)

---

[13]See further Chapter 5.

(Continued)

world per capita and has one of the lowest dispersion rates between high and low incomes. The building of the oil industry has been controlled by the government but has gradually opened up to private capital within a mixed economy format.

Now that fossil energy (oil, gas, coal) has to be reduced for environmental and health reasons, everyone is looking for replacements. Two alternatives have been aggressively promoted: ethanol based on agricultural products (such as sugar cane, corn and potato) and windmill power which requires constant wind. More recently, solar cells have popped up as the solution. None of these options fulfil the sustainability and economic goals. Despite this, they have been favoured by EU governments, mainly out of ignorance paired with heavy lobbyism and corruption. Sweden and Norway were early in introducing electricity by exploring hydroelectric power. Nuclear power is also promoted with the claim that we can now build safe plants and take care of the waste. For Sweden, methanol, made from wood, stands out as the ideal option both from an environmental and an economic perspective. As the sale of wood goes down continuously, due to less consumption of paper, major suppliers, among them Sweden, must search for alternative uses.

During the past 8 years, a Swedish company, Varmlandsmetanol AB, in cooperation with the German ThyssenKrupp Industrial Solutions GmbH, has developed a concept for manufacturing methanol from wood biomass. The entrepreneur is Dr Björn Gillberg, a scientist and, since the 1960s, an investigator into environmental problems and sustainable solutions. The development has resulted in the design of a complete methanol factory. It is automatic and has no negative impact on nature. The only by-products are heat which can be used for heating houses, and wood ash which contains all the minerals found in wood and can be returned to the woods. The first factory design is complete and licences and delivery agreements have been secured as well as environmental certification.

Today, finance and taxes pose obstacles. So far the development of the Swedish methanol company has been based on smaller emissions of stock, a small staff and low cost. No political party in Sweden has taken an interest in the project, and national media have ignored it while local and regional media report it. Politicians, all the way from the extreme left to the extreme right, and the national media keep praising windmill power, having fallen for lobbyism and special interest groups instead of rational arguments. News media and politicians in Sweden have little interest in knowledge and fall back on populist opinions. The other issue is that energy is a tax object that gives a high income to governments, who are afraid to lose this income. This again is just convention and lack of innovative thinking. If we change the fuel for cars, for example, tax rates can be re-calculated, be based on the new situation and open up for new solutions. It will be necessary anyway as goals to substantially lower pollution are set by the UN and the EU. Successful Swedish industry was built on long-term investment but this tradition has got lost.

Methanol can be produced at reasonable cost and there is unlimited raw material in Sweden and there will be so forever. It would take 20 years and 50 factories (replicas of the first factory) spread in forest areas from the south to the north of Sweden. In this way the raw material would always be close to a factory and the methanol would be distributed in the region of the factory; no big transport would be needed. It takes 2–3 years to build a factory, requiring a workforce of 700 people. As during the first 20 years the building of 2–3 factories annually would be in progress, 1,500 to 2,000 full-time jobs would be created. Operations and maintenance of the 50 factories would provide 10,000 permanent jobs. This would take place in sparsely populated areas, meaning that small towns and the countryside get an injection of work prospects and young people are not forced to move to metropolitan areas. In addition, it would attract other firms and public services: shops, restaurants, local transportation, doctors, dentists, etc.

So why does it not happen? Politicians keep chanting the innovation, entrepreneurship and scientific research mantras. Sweden's government as well as the EU gave huge support to methanol research although everything was already known.

When governments these days offer money for research, they have certain priorities or rather hang-ups: 'life science' (mainly medication), IT-based products, and leisure such as computer games, events and tourism. They believe we live in a postindustrial era dominated by the service sector. Official statistics are supplier-oriented while consumption-oriented statistics would give a totally different picture. A former prime minister even proclaimed that Sweden does not need manufacturing in the future and a new prime minister claims we do but only says so in general terms. The production of methanol is the first major manufacturing proposal in half a century in Sweden.

The financial sector does not support long-term sustainable investment, but wants high payback in 3–5 years. An industrial project is long term and requires high investment which only a nation can handle, like the government in Norway. The EU tries to put up obstacles when governments support industries, suspecting that it will interfere with free EU competition.

Sweden has unique conditions for methanol production. In 20 years from now, Sweden would not have to import any oil and could later export fossil-free energy and fulfil the sustainability and environmental goals which the same politicians in their public rhetoric have at the top of their priority list but totally disregard in practice. It only ends up in bureaucracy and legal technicalities. For example, a tax was recently introduced on all biofuel when more than 5% is mixed into petrol and diesel. In this way, the biofuel is taxed for carbon dioxide in the same way as it is for fossil fuels – but it does not produce carbon dioxide emissions. Pragmatic wisdom is absent.

In business there are usually risks when a new company is established and there are uncertainties about the future. With Varmlandsmetanol there are none. The building of the first factory could start immediately and the market is there. The obstacles come from peripheral institutions which fail to fulfil their function of infrastructural support: government, financial institutions and the EU.

This comparative case raises several basic and crucial questions: Is the demand for innovation and entrepreneurship mere rhetoric? What can we do to encourage innovation and entrepreneurship in practice? Are we afraid of change, although we talk about change coming faster and faster? How can we stop lobbyists and others taking over important national interests just for the benefit of special interest groups? How much is merely controlled by persona factors? And what are the roles of the EU, the national government, financial institutions and universities?

Knowledge can be long-term stable as well as ephemeral. Innovation, new knowledge, is important but it should not be a cause in itself. Some things do not need innovation but rather maintenance and incremental improvements.

Visions and overriding strategies without an action plan and hands-on work are empty words. The innovator – the creator of the new knowledge – is often not the person of action and street wisdom needed to turn an innovation into a value proposition that the market will accept. Treating customers, citizens, intermediaries and other stakeholders as co-creators also means that entrepreneurs are needed in business to sell at a reasonable profit and in government to help politicians make decisions accordingly.

> Plans are only good intentions unless they immediately degenerate into hard work.
>
> (Peter Drucker (1909–2005), often called the founder of modern management; see further Box 6.1).[14]

Let me once more refer to my old school master when addressing our mathematics class: 'When you think you have solved a mathematical problem, ask yourself if the solution makes sense.' Perhaps you thought you had followed the rules of mathematics and gone by the book. A bureaucratic mind settles for that: 'I have done everything right!' Yes, but you may have been distracted and missed a tipping-point detail like writing a minus where there should have been a plus.

Businesspeople are under constant pressure to meet deadlines, enhance shareholder value and satisfy customers not to lose them. This is not true in monopolies and many government organizations where decisions, actions and results are often sadly lacking or being routinely delayed, causing dissatisfaction and injury to customers, citizens, employees and others. Particularly in government organizations, political control, outdated regulations and persona factors such as lack of motivation, dislike of colleagues, an urge for power, etc., can severely impede quality and productivity. Just following a bureaucratic ritual – 'go by the book' – is rarely sufficient.

There is theoretical knowledge that

- provides maps for practice and action, or
- lives its own internal life, screened off from the real world – *pure theory*.

To reduce uncertainty when knowledge is lacking about the future, one can:

- monitor an issue and get early signals if the development is not satisfactory and then quickly change decisions, plans and action; but also
- be prepared by designing alternative scenarios and identifying which decisions and actions may have a crucial effect on the outcome and what alternatives may exist; and then
- be prepared for quick action when suddenly called for.

---

[14]Haas Edersheim, 2007, p.x.

Most of the daily adaptations we have to make in an organization or in our private lives are incremental and well within our paradigm and experience. But when incremental changes accumulate – often without us noticing – they may lead to a sudden tipping point and discontinuity, leading to a paradigm shift. Our business mission may turn out to be no longer viable. Change can also be unforeseen and abrupt when, for example, a competitor offers an innovative value proposition that is quickly accepted among buyers. The IT market is full of such examples.

It can be a strength to have worked long and have lots of experience. But when something novel occurs it can be difficult to understand and accept it, especially if it is contrary to our current understanding. Our knowledge has lost relevance but we still cling to it. When new tech is involved, it is easier to change and lack of experience becomes an asset. To learn something new, you often have to *unlearn* the old, which may have taken your whole working life to build up. Young people have nothing to unlearn.

There is also considerable *inertia* and *resistance*. I have recent experience of reactions to innovation in business and management concerning both the free market and governments that only reinforce an experience from long ago: people are reluctant to accept innovation. There is no fast and continuous change. Innovators and entrepreneurs have just as difficult a time in getting the novel accepted today.

I once participated in a *brainstorming* session with a small group of managers at an international firm headquartered in London. Brainstorming is an organized way of stimulating positive and constructive thinking, however crazy. Ideas should be constructively received; you should try to pick up on an idea, see it as an opportunity and move it forward. It is the opposite of *brainwashing* which restricts our minds. However, we are so used to focusing on fault-finding and problems that constructive brainstorming requires training. After a while, when every idea had been killed off, one of the managers concluded: 'Gentlemen, this is the kiss of death before birth.'

We also have a wealth of knowledge that is rarely taken care of by anyone. For example, PhD and masters theses and books and articles by senior professors may contain seminal contributions that never reach a wide audience. Research has to be marketed and academic articles are hardly read by practitioners. Some academics are good at this and become respected professors at top universities, superstars on the speakers' circuit and highly paid management consultants. But it is not a self-regulating mechanism that separates the excellent from the mediocre and the bad. Total Quality Management (TQM) programmes have opened up for improvements, both incremental ones and innovation, and many organizations have benefitted from them. The programmes often degenerate into reports and measurement exercises rather than actual improvements of organizational cultures and researchscapes. They add to the number of meetings, reports and conferences; their outcome is words and numbers mega-babble instead of action and results.

Conventional categories and approved methodology have become so taken for granted that no one questions their meaning. We have already noted that truth is not a voting issue and can only temporarily rest on consensus and compromises between experts – intersubjectivity. But when a research 'truth' becomes institutionalized with chairs, departments, buildings, money, journals, courses, textbooks, etc., the temporary becomes permanent.

There are conflicts between:

- what is better and what should replace the established

- innovation and the established

- the established paradigm and a new paradigm

- intellectual issues and persona issues

- fads, fashions, images and hype, and the solid and the genuine

- welcoming the new with an open mind and the risk of being taken for a ride.

Not all innovation is good. New chemicals and drugs, for example, can cause suffering around the world in many ways, although they can also find good applications.

Re-inventing the wheel refers to something that is presented as an innovation but has been known about for a long time. It may have been forgotten; it is *lost knowledge* and *lost pragmatic wisdom*. Business and management are full of re-invented wheels but also of square wheels and other non-circular shapes. Looking back at the old philosophers of science, one can find so much wisdom that we do not apply.

An entrepreneur is a person who changes something and makes it a success. When we believe in something and go for it with all the drive we have, it may bear fruit even if it seems impossible. Before they are successful, entrepreneurs have usually failed several times but learnt from their failures.

> If I have a thousand ideas and if only one turns out to be good, I am satisfied. (Alfred Nobel (1833–1896), founder of the Nobel Prizes, who registered 350 patents (innovation) and had a sales success that made him one of the richest men in the world (entrepreneurship))

Machiavelli published his book *The Prince* in 1513. Its message has endured, although we may wish it had not. It was based on experience and reflection. Presidents, CEOs and others in high positions get there and stay there by applying lessons from Machiavelli. Keywords are power, rhetoric and control. Leadership is a phenomenon that has eluded capture and keeps doing so. What is it really?

Recently, I read about a high-profile consultant who claimed that he had condensed the most pivotal qualities of a great leader. One was 'Do the right thing at the right time.' Who can object, but what does it tell you? If you negate the statement it becomes: 'Do the wrong thing at the wrong time.' Both statements seem equally banal. In these days when innovation and entrepreneurship are the lead words everywhere, it is wise to listen to Machiavelli:[15]

> There is nothing more difficult to take in hand, more perilous to conduct, or more uncertain in its success, than to take the lead in the introduction of a new order of things. Because the innovator has for enemies all those who have done well under the old conditions, and lukewarm defenders in those who may do well under the new. This coolness arises partly from fear of the opponents, who have the laws on their side, and partly from the incredulity of men, who do not readily believe in new things until they have had a long experience of them. Thus it happens that whenever those who are hostile have the opportunity to attack, they do it like partisans, whilst the others defend lukewarmly, in such wise that the Prince is endangered along with them.

Machiavelli's advice is pragmatic. We have to

> inquire whether these innovators can rely on themselves or have to depend on others … can they use force? In the first instance they always succeed badly, and never compass anything; but when they can rely on themselves and use force, then they are rarely endangered. Hence it is that all armed prophets have conquered, and the unarmed ones have been destroyed.

Without entrepreneurship, a major innovation may never reach the market. The name of Joseph Schumpeter (1883–1950) is associated with the need for innovation and entrepreneurship.[16] He claimed that capitalism drives innovation and that breakthrough innovation requires *creative destruction*, abandoning the old for the new. It refers to an innovation that creates a new market and new value networks. Such examples are the 'no frills' airlines that started to grow at a rapid rate in the 1990s. Southwest Airlines in the USA is the role model and Ryanair and Norwegian are successful examples from Europe. Their dramatically lower prices, even giving away tickets for free, a dynamic pricing model based on the number of unsold seats, and maintaining a slim organization have gradually disrupted the mode of operation of large full-service airlines and created a whole new market for flying. Other examples can be found within IT. Such innovations are not only beneficial, they may force the closure of well-run companies with great service but who are locked in a

---

[15]Machiavelli, *Il Principe*, Chapter VI. English translation available at www.gutenberg.org

[16]See Schumpeter, 1950.

business model that cannot handle the price competition of the innovation. Many people associate innovation with new technology but it is probably more often about taking existing knowledge and innovating a business model which can better exploit it.

How entrepreneurship works is best seen where it happens. Innovators and entrepreneurs are often perceived as difficult people – that is so because they break with the mainstream and the established order and therefore live in a stressed and turbulent situation. Steve Jobs, co-founder of Apple, left the company and was later called back as CEO to save it. He launched a series of innovations, among them the iPad and the iPhone, and made Apple the world's most valuable company on the stock exchange in 2011, a spectacular turnaround. The same year, at the age of 56, he died of cancer. *Fortune* described him as 'the greatest entrepreneur of our time … brilliant, visionary and inspiring'. Jobs was both an innovator and an entrepreneur but he could only implement this by being extremely demanding of his organization. More often, the innovator and the entrepreneur are not the same person. Ingvar Kamprad, the founder of IKEA, did not invent the selling of prefabricated furniture parts to be transported and assembled by the customer. But he invented and has continuously improved a business model that made it work on a grand scale. In 2016, at the age of 90, he was one of the richest men in the world, but he has recently moved back to his home town in Sweden and handed over the chairmanship of the company to his youngest son.

Serendipity means accidental discovery. You are looking for one thing and find another. You may experience this as failure, but wait a minute! Take a look at what you found to see if it may be useful for something else. An example is the 3M product Post-it, the set of small yellow pieces of paper with glue at the back. The glue allows you to attach it, but also to take it away and stick it down again. I use Post-its all the time to tag pages in books and newspapers which I want to go back to. The 3M researchers were doing research to develop the strongest glue in the world but found the opposite – and a successful innovation was born.

A scholar must also ask 'What exists?' and 'Into what categories can we sort existing phenomena?' These are basic questions in *ontology* where the Greek 'onto' means 'being'. Do we find a pseudo-world or a real world? The 1999 science fiction movie *The Matrix* was about the real world having been captured by computers which have created a simulated world for us to live in. Analogous with this theme, Hastings (2013) called his critical book on marketing *The Marketing Matrix*. Business has designed a pseudo-world for citizens to programme them to maximum consumption, with the illusion that we can only be happy if we have the latest wide-screen TV, the latest fashion in clothing and the right brands of anything from cola to cars. So ontology is about the existence of reality. A distinction is made between *realists* and *nominalists*. Realists claim that the real world exists as an objective entity, irrespective of the individual. Nominalists claim that reality is subjective; it is interpreted through our senses by means of terms and concepts (like relationship marketing), categories (like goods and services), models (like an organizational structure) and theories (like the microeconomic price theory). So there are many views on 'reality'. In summary:

- Only the external world provides reliable evidence; extrospection alone takes us to true knowledge. It exists as an objective entity, irrespective of the individual.

- Only one's own *mind* is sure to exist; the external world cannot be known and might not even exist in objective terms.

- Reality is subjectively interpreted through our senses and we cannot separate ourselves from what we know.

- Reality, as we know it, is constructed intersubjectively through meanings and understandings developed individually, socially and experientially. In this way, reality becomes a majority voting issue.

- Both introspection and extrospection contribute to knowledge.

Right or wrong, in business and management we have to assume that there is a real world in which we operate. We have to make things happen and constantly doubting that reality exists makes our lives onerous. We have to remain pragmatic and leave the deeper existential riddles to another discourse.

To become a scholar, however, the researcher must pose the questions 'What is knowledge?' (the known) and 'How is knowledge acquired?' (the process of knowing). These are basic questions in *epistemology*, a term which stems from the Greek *episteme*, meaning 'knowledge, science', and *logos*, here meaning 'study of'. But do not facts constitute the 'real reality'? *Management by fact* – instead of *by opinion* – is a cherished slogan in corporations. Within the positivist paradigm, you are expected to deal with facts. If they cannot be found, certain data, especially stylized numbers, becomes *facts-by-appointment*, creating an illusion of the real world.

T-Shaped Research

Scientists used to be well-rounded and some have already been mentioned. One of the most versatile was Copernicus (1473–1543) who dethroned *earth* as the centre of the universe. He was a mathematician, astronomer, physician, classical scholar, translator, artist, priest, lawyer, governor, military leader, diplomat, economist, traveller and speaker of 4 languages. We do not make scientists like that anymore. With today's accumulation of knowledge, it is too much to be handled by a single person. All the same, originality and innovation seldom come out of a group. Those who began Microsoft worked in the most powerful computer environment in the world, IBM, but had to break out to implement their ideas. Apple started out in a garage and so did Amazon.

A common distinction is that between *generalist* and *specialist*. The generalist knows little about a lot and may, that way, be able to lead an organization consisting of specialists who each know a lot about a specific area and work in specialized departments but cannot overview their contribution to the whole; they *sub-optimize*. True leaders make syntheses of recommendations from specialists to *optimize* the activities of organizations and research, or more realistically: *find satisficing solutions.*

Today, people are specialized in smaller and smaller topics – a practical necessity, yes, perhaps. Even at a business school, a lecturer may have little idea about what his colleague in the next room is working on. Details are studied at great length with increasingly refined techniques but need to find their place in a broader context. It is hoped by researchers that details can be added together to build a whole and then find improved mid-range theory and grand theory. It is a hope in vain; it is regression to the Scientific Revolution and positivism and the mechanistic world. The whole is not just the sum of its parts. Academics are in for a great challenge. Every year, they get thousands of journal articles and other publications and most are destined to live a lonely life. Articles today are not necessarily there to be read or add to knowledge but to give career entries in a person's résumé. If specialization occurs, it is important to see where in a larger context it belongs and how it integrates with other tasks. Network theory and systems theory offer help to find holistic knowledge.

In the IBM Service Science programme, the T-shape is used as a knowledge metaphor. The vertical bar of the T represents depth and speciality, and the horizontal bar width and the ability to see the whole. Figure 4.5 shows the T as an individual who is deep in one area and combines that with a generalist view. Research is increasingly developed in teams and dependent on the combined efforts of many people, many Ts, that represent different types of depth and width. By merging them, we get a network of Ts and we may be able to gain synergy effects. Interdisciplinary research in the social sciences can easily become an organizational burden with built-in conflicts: internal competition instead of team spirit, collision between methodological traditions, budget issues (who should pay what?), too many views and too much diluted consensus. This may all end up in non-productive babble.

According to Service Science, it is time to co-create the 21C (21st century) Talent, the T-shaped university graduate and the lifelong learning professional.

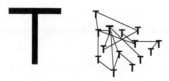

Figure 4.5 The T-model illustrating specialist and generalist knowledge in an individual (left) and a network (right) of collaborating people who integrate their resources

IBM's initiative to build a Smarter Planet requires co-creation between stakeholders (IBMers, customers, partners and others); disciplines (people from engineering, management, the social sciences, the humanities); people from all sectors of society; and people from all countries. Do universities and companies provide this today? No.

There are *genuine experts* and there are those who charge high fees for little value being added, if any at all. They may just be well-paid 'hostages' to instil trust through their celebrity image and rhetorical skills. Expert is a dangerous word because it includes true and serious experts with sound judgement as well as *experts ad absurdum* who follow rituals but do not focus on outcomes. Experts, be they university researchers or business professionals, must venture to deviate from an established ritual when they see it is not working and use their tacit knowledge.

> Sooner or later we all get professionally deformed. (Herbert Tingsten (1896–1973), professor of political science and editor-in-chief of Sweden's biggest newspaper)

Expert knowledge is context-dependent in the sense that the expert must understand why, when and where to use a solution or perform an activity. Experience can only be acquired in actual cases. Academically acquired knowledge is usually generalized beyond what the substantive data offers and the student does not come into contact with the variations in context that appear in real life. Therefore, the practice of poor 'book-smarts' must be combined with pragmatic 'street-smarts'. A common complaint against young MBAs is that they are too book-smart and do not see what is really important and how it should be tackled; they need experience to become skilled.

Specialization may be very productive, which was noted by Adam Smith who introduced the specialization of labour. This in turn required trade. Again, the question is not either/or; it is the balance between performing many operations and just a few. Specialization has often gone too far in working life, making people bored or sick or lose the view of their contribution.

There is a difficult trade-off between how innovation is created by independent basic and long-term researchers, totally uncontrollable processes and dedicated entrepreneurship, and bureaucratically controlled law and order. Today, the financial aspect is trying to take charge in controlling research through the allocation of money. In this finance-centric world, science follows the money rather than the important research issues.

A long-lived notion is that change is ever more rapid. I have heard this since I first started out in business. Some things move fast during a period, like the integration between computers, mobile phones, TV and cameras do now. However, many issues that were on the agenda in the 1960s are still here, like how to measure the financial effect of marketing, how to make companies understand customers, and how to manage a merger between companies so that true synergy occurs.

5

WHAT SHOULD RESEARCH AND SCIENCE BE?

This chapter is about my perception of what research and science should be. These are high-profile phenomena in our times and the 'emperors' of the modern knowledge-based society. But when does the emperor wear clothes and when is he naked? Science is categorized as quantitative and qualitative, and the social sciences, the natural sciences, the humanities and, recently, life science are seen as categorizations that should be abandoned.

As you know by now, I see all important and complex concepts as fuzzy sets. Many terms, concepts and categories have been launched in different time periods in research contexts, and many are just very slight variations of one another. When they have become obsolete, they have a tendency to keep hanging around. These are reasons why methods books can stand out as confusing.

It is vital to understand where science and research can contribute useful knowledge and where it cannot:

- There is knowledge that we can acquire if we make an effort.
- There is knowledge which is hard – sometimes even impossible – to acquire. We may lack access to pertinent data, but even if we have it we may lack the ability to organize the data in meaningful patterns, i.e. in theories.

The conclusion is that we sometimes know very well what we are doing, sometimes know it reasonably well and sometimes, frankly, we have not got a clue, even if we have practical experience and deploy a battery of research methods.

In Chapter 1, two purposes of case theory were defined:

- learning about and handling a particular case and situation
- theory generation to arrive at more generally applicable knowledge.

To show the confusion about what science is, the following types will be discussed below:

- *Genuine science* is the good guy, the systematic, serious and honest effort to under-stand the world we live in and how we can manage and improve our lives.

- *Scientism* is the extremist; it is synonymous with an overreliance on methodological ritual and convention, while the value of the research results is secondary.

- *Pseudoscience* poses as science but is not.

- *Fraudulent science* is a villain.

- *Science fiction*, finally, is a designation for speculative future science that seems impos-sible now but can become reality. It will not be brought up further here.

What is what can be disputed. What is pseudoscience for some can very well be science for others. And fraudulent science often passes as science because the fraud is not exposed and can even be protected by individuals and special inter-est groups. In Chapter 4 we learnt that knowledge is hard to catch but we have to make the best of it. After all, we strive for survival and try to reach an acceptable state of well-being. This is what pragmatism is about.

At the same time as science is claiming superiority in knowledge develop-ment, scientists behave in ways that are inconsistent with their claims. Here are some of my experiences:

- They disagree, sometimes aggressively, on major issues. They say things like 'what is true today may not be true tomorrow' and claim that this is evidence of progress. Why is that so if science is so superior to all other ways of acquiring knowledge?

- When as a consumer you suspect that a product is unhealthy (such as genetically modified food (GMO)) they say: 'That has not been scientifically proven.' No, because it has not been studied, so how can it then be proven? It should be up to the scientist and the producer to prove that it is not harmful and show social responsibility by assuming the burden of proof. Instead, by using smart one-liners they try to impress people and keep them quiet. This is non-scholarly behaviour.

- When you keep demanding an answer, instead of entering into constructive dialogue, scientists sometimes get irritated, angry and abusive or refer to your claims as super-natural and paranormal and thus beyond the reach of science.

- Persona factors – the quest for power, personal goals, talent, hang-ups, etc. – are mixed into scientific research and even take over. Many hard-nosed Western scientists realize the shortcomings of science, but they feel they will lose prestige if they admit it and try to cover up insufficiencies instead of displaying them and taking hands-on action.

Science and *art* are often presented as conflicting categories, with talk in terms of *either* the natural sciences *or* the humanities. It is the same either/or conflict that exists between explicit and tacit knowledge. But their dependency is also recognized, while the London School of Economics (founded in 1895) has the positivist motto 'To Understand the Causes of Things'; the logo of the Royal Institute of Technology in Stockholm (founded in 1827) carries the inscription 'Science and Art'; and the University of Oxford, the second oldest university in the world (from 1167), keeps its motto 'The Lord Is My Light'. To boost its image, the film industry established the Academy of Motion Picture Arts and Sciences. It is best known for the Oscar Award but also for developing film technology. Russian film director Andrei Tarkovsky[1] writes that 'art, like science, is a means of assimilating the world, an instrument for knowing it in the course of a man's journey towards what is called "absolute truth"'.

The following sections deal with the different types of science. They are followed by sections on the terrorism of received categories and notes on definitions. The chapter concludes with a recommendation that case theory is appointed the diamond standard of research in business and management.

Genuine Science

One of the Swedish representatives in the EU returned from Brussels where the controversial issue of GMO had been on the agenda, as it has been for many years. She was now convinced that GMO is good for humanity. Her message to the news media was: 'We must trust science!' Is this a credible conclusion or should it be: persistent and skilled lobbyists win in the end because the decision-makers, those politically appointed, are less competent?

She is known to be smart and has extensive experience of international negotiations. What she has actually achieved except for being diligent and having been around for a long time I do not know. But what did she mean by her statement? I would have liked to have asked her, but politicians in Sweden are difficult to approach and if you do they give vague answers and seem little interested in what you say. They take on too much and just cannot handle it.

My conclusions are: she has no idea what is meant by science and has no experience of scientific research but has the official power to push the introduction of GMO in Sweden. If I required brain surgery, would I allow myself to be operated on by a person who knew nothing about brain surgery? Would I allow myself to be flown by a person who is not a skilled pilot? Would I accept those people just because they mean well? Of course not.

There is no general consensus about what science is, not even by scientists, although there are those who claim they know. If scientific research were the ultimate and clear answer to the riddles of humanity and the universe, it would

---

[1] 1986, p. 37.

be great but science is fuzzy and ambiguous. It dwells in a zone of instability which is equally a zone of opportunity. How should we behave?

Although most people have little idea about science, it is a commonly held opinion that science is good, and even the crown of the human quest for knowledge. Science has become a premium brand. But how we identify true knowledge and tell it from noledge is a critical issue. The answer is far from straightforward.

When you meet people who claim – in an authoritative voice – that they know what science and knowledge are, watch out. You are in bad company. Characteristic of excellence both in research and practice is a reflective mind: we need *the reflective researcher,*[2] *the reflective practitioner* and *the reflective user of research*. Life is complex and confusing, data is incomplete and deadlines prevent us from acquiring sufficient data – and very often such data is inaccessible, even with unlimited resources. We have to act despite the imperfections or we get nothing done. We have to take risks.

In business and management, we must give priority to pragmatism. But even so, constant reflection and curiosity should accompany us throughout our personal and professional lives. If not, we may very well reach the status of mediocrity – but not of excellence. The scientific journey requires our presence here and now. It is important to emphasize *constructive dialogue* which is *win-win interaction*. Avoid *debate* which follows a *win-lose* strategy: Who won the debate and who lost? External reflection – *extrospection* – goes hand in hand with internal reflection – *introspection* – where we use our persona and tacit knowledge.

Science claims to deliver the Rolls-Royce of knowledge, the highest quality possible. The latest buzzwords are evidence-based medicine and life science, which, except in some very specific applications, I discard as public relations stunts for profit. Big data is another buzzword which may have an important contribution to make but we do not really know yet.

My personal stance is that science should be

- systematic
- innovative
- transparent
- honest.

Science should further

- offer useful knowledge
- be supportive of the welfare of society
- require commitment beyond being a mere career path.

---

[2]Schön, 1984.

These criteria must be seen together. Systematic and innovative, especially, are often incompatible. Systematic indicates law and order; innovative means disturbing the order. Still, systematic and innovative need each other; they have a both/and relationship.

Role-model mainstream scientists are described as logical and rational, with analytical and critical minds, searching for evidence that unambiguously proves their hypotheses as right or wrong. This is an archetype, *the scientific man*, who is just as unreal as *the economic man*, whose completely rational behaviour is assumed in economics. Behavioural economics had 'discovered' that human beings also have emotions and cognitive limitations and lack perfect information, but at times have to make immediate decisions and act quickly. The terms *bounded rationality* and *satisficing* are ascribed to Herbert Simon. He said that we could strive for an optimal decision as an ideal, but more realistically we see the rationality bounded and have to settle for a satisficing outcome. It is pragmatic wisdom. What goes on in our minds is sometimes a black box even to ourselves; it is tacit. In business and management practice, however, emotions and non-rational behaviour have always been recognized.

Even if we want our understanding to 'rest on scientific grounds' as the slogan goes, the lack of such grounds and a pragmatic attitude force us to rest on a mix of objective, subjective and intersubjective bases. Awareness of this dilemma is necessary to make us search for better knowledge; complacency will block our progress.

Scientism

Scientism is science stretched ad absurdum. Science becomes methods rituals, and its advocates drive a hard bargain. Scientism will be discussed based on the science criteria proposed by Mario Bunge, the campaigning of Richard Dawkins, and evidence-based research. It concludes with Paul Feyerabend's warnings against rigidity in the use of the scientific method.

The Bunge Syndrome

Professor Mario Bunge is the epitome of the versatile and successful scientist who has devoted his life – he turned 97 in 2016! – to the philosophy of science and research methodology. He has published extensively, has 16 honorary doctorates, has won the most prestigious awards and is a member of scientific societies around the world. He has not sought celebrity status among the common man.

He is a ruthless prosecutor of what he calls charlatans in science. In his 'Charter of Intellectual Academic Rights and Duties', he presents 10 'commandments' of science.[3] The intentions are commendable; we are all longing for clear guidelines that will set us on the right path. He is an atheist but denies he is a classic positivist. Let's see.

Commandment no. 6 reads: 'Every academic has the right to discuss any unorthodox views that interest him, provided those views are clear enough to be discussed rationally.' But who determines what is 'clear enough' and what is 'rational'? Such criteria correspond to regulations in a bureaucracy and do not open up for theory generation and innovation. At the same time as Bunge is emphatically rejecting subjectivity and discarding interpretation as mere guesswork, he makes continuous subjective interpretations and evaluations of a diverse range of research. He is right in doing so if he is guided by reflection and dialogue, including high ethics and good intentions. But he denounces the right of others to use their good subjectivity, pragmatic wisdom and persona. Hence, his discussion does not qualify in the complexity paradigm.

He wants to separate science from the 'bunk' that has infiltrated academe, disguised in false scientific clothing, 'a postmodern Trojan horse' the most lethal enemy of all, the enemy within. In his 15-page text, on well over 100 occasions he applies abusive designations to those who deviate from his norm. They represent mysticism, freewheeling, deceit, anti-intellectualism, guts over brains, instinct over reason, contrived wilful ignorance, gobbledygook and much, much more.

These are certainly not criteria from the methods literature. Is it not below the dignity of those who consider themselves scientists to regress to such jargon? Whatever you think of their message, it scares me when people like Bunge, Marx and others are abusive when trying to make their point. They degrade science to scientism.

The Dawkins Crusade

Richard Dawkins is best known in science for his early contribution to genetics. He further developed the concepts of *genotype* (our heritable and unique genes) and *phenotype* (our observable physical characteristics and behaviour), and the interaction between the two. He later became Professor of Public Understanding of Science ('Popular Science') at the University of Oxford, UK. His list of scientific achievements is impressive and his paradigm is the same as that of Bunge: positivist and atheist. But unlike Bunge he has become a media celebrity. Being in marketing myself I conclude that he has been heavily coached in PR, lobbyism,

---

[3]Bunge, 1996, pp. 110–111.

branding and media behaviour. He turns science into light entertainment. In this respect he is Bunge's antipode.

I watched a TV show where he toured Australia with another highly regarded professor. They were whisked in and out of airports, into limos, entered huge auditoriums where they were presented as the James Bonds and Elton Johns of science. They sat on the stage with a bishop, arguing against his belief in God and religion. The arguments were one-liners, sound bites and slogans. Perhaps it is the fault of the TV producers, but I could not find much intellectual content in their statements. They said that through scientific study you can find out and test anything. *But they never defined science and scientific research and most people are so impressed by these words that they do not ask what they mean.* When referring to truth, even such scientists fall back on subjective expressions like 'what is plausible, rational and reasonable'.

When 150 years ago Charles Darwin explained the evolution of species as *natural selection and the survival of the fittest,* his logic seemed convincing and was accepted by the scientific community. What he said simply means that we are all – human beings as well as animals – predators.

As an alternative to Darwinism, those with a religious approach to life suggest *intelligent design* or *creationism* – that is, that there are aspects of life that can better be explained as a *planned cause* directed by some kind of mastermind. A study conclusion was recently reported that atheists are more intelligent than religious people.[4] The project involved a statistical meta-analysis of 63 studies done over many years. Such a study is highly unreliable and may completely lack validity. The research question 'Are atheists more intelligent than religious people?' is not meaningful. It offers 'rigorous noledge' and does not add to useful knowledge. 'Atheists versus religious people' becomes a play with forced abstractions and fuzzy categories; it is loaded with methodological difficulty. For example, several people may belong to a church from childhood but do not take a deeper interest in religion; it is more a social and family thing and provides rituals for weddings, funerals and such like. The meta-study showed that perhaps half of all scientists have religious beliefs and half reject religion.[5]

My preferred term is *spiritual* to religious because 'religious' is associated with a certain church. By rejecting all those who are spiritual, such thinkers are not just buying into Darwin, they are appointing themselves supermen who, like James Bond, have a licence to kill, in this case ridicule their colleagues. They follow in the footsteps of Karl Marx who branded those 'unscientific' who did

---

[4]Zuckerman, Silberman & Hall, 2013.

[5]The term *agnostic* refers to those who take a more humble stance and say they are uncertain about the existence of a higher power.

not think that all misery could be explained by class differences and eradicated by socialism. Political beliefs are similar to the religious ones and in the history of mankind both are linked to wars: who conquered and killed who and who was the 'great leader'. This has not changed. The only difference from before is that we now have more advanced technology with which to kill people or force them to do as we say.

Competition is Darwinian; the best companies win and the others die, as reflected in the ABBA song 'Winner takes it all'. There is a *belief* in certain business and political circles about the totally free market where hypercompetition acts as an objective referee. But competition is only one of many dimensions of success and it is sometimes beneficial but also sometimes disastrous for the service to consumers, citizens and society at large. The other extreme is a planned economy where everything is controlled by almighty governments. The economically most successful nations apply a compromise between free competition and regulation, sometimes referred to as a mixed economy. It is both/and, not either/or. In 2015, US marketing professor Philip Kotler published a new book, *Confronting Capitalism: Real solutions for a troubled economic system*. Marketing is a way to handle competition and during his long career Kotler has acquired the reputation of being the leading representative of marketing thought. He gives the following reasons for writing the book: he wants to understand the capitalist system himself; he has found that the system has 14 major shortcomings; he wants to propose solutions to the shortcomings; he wants to make his text accessible to anyone; and he believes that marketing is one of the bedrock concepts of a functioning society but that it has been neglected by economists.[6]

In a book for youngsters, *The Magic of Reality: How we know what's really true*, Dawkins (2011) warns against the evils of 'anti-scientific fairytales'. The book is made for the computer game and monster generation of young people and is filled with artistic illustrations. More than emphasizing his message, the illustrations draw the attention away from it. Science is turned into trendy entertainment.

Dawkins claims that you can understand reality in the following ways:

- *Direct use of our 5 senses: sight, smell, touch, hearing and taste*: What says that there are only 5; could there not be 6, 7 or more? Animals have developed their senses differently and have other senses. How about a musician's ability to perceive and reproduce the most subtle nuances of sound, and those with the ability to intuitively understand mathematics? We also know from witness psychology that, for example, 'sight' is highly deceptive.

- *Indirectly with the aid of special instruments*: much of what physics is about cannot be seen so we need sophisticated instruments to study what our 5 senses cannot help us with. As private people, we use TV and telecom daily; the signals are around us but we need TV sets and phones to pick them up.

---

[6]Kotler, 2015, pp. 1–2.

- *Indirectly through models that can be tested for their ability to make correct predictions*: the models are designed to replicate reality and can consist of words, equations, graphics or computer simulations. But predictions can only be made with high probability in very limited instances – a problem dealt with in chaos theory.

Then Dawkins defines 4 types of magic:

- The title of his book contains the word *magic*. By *real magic* he means what can be understood through scientific method.

- *Supernatural magic* is found in myths and fairytales. Yes, but great myths and tales are often based on real-life experience and provide metaphors – models – that communicate something of value for understanding reality. Great examples are the tales of Hans Christian Andersen. His stories *The Emperor's New Clothes* and *The Ugly Duckling* succinctly uncover general aspects of human behaviour.

- *Stage magic*, as performed by professional magicians, who do not claim they do real magic; they use the shortcomings of our 5 senses to fool us for entertainment. But Dawkins just recommends that these senses be of use in science. American magician James Randi, a true believer in mainstream and positivist science, has been called in by scientists to unveil dishonest research and has done so in many cases.

- *Poetic magic* can be falling in love or watching a spectacular sunset.

Dawkins says that true science is constantly on the move, which also means that today's truth may be tomorrow's untruth. He is willing to change his mind if there is new evidence – but again the problem arises: What should be considered evidence? What he says may sometimes be true, sometimes not. A lot of science is simply loudmouthed and arrogant and does not keep searching for or listening to new observations. It is driven by persona factors such as the financial aspect in its worst form – extreme greed – and knowledge that may be a financial threat to powerful organizations is kept away from the public and from further research.

At the opposite of what true science discovers, Dawkins sets the *supernatural* or *paranormal*. He determines for us what is natural and normal. 'Norm' comes from the carpenter's square, a tool for creating right angles. It became the most common and desired state or form. There is also the unfortunate concept of *parapsychology*, meaning psychology alongside the recognized academic discipline. It studies telepathy, near-death experiences and many other phenomena. By tying them to mainstream psychology and positivist research (such as randomized experiments), the phenomena cannot properly be studied on their own terms. They belong to another paradigm. His methodology is claimed to be perfect: How come?

I do not know what makes Dawkins tick. His brand earns him money and accolades, which can be acceptable persona virtues within limits. He could also *believe* in what he says – it is science turned into fundamentalist religion. It could also be that he is a well-paid lobbyist by certain pressure groups and companies to keep up the public belief in what they are doing and to encourage politicians to allocate funds to certain types of research. I do not know. Let him apply his perfect scientific methodology to himself and 'prove' his case.

Unfortunately, Dawkins uses subjective ideas and circular reasoning by saying that the supernatural is 'beyond the reach of natural explanation [and] beyond the reach of ... the well-established, tried and tested scientific method that has been responsible for the huge advances of knowledge we have enjoyed over the last 400 years or so'.[7] Note then that the use of these methods also causes suffering, and that chemicals through food, water, soil, medication and air keep poisoning the earth, threatening health and even killing people. He uses the expression 'real evidence' against what he calls 'supernatural'. Nothing of this is objective. What if – and most likely so – there are lots of natural things in the universe that defy his 'scientific' man-made methods and require other insights to be understood?

Within the complexity paradigm and case theory, I would like to include a different kind of meta-analysis. As we proceed to generate theory from cases, we can rarely reach the saturation point on our own but can benefit from existing cases and those made by others. We could avoid the bias inherent in only taking cases that have been published in top journals and decide for ourselves whether a case qualifies or not, thus avoiding the risk of the publication bias. We could also avoid the bias of a specific agenda and advocacy by doing purposeful sampling.

Bunge stated that every academic has the right to unorthodox views provided they are 'clear' and 'rational'. We can add another quality in vogue: 'rigorous'. In a recent essay, 'Is it a Theory? Is it a Law? No, it's a Fact', Dawkins makes the same mistake as Bunge and others.[8] His message is that Darwinian evolution is a FACT. But fact holds the same subjective loading as 'rational', 'reasonable', etc. – it is a fuzzy set and it is contextual. So we land in more 'famous last words' and a dead end.

We now proceed with another hard-pressure sell in 'science' – *evidence-based medicine*. It is spilling over into the social sciences and business and management so I want to draw your attention to it. The medical-industrial complex, consisting of pharmaceutical companies, pharmacies, hospitals and other clinics, doctors and nurses, and researchers, is also a growing and highly profitable economic sector.

---

[7]Dawkins, 2011, p. 23.

[8]Dawkins, 2015.

Evidence-based Research

In the book *Hard Facts, Dangerous Half-Truths & Total Nonsense*, two Stanford University professors ridicule those who make decisions in organizations because they do not understand how to use science.[9] The book launches evidence-based medicine as the role model for *evidence-based management*. In another book, *Bad Science*, the author claims that evidence-based medicine is 'the ultimate applied science, contains some of the cleverest ideas from the past few centuries, it has saved millions of lives'.[10]

It sounds like *the silver bullet*. No, that is not enough – evidence-based medicine is launched as *the gold standard of science*. Being in marketing I smell the recommendations of premium-priced public relations consultants and lobbyists. The outcome of the books is scientism. Even if the intentions are commendable, they offer an overstressed message.

The word 'evidence' can mean data, facts or proof, or all of them. Evidence-based medicine consists of randomized, controlled experiments offering statistical probability estimates of the outcome. The results are sometimes followed by *meta-analyses*, meaning that several experiments are compared in order to establish reliability (replicability).

Advocates of evidence-based medicine distrust medical practitioners – your doctors – for using their experience and judgement, i.e. a combination of explicit and tacit knowledge and not scientifically proven therapies. In reality, what is 'scientifically proven' is not objective but operationalized constructs offering probabilities and averages, and thus it has reduced validity. It may fit instances of simple causality but not complex, multi-factorial causality.

The Greek physician Hippocrates (460–370 BC), usually named the father of Western medicine, founded his theories of disease and treatment on a limited number of patient cases. In retrospect, we can conclude that Hippocrates, Freud, Marx and others have been both right and wrong, but their 'impact factor' – to speak the modern language of academic research – has been extremely high.

Medical practitioners were once expected to follow the guidelines of 'what is used in professional circles' and 'science and established practice'. Hippocrates advanced the systematic study of *clinical medicine* by summing up medical knowledge and prescribing practices for physicians – this is known as the *Hippocratic Oath*. In a modern version of the Oath, two of the tenets are:[11]

---

[9]Pfeffer & Sutton, 2006.

[10]Goldacre, 2009, p. x. Other sources for this section are Timmermans & Berg, 2003; Staal & Ligtenberg, 2007; Bohlin & Sager, 2011. See also Crossen, 1994, about the manipulation of fact.

[11]Created by Dr Louis Lasagna, Tufts University, Massachusetts, 1964. See also a discussion by Lasagna on ethical issues in medical treatment. The New York Times, 1964.

- 'I will remember that there is art to medicine as well as science, and that warmth, sympathy, and understanding may outweigh the surgeon's knife or the chemist's drug.'

- 'I will not be ashamed to say "I know not", nor will I fail to call in my colleagues when the skills of another are needed for a patient's recovery.'

This is a humble and holistic approach to the profession and to its potential benefactor, the patient; it demonstrates pragmatic wisdom. Each patient used to be an individual case, and then increasingly grew into a statistic coming out of a randomized experiment with mice. Medical science lives under the illusion that numbers make it scientific. But human individuals cannot be treated in crude categories; they are not averages, approximations, distributions or decimals in statistical tables. The revised Hippocrates guidelines recommend that science, intersubjective consensus and doctor persona are elements in the treatment of patients. But in the future the behaviour of medical staff shall be standardized and adhere to what has been published in peer-reviewed, international and top-ranked medical journals. The goal is *evidence-based practitioners* and patients should be dedicated *evidence users*. Critics have described this as 'the fast-food option in science', where procedure and not the effect on each individual patient is in focus.

Many doctors do not use the best scientific methods and offer outdated therapies. Doing experiments in a lab is just the start of a possible value-adding process. Even if new research is based on advanced methodology and techniques, it has no value until it is transformed into clinical practice so that patients can benefit from it. In an interview, Dawkins said that if *alternative (complementary)* medicine comes up with something new, it will be tested by Western medical science and, if found to be working, be quickly used to treat patients. He is wrong; new knowledge may be delayed for decades or never reach the market – the patients – and obsolete knowledge stays on. Traditionally, medical staff learnt both through formal education and patient encounters under the guidance of senior colleagues. Today, formal training has taken over. As the personae of doctors and their environments vary greatly, patients will be exposed to treatments all the way from excellent to mediocre, harmful and lethal.

My standpoint is as follows: the *concept* of evidenced-based research is not new – scientists have always looked for evidence and facts – but the *term* evidence-based makes it sound like an innovation. On a more sensible interpretation, evidence-based medicine is a supplement to other knowledge in consultations between patients and healthcare staff.

Evidence-based research stays within the positivist paradigm and does not qualify for the complexity paradigm. Elements from it can be of value in specific cases but it has no general value, and it is certainly no 'gold standard'. In the practice of research, evidence is a combination of subjective values and raw data.

What data you should define and promote to evidence depends on your problem, intentions, creativity, time, money, concepts, theories, and so on, i.e. the context in which it belongs. This goes for business and management as well as for physics and medicine.

The reality is that there is no single superior way of handling the complexity of the human being. Evidence-based medicine is customized in studies of the effect of medication, simply put: pills. Other parts of medicine that cannot be exposed to randomization and experiments are excluded, for example most of surgery. Evidence-based does not apply to serious alternative medicine which is not based on the Western medicine paradigm and is stamped as 'quackery'; alternative medicine is rejected despite the fact that patients get well. Western medicine refers to this as imagination; the patient is simply stupid. It has been given a 'scientific' name – the *placebo* effect. Medicine becomes business and the strategy is 'more pills to the people' to boost the profits of 'Big Pharma'; value for the patient is not the first priority. The placebo effect is defined as an effect which is reached by a therapy that has no proven 'objective' – meaning 'physical' – effect but all the same makes patients healthier. It is continuously misused in medical science. It is known from experiments with 2 groups of sick people, where 1 group gets a pill that is known to heal (or, more commonly, to reduce symptoms) and the other gets a 'sugar pill'. Both groups are told they are getting a new potent drug, but those in the 'sugar pill' group get better as well. It shows that what people believe – their mental disposition – is equally as important as the carnal aspect. Unfortunately, placebo is used in medical science as a garbage can for what cannot be explained by narrow testing techniques. It could just as well be that neither of the pills had any effect and the patient has self-healed. It is a convenience explanation that frees scientists from ignorance and mistakes and makes them feel great. What it amounts to is the arrogant attitude that medical doctors are clever and patients are ignorant. Recently, the Karolinska University Hospital in Stockholm spent a lot of money and several years on investigating placebo. They found that there is nothing magical about it but rather that there is always a combined reaction of the physical and the mental. Then they say more research is needed. Why? My conclusion is that placebo can have a meaning in specific cases but the concept is not generally applicable.

But the random experiment is not even enough to test medication. Patients for whom there is no approved remedy may be asked to try a new medicine which may have a healing effect or, more commonly, slow down the progress of their disease. But it can also have unknown side-effects. Doctors are paid to recruit such patients who think they have nothing to lose and a chance of gaining something. This may be reasonable but is just a commonsensical trial-and-error strategy; it is not evidenced-based medicine.

Evidence-based research does not uncover the *synergy effects* of taking several different pills. As far as we know, Elvis Presley and Michael Jackson did not die from drug abuse at the ages of 42 and 51 respectively, but from the use of too many pills legally offered by several doctors whose prescriptions were uncoordinated.

How to organize healthcare, measure its quality and productivity and how to finance it are issues that concern business and management. It is not my intention to go into the intricacies of healthcare, but only to establish that it consists of an extremely complex network of relationships and systems with many interacting stakeholders. Hospitals and doctors know a lot and can achieve a lot in *absolute terms* – but *not in relative terms*. This means that most of what they need to know and do is yet to be found out, for example how to cure flu, cancer, Alzheimers and AIDS. It does not matter how you organize or finance healthcare if doctors and others do not know what to do. All the same, the brand 'medical science' carries with it iconic prestige and there are continuous and planned promotion campaigns in the media announcing that medical science is making tremendous progress. Although there is progress in specific areas, progress in general is slow.

Both established practice and science can make contributions – and mistakes. Evidence-based research leaves out the observations of reflective medical practitioners who discern patterns among their patients using both explicit and tacit knowledge. A single case can be seminal and if a practitioner finds several cases they should be further studied, not as statistics but as in-depth cases. This is not done today in medicine and practitioners who deviate can get punished – they have difficulties publishing in top journals and getting research money to further verify their results. It is therefore easy for those who get money to say: 'You do not have any scientific evidence to confirm your claims.'

Evidence-based research promises to be the panacea, the safe handle to hold on to. The reliance on randomized, controlled, empirical and generalized research as the 'gold standard' is inadequate. Even combined with meta-analysis, it is only functional in specific instances.

As randomized experiments can be applied in very few situations in business and management, evidenced-based research adds little to our research agenda.

Feyerabend's Attack on Methods Rigidity

An early warning against scientism was Paul Feyerabend's seminal book *Against Method*.[12] He goes far in defending researchers' right to pursue their own ways in the search for valid results. His antagonists label his expression 'anything goes'

---

[12]Feyerabend, 1975, quotation from p. 175.

as total and irresponsible anarchy. If they had read him with an open mind, they would have found that he only rejected the dogmatic use of rules and the single prescriptive scientific method. In the book he asks:

> For is it not possible that science as we know it today, or a 'search for the truth' in the style of traditional philosophy, will create a monster? Is it not possible that an *objective approach* that frowns upon personal connections between the entities examined will harm people, turn them into miserable, unfriendly, self-righteous mechanisms without charm or humour? 'Is it not possible,' asks *Kierkegaard*, 'that my activity as an *objective* (or critico-rational) observer of nature will weaken my strength as a human being?'

Feyerabend pointed out that the *consistency condition* used in the positivist paradigm – that new theory should be consistent with established theory – will only make defunct theory and cherished prejudices live on. His criticism is in line with paradigm thinking and GT's avoidance of received theory. Feyerabend advocates pluralism and a multi-methods approach. He concludes that established theory makes claims far beyond its capacity and that science does not deserve a privileged status in knowledge development. He was upset by the condescending attitudes of established scientists to alternative traditions and critical of the lack of knowledge of philosophy shown by the generation of physicists that emerged after the Second World War; he even called them 'uncivilized savages'. Today, however, I find that his conclusion is more characteristic of medical research, whereas physics develops in many innovative directions and risk-taking than the social sciences.

We have to ask ourselves: Are we educating measurement technicians instead of scholars and reflective researchers? Are we breeding Frankenstein monsters and robots?

Pseudoscience

Pseudoscience, also referred to as *fringe science*, even *junk science*, is knowledge that claims to be correct but is doubted by many. It is doubted primarily because it has not come out of a conventionally approved research technique; it has the 'wrong' image and brand. Those who criticize it do not look at outcome in the first place but question the ritual around it, that the research technique does not properly relate to 'approved' theory and that it is not published in a top journal. So those who criticize pseudoscience are very much victims of their own pseudoscientific criteria.

What is true science without being scientism, and what can be labelled junk science without rejecting the unknown and innovation that go against the mainstream and the intersubjective consensus of the established elite? Such diverse personalities as the Nobel Laureates in the Economic Sciences Gary Becker and Milton Friedman, and philosophers Herbert Marcuse and Michel Foucault, are bunched together as charlatans by Bunge.

The terms pseudoscience and junk science suggest that something is being inaccurately or even deceptively portrayed as science. Those accused of practising or advocating pseudoscience naturally dispute the characterization. They may be mistaken but they may be right in the end. It raises the dilemma of how to receive innovation without being swindled and at the same time not stopping progress.

There is no simple answer and as scholars we have to watch out. The fight is about the risk of accepting junk and the risk of rejecting the brilliant. Neither of these risks makes us comfortable, and when something goes wrong it is easy for anyone to come up with seemingly rational criticism. Being on the safe side and rejecting the unknown mean no progress; being too freewheeling and jumping on every hyped-up bandwagon aren't progress either. Those who warn against the new can always celebrate how clever they are if it does not work. If it later proves to be correct, they are seldom held responsible for the damage they may have caused.

In business and management, *postmodernism* represents a reaction against the objective, absolute and single truth and the notion of the constant progress of society. It has been accused of being pseudoscience – but it lives on. It perceives realities as social constructs that are contextually dependent and subject to change. It emphasizes the role of communication, power relationships and motives. It rejects either/or categorizations in favour of simultaneous both/and realities and pluralism. Postmodernist thought is a departure from the *modernist* scientific mentality of objectivity and continuous progress. It is used in *critical theory* for work in the humanities as well as in business and management.[13]

Peter Medawar, Winner of the Nobel Prize in Physiology/Medicine in 1960, is reputed to have said that psychoanalysis is the 'most stupendous intellectual confidence trick of the twentieth century'. We can all have doubts about the conclusions and therapies of psychiatrists and psychologists – but can Medawar offer a 'scientific' alternative? In a much publicised trial in Norway in 2012, a man killed 77 people and blew up government buildings. A major issue was: Should he be considered ill and unable to take responsibility for his misdeeds and be sentenced to mental health treatment? Or should he be considered sane and responsible and receive a sentence for murder? The defence lawyer claimed that his client was mentally ill and so did the first psychiatrists who examined him. This raised public doubt and a second team of specialists was called in who declared him sane and responsible. Science in psychiatry and medicine cannot

---

[13]For postmodern research, see Holbrook (2003).

sort this out. A poll was taken among Norwegian psychiatrists and psychologists and 60% claimed that he could be held responsible, 15% that he was disturbed and could not be held responsible, and 25% were undecided. But a vote is no scientific ground. Much of 'science' is just intersubjective consensus among a limited group of voters.

It not only shows how brittle 'scientific grounds' are as a criterion but also that there is something more to understanding than what comes out of intellectual reasoning and testing. The final decision may rest on persona factors, judgement calls, political pressure, public demands and other considerations. The felon admitted what he had done and there was evidence to corroborate his confession. Then there is no basic need for a trial except for two things: Why did he do it, and did he have accomplices? He claims that it was a political act, that he is sane and that this is his protest against where the government is taking the country. The final verdict has to rest on a pragmatic solution but cannot be claimed to 'rest on scientific grounds' – because such grounds are not known to us.

Fraudulent Science

In 2012, the Japanese Hisashi Moriguchi – representing medical science – was found guilty of fraud in stem cell research. He claimed that he had cured 6 patients with injections of reprogrammed heart-muscle cells. It turned out that he had not, but also that he had a history of previous frauds. To boost credibility, he referred to colleagues and cooperation with Tokyo University and Harvard. They both denied involvement. He has been able to publish in 'top journals' and been invited to speak at conferences without anyone suspecting anything.

This is not an isolated instance but a growing problem in all sciences. If such a thing is revealed, the risk is high that a university or journal will make efforts to cover it up in order to save its image. If the idea of true scientific research was pursued, the academic body would immediately announce the fraud to the public. The scientist has been accepted on trust. It is a dilemma: Can we trust anyone? We know from experience and explicit research that trust and commitment are necessary to make human relationships work, for example between a boss and an employee or a supplier and a customer. As business is the object of competition, companies must keep certain knowledge to themselves or it may be used by competitors who have not spent resources on bringing it about. The negative side is that it can lead to unwanted monopolies and premium pricing. Patents, licences and copyrights are there to protect the inventor for a limited period but they are also systematically violated through pirate copies.

Among academic researchers, there is also the trust of colleagues. The conclusion of Zetterberg[14] is pragmatic – we simply have to trust what scholars do. When you cannot find something out for yourself, you have to go on trust. But the worst crooks are those who do not look like crooks but instil deep trust – 'confidence tricksters' or 'con men'. Today, academic institutions, political parties, governments and businesses are deeply involved in building their brands and claiming qualities they do not have.

We cannot entirely trust anyone to be 100% competent. Researchers may take erroneous steps during a study, misunderstand the theory and research procedures, and force biases on the reader. It can be plain mistakes and ignorance but also intentional and an expression of low ethics. The journal review system is a way to check this and to improve research, but can we trust reviewers? Most are trustworthy but some are not; we do not have the resources to check their credibility.

There is plenty of deliberate fraud in science and most of it is never discovered. The check and double-check culture gives rise to an eternal chain of auditing, like in a dictatorship where no one is trusted and each and everyone is assigned to check on neighbours and report deviant behaviour. How long should the chain be? And is it productive? To secure reliability, Yin[15] recommends that case study researchers should imagine auditors looking over their shoulders. I see his point but it would ruin my creativity. It reminds me of George Orwell's dystopian novel *Nineteen Eighty-Four* where the State – Big Brother – controlled 'thoughtcrimes' through planted microphones and video cameras. And with today's technology we can be controlled much more easily.

The first question is how a study is financed. Are there special interests lurking in the background? Do the funders have an agenda which they want to have scientifically ratified? Research and science are increasingly used as a marketing tool to boost the image of products. For example, there are recurrent articles in the media about how healthy it is for people, especially older ones, to drink a glass of wine per day. It will prevent heart attacks, cerebral haemorrhage and blood clots and in general make them happier. The authors of such studies are academics at universities. Are they financed by wine producers, perhaps disguised as an independent research foundation? What lobbyists, public relations consultants and journalists were used to claim that mobile telephony causes no harm, that fertilizers cause no environmental problems and that GMOs will eradicate starvation?

But how about those who claim they have psychic powers such as being able to talk to the deceased? Are they just magicians deceiving people? But what

---

[14]Zetterberg, 2013, pp. 75–79.

[15]Yin, 2014, p. 49.

about all the evidence (a large literature) from people who claim they have received messages – through their hearing, which is 1 of the 5 senses that we should trust – with the help of a genuine medium? Near-death experiences are reported by many who have almost died of an illness and it is quite common that people have premonitions about something that has happened or is going to happen to a close friend or relative.

The Terrorism of Received Categories and Concepts

To many, science seems to be just one thing: categorizing (classifying) data and putting it in boxes. Some property is given the status of overriding, while some scientists even follow tradition and folklore. Categorization keeps terrorizing science, it seems forever. In my experience, categorization as it is done today is a threat to science; everything is made one-dimensional. It is a common standard to divide research into quantitative and qualitative; and into social sciences, natural sciences, the humanities and, more recently, life science. I find the categories counterproductive and want to abolish them. The following sections explain why.

Quantitative and Qualitative Research

An overriding categorization of the social sciences is that of quantitative and qualitative. I have already mentioned that I consider the division non-scientific. All quantitative research includes qualitative and subjective assumptions and conclusions, as the research edifice showed. Interestingly, the modern natural sciences and mathematics represent a shift and today they are just as concerned with qualitative features as with the quantitative values of variables.[16]

The war between sterile categories is counterproductive when it comes to enhancing pragmatic wisdom. I am fed up with the artificial quantitative/qualitative research conflict. Instead, I support *mixed methods research*, meaning that you can use whatever paradigm, technique and language you believe will boost your chances of answering the research questions and getting useful results.

A common way of showing the difference between quantitative and qualitative research is to say that quantitative research asks *How many? How much? How often?* while qualitative research asks *What? How? Why?* All these

---

[16]Capra, 1997, p. 134.

questions can be important and you should use the methodology that best answers them.[17]

A widely held opinion of quantitative researchers is that their methods elevate business and management disciplines to rigorous science.[18] *Rigour* is a high-status word. If instead we say *rigid*, the status depreciates: who wants to be thought of as rigid? But rigour and rigidity both stem from the Latin *rigidus*, meaning hard, stiff, rough and severe. Most people agree that bureaucrats and the legal profession are characterized by the type of rigour which easily transcends into rigidity through hard-nosed adherence to principles and procedures. There is a widespread perception among academics that once the methodological procedure stands out as rigorous, validity is secured. Yes, the validity of the research process may be high but not that of what I stress is the hallmark of science: validity and relevance of the outcome.

Rigour and *lenience* should be seen as both/and concepts. Human life is so complex that laws that are supposed to work for everyone more often than not just work for a majority and leave minorities out in the cold. If the survival of a person or a company is at stake, the true bureaucrat says: 'I'm sorry about that. I understand your problem but we have to follow the law.' At one time, the *spirit* of the law was what counted and not just the *word* of the law. We know that it is difficult to find the best word for a phenomenon. Add to this the fact that bureaucracy and the law usually work very, very slowly and can prolong suffering for years. Again: 'Sorry!' And the laws and regulations just as often free offenders because of technicalities or ignorance.

Interpretation – where the explicit and tacit unite – is necessary; mere explicit *analysis* is not sufficient. Most things in our lives have to be interpreted. Sometimes I hear those trained in statistical analysis and who are beginning to explore qualitative research, say that they will turn the qualitative stuff into quantitative. This is an outright misunderstanding; it is just more 'conjecture'.[19]

We come to what I include under tacit knowledge and pragmatic wisdom. Rigorous safety rules are sometimes called for, such as in nuclear plants and airplanes as mistakes can cause disasters. Sitting in with pilots on passenger planes on numerous occasions, I have found that a lot is left to the pragmatic wisdom of pilots and their judgement calls. Even if there is an automatic computerized pilot, not everything can be prepared for with scrupulous rigour. In an emergency situation, the combined explicit and tacit knowledge increases the chances of a happy ending.

---

[17]See also Coviello, 2005.

[18]See e.g. Saunders, 1999, p. 85.

[19]See further Chapter 10 on analysis and interpretation.

The statement that quantification takes marketing to rigorous science could be turned around and broadened as follows: qualitative methods take management and business research from rigid ritual to art and understanding. Or better: both methodologies, used with sound judgement, can make contributions to knowledge and the understanding of a complex reality.

Within the complexity paradigm, I argue that:

- being quantitative can sometimes raise the scientific value of research – but only sometimes

- quantitative methods cannot achieve scientific excellence without a clear awareness of their qualitative dependency

- a merger of the best of both worlds – rather than a one-sided acquisition – will add substantial synergy to research in all business and management disciplines.

My view resonates with the words of the MIT Sloan School of Management professor John Van Maanen: 'many of the promises associated with the quantitative study have come up empty. Counting and classifying can take one only so far. Meaning and interpretation are required to attach significance to counts and classifications and these are fundamentally qualitative matters. The approaches are then bound together, neither capturing truth alone nor trumping the other.'[20]

Although it is tremendously important how you find your data, it is just as important what you do with that data. In reports based on qualitative research, data *collection* is usually described, sometimes at great length, whereas analysis and interpretation stand out as the Achilles heel. I prefer the concept of *generating* data, as data is not just there to be collected; data is shaped in the process and in this sense analysis and interpretation have already begun.

The quantitative and qualitative represent *languages*, one based on numbers and the other on words. The battle between them reminds us of a civil war. In some bilingual countries, there have been wasted resources and immense suffering when one language has tried to get supremacy over the other, 'proving' it is the better and historically more justified.

When quantitative researchers characterize qualitative research, the majority routinely do it in terms of statistics and mathematics. They use the numbers language and its grammar as the benchmark. But it is obvious that you cannot explain a computer with steam engine concepts or tennis in terms of golf. You certainly cannot handle complexity research within a mainstream paradigm of classic positivism.

Here is an example of how quantitative and qualitative data were used in a mixed methods research programme:[21]

---

[20]Van Maanen in Gummesson, 2000, p. x.

[21]Mason, 1994, quotation from pp. 90, 91 and 101.

> The first stage was a large-scale interview survey (978 respondents), using a statistically representative sample of the population ... The second stage ... involved a more qualitative study, where we conducted 120 in-depth, semi-structured, tape-recorded interviews with 88 people ... we anticipated that these would tell us about different aspects ... We were ... concerned with people's reasoning processes, and with the way their experiences ... had developed and changed over time. Survey methods are not very amenable to answering such questions.

To live up to its claims, quantitative research has to limit itself to a few factors and links, although there are techniques like structural equation modelling (SEM) that allow for a few more variables and interaction between them. Factor analysis, path analysis and regression analysis are special cases of SEM. Lisrel, an acronym for linear structural relations, is a widespread statistical software package. Without being a technical expert of Lisrel, I have been exposed to the outcome of such studies.[22] The seemingly precise diagrams and indices of dynamic relations between several variables have severe limitations. First, ambiguities have been removed so that equations become linear; second, the outcome is highly vulnerable to the choice of assumptions; third, we are offered probabilities and not conclusive evidence; and fourth, the equations are not robust as tiny changes can make the results collapse. Linear means taking out complexity, especially 'small' factors, but we know from the natural sciences that small factors can trigger a tipping point. So, quantitative manipulation does not elevate business and management theory to a higher level of validity, relevance and generality. The outcome can be suggestive but has to be followed up by, for example, case theory.

During my first semester at the Stockholm School of Economics, a reputed school that celebrated its 100th anniversary in 2009, I became suspicious of official statistics. We studied the statistics of industries, exports, imports, GDP, and so on, by means of approved indicators that allegedly painted a picture of reality. I became even more suspicious when we were taught techniques for doing statistical surveys based on random samples and processed with sophisticated methods like regression analysis. I was suspicious of microeconomics and its equations and graphs. I thought that all this, at best, gave uncertain images of reality. I then thought that maybe, with further studies and business experience, I would understand this better. But I do not; my experience rather supports my first impressions.

I am not saying that all statistical research is inadequate. I used surveys as a product manager in a consumer goods company in one of my first jobs. But I had to adapt them for practice and could not always live up to all their demands. I also began to observe the persona factor of research. For example, my manager wanted a study but when the results went against his pet ideas he locked it up

---

[22]See a critical discourse on SEM and surveys by Woodside, 2010.

in a drawer or had it shredded. To survive in the organization, he played a political game rather than try to find the truth about markets.

Turning words into numbers, making the qualitative quantitative is no panacea; it is a chimera. Quantitative and qualitative can be used as two of many properties of a study but neither earns a place as an overriding category.

> There is no such thing as philosophy-free science; there is only science whose philosophical baggage is taken on board without examination. (Daniel Dennett in *Darwin's Dangerous Idea: Evolution and Meanings of Life,* 1995: 21)

Our minds are littered by obsolete overriding categories: theory/practice, researcher/practitioner, goods/services, supplier/customer and more. Traditional socio-economic variables – age, gender, income, etc. – still have an influence although the value is doubtful. Now they have even been reduced to age and are almost only about young people – the new generations. These are given fancy names: Generation X, Generation Y, Generation We, Global Generation, Generation Next, Net Generation, Generation 9/11, Peter Pan Generation, and now the Millennial Generation – those growing up after the year 2000. Age does not automatically earn the rank of overriding variable though it may be useful as a property among numerous others, but it is very convenient for statisticians.

It took a long time for me to discover that I was a victim of received categories. Had it not been for Barney Glaser and GT, I may still be trapped in the conventions of categories, treating them as godsend absolutes.

A lot of research just reports categorizations, or new empirical data is thrown into approved but often irrelevant categories. Such categorizations are usually presented as crisp while they are fuzzy. Western science is full of stereotyped concepts and categories that have survived a natural death or been invented without being of import. An example of the way national statistics keep misleading politicians and the media is the categories that are used to indicate unemployment, economic growth, inflation, etc. They are stylized boxes that do not reflect reality; their validity is unknown. They give rise to meaningless research purposes and research questions, and consequently the conclusions are empty – even worse: deceptive. Still, they are kept, decade after decade.[23]

In a dynamic and unstable world, statisticians want static and stable boxes to facilitate data comparison over time and between nations. But reality does not consist of a set of boxes. For example, milk in the 2016 statistics is not the same product as milk in the statistics from the 1930s. The source of milk, the cow, did not get penicillin and oestrogen to stay 'healthy' and grow faster and it did not eat grass polluted by pesticides. The milk was not homogenized and pasteurized

---

[23]Criticism of this has been intense for decades. A recent contribution that has attracted attention is Karabell, 2014.

and treated to stay fresh for months. It was locally produced and consumed and not transported or stored. There were no light variants and no gene modifications. It may not even be true that what is called milk today comes from a cow. So milk has changed and the product is not comparable over time. But statisticians whose job it is to make reality visible to us, keep spending tax-payer money on meaningless numbers, thus deceiving the public.

Because of the fuzzy definitions and stylized categorizations, official statistics open up for fraud. For example, it is common in international trade to avoid or reduce customs tariffs and taxes by classifying exports in 'creative' ways. In addition, the smuggling of goods is widespread and within the EU it is hard to detect. The complexity of the supply chain makes it difficult to uncover the fraud.

Social Sciences, Natural Sciences, Humanities – and Life Science

By tradition, the main categories of higher learning, science and research are the natural sciences, the social sciences and the humanities. Recently, the term life science has been launched. These are epitomes of fuzzy sets but we use them in daily language and to categorize disciplines at universities. What do they tell us?

The humanities are associated with culture, but culture in turn has been standardized into equally fuzzy categories. A section called 'Culture' in my daily newspaper contains articles and pictures on painting, architecture, sculpture, literature, music, film, television, etc. – a mix of serious culture and entertainment of little substance. Originally, culture and cultivation came from cultivating a piece of land or the soil and were broadened to embrace our minds, faculties and manners. As a student, I hitchhiked through Germany. Walking along the road waiting to get a ride, I passed a field with the sign 'Es ist verboden die Kultur zu betreten' ('It is forbidden to enter the culture'). If we accept the original meaning of culture as growing something and tending to it for the benefit of people and society, the bulk of TV, for example, is not culture. Violent movies where murders are shown every few minutes with detailed instructions on how to cut someone's throat are not culture. And neither is entertainment based on dirty jokes, profane language and sexual innuendo. Can you really talk about a drug culture seeing sick young people injecting heroin? Are reality shows, where people are insulted and ridiculed in front of millions, culture? To me, culture has something to do with the original meaning: to cultivate something for our good.[24]

> Culture is the sanctity of the intellect. (William Butler Yeats (1865–1939), a pillar of the Irish-British literary establishment)

---

[24]Geertz, 1973 and Gross, 2012.

In quantum physics, a micro universe is studied to find the smallest building blocks of life, among them molecules, atoms and quarks. In 2012, the Higgs particle was proven to exist through one of the costliest experiments in history. A complex facility was built by the European Organization for Nuclear Research (CERN) in Switzerland, costing £10 billion!

Suppose the social sciences and the humanities had the same kind of money, would we then understand human behaviour better? Or are objects studied in physics more complex and demanding? No, human beings are a combination of physical and mental capacities with billions of cells that represent a micro universe. Body and mind interact and humans interact in social life. For example, bad results and disorder in school have been found to be just as much the outcome of junk food and sugary drinks as of bad teaching and low intelligence in students. Sugar gives schoolchildren temporary hyperactivity, and a lack of vitamins and minerals gives them low levels of energy.

The social sciences and, to some extent, the humanities have taken over parts of traditional mathematics and statistics and sometimes appointed the numerical language as superior. Those who have tried to adapt the *modern* natural sciences to the economic sciences have been neglected by the mainstream, or have even been accused of pseudoscience.

The conventional categorization is harmful to the progress of science. The categories are historical and have lost their ontological meaning, and none of them is a crisp set; each is split up into numerous disciplines. They preserve traditions, privileges and prejudices and create civil wars within science. As long as I can remember, cross-disciplinary research has been on the agenda but has met with problems. If you say cross-disciplinary, you have already set up boundaries to cross and people tend to defend their turf. An obstacle is the researchscape in which you belong and its traditions, culture, favoured research techniques, and budgets.

The newly launched life science is making it worse as it limits itself to high-tech, medicine-related science. Within that limited field, it can probably neutralize some of the differences, though. *But should not all sciences be about life; what else could they be about?* By letting them join forces for a common cause – to learn about life, reality and society – we open up to methodological creativity and deeper knowledge. Quantitative/qualitative and natural/social/human earn a place among many other properties of research, but should be dethroned from their current status of overriding categories.

Life science could develop into a concept for erasing borders between the natural and social sciences and the humanities. But is it just a fancy name? My guess as a marketer is that the expression was invented by a public relations agency and promoted by lobbyists to help Western medicine, genetics and chemistry stand out as more attractive and human-friendly.

We may not be aware of it but the social sciences have borrowed several terms, concepts and techniques from the old natural sciences. One example is *triangulation*, which is used when research data has been generated by different techniques, for example a statistical survey, personal interviews and documents, and/or been exposed to more than one analytical process. Triangulation is a technique in navigation, surveying and civil engineering. It is based on the fact that if 1 side of a triangle and 2 angles are known, the whole triangle is unambiguously defined and distances can be established with precision. In the social sciences, triangulation is just a metaphor. It is not sufficient to say in an article that 'we used triangulation', even if it may sound impressively scientific. Explain what you have done and why and what effect you think it may have had on the value of your research. As has been mentioned, I prefer the expression *mixed methods approach*.

The original triangulation is based on the geometry developed by Euclid (300 BC). He suggested a number of standardized shapes – the straight line, square, triangle, circle, and so on – which are very useful in special cases. But they do not consider the irregularity of complex natural and social structures and offer only crude structures for business and management, like the 2 x 2 matrix. Traditional geometric shapes are also rare in nature – a cloud cannot be described in these formats, but neither can a tree branch nor a coastline. *Fractal geometry* was developed by Benoit Mandelbrot in the 1970s in his computer experiments at IBM. He offered complex and realistic descriptions of physical forms, based on the observation that each part of the whole is built on smaller parts which are reduced-size copies of a whole structure (self-similarity). In business and management, these have been used to give more valid descriptions of organizational behaviour in general and specific phenomena such as a stock exchange. Fractal geometry is part of the modern natural sciences and complexity theory. But when did you last see a reference to Mandelbrot in a business and management journal?

In the humanities, for example, Jackson Pollock's modern paintings appear as chaotic dripping and splattering but computer analysis has uncovered fractal patterns. Such patterns are also prevalent in African art, design and architecture. Mandelbrot should be recognized for bridging the gap between art and mathematics, showing that these worlds are not mutually exclusive. His discovery continues to provide fresh and unexpected insights into some of the world's most difficult problems by altering perspectives, challenging preconceptions and revealing connections previously invisible to our senses.

Old mathematics is not modern mathematics and the physics as perceived by mainstream social scientists is not the physics of frontline physicists: 'Physicists in particular have entered into a new stage of their science and have come to realize that physics is not only about physics anymore, about liquids, gases, electromagnetic fields, and physical stuff in all its forms. At a deeper level, physics is really about *organization* – it is an exploration of the laws of pure form.'[25]

---

[25]Buchanan, 2003, p. 165, italics added.

The natural sciences can do wonders like taking us to the moon. Hence the expression in softer sciences: 'This is not exactly rocket science.' Why isn't it? What is stopping us?

There is also an overreliance on the general and standardization, and a denial of the individual and particular, and of the need for variety and diversity. We are exposed to superficial and ephemeral overgeneralizations at the cost of confronting the particular. There is a 'general' idea that technology is the way to solve problems in society, and the majority of research money around the world is allocated to the natural sciences and the technology that may come out of them.

Overriding Category – Or Just One Property among Many

In books on methodology, authors show reverence to earlier work. You should of course give credit to seminal contributions to your subject, but you should not feel forced to cite references which you are not comfortable with, just because they are considered standard references. When you submit articles, you may however be forced to do so as the bibliometrics regimen demands it.

Forming categories is an important ontological issue. In a complex reality, categories can assemble similar phenomena under one hat and make them simpler to deal with. This is helpful in life in general as well as in research. For example, customers are categorized as consumers (households) or organizational buyers (companies, government) based on the observation that B2C/C2B (business to consumer/consumer to business) marketing and B2B (business to business) marketing are different in some respects. But, in other respects, keeping up the categories as overriding is unscientific.

If something belongs to a category, it is associated with at least one distinguishing property. If people are classified according to age, this may be useful in some cases, for example in manufacturing certain products. But if age is allocated properties which are sometimes true and sometimes not, the category has lost its distinguishing power. Useful categories should have *minimal intra-variation* and *maximal inter-variation*, although a certain amount of approximation – fuzziness – is unavoidable.

Watch out for taken-for-granted and counterproductive categories and try to weed them out, even if you meet with resistance. A routinely used category in business research is company size. 'Fortune 500' companies, listed in the business journal *Fortune*, are the biggest businesses defined by number of employees and revenue. Small and medium-sized companies (SMEs) form other and very crude categories. Statisticians may sometimes (but not as a rule) have reason to state the size of a firm in this way; it might offer some macro data of interest. But if you are doing case research of specific companies, firm size only contains superficial information of limited relevance. As was described in Chapter 2, companies today are networks, many functions are outsourced, service is bought instead of produced in-house, with the advent of the Internet even a big business can be operated by very few people, and so on.

Some of these categorizations may have been important overriding socioeconomic variables in a different economic and political context, but today they are just some of many characteristics, sometimes of importance and sometimes not. They are part of our cultural heritage and have sneaked into the researchers' paradigm – usually without them reflecting on it. From there, they tacitly control research questions and the purpose of research. Many of them have had tragic consequences, like racial and gender tensions, and we see them in the headlines every day. With better categories, research could be made more valid and relevant.

Unfortunately, the either/or mind is dominating Western science just as it is dominating many of our institutions and organizational structures. But there is opposition from many directions, including the sciences. It could also be both/and. This is found in both Western and Eastern philosophies. An example from the West is the *dialectic* approach which deals with the unity and conflict of opposites; in the East there is *yin and yang*. The obsession with opposites and conflict is a curse of Western science and is detrimental to its development. It drives itself into a corner of technicalities, instead of opening up a world of understanding and insight – which is, after all, the original mission of the scholar and scientist and the rationale for education. The either/or fallacy is one of the biggest impediments for scientific development in the social sciences.

By routinely stylizing their equations and constructs and reducing human beings to numbers, statistics, percentages, averages, distributions and probabilities, and neglecting minorities, anomalies, variety and diversity, we end up with contextless fragments of social constructs that address anonymous masses and not human beings. The constructs are difficult to relate to reality. Statistical categories are arbitrary and full of compromises, the data sources are often unreliable, and the presentation in numbers and diagrams can be used to stress or hold back information. Examples are relative measures that may be used in very specific instances. Used in general comparisons, they cover up more than they uncover. For example, 'only' 0.1% of China's population is 1.3 million individuals, while 0.1% of the population of the Republic of Ireland is 4,500 individuals. Further, a 'negligible' small factor can be the tipping point that disrupts an approved theory or collapses an elegant structural equation. A straightforward causality between an independent and a dependent variable is a special case; causality is seldom restricted to a dyadic relationship and truly independent variables are the exception, as they are all embedded in a network context and may have several roles.

We have already met Feyerabend's concern that philosophy has cocooned itself into a shell and that physicists lack knowledge of philosophy. Hawking[26] is also concerned and says that 'philosophy is dead. Philosophy has not kept up with modern developments in science, particularly physics' (p. 5). He further says that 'Many notions of today's science violate our everyday experience and common sense' (p. 7). He has devoted his life to theory generation. In his memoirs,[27] he explains how he has been trying to connect the theory of relativity (a theory of the macro world, like galaxies) with quantum physics (a theory of the micro world, like atoms) into a unified quantum theory of gravity. Such efforts are sometimes referred to as 'the theory of everything'. Scientists have designed a massive system of equations – but they could not solve them. What did they do as the next best thing? They tried to *guess* the solution! Hawking further says that it is *impossible to be rigorous* in quantum physics because it rests on an extremely fragile ground.

This is not what we hear from quantitative researchers in the economic sciences, but natural scientists who are in the forefront admit it and live with it. In the *modern natural sciences*, disputes about new theories can go on for decades and be quite agitated. Hawking *believes* in scientific rationality but is not entirely sure of what it is. He and other natural scientists are technically skilled in mathematics and carry out controlled experiments, but both Hawking and Einstein are also highly creative and speculative. Hawking[28] writes, for example, 'if you *believe* that the universe is not arbitrary'. He does not say *know*; the research springboard for Hawking is still a *belief* (in contrast, Dawkins claims he *knows*).

Hawking opens doors to re-search, re-search and re-search. At the same time, he strives to find evidence through experiments and mathematics. Physicists have not answered the age-old existential questions of the origin of everything, what reality is and how we can know anything at all. They like to say 'not yet', indicating their belief that it is just a matter of time and other resources. It struck me first when reading about network theory in books on physics and mathematics that the natural scientists were neither afraid of complexity nor of daring speculation. With the possibility of being accused of not being rigorous, social scientists in general are scared of complexity as well as of speculation. At the same time, they *believe* that the natural sciences can establish, without a shred of doubt, what is true and not true. How come this happens when physics receives accolades as the superior science based on evidence, controlled experiments, mathematics and clear causality?

---

[26]Hawking & Mlodinow, 2010.

[27]Hawking, 2013.

[28]Hawking, 1996, p. 14.

Physicist Max Tegmark (2014) concludes that mathematics is not just a language that describes reality but *is* the 'real reality'. We also have those who claim that words, as the media through which we communicate, are the reality. Mathematics, as used in the economic sciences, certainly is not reality. It is a more precise, yet incomplete and stylized image of reality and the words used are open to numerous interpretations.

A current belief in physics is that there is not one theory of everything but a network of theories each addressing specific issues. Further, the phenomena are fuzzy and connected through overlaps. It seems most adequate for business and management; there is not a single all-embracing grand theory but several grand theories. *M-theory* suggests that there may be many universes, even an infinite number constituting the *multiuniverse*,[29] and that they were created out of nothing without the need for a God or any other intervention. It is unclear what M stands for but master, miracle, mystery or magic have been suggested. It is rather a network of theories that provide aspects of physics. Hawking does not *believe* in God and says that the Universe can create itself out of nothing; it is spontaneous creation. But what does 'nothing' mean? It reminds me of the immaculate conception from the Bible. My conclusion is that Hawking is not entirely comfortable with his ideas and keeps searching.

Hawking further says that before the Scientific Revolution 'ordinary experience and intuition were the basis for theoretical explanation'[30] (p. 66). M-theory tells us that the conventional dimensions of the physical world (length, width, height) plus time have to be expanded into 14 (superstring theory). We cannot visualize these dimensions; they are part of model-dependent realism and the uncertainty within quantum theory. We can easily see that this is not the classical physics that social scientists envy; it is the modern physics of the last 100 years.

'Classical science is based on the belief that there exists a real external world whose properties are definite and independent of the observer who perceives them' (p. 43). Our reality is model-dependent, meaning that our 'mental concepts are the only reality we know. There is no model-independent test of reality. It follows that a well-constructed model creates a reality of its own' (p. 172). In modern science, 'Both observer and observed are parts of the world ... and any distinction between the two has no meaningful significance ... According to the model-dependent, it is pointless to ask whether a model is real, only whether it agrees with observation' (p. 46).

We have recognized in business and management that the whole is not the same as the sum of its parts. The purpose of mergers and acquisitions is to create synergy effects, often described as 2 + 2 = 5. However, mergers and acquisitions

---

[29]Hawking & Mlodinow, 2010.

[30]Hawking & Mlodinow, 2010.

are difficult and may equally result in 2 + 2 = 3. It may be sufficient to conclude, as Hawking does, that 'there are many instances in science in which a larger assemblage appears to behave in a manner that is different from its individual components' (p. 67).

Hawking supports the complexity paradigm, saying that 'The behaviour of things on earth is so complicated and subject to so many influences that early civilizations were unable to discern any clear patterns or laws governing these phenomena' (p. 171), and further that 'The laws of nature tell us *how* the universe behaves, but they don't answer the *why*' (p. 171).

Something, someone or nothing – whatever 'nothing' means – created and influences the world but we do not know yet why, or perhaps we never will. As Hawking says, there may be many universes, each with their own story.

To add to the adversity from mainstream scientists, in the 1970s physics professor and Nobel laureate Hannes Alfvén began to worry about the dangers of nuclear waste and that we were letting loose forces beyond our control. The nuclear catastrophes at Three Mile Island in the USA (1979), Chernobyl in Ukraine (1986) and north-east Japan (2011) show that Alfvén was right. Apart from being a creative scientist, he is a great example of someone who transcended the artificial boundaries between the natural sciences, the social sciences and the humanities. To broaden his understanding, he also studied the history of science, oriental philosophy and religion. Some claim that the task of scientists is to expand our knowledge but it is not their task to tell society how to use it. That is up to the politicians – but what do politicians understand and what are their driving forces? Those scientists who have taken ethics seriously and protested against the misuse of science, have often been ridiculed by their colleagues.

Science is usually required to verify its claims. Karl Popper turned it around and said that theory should be designed so as to allow *falsification*. He uses two examples of well-known theories that do not allow falsification: Freud's psychoanalytic theory and Marx's theory that the conflict between the classes caused by capitalism will eventually give in to socialism and communism. What Popper objects to is that whatever happens when these theories are confronted with empirical data, the theories claim they have an explanation.

There are many seminal books that question mainstream science and the absolute belief in science as solid knowledge. They teach us that what we call knowledge may work and may not, that it plays hard-to-catch and can best be explained by case theory.

All types of methodology and its techniques are in some ways imperfect. When we work with applied sciences like business and management, we have to get things done even if it will not be perfect. We have to settle for it being satisficing – the best we can do within pragmatic wisdom.

We can criticize a methodology from the standpoint of the complexity paradigm:

- when it claims it can do things it cannot do
- when the technique and its rituals take priority over the possible outcome and its usefulness to solve a particular problem or to generate higher level theory
- when quantitative methodology is presented as the benchmark for superior science; language – words or numbers – is not a natural overriding property.

On Definitions

General Definitions, Operational Definitions and Social Constructs

In research, we want definitions that closely reflect what we are after (valid and relevant) and that it is possible to work with (operational). General definitions may be too fuzzy and inclusive. To address this dilemma, *operational definitions* and *operationalization* of variables have been introduced. Being operational means that the definition of a variable is tied to a certain measurement technique. A clock offers an operational definition of time and a budget period for a firm may be operationally tied to a month or a year.

If the goal of an enterprise is long-term survival and growth, it must make a profit. The general definition of profit as revenue minus cost is not sufficient in research, as neither revenue nor cost is an unambiguous and static concept. The price of stock at an exchange is based on several factors of which expectations about future profits are important. So the price of stock becomes an operational definition of a company's perceived value and profits. Amazon.com did not make a profit during the first 10 years but selling books (and later other products) on the Internet was considered by the stock market as viable for the future – and it turned out to be right. The same expectations were held about all those companies that crashed during the dotcom boom around the year 2000. The annual report of a public company shows a balance sheet and a profit and loss statement, checked by allegedly independent auditors and reviewed in the business press. But it is full of numbers, footnotes and comments that make it a jungle even for the expert.

The further a study is operationalized, the more of the complexity of reality is taken away and hence validity is reduced. It then offers noledge, an illusion of knowledge consisting of rigorous derived ignorance.

Social constructs are used in the positivistic social sciences. In business and management, we take over almost all methods from other social sciences – but these are not designed for the business and management context. A social construct is made up in the researcher's mind; it is not the thing-in-itself. It is hypothetical and does not necessarily exist or is not observable but still guides the research. Within the positivist paradigm, researchers in the economic sciences seem too preoccupied with constructs and operationalization, rather than with coming up with anything of value. It is a way of demanding precise definitions of a fuzzy reality. It has also become a way to hide from reality and offer research that is not generally applicable. Even if the weaknesses of the operationalizations are explained in scientific reports, they are often neglected by the reader.

Social constructs are used in business and management research. But do we use the 'right' ones? As they are social perceptions, they are not absolutes but represent an ontological relativity and anyone can claim that almost anything is right. Social constructs are forced on us by an elite of professors or businesses that currently reign the discipline; they are established and taken for granted. This is of course not in line with innovation and entrepreneurship. We encounter the oxymoron of wanting the new and rejecting it at the same time.

Leaning back on the past chapters and not going into what recent methodologists and philosophers[31] have said, I would like to conclude as follows. I have continuously returned to the need to recognize real-world complexity and not fall for the convenience of armchair deductions and old references. This requires the merger of explicit and tacit knowledge, fuzzy set theory, chaos theory, validity, relevance, pragmatic wisdom and mid-range theory. We must strive to get close access to real-world data – and this is rarely achieved through statistical surveys, statistical conjecture, interviews or detached observation, i.e. the data-generating and analytical techniques offered in the social sciences. It requires presence where the action is.

Instead of diving into the cold waters of reality, researchers seem scared and search – desperately search – for ways of not having to dive into the water. They find all sorts of intellectual reasons to stay on shore and just look at the water. What they see is the surface. Sometimes the water is clear and they can see into the water; sometimes it is muddy and they see nothing. An iceberg is 90% under water, so they settle for the tip of the visible 10%.

Generic Definitions and Definitions by Comparison

When you want to define something, you can make *comparisons* with something familiar by using *metaphors* (*analogies*), like explaining in what way goods are different from services, how qualitative research is different from quantitative research, and how the social sciences differ from the natural sciences.

Such comparisons should be made with caution. They are easily taken too far, overstressing a single dimension, and even if they can shed light on an issue they can create clichés that become accepted convention and block improved understanding, innovation and theory generation. They can mislead practitioners into focusing on the wrong problem and coming up with the wrong recommendations.

---

[31]See Berger & Luckmann, 1966.

Comparisons and metaphors may be used to illustrate or facilitate the understanding of abstract and complex concepts; they have a pedagogical mission but no more. In service research, services were defined as deviations from goods and not on their own merits. Something else was used as the reference point. It gave service research an initial euphoria which developed into a constant hangover. Even if current service research embraces a new paradigm, many researchers cling to the differences, still not being able to define them, just referring to articles and books of the past.[32]

Instead, one should strive to find and understand the *generic traits* of a phenomenon. Generic has the same root as genes, the unique combination of building blocks that make up a living species and individuals.

Case Theory as the Diamond Standard of Research

Quantitative research is presented as the crown of science in business and management and evidence-based research is now sold as the gold standard of science. I would like to introduce case theory as the *diamond standard* of research. Why?

Medicine once built on cases but today the case has lost it status and been replaced by statistical experiments. Within the spirit of positivism, their chosen explanation is that cases are too few to allow for statistical and descriptive generalization; and these are the only generalizations they allow.

I am not going to go into further comparison between the claims of evidence-based medicine and case theory. Instead, I will explain why I consider case theory more productive than statistical studies. I will not hire expensive PR consultants to find a name for it, just give it one: *the diamond standard*. It is symbolic not because diamonds are expensive, just as gold is, but because diamonds:

- reflect the sun and its spectrum of light
- have numerous facets
- are a product of nature that took 1000s of years to produce under very heavy pressure
- are hard, solid and resistant.

Gold, on the other hand:

- glitters and is used to demonstrate wealth
- is a soft metal that has little use unless combined with other metals.

Where does this take us in research and practice? Business and management are meant to help us make decisions, manage our lives and help others. They live under many imperfect conditions so we have to settle for working simplifications

---

[32]Lovelock & Gummesson, 2004.

and mid-range theory. When I look at the huge amount of effort that has been made over the millennia to understand what knowledge is, and not least the flood of articles with variations of methodologies that are increasing at a rapid pace today, it is easy to sense desperation. We want to understand how we can acquire knowledge to run businesses and other organizations, to manage our lives as citizens and consumers and to lead a good life. We are not there. Are we chasing a fuzzy and moving target that keeps dodging our efforts? Sometimes we catch up on specific points and sometimes science offers true innovation. But what is meaningless innovation and a media hype, fad and fashion? In other areas, we don't go forward very quickly, if at all. We have to do the best we can; this is being pragmatic. We can remain conventional pragmatists with little progress or we can be true professionals and apply pragmatic wisdom.

It may seem discouraging to some but hopeful to others. The prime mission of science and research is to address complexity and keep taking steps towards grand theory and its extension into simplification. We can then better overview all the data that we need to understand the core of an issue and be able to manage it. We have reached a state of condensed simplicity without losing in content. This happens in the natural sciences. Examples are Einstein's condensed energy formula $E = mc^2$ has already been mentioned. But does this simplification happen in the economic sciences? I do not think so. But why should it not? We just have to work in the right direction. Here is a summary of strategies:

- Direct academic research towards higher abstraction zones with grand theory and condensed knowledge and simplification as the ultimate goal.

- Rethink methodology so that it can better handle complexity and increase understanding instead of promoting ritualistic techniques.

- Accept the uncertainty of innovation and do not fear failure. The current strategy of playing safe will never open up for the new and will never allow paradigm shifts.

This is what this book is about and where case theory can make a contribution. Even then the search for relevant data is a gargantuan challenge – and an opportunity. A problem is that incremental additions to knowledge must reach a certain number to show existing variety and and diversity. It requires moving up towards grand theory. Only then can we find the soul of an issue. We then condense knowledge – and find simplification. If we exclude complexity at an early stage, turning a non-linear reality linear by reducing the variables and their links or by introducing assumptions to get everything into equations and categories, we lose the phenomenon in the process. We have to find patterns in the rich cases we encounter, and patterns can gradually and iteratively take us to higher zones of understanding.

6

THEORY GENERATION – AND TESTING

A major task for research is to generate better theory, all the way from substantive theory to mid-range theory and general, abstract theory – grand theory – and then to offer actionable simplifications. This is also a way to test theory, not by finding shortcomings in extant theory but by offering better theory.

Whenever there is a problem with a company or a government agency, they say things like 'We will change our routines', 'We have to establish stricter laws and regulations', or 'We will appoint a committee and start an investigation'. It is more sorcery than a promise to act. We need to know when it will be implemented, if it will lead to improvements and how we can monitor the developments and make revisions.

An applied science like business and management needs theory that is supportive to action and results. It can benefit from basic academic research. We should not start a simplification process before we have understood an issue, be the understanding explicit or tacit. If you stylize data and add assumptions to make a problem amenable to 'rigorous' research techniques, then validity and relevance are jeopardized.

For a long time, the lack of theory generation on higher levels has been a major problem. Few academics engage in it; they are rather dissuaded to do so. It is easier to earn career points on empirical studies based on conventional research techniques and established theory. If you want to play safe, 'me-too' and 'more-of-the-same' are the smoothest career paths. If you want to make a difference and take science further, you must be willing to challenge the establishment, confront resistance and be stimulated by it.

The theory problem consists of several parts:

- Knowledge about theory generation is poor among researchers in business and management. Research techniques, especially quantitative techniques, are taught as a cure-all, which they are not. But some business schools are well versed in alternative and more daring methodologies.

- Most research is about fragments that may be interesting in themselves but without tying them together into a context they make little sense. With the exponentially growing number of published articles forced by new academic promotion and grants systems, and by quantitative bibliometrics techniques, established journals have increased their annual number of articles and new journals and conferences are continuously being started up. The number of papers is so huge that even in your own sub-discipline you cannot follow them and see the relationship between them.

- The still dominating research paradigm in business schools and among too many journal editors is that of the natural sciences, especially physics, from the 400-year-old Classic Scientific Revolution. Although the modern physics of the past 100 years embraces certain elements of the past, the modern scientific paradigm is very different; it is part of my complexity paradigm.

- Journals in general make it difficult to publish theory-generating articles. They encourage research based on the past and on fragmented theory. Syntheses of substantive and mid-range theory research in the direction of grand theory are in short supply.

- Business and management theory is traditionally about *data collection, analysis* and *conclusions*, whereas *action* and *results* are left dangling. Theory should also be about getting things done and making sure that the outcome is satisficing. This view is evident in Peter Drucker's pragmatic wisdom (Box 6.1).

Box 6.1   Peter Drucker

Drucker became an icon among managers and many professors. The overwhelming part of his messages and continuous publications from the 1930s until he passed away in 2005 (at the age of 95) had a major impact. His death was reported with headlines and articles in the international business press. Once in Manhattan I went to the bookstore of the American Management Association. It had a bookshelf for each discipline within business and management: corporate strategy, costing, organization theory, and so on – and then one called Drucker. He had become his own discipline! It was a demonstration of his status as a thinker and visionary. Some years ago I was invited to the Vienna University of Economics and Business and stayed in a hotel in its neighbourhood. Every day I walked by a house where Peter Drucker had lived. Just seeing it instilled a feeling of responsibility in me: I have to say important things in my lectures! Austrian economist Joseph Schumpeter, known for his ideas on innovation and entrepreneurship, was a friend of the Drucker family and little Peter was exposed to his ideas from childhood.

   Following a PhD in law, Drucker worked in finance and then became a journalist. The 1930s turbulence in Europe made him leave for the USA where he became a professor of management at New York University and a prolific author and management consultant. He brought his experience from organizational life with him and showed an ability to conceptualize what was happening in society, business, governments, NGOs and households. He took a serious interest in a wide range of the social sciences as well as in the humanities.

(Continued)

His way of writing appealed to managers and he became their most read author. In certain academic circles, he was not considered 'scientific' enough but he definitely earns a place within the complexity paradigm. He generated theory by making syntheses of his experiences, having constant interaction with managers and others, and making keen observations.

Drucker was a pragmatist with a holistic view. He contributed to mid-range theory but also to grand theory by conceptualizing overriding phenomena that were in the making. Among his many contributions were the promotion of decentralization and outsourcing for simplification of work in large and complex organizations; knowledge as the unique resource and the introduction of the term knowledge worker; the importance of discontinuities and paradigm shifts caused by innovation and entrepreneurship; and a business being there to create and serve customers. He preached that maximization of short-term profit for the firm, its shareholders and managers was not the ultimate goal of businesses. They should show corporate social responsibility, be good corporate citizens and contribute to the well-being of society. He saw the necessity to balance needs and goals to satisfy all stakeholders. He was sceptical of economists whom he considered unable to explain and understand what was going on in economic life.

Some years ago, I suggested that 'theory must reinvent itself and be refined, redefined, generated, and regenerated – or it will degenerate'.[1] This could serve as a sound bite for my conviction that generating theory on gradually higher levels is one of the most important tasks for business and management scholars. It is pragmatic. Not so in the short term where immediate decisions have to be made under time pressure, but in the long run where it can open up for simplicity and better mid-range theory.

At a conference in the UK, I listened to presentations by professors and business executives on customer satisfaction and how to manage and measure it. The presenters offered a wealth of 'truths' and observations that mostly stood out as relevant and credible. Some were based on particular cases and experiences, some on surveys. What was lacking was the connection between the parts and the possible contributions to higher level theory. It offered a *smorgasbord* of fragmented knowledge, a bit of this and that. Smorgasbord research will not do. You need coherent theory that links the salmon, ham and asparagus together. Theory 'boils down' huge amounts of data to the core of an issue. This can happen through intuitive understanding, which characterizes much of innovation, and may take a long time to prove and make explicit. Displaying diagrams with boxes and arrows is not enough, even if you add quantitative measures and go as far as to use structural equations. It stays put in substantive and mid-range

---

[1]Gummesson, 2005, p. 317.

theory. Today, we can transmit so much data without giving it meaning, and computers can do numerical computations that humans cannot do because it would take too long. It is predicted that big data will take us even further.

A dividing line in research is whether one should *test extant theory* or *generate new theory*. Positivists draw a sharp line between *theory generation* (discovery) and *theory testing* when a theory is *verified* or *falsified*. They claim that discovery is often just a *happening* characterized by subjective hunches or *serendipity* (you search for one thing but find another that is also useful). Rigorous testing as postulated within positivism is also used in business and management research but within the complexity paradigm it is not sufficient. My interest is theory generation and, as a natural consequence, I test the new and old by comparing the two. All theory is temporary but the time span can be short or centuries long. When new and better theory has been generated, it should naturally replace extant theory. There are many persona-influenced reactions like 'Not invented here', 'We have not done that before', or 'This will not be problem-free', but there is also the fear of losing a position or the uneasy feeling that you will have difficulty in learning to master the new.

Despite the fact that innovation and entrepreneurship are current buzzwords, resistance to improvements can be very strong. The old expression is 'resistance to change', but we also have meaningless change all around us, for example some updating of software or governments passing new legislation that can never be implemented. For businesses, it is most often to force us to buy more through 'planned obsolescence' (most blatantly illustrated by the IT industry); for governments, it is a way to make citizens believe they are doing something. Resistance to change can therefore be highly justified. What is not justified is 'resistance to improvements' and by that I mean real improvements.

Even if scientists do not abandon a theory at the same time as they encounter data that contradicts it, the reasons can be constructive. They may be exposed to hype or fad and fashion, or existing theory may remain valid in specific instances. Further, more often than not there are shortcomings in new theory as it takes time and resources to complete it.

We have very few grand theories in business and management although some are striving in that direction. It is more of a direction; go for the stars and you may reach the treetops. In 1957 the Soviet Union launched Sputnik, the first man-made satellite, and caused a political crisis in the USA. Three years later, US President John F. Kennedy gave the order: 'Put a man on the moon!' Resources were allocated and in 1969 Apollo 1 landed on the moon with 3 astronauts and for the first time human beings walked on another planet. This is true rocket science. But why can we not develop rocket science in business and management, a science that can guide us through 'social space'? We may then have to look at human behaviour differently. As mentioned, they allocated £10 billion to find the Higgs particle, and to find out how people *really* react to warnings against cigarette smoking, a neuroscience experiment costing US$6 million was set up.[2] By extending the scientific narrative to network, systems and fuzzy set theory, we add graphs, mathematics and computer simulation to the narrative. Experiments are extremely rare in business and management as they are costly and only suited to very select cases.

Researchers often present 2 variables and a simple link between them as theory. A simple link between 2 variables cannot usually represent the complexity and variety of the real world. It may be a premature simplification with appealing face validity but no genuine validity. *Validity* is a descriptive and static noun. Lyn Richards, who is behind the computer program NVivo for analysing qualitative data, treats it as a gerund verb – *validating* – with the emphasis of the active process of ensuring meaningful conclusions. It is noteworthy that marketing is a gerund verb, while its sister discipline, organization theory, is a noun;[3] accounting is a verb but finance is a noun; and manufacturing is a verb but operations management is a noun. We can wonder what effect, if any, these different terms have on our brains: time to call in neuroscience.

Mid-range theory is sometimes well grounded in real-world data; it has reached a certain level of bounded generality and abstraction but may have a long way to go to become truly general. Sometimes it is not well grounded in solid data, and then it can be grossly misleading, even if it has acquired status through top journal articles and many citations.

In the methodology literature, *validity* appears in several variants. I only use it in its basic sense to refer to how well a study pinpoints what it sets out to investigate and not something else. *Pure theory* is not smudged by the complexity of the real world and its fuzziness; it is theory for its own sake. It is based on operational definitions of constructs, simplifying assumptions and stylized data so that rigorous experiments and equations can be designed. Pure theory can be temporarily useful to insulate variables and to make us see something in a brighter light. The problem arises when pure theory is perceived as generally applicable and the users do not realize its limitations. It is only auxiliary. An example is when the operational definition of intelligence as 'what you measure in an intelligence test' only covers certain cognitive abilities but not creative, emotional and social abilities. Another is microeconomic theory that assumes that all customers and all products are the same.

When we ask for empirical data as a ground for theory generation, we do it to achieve validity. We should be able to say that the theory is grounded in real life and that the theory can guide us in the real world; the theory becomes a map.

---

[2]See Box 9.9.

[3]Czarniawska, 2008, has suggested the term *organizing* but it is difficult to change established terms.

To draw a map, you need to know where the land and the sea are, where there are mountains and valleys, what roads look like, and so on. To communicate useful information, maps are stylized graphic diagrams of geographical areas. The most common world map is the Mercator projection where the spherical earth is made flat. It is practical; it is easy to read and you can carry a flat map while it is hard to carry a globe. But the size of areas shown on the flat map lacks validity. The further you get from the Equator, the larger the territory becomes on the flat map. Greenland, situated close to the North Pole, looks as big as Africa which is situated on the Equator. The truth is that the area of Africa is 15 times the size of Greenland. Russia is about twice as big as China or the USA but on the map it looks like it is 5–6 times bigger than each of these nations.

To compare area size properly, consult a globe. But even the globe is an approximation of area shapes and sizes. To compare with an extreme, according to modern fractal geometry the coastline of a country is infinite as it can include every little detail down to a grain of sand. This level of detail may be helpful in certain scientific studies but it is not helpful for action in real life. In the military, we were out in the forests and needed very detailed maps of small roads, paths, swamps, heights, etc. If you travel by car, you need road maps which are obvious simplifications of the fractal geometry map and the forest map. So validity is related to our needs and intentions. We need simplifications accordingly, but they must be a condensation of substantive real-world data.

So where is the optimum or the satisficing compromise? As business and management disciplines are about how to orient ourselves in the real world, make decisions, take action and achieve results, we need to find a satisficing level.

> Simplicity is the ultimate sophistication. (Leonardo da Vinci (1452–1519), Italian universal genius)

Theory Generation and Testing as Iterative Processes

The conventional recommendation within the positivist paradigm is the testing of hypotheses or propositions. Too many articles are a show-off that the authors are technically skilled in statistics. The contributions made to the understanding of business and management in theory and/or practice are usually meagre, if any, and genuine innovation is even rarer. In contrast, I agree with Walton who says that 'case studies are likely to produce the best theory'.[4]

If big data and artificial intelligence fulfil their promises, we will not have to bother about theory generation and testing. The grand patterns of data should

---

[4]Walton, 1992, p. 129; see also George & Bennett, 2005.

come out of the computer. Waiting for this to happen – if it ever will – we need theory generation.

I first heard about research as *trial and error*. The expression does not seem to be around in methods books but it is what we do in our daily lives to build up experience. I use computers but I mainly have tacit knowledge of software logic. If I am going to do something I have not done before, I try whatever pops up in my mind and if it does not work I try something else. It often works after a while. If I come to a full stop, I call a friend or a support team; I rarely understand the 'Help' program.

In theory generation, I do very much the same although more systematically; it is a *constant comparative analysis*. I come up with a new concept, category or theory and test it by comparing it with what there already is. If my new theory does not come out as better, I try again. I mention this because theory generation may sound scary, but when you reduce it to systematic trial and error and constant comparison it may seem friendlier.

Figure 6.1 will guide you through my perception of the theory-generation process. The purpose is to facilitate understanding of theory within a pragmatic approach where complexity is recognized as a reality, but also where theory can help us turn complexity into actionable simplicity. Combining explicit and tacit knowledge is a necessity for pragmatic wisdom.

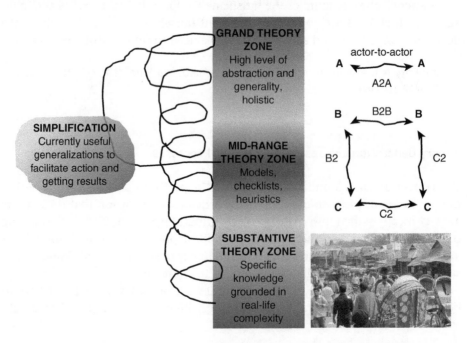

Figure 6.1 Theory generation and testing as iterative processes (© the Author)

Figure 6.1 shows a mental model for generalizing and validating theory. It is iterative, dynamic and fluid, and the substantive, mid-range and grand theory zones and positions are not forever fixed. The thinking is in line with fuzzy set theory.

The Substantive Theory Zone

Look at the middle column of the figure where 3 zones are found. It starts at the bottom with *substantive theory* grounded in real-life complexity. It is specific theory; it cannot automatically be generalized beyond the data on which it is based. It is meant to fulfil the particularization task of case theory which was discussed in Chapter 1. But Flyvbjerg says that 'One can often generalize on the basis of a single case … formal generalization is overvalued',[5] and Eckstein[6] that case studies can be used to test theories but is then more guided by pragmatic considerations than by strict logic. In his treatise on social costs, Coase (1960) used 3 main cases. One was fictional and is a simplified example to illustrate his ideas. He did not use quantitative research. He concludes that the value of laws and regulations is highly overrated and something which we can see around us all the time, and he claims that defining transaction costs is a better choice. Coase displayed pragmatic wisdom. For a quick test, take your substantive theory and try to apply it to a real case that you already know reasonably well and see if there is a 'fit'.

The Mid-range Theory Zone

Mid-range theory can be grounded in explicit research and substantive theory but can also be the outcome of tacit knowledge. Mid-range theories materialize in models, frameworks, checklists, algorithms (advanced step-by-step checklists) and heuristics (rules of thumb). They are useful for action and can provide stepping stones towards grand theory.

Michael Baker, Emeritus Professor of the University of Strathclyde, UK, and a leading spokesman for marketing for decades, has roots in both theory and practice. In referring to his studies at Harvard Business School (HBS), he says:[7]

---

[5]Flyvbjerg, 2006, p. 228.

[6]Eckstein, 1975.

[7]Baker, 2012, p. 1.

Lacking the ability to control the context in which most decisions concerning behaviour occur, the researchers and teachers at HBS wisely decided that they would confine themselves to offering advice that worked, or not, in the past based on observation and experience. This approach resulted in the decision to use a clinical 'case' method of instruction, that emphasises the need first to describe the nature of the problem to be solved, in as much detail as possible, as a basis for prescribing a course of action(s) to be taken in order to achieve a 'cure'.

This was about cases for teaching purposes but it also defined the concept of *currently useful generalizations*, which is applicable to research as well. Baker refers to the necessity of finding evidence for such useful generalizations and developing them further. They are an example of pragmatism corresponding to mid-range theory. We need them temporarily. The problem is that if they become popular and are sold through textbooks and consultants they become permanent and are hard to get rid of, even when better knowledge becomes available.

Later, Baker reflects on the standard of business schools and journals and the criticism in the 1950s that they were less scientific than other disciplines:[8]

Following the publication of reports by the Ford and Carnegie Foundations, substantial funding was made available to encourage US business schools to emulate the standards and procedures associated with other established fields of study. The immediate effect was to promote the adoption of positivistic and quantitative research processes associated with the physical sciences at the expense of interpretivistic and qualitative approaches adopted by the social sciences. The effects are still widely apparent today.

The Ford and Carnegie Foundation report is long outdated and its reference to physics is from the Classic Scientific Revolution, the same foundation as Thomson Reuter uses for bibliometrics. As has been pointed out, the modern physics of the past 100 years is different. It also shows that the categorizations of the natural and the social sciences and the humanities should be abandoned. The complaint about business schools was that their teaching was based on practice and lacked theory. My complaint is that in adhering to the now obsolete conclusions of the 1950s, too many business schools still confess to quantitative positivism and are backed by bibliometrics. But the theory/practice categorization is also misguiding us. What we learn should be put to use for our benefit and not just be a career path in isolated academies. What is the use of scientific research in medicine if it cannot help patients by mitigating, curing or preventing disease? Physics is used to build machines, and sociology to better understand society and its organizations.

Heuristics refers to experience-based techniques for problem solving, learning and discovery. Heuristic techniques are used to speed up the process of finding

---

[8]Baker, 2015, p. 272.

a satisfactory solution, where exhaustive search is impossible; it is an educated guess, intuitive judgement and *common sense*. Heuristics are formed through *trial and error*, and can be used in everything from matching bolts to bicycles to finding the values of variables in algebra problems. They are often called 'rules of thumb' and are part of everyday life.

An *algorithm* is a set of rules that precisely define a sequence of operations. We meet it daily in the form of computer programs. Even a tiny shortcoming in a website can sabotage the whole process of ordering an airline ticket. You cannot get the process right without trial and error and interaction between suppliers and users – and it may take many years. It shows how difficult it is to chart a sequence of events when they have to be 100% explicit. In real life we can handle this through experience, most of which is tacit knowledge. A *checklist* is a practitioner variant of an algorithm where explicit and tacit knowledge support each other. Even if pilots have lifelong experience of take-offs and landings, they use checklists; missing a tiny detail can cause severe problems.

As it was the gap between theory and practice that once got me started on the academic track, I should ask myself if research in business and management has any impact beyond the academic environment. As business and management are applied sciences, it should have an impact. I will say a few words about good impact, bad impact and no impact. Even if we can make lists of variables – quality dimensions, properties of the entrepreneur, success factors – they do not seem to have much predictive value. There is something lacking.

Professors and consultants are often accused of lecturing on what should be done – but not being able to do it. Going back, knowledge was not created from logical analysis and concepts; it came to each person through doing. It was based on imitation of others, trial and error and observations of patterns through experience. The original meaning of 'empeira', from which the term empirical is derived, referred to knowledge through experience. In Greece, the separation between doing and thinking is accredited to the sophists, literally 'the wise guys'. They contemplated, analysed and reported. They influenced and persuaded others to do the job. Abstract conceptualization and generalization emerged, separated from hands-on action. We all experience this as a major problem. We have a bright idea that is going to make us rich but we cannot implement it; the idea gets no support from politicians, financiers, consumers and others. Those who determine policies in the boardrooms may not be close enough to their frontline staff and customers to know whether their decisions are implementable. Researchers rely on stylized and operationalized statistical data that may be depleted of its original richness and variation. Politicians use such data to make irreversible decisions with long-term effects.

We need to use research *short term* to continuously solve current real-world problems and be of assistance to business and society. But we also need *long-term* basic research. It can be curiosity-driven from ideas and hunches about new approaches and solutions or syntheses of knowledge on a higher level of abstraction. It may not stand out as practical until after some time. In the natural sciences, you find everything from high-level long-term basic research to very hands-on short-term applied research.

This leads to options for technological advances that were not planned or not even imaginable. Michael Faraday, one of the great chemists and physicists (1791–1867), is reputed to have responded to the question 'What is the use of basic research?' with the words 'Sir, what is the use of a newborn child?' Basic research is often linked to a paradigm shift and easily becomes controversial.

Kurt Lewin, pioneer of action research, is reputed to have said that 'there is nothing as practical as a good theory'. Or, in other words: 'A good map will take me to my destination quicker and safer.'

Applied research is the use of existing knowledge, tried techniques, and checklists. It is also usually planned and there is a schedule that you should try to keep to. Basic research can be time planned in short batches, but often there is no way to know if it will be ready this year, next year or many years ahead. If a new discovery is made, the road to application may be short or long.

Box 6.2   Examples of Widespread Mid-range Theory

Here are some mid-range theories that have been around for decades. Their strength is that they simplify the complex and help us decide and act; their weakness is that they may make us jump to premature simplifications with face validity but lacking genuine validity:

- As shown in Box 3.1, corporate strategy is a bewildering field aiming to make a company successful in an uncertain future. Several efforts have been made to simplify the process and help management make decisions. Among the best known are the 2 × 2 *SWOT matrix*, helping to identify an organization's Strengths, Weaknesses, Opportunities and Threats; *The Boston Consulting Group Model*, a 2 × 2 matrix, above all known for its definition of 'cash cows'; and *The Directional Policy Matrix*, extended to 3 × 3 dimensions which you can read more about in Box 6.7, where the usefulness of strategic matrices is also analysed more generally.

- Harvard professor Michael Porter became a celebrity through the *Value Chain* and the *5 Forces of Competition*. These theories have dominated the literature on competition and strategy from the 1980s. During the global financial crisis that began in 2008, they gradually lost their pizzazz among executives. The crisis resulted in bankruptcy in 2012 for Porter's Monitor Group of premium-priced consultants backed by the Harvard brand.[9] The value chain is essentially linear

---

[9]See the analysis by Stewart, 2009.

and production and supplier centric and does not embrace the customer and the broader value network of integrated resources of numerous stakeholders. Value is further used in the same meaning as cost, assuming that higher cost products have higher value which shows in the expression 'value-added tax' (VAT). Higher cost, though, is often just the result of low productivity. The 5 forces model postulates that successful competition and sustainable profits are the result of managing the forces well. It is a mid-range theory allegedly coming out of grand theory. In reality, all business is in a state of flux with shorter or longer cycles and can only be permanently sustainable if enjoying monopolistic dominance – which is inconsistent with the hailed idea of free market competition. Another major criticism against the model is that it may explain the past but not predict the future. Porter's theories are accompanied by extensive texts and also empirical research which explicitly shows many of the intricacies of competition, but the outcome does not qualify in the grand theory zone. It was once a sound reaction to the highly stylized models of competition from economics but was not the final answer. The old economics models and Porter's models are still taught in business schools and fill textbooks.

- *The 4Ps of marketing*: Product, Price, Promotion and Place. These concepts together with subgroups are claimed to condense the essentials of marketing strategy, thus representing mid-range theory as coming out of grand theory. But its substantive base was limited to mass-manufactured and mass-distributed consumer goods and never had grand theory status. The 4Ps still form the structure of most marketing textbooks. They are challenged by a new logic of service which is addressing complexity through systems and network theory with relationships, networks and interaction as key concepts (see Box 6.5).

Mid-range theory can easily park itself in its zone and not develop further, especially if the theory has received acclaim and its originator has become an academic celebrity, much like a Hollywood star. You get *stuck-in-the-middle theory*. This is where support from grand theory comes in, and is a reason for putting the majority of academic resources into getting bits and pieces of research together, finding regularities in complex patterns and sending them back in simplified and manageable form.

You cannot make abstractions unless you have – explicitly or tacitly – understood the molecules and electrons and genes of business life. Your understanding may start as a hunch – tacit knowledge – but to communicate it you need to show its superiority in practice and at best turn it into explicit knowledge. Unfortunately, crude statistics are used to build abstract and linear models and theories of alleged general value. With low quality of the substantive data, you cannot make good abstractions; errors will multiply. One should have a balanced view on generalization – 'to use it but not to overuse it'[10] – but both researchers and practitioners need *grand theory*. If you make it to the grand theory zone, you

---

[10]ECCH, 1997.

are on a high level of abstraction and the theory is generally valid. In physics, both the theory of relativity and quantum theory are perceived as grand theories; the generality is comprehensive. As the Hawking case showed, the next step is to find one or more theories that unify these two on an even grander scale.

The road from hunches or raw empirical data to grand theory resembles the drunkard's zigzag stumbling from one lamppost to another. It is an *iterative, non-linear process* which is illustrated by the shaky, spiral-like pathway to the left in Figure 6.1. Grand theory can send down simplifications to the mid-range zone in a form that opens up for practical application and improvement of extant mid-range theory.

To the right of the figure is an example. We recognize the photo of a complex environment that illustrated a non-linear society in Figure 3.2, a busy village street with cars, bicycles and pedestrians moving in several directions. There are houses but we cannot see what is happening inside them. We may want to understand more about how people live in the village, what they consume, how the shops are organized, how transportation works, etc. In the mid-range zone is a diagram that shows combinations of Bs and Cs – businesses and consumers. B2B means interaction between two business firms or a network of them; and B2C supplemented by C2B (consumer-to-business) accentuates that the initiative can come from either direction – the business or the consumer. C2C interaction is increasingly more powerful, not new but spurred by social media and the Internet. All this is interconnected, here illustrated as parts of the same square. But all the Bs and Cs can be further generalized to As, *actors*, and to A2A (actor-to-actor) interaction which is shown in the higher theory zone. What have we gained by this? We have been able to discern complex patterns, to conceptualize them into B and C combinations and from that found that there is yet a higher level. The As can embrace all actors in complex networks of stakeholders.

Box 6.3 is an example of a very complex and demanding issue, namely assessing the value of mergers and acquisitions. It is in the application of mid-range theory that detailed checklists are important.

Box 6.3   Due Diligence: Mid-range Theory for Practical Purposes

Due diligence is an approach practised by consultants, brokers and others who prepare their clients for a major investment in stock or a merger or an acquisition. Preparation for and implementation of such investment is costly, and the consequences if it goes wrong can be devastating. Many mergers and acquisitions are failures, perhaps even the majority of them. Without due diligence, the number of failures would probably rise dramatically.

A recent example is when in 2012 Old Mutual, a South African international insurance company with headquarters in London, sold the insurance company Skandia, which it had acquired some years earlier, to Skandia Liv, a life insurance and retirement savings company headquartered in Sweden. Skandia Liv has now become a true mutual insurance company, meaning that those who save money for retirement own it. There are no shareholders who can demand dividends; the yield goes to the savers. After 3 years, the yield has been exceptionally high, despite the fact that savings in banks and ordinary insurance companies have only given a guaranteed yield of less than 2%; in Skandia Liv it has been several times higher than this.

The sales sum was £2.25 billion. The buyer and the seller each paid £6–7 million in fees to financial consultants and law firms, and both had considerable costs relating to their own personnel who were engaged in the deal. The acquisition process went smoothly, but even so it took over a year to complete. Having been involved in the process, although in a minor role, I had an opportunity to follow events and get privileged information. Having the majority of my retirement savings in Skandia Liv for decades, I am also an 'owner'.

Due diligence is an example of mid-range theory based on diverse theories and practical experience turned into checklists of what to find out and what to do in the evaluation of a company. The designation refers to paying due attention to the important factors in the investigation of a company. If the investigators have shown due diligence and disclosed what they found to a client, they cannot be held responsible should unexpected information surface at a later stage. They have done what they could. This is of course no precise science but it seems to be as far as we can get. Serious brokers and dealers have institutionalized due diligence as standard practice for the stock offerings in which they involve themselves. It includes the buyer's examination of a potential target for merger, acquisition, privatization or a similar financial transaction; a reasonable investigation of pivotal future matters; and asking and answering the key questions: Should we buy? How should we structure the acquisition? How much should we pay?

The due diligence process, which is partially contingent on the specific situation at hand, covers financial, legal, labour, tax, IT, environment, and the market and commercial situation of the company to be acquired. In addition, it may include intellectual property, real and personal property, insurance and liability coverage, debt instrument review, employee benefits and labour matters, immigration, and international transactions.

Each of these areas is in itself demanding to investigate and in need of additional checklists and guidelines. But it is not just a mechanical and automatic analysis. The areas are interdependent and the person who interprets the findings, draws the overall conclusions and makes recommendations, must have professional experience that has matured to pragmatic wisdom and the ability to make sound judgement calls.

The outcome must not just be a report of all the complexities but also a synthesis of the essentials and a clear account of possible risks. It should be complexity turned into manageable simplicity.

Generalization in the Grand Theory Zone

Let us start by summing up from previous chapters. Mainstream positivists advocate that case studies cannot form the basis for *generalization* but only show what is particular in a certain situation – *particularization*. But there are similarities between cases which can be used to show the general and there are differences to show variety. By merging general knowledge with particular knowledge, answers can be found. Generalization is in a both/and relationship with particularization.

For quantitative researchers, it seems to go without saying that their studies are generalizable if they fulfil certain statistical requirements. We must then remember that they can only generalize within the context they have studied. For example, a survey of the satisfaction of mobile phone customers using Vodafone in the UK based on a statistical random sample is just 'The Case of Vodafone Mobile Phone Users in the UK'. It cannot be generalized beyond its narrow limits and often not even inside these limits as survey data usually stays on the surface of customer needs, wants, motives and behaviour. A survey or experiment is a single case although based on the logic of a numbers language instead of a verbal language.

Statistical tables, procedures and equations are stylized and built on limiting assumptions to make statistical processing manageable; on samples where lower and lower response rates may impair the outcome; and results are presented as probabilities and distributions. Quantitative research uses elaborate tricks to give uncertain and ambiguous 'knowledge' a pseudo-precise identity. Through the operationalization of variables, averages and normal distributions, 'exact' indices and numbers are offered to account for deviations. Behind the fancy language and indexes, you find 'precisely perhaps' and 'exactly approximate'; the outcome is turned into fuzzy sets. There is constant reference to 'rigorous' research, despite the fact that the 'rigorous' process includes assumptions, judgement calls and an unknown number of errors. What remains is 'rigorously' derived non-knowledge – already referred to as *noledge* – posing as hard-core knowledge. And at the end of their articles in 'top' journals, these quantitative researchers seem to repent and apologize, entering a state of anxiety and say that more studies are needed to secure reliability. If those who replicate a study come from the same research tradition as those who did the first study, this 'test' is no more than a self-fulfilling prophesy.

Even if *statistical generalization* can establish quantities, it offers little understanding of a phenomenon. We have already established that statistical studies primarily answer questions about how much, how many and how often. The black box model in Figure 4.3 laid this out. We should also remember that the generalization of, for example, a group of 1,000 men which says that 36% of them go to a bar and have a drink after work, cannot be reversed. We cannot pick one of the individuals and predict if he will go to a bar or not. We may say that with a 36% probability he may do so – but a guy either goes to a bar or he does not. So the result may have predictive value for mass behaviour but it has no predictive value for individuals.

We also suffer from *overgeneralization* and *oversimplification* based on numbers. The whole of society is assessed by such numbers. For example, in the election campaign in Sweden in 2014 the opposition claimed that the government had run the Swedish economy into a situation of uncontrolled and growing debt and poverty, while the international organizations which rank the financial 'health' of nations put Sweden among the very healthiest. Financial health is a complex phenomenon which cannot be generalized into a single number and it is full of assumptions and judgement calls.

In the scientific world, bibliometrics and the impact factor are increasingly being used. A single number is presented as if it held the objective truth about a person's suitability to be an academic educator and scientist, and it is used to rank applicants for higher positions in universities. The number is appointed an almighty God. But a single number cannot embrace the complexity of what it takes to be an educator and a scientist. It's a simplification ad absurdum and here Bunge's expression 'gobbledygook' seems justified. A single number can establish who won a race in the Olympics, but that is a different kind of race.

Case theory is geared to understanding. It is sometimes referred to as *analytic generalization* that certain patterns are found to exist but not how often and to what extent. But what do we want: to understand the mechanisms of a phenomenon or to count heavily stylized details? My conclusion is that quantitative research has monopolized the word generalization without scientific support. Unfortunately, it has become so dominant that academic researchers and others are socialized into it without stopping for a moment to say: 'Hey, is this really right?' Unfortunately, academics are gullible when it comes to definitions and categorizations.

The usefulness of statistics for generalization is grossly overrated and the mainstream perception that single cases cannot be used for generalization is equally underrated. Even a single case can be used to generalize. More commonly, it is the starting point for a series of case studies to find variations and include them in progressive theory generation. The strategies are *purposeful sampling* (also called *theoretical sampling*), *saturation* and *constant comparison*. Purposeful sampling means that you start with a single case, then select a new case that you consider in some respect different from the first and therefore can add new data. You go on trying to find differences until you reach a point where you get no additional information from the last few cases. Then you have reached the saturation point. You can also compare what you have with relevant research by others, archival data and existing theory.

To elevate statistical generalization to science and treat case theory as pre-liminary, explorative, conceptual or anecdotal does not make sense. Numbers rarely speak for themselves; they are context-dependent and have to be both analysed and interpreted. When a survey is presented in a scientific article, it is followed by a discussion section, which is an effort to interpret and reflect on the numbers and draw inferences. To do so, judgement calls must be made, but despite the rigorous process of statistical data generation, it often ends up as speculation or non-actionable advice.

Business and management operate under uncertainty and risk, part of which can be the outcome of chaos theory. A company resides in a complex situation where networks of influences occur. Some can be controlled by the company, some cannot. There can be major discontinuities. One was the oil crisis of the 1970s when the price of energy rose to an all-time high and stayed high. The fall of the Berlin Wall and the dissolution of the Soviet Union suddenly occurred around 1990 and were totally unexpected, even among political and military analysts, the foreign diplomats with access to government circles, and the jour-nalists in place. In 2008 the long-lasting global financial crisis broke out. During 2009 car sales dropped by 50% – and the car companies could not do anything about it. In 2011 a strong earthquake followed by a huge tsunami hit the east coast of Japan. It had a long-term effect on the whole of the Japanese economy.

If we want to understand the complex reality of business and organization, we should come up with case studies that go into substantive detail. Arrival at the saturation point requires a judgement call from the researcher. We then have a chance to spot similarities and differences and build higher level theory, and in the same process test extant theory.

The following boxes show different types of theory generation. Box 6.4 is an account of theory developed from empirical case studies.

Box 6.4   Theory Generation Primarily Based on Cases

The Nordic School: Service Theory[11]

Northern European scholars, especially those from Finland and Sweden, have felt free to use cases to design their own theory without falling back on positivist requi-sites. Starting in the 1970s, contributions include an alert to *services* being neglected in business and management theory as well as in economics. There was dissatisfac-tion with service quality everywhere – both private and government service – and complaints were raised that service productivity did not improve while productivity

---

[11]Based on Gummesson & Grönroos, 2012. See further the e-book anthology edited by Gummerus & von Koskull, 2015.

in manufacturing was constantly on the rise. The marketing literature hardly mentioned services, despite the fact that in developed countries more than half of the population was employed in what national statistics call the service sector.

Case study research was made up of professional service and consumer service, leading to a new conceptualization. The cases showed that there was considerable interaction between suppliers and customers in both service production and service consumption, while goods were manufactured without customers being present. Individual researchers had made similar observations before that, but these had never caught the attention of business and management education and had not been followed up by further research. In the 1970s, however, researchers in many parts of the world started to investigate service. We don't know why this happened – was it just that 'the time was ripe'? But over the next 10 years a critical mass of international service researchers emerged and today service research is a major field. As Box 6.5 will show, service research has entered a new paradigm during the third millennium.

Nordic School methodology was characterized by induction, case study research and theory generation to better address complexity and ambiguity in favour of validity and relevance. In other countries, efforts were made to connect new service thinking to extant theory. Quantitative methodologies were used to learn about customer satisfaction. One of the tenets was that goods and services were different and services were defined on the conditions of goods. This led to empirically unsupported conceptualizations, such as goods are tangible and services are intangible.

The IMP Group: B2B Marketing and Management

The Industrial Marketing and Purchasing Group (IMP) has performed case study research since the 1970s with the purpose of both understanding specific cases and generating general theory. It originated at Uppsala University, Sweden, and has spread internationally but its heartland is Europe. The state-of-the-art synthesis of their general findings says that B2B should be addressed as relationships, networks and interaction. IMP has sustainably generated and continuously improved B2B management theory for over 40 years. In the following quote, IMP researchers use the metaphors of the jungle and the rainforest to explain their standpoint:[12]

> Traditionally, the jungle metaphor is most frequently used in attempts to capture the soul of the business landscape. It pictures a landscape characterized by deadly competition between the companies that populate it. An alternative metaphor ... of the rainforest indicates that a basic feature of the business landscape is the intricate interdependencies between the companies that populate it ... that companies are involved in many different forms of cooperation and are not simply rivals ... [identifying] three typical features that emerge from it: the variety, motion and relatedness of the business landscape.

(Continued)

---

[12]Håkansson et al., 2009, p. 1; see also Gummesson & Polese, 2009.

So far the metaphor. IMP research consists of hundreds, even thousands, of cases, some very deep-going. The researchers noted that B2B marketing could not be studied without considering general management and the functions of purchasing, engineering, manufacturing, among others, and that it had to be seen from an international perspective. IMP has engaged researchers from all over the world. It has stayed within B2B although it recognizes that its results may be relevant for marketing in general.[13]

New theory can also be generated using existing studies to make *syntheses* in a higher theory zone. This not only means including the viable pieces of current knowledge and merging them into higher level concepts and theory, but also dropping the irrelevant parts, however established they may be in the literature and in practice.

We have already learnt that prior to the 1970s management and marketing theory was directed at manufacturing and the distribution of consumer goods through retailing. I refer to it as *Paradigm 1*.[14] The *Paradigm 2* period (the 1970s to the 1990s) is characterized by a divide between goods and services and between B2B and B2C/C2B. It primarily consists of theory fragments in the mid-range zone and lacks the link to grand theory. Paradigms 1 and 2 still dominate the mainstream thinking of academics and practitioners. However, the beginning of the 2000s is characterized by *Paradigm 3*, based on integration and interdependency between goods and services.

Service-dominant (S-D) logic is an example of long-term grand theory generation through syntheses and the Service Science of practice as the outcome of grand theory (Box 6.5).

Box 6.5   Theory Generation and Syntheses of Extant Theory Fragments

Service-Dominant (S-D) Logic

The taken-for-granted categorization of suppliers and customers used in mainstream research does not reflect today's reality; it is a reminiscence of old economics. The discovery of the role of ambiguity is not new but has only recently

---

[13]See further www.impgroup.org

[14]The paradigms are further explained in Gummesson, 2012 and 2017.

been conceptualized in higher level theory – *service-dominant (S-D) logic*.[15] In S-D logic, customers are defined as active *co-creators* of value who *integrate their resources* with the traditional suppliers and other stakeholders. Suppliers do not sell goods or services but make *value propositions* which buyers may find tempting or not. Service is the application of *knowledge* by one stakeholder to another in *networks* and *service systems*; it is *service-for-service exchange*. Value for households is *value-in-use* and for business firms *value-in-exchange*. As there are networks of stakeholders involved in value co-creation, it is not limited to a few uniform categories. The concept *value-in-context* has a more general application. It is a complex *value network* of all those involved in producing service, including customers, in an *actor-to-actor relationship (A2A)*. For example, the value of a car as seen by the buyer is partly the manufactured product but primarily the transportation service that customers get from their interaction with the car.

The focus is on the outcome which is referred to as *service* (in the singular) and *value* to the network of involved stakeholders. S-D logic is an emerging higher level theory. It aims to capture evolutionary thinking about value and service and is subject to ongoing, open-source development. A large number of articles, book chapters and books on the topic are continuously being published. S-D logic is applicable to both B2C/C2B and B2B markets. Many of the properties, such as resource integration, have been treated in B2B research by the IMP Group but have not really been treated in B2C/C2B. Earlier service research contributed to the concept with a special case, the *service encounter*, in which the customer and service provider interact.

I personally tried to design higher level service theory starting in the 1980s. Most of its critical elements were there and I had seen through several of its hypes – and yet failed. When reading the script of their first article on S-D logic in 2003, I found that the authors, professors Bob Lusch and Steve Vargo, had done it. They offered the beginnings of a new, grand theory of service. Lusch was a long-established marketing academic in the USA and Vargo had started a travel agency and run it successfully until he decided to do a PhD. They were lucky to find each other and have now worked together for 20 years, during the past 10 years with extremely high intensity and stamina. They are both from the USA but their minds are global; they acknowledge international research, use it and refer to it.

In many service research circles, S-D logic has been perceived as a threat while it has been hailed as a quantum leap by others. Together with IBM's long-term research programme to change from computer science to services science and address society as a network of services systems,[16] and the contributions from network

(Continued)

---

[15]Vargo & Lusch, 2008a, 2008b; Lusch & Vargo, 2014; Löbler, 2013; see also www.sdlogic.net

[16]Maglio & Spohrer, 2008; Maglio, 2011; Mele & Polese, 2011; see also http://service-science.info/ and for the journal *Service Science*: http://servsci.journal.informs.org/

(Continued)

and service theory and its translation into *many-to-many marketing*,[17] we have the basis for a new logic of service and a paradigm shift in management. It is working its way up the grand theory zone. It has already contributed to mid-range theory by redefining goods and services as service, and products as value propositions, and by explicitly emphasizing the co-creation of value and resource integration. This is pragmatic and can be applied in practice. With a series of substantive cases in the future, the authors will be able to make mid-range theory more practical and move up the grand theory zone and send back new knowledge to the mid-range zone. The testing of S-D logic will primarily be an issue of continuous conceptual improvements and empirical case studies.

Service Science

Something then happened which I have never encountered before: theory and practice met. It was love at first sight and the love affair turned into matrimony. S-D logic was observed by IBM who immediately saw its potential. Lusch and Vargo did not have to convince anyone. In the early 2000s, IBM had started to rethink its business mission. It gradually lost its IT dominance when the mainframe computer market (mainly a B2B market) changed and the consumer market began to grow in a new digital era with the laptop, email and the Internet. The winners were garage upstarts like Apple and Microsoft, and IBM approached a major crisis. At the same time, the role of IT in organizations changed from mainly being about efficient office machines to become an integral part of management. IBM today is a management consulting firm with 360,000 employees.

IBM had been early to embrace the concept of computer science but began to realize that computer science was about computers – machines – and not about service and value-in-use for customers. It gave birth to a long-term research programme, Service Science, Management and Engineering (SSME), usually just referred to as Service Science. Jim Spohrer, who graduated in physics and had a PhD in computer science and artificial intelligence, is the driving force in Service Science and the Director of 'Understanding Cognitive Science' The Service Science programme involves 500 universities around the world and numerous businesses and governments. Jim worked for 10 years under Steve Jobs at Apple before joining IBM.

Jim explained: 'When I started up Service Science I did not know the first thing about service or where to turn. It was natural for me to contact schools of technology but they did not know either. Then I found that business schools around the world had worked intensely with service management and marketing education and research for over 20 years. They taught me totally new things. At about that time, in 2004, the first article by Vargo and Lusch had been published and became an immediate hit. I met them and realized that this is what I am looking for, a grand theory of service in the making that strives to get the many fragments of knowledge together.'

---

[17]Gummesson, 2017.

It will still take time to transfer S-D logic into Service Science and implement the ideas. Spohrer, Lusch and Vargo keep writing and speaking at conferences, stimulating co-authorship with academics and practitioners around the world. As IBM is a business firm, it has to transform the grand theory into mid-range theory and implementable consulting assignments. The new way of approaching service will keep developing and empirical cases and consulting assignments will progressively provide data. My prediction (but watch out for predictions!) is that service thinking will radically renew both economics and the business and management disciplines, and improve their ability to match reality and provide guiding maps. Case theory will provide a methodology for progress.

Box 6.6 reports on grand theory efforts using mixed methods approaches and offering simplifications for pragmatic use within the mid-range theory zone.

Box 6.6   Mixed Methods Approaches

The Resource-advantage (R-A) Theory of Competition

R-A theory is a grand theory contribution with pragmatism in mind. Originated by Hunt and Morgan (1997) and further developed in numerous publications, it integrates contributions from several fields within the economic sciences, both economics and the behavioural aspect of business and management. R-A theory is condensed into 9 foundational premises:

1   Demand is heterogeneous across industries, heterogeneous within industries, and dynamic.

2   Consumer information is imperfect and costly.

3   Human motivation is constrained self-interest seeking.

4   The firm's objective is superior financial performance.

5   The firm's information is imperfect and costly.

6   The firm's resources are financial, physical, legal, human, organizational, informational and relational.

7   Resource characteristics are heterogeneous and imperfectly mobile.

8   The role of management is to recognize, understand, create, select, implement and modify strategies.

9   Competitive dynamics are disequilibrium-provoking, with innovation endogenous.

(Continued)

(Continued)

R-A theory reflects the loop in Figure 6.1. It contrasts with conventional economics theory as it is not presented as pure theory with stylized data, social constructs and limiting assumptions required by the numbers language. It is also based on realistic substantive research to a much greater degree than is traditional economic theory. In comparison with the 5 forces theory mentioned earlier, R-A theory is more complex and fuzzy. It is being developed further by its originators and others.[18]

Contemporary Marketing Practices (CMP)

Another classification is based on extensive empirical data from practitioners. It has led up to a schema of *Contemporary Marketing Practices* (CMP), positioning relational approaches in a context of different dimensions of current marketing.[19] The first is *transaction marketing*, the traditional approach in marketing management. It is a zero-relationship situation which is focused on making each single transaction profitable in the first place and with no planned effort to create long-term loyalty. The second is *database marketing*. It is a more elaborate version of the mailing list and the salesperson's box of cards with notes on each customer, now charged with IT; it represents the most common type of CRM. The third step on the relationship scale is *interaction marketing*, which involves face-to-face interaction as is common in the service encounter and in B2B cooperation between buyers and sellers. Fourth, there is *network marketing*, addressing the complexity of multiple relationships between many stakeholders and which I call many-to-many marketing.[20] Finally, *e-marketing* has been added, embracing interactive technologies that allow for a dialogue between suppliers and their customers.

These are examples of theory generation based on cases and syntheses of extant theory with ensuing further conceptual development. So theory can be generated in many ways as long as it sees knowledge as pragmatic wisdom. Pure theory based on crisp sets and heavily stylized data cannot fulfil the demand, although it may provide fragments of useful input.

The business and management disciplines are in need of more innovative and daring research, quantum leaps and paradigm shifts. As social scientists look up to old physics where causality and clear testing are possible and the outcomes are indisputable, it is again appropriate to remind ourselves of Einstein's repeated emphasis on the importance of raising new questions and see problems from

---

[18]Hunt & Madhavaram, 2012.

[19]Coviello, Brodie & Munro, 1997; Brodie, Coviello & Winklhofer, 2008; and Brodie, Saren & Pels, 2011.

[20]The reason for my preference for many-to-many marketing is that network marketing is often used to denote direct selling or multilevel marketing, i.e. marketing door to door or at home parties.

new angles. This is a broader, overriding alternative to the current piecemeal contributions where details and simplistic causal relationships between two or a few variables are studied in a contextual vacuum, deprived of real-life complexity and dynamics. The research tradition is more ritual-oriented in an effort to stand out as 'scientific', and less result-oriented, which is increasingly institutionalized through bibliometrics. Conventional science likes to give the impression that it will be able to explain absolutely everything; we have already met Dawkins and evidence-based research where science is appointed the winner, just given more time and money. A more humble view is that there are things that cannot be explained by man through science.

Case theory treats theory testing as a companion to theory generation and some examples have been given. Box 6.7 concludes this chapter with an example of a case study of the application of a mid-range theory model used in a specific case and the conclusions that are drawn about the generality of the model. To generate quality data, the researcher needed close access to the specific practical application. Therefore, management action research was used.[21]

Box 6.7   Testing a Strategic Planning Model through Management Action Research

In a consulting assignment, I was working on the restructuring and turnaround of a group of textile companies. The parent company demanded that the management teams of its subsidiaries use a specific strategic decision model in planning for the next 3 years. The model was a version of the Directional Policy Matrix mostly associated with Shell and General Electric. Among similar 'portfolio models', the one created by the Boston Consulting Group is probably the best known. The purpose of these models is to find a satisficing combination of markets and value propositions for the next few years.

The model is an example of mid-range theory, a simplification that could facilitate business practice. It offers a 3 x 3 matrix. On the vertical scale are *market conditions* graded as excellent, medium and poor; on the horizontal scale, *competitive strength* graded as weak, medium and strong. To facilitate the group's focus, arrows can be drawn to show future direction, for example going from excellent market conditions to medium conditions because of a falling market.

I had used similar decision matrices in previous assignments. The advice offered in the literature, as well as the way the models structured strategic problems, left me with some questions unanswered. As a result of these doubts and the opportunity that arose, I decided to study the process of model usage with the goal of testing the model, to perhaps improve it or replace it.

(Continued)

---

[21]Based on Gummesson, 1982. Management action research is treated in Chapter 9.

(Continued)

The work with the model was carried out in management teams where I acted as secretary, external advisor and the devil's advocate. Being responsible for writing the report on future strategy, I had privileged access to all internal documents and to all employees, including top management and representatives of the president's office in the parent company. By being at the company for 3 days per week with an office of my own, I also had access to informal contact with the staff.

I found a number of things that had to be considered in using the model. Here are the overriding and general conclusions:

1. The model had *analytical* qualities by structuring the complex problem of strategic planning. These were the qualities emphasized in the literature.

2. In addition, I found that the model had *non-analytical* qualities:

    o   *Illustrating qualities.* Its graphic design gave an immediate visual understanding of the most important factors and their links. You could also say that its simplicity made it seductive and gave the impression that the strategic issue is more straightforward than it is.

    o   *Communicative qualities.* As the model presents a series of concepts and links between them, the strategic planning group can focus its attention on these and leave others out and make group communication more efficient.

    o   *Concretion qualities.* Strategic issues are complex and confusing. It is easy to land in discussing principles and dodging the real burning issues. By drawing arrows and making notes in the matrix, everyone became focused on the same issues and specifically tied to one of the products.

    o   *Legitimizing qualities.* Strategic issues are not a daily concern. The head office demanded that each profit centre make a 3-year rolling plan in May each year. This forced managers to devote their time to strategic issues in an organized form.

These non-analytical qualities were not present in the literature. Could I have discovered them by using interviews and direct or participatory observation? I don't think so. Because I had to write a report and present it to the management, I also felt a deep responsibility to make a useful contribution. The social interaction in the group, my direct advice and recommendations during the discussions, where we were often arguing, demanded more of me. I had to pay attention to the fact that the staff knew about the realities of textile manufacturing and trade and I did not. They could be stuck in history and conventions so I had to challenge some of the things they said with regard to the future.

With the thousands of articles and books published on business and management every year, the challenge is to see a pattern in them. The majority of articles offer empirical studies linked to extant theory. The article results are rarely conclusive but require additional research. As even a fragmented study can be resource-intensive, at the end of the article the authors urge others to continue their research. We need more theory-based and theory-generating articles so that we can get a firmer grip of what we are doing in the economic sciences, as well as open up for improvements and innovation. My advice to editors: Stop the flood of articles based on fragmented empirical research and shallow data from statistical surveys; reject articles based on unrealistic assumptions, premature simplicity, stylized data and where very few variables are considered; and encourage articles that add syntheses and theory of the complex reality.

All truth passes through three stages. First, it is ridiculed. Second, it is violently opposed. Third, it is accepted as being self-evident. (Arthur Schopenhauer (1788–1860), German philosopher)

7

INTERACTIVE RESEARCH

This chapter explains the meaning of interactive research and its central role in the complexity paradigm. It is akin to network theory and systems theory, which are explained in the last sections.

As mentioned in Chapter 1, the methods literature and the philosophy of science are important. But my platform for this book is, first and foremost, my personal experience and reflection as a professor; 25 years in business and government organizations as an employee, executive, consultant and principal in a partnership; and as a consumer and citizen. As consumers, we are 50% of business life, and as citizens we are 50% of government. Over the long term, businesses and governments cannot deliver more than consumers and citizens can use.

A major lesson is that *interaction* should play a leading role in research. I have come to see life and society as *interaction in networks of relationships*. It is my conviction that the researcher has to be involved and interact with the research data and its sources. If researchers remain detached observers and listeners, they do not take full advantage of their persona. *Interactive research*[1] is therefore in the core of the complexity paradigm and case theory.

Interactive research requires win/win reflection and dialogue in contrast to win/lose hard sell and persuasive debate or a courtroom atmosphere. Individual reflection and dialogue may be the most powerful tools in science. Dialogue does not come from the exchange of information between two people as the prefix 'dia' might lead us to believe. 'Dia' in this context means 'through', so dialogue is 'understanding through the exchange of information with others'; it is win/win. Debate is about arguing for the sake of winning rather than for the sake of understanding. It is about win/lose. It has its roots in an old French word meaning quarrel, dispute, disagreement or contest.

---

[1]The term interactive research may be used differently by others.

Whereas a dialogue is benevolent and constructive, debate and the dialectic process are confrontational and focused on persuasion: I am suspicious, prove your point, convince me! It starts with a thesis (a statement), continues with an anti-thesis (a counter-statement) and ends in a synthesis and compromise (a joint statement). There is no dialogue in the courtroom, there are street-smarts and book-smarts and any kind of smarts you can dream of; there is dialectics. Do not get provoked and defend your work in a debate. As a scholar, you are not on trial for murder. Quietly ask questions instead, and when your attackers cannot answer they will soon start scolding you. When pushed into a corner, those 'objective' scientists end up by referring to 'approved' procedure, attaching degrading labels to their antagonists – sloppy, illogical, subjective, New Age, anecdotal, journalism, speculation, advocacy – or simply getting angry or scared, or taking an authoritarian stance, or being unwilling to indulge in further discussion. I have already referred to this as the Bunge syndrome.

My conclusion is supported by studies of *network theory* and *systems theory* and their applications. Instead of searching for strict or partial causality, I search for the understanding of a systemic whole, a context with individual and complex patterns of interactive relationships. It does not mean that everything is interactive, but interaction has stood out as a neglected key element. Important guidelines throughout my research are close access to reality[2] – which requires researcher involvement – and high validity and relevance. In the words of S-D logic, it is about co-creation and resource integration which include both interaction and what the parties do independently of each other.

In the ancient Veda philosophy of India, the unfolding of knowledge is described as a synthesis of the *knower* (the researcher), *the known* (what we know about an issue) and the *process of knowing* (the research process and its methodology).[3] The prime object of methods books is the process of knowing. However, within the complexity paradigm the knower is in constant interaction with the known and the knowing; he/she is their carrier. In that sense, I agree with those who consider the researcher the number 1 research instrument.

Within the complexity paradigm, several types of interaction have a central role. There is interaction between:

- the researcher and the object of study and its actors – extrospection
- the researcher and his/her consciousness, tacit knowledge and other qualities of the inner self – introspection
- people in your researchscape
- substantive, raw empirical data and general concepts

---

[2]Access is treated in Chapter 9.

[3]Gustavsson, 2003.

- the parts and the whole, the individual and a system

- words, numbers, body language and tacit language

- the researcher and audiences

- data, analysis, interpretation, conclusions, recommendations, decisions, actions and results.

Box 7.1 is an excerpt from a case narrative of doing field research and learning through interactive processes.

Box 7.1   Interaction in Field Research Practice

My first visit outside Europe occurred several decades ago when working on a United Nations consulting assignment, evaluating UN efforts to help developing economies increase their foreign trade. After 2 weeks interviewing UN staff in Geneva, Switzerland, and planning the assignment, I went on an 8-week field trip to countries in Asia, Africa and Latin-America.

The first stop was New Delhi, India, where I arrived on a pitch-dark evening. The taxi was a battered Morris with two people in the front seats. I was worried what the second guy was doing there. Were they going to mug me? I later learnt that two people often shared a taxi business and also slept in the taxi at night – my first confrontation with a business model of a poor country.

The hotel was a top-class traditional Indian hotel, the Ashoka, booked by the UN. The fact that the lights went out, on and off, was normal, as I learnt. I slept well but worried about what I was going to eat and drink; I did not want to begin my long journey with a stomach disorder. Breakfast next morning was in a grand room with a band playing soft Indian music. It was an English breakfast with a fried egg, small sausages, mushrooms, toasted bread and tea.

Then I had to prepare for my 11 o'clock meeting with the Department of Trade of the Indian Government. I had designed a long questionnaire for the evaluation, asking questions about their trade practices and what they would like the UN to do for them. I went out into the busy street to wait for the taxi the hotel had ordered and was immediately surrounded by kids begging for money. Some even put their hands in my pockets. I did not want to be rude, but that was my problem; they felt encouraged. In the evening I had dinner with the Trade Commissioner of the Swedish Embassy and he told me that I had to give them a nasty look and hiss out my discontent with an angry 'Pssst!' That would show that I was an experienced Westerner and nobody's fool. I did so next time after some hesitation but it worked. They were gone in a split second.

The taxi could not find the exact building and let me out in a muddy and littered street. I walked through a group of pigs and then tried to ask people for directions. It was hot and smelly. Finally, I found the building and the people who received me were nice and seemed happy to answer my questions. But I was not sure they found the questions relevant. I wondered afterwards if I had really got any pertinent information or whether they were just trying to please me. I was, after all, representing the UN and they needed UN financial support.

I spent 4 days in New Delhi and 2 days in Bombay. Then I went to Kuala Lumpur, Malaysia. I carried a pack of interview forms which I had carefully prepared in accordance with what I had learnt at business school and as was the practice at the consulting firm. Reflecting on the week in India during the flight, I felt that the forms were heavy but not helpful. I took a decision: throw away the forms; and made a 1-page interview guide as a checklist. I could add and delete issues on the checklist as I gradually learnt what it was important to bring up. I also found another thing when looking through my assignment plan. I had spent 2 weeks of preparation in Geneva, was beginning my 8-week field trip, and coming back I would have 2 days, no more, to analyse, draw conclusions, write a report and make an oral presentation with recommendations. A UN employee had made the plan for me and I had not considered it in depth.

My next decision came out of desperation. The worst thing a consultant can do is to exceed the budget and have to work without being able to invoice a client for the time spent, as well as having to postpone the reporting. The standard format for a study was strictly positivist: collect data, analyse the data, draw conclusions, make recommendations and present a report. I had already begun to doubt the validity of this linear format and adopted an iterative approach, and the phases of research became partially interactive and simultaneous. So I said to myself: start doing all this now, after the first week. I did not just record the data, I also drew conclusions. The key was to revise the conclusions with an open mind when I had more data. If I committed myself to conclusions too early, they would block my perception and bias the report. I was going to do over 100 interviews but decided to revise and expand my report every evening.

It worked. When I landed in Geneva, I had a handwritten report ready for typing. It left me a day extra to party with my friends. I also learnt that the highly paid UN official who had planned my trip had never set foot outside Europe.

Here are interaction-related lessons derived from this field experience that are of general interest in case theory:

- I had to interact with an environment that was new and sometimes puzzling to me. It required asking people and it made me worry at times. You need extrospection but you must balance it with introspection.

- After the first week, I let common sense take over and throw away the lengthy questionnaire.

- Research is not linear, but in part it is iterative. Starting to write the report at the beginning of the field trip was a lucky move.

- You need practice, field experience and experience of report writing to be able to apply the demands and advice of methods books.

- Did I ask the important questions? And did I get true answers? When in doubt, I must keep asking and rephrasing my questions.

- How much should I trust the convention and the methods books and how much my personal experience and common sense?

- To understand how one gets information in interviews, one has to interact closely with the respondents and not just mechanically ask a question. Those who do the interviews are often not the same people who design the questions and the response alternatives. It means that those who are going to plan an interview do not have any interactive and first-hand impressions of the interviews.
- One has to understand initially or be open to and learn about the context in which the research takes place.
- Planning is important but flexibility as you go along is too.
- Writing the report and doing the analysis and drawing conclusions continuously, the interviews and the data were still fresh in my mind. It is amazing how dull field notes and memos stand out to be after some time.
- The more people I talked to and the more I reflected on the material, the more clearly I saw the gaps in my knowledge and could revise my interview guide accordingly.
- Doing research is not just intellectual; it requires an adaptation to new environments and the handling of many practical issues.
- Had it been today and had I been able to design the research plan, I would have made 8 cases, 1 for each country, going into the detail of specific trade projects or trade problems. It would have left me with grounded, substantive data.

Support for interactive research is offered by the relationship-based theories of B2B marketing, the new service marketing and management, and the interaction that naturally takes place in the delivery of service.

For example, when you fly you are an active co-creator of the service when you buy a ticket, check in online, drive to the airport, park your car, walk to the security control, load your things on a conveyor belt, and take off your jacket, sometimes even your belt and shoes. You then walk to the gate, wait for boarding, walk into the aircraft, find your seat, stow your hand luggage on a shelf, and buckle up. If you go on a 1-hour flight, you probably spend 3–5 hours ordering the ticket, getting to and from the airports and waiting there. This means that most of your interaction is with other people than the airline and its staff. Further, you are present during the flight and the narrow aisle forces passengers to show consideration to each other (C2C).

This forms a background to *network theory* and *systems theory*. As has been noted already, the roots of words like network, system, ecology and complexity have close affinity. They all stress the importance of addressing the parts and the whole. Together with the other characteristics of the complexity paradigm, we end up with the scientific narrative going beyond the merely verbal 'story'.

The chapter proceeds with reviews of network and systems theory.

Network Theory

A network is often set up as the opposite of a *hierarchy* – but a hierarchy is actually the simplest form of network. It is 2-dimensional and is an expression for an authoritarian chain of command. As an employee, you are over some and under some and some are on the same level as you. A network is usually multidimensional and the context determines which and how many dimensions are pertinent in each case. There are also networks of networks and some of these are more powerful than others. So the concept of hierarchy is critical to defining networks; it is both/and.

You sometimes hear that a network or a system provides just a *structure*. This is not the whole story. The misconception may come from the graphs that are used to show networks. A danger of graphs is that they are static snapshots and do not show the dynamics, and they are images and not the real thing. In networks and systems, processes are going on, things are changing, power may move from one actor to another or the strength of each one's power may change. Interaction is a keyword in networks as numerous nodes are dependent on each other and each interaction can have an influence. Sometimes a change in a minor variable can cause a major change by sending ripples through the network. For example, a supplier has a long-term B2B relationship with a customer and regular purchases take place with little variation between them. Then the customer goes bankrupt or decides to use another supplier and this becomes a major change.

As told in Chapter 2, to describe the operations of a company today you have to show its network. This can be done with varying degrees of sophistication. The first step is to offer a basic graphical sketch of nodes and links that constitute a certain business, and to lay bare its complexity. This graph can be further explained verbally in the narrative. Most current case research in business and management is at an early stage of sophistication. Traditional case study research is verbal, but with network and systems theory it is possible to add more advanced graphs and mathematics and even to do computer simulations. These are extensions of the verbal language of the conventional case narrative. Network theory offers a bridge to the natural sciences and helps erase the irrelevant social sciences/natural sciences categorization.

Companies are legally defined entities but their actual operations happen in networks and systems. They include internal as well as external interaction. Big companies consist of divisions, subsidiaries, part-owned companies, alliances, and so on. A small company, especially with the help of the Internet and mail order, can have an extensive network of partners even if run from the owner's home. The core of what we perceive as a big company can be a name and a brand managed through a small group of people who control the network of operations through other entities and are ultimately controlled by banks and risk capitalists on Wall Street or in the City of London. To state how many people are engaged in the operations is possible by applying network and systems thinking. Still today, company descriptions are guided by the industrial era structure where the Ford Motor Company consisted of Henry Ford as president and sole owner, surrounded by a small group of managers and engineers and then 1000s of workers. The counting of people on the payroll was an easy way to describe size. Not so any more.

Network theory offers an attitude to business and management and techniques to address complexity. By accepting the network lenses of nodes and links and other concepts and properties that network theory has brought to the fore, we can see management in a new and productive light. It allows us to work on different levels of sophistication, including verbal and theoretical discourses, field studies and graphics, all the way from hand-drawn sketches to computer-generated patterns, mathematical and statistical studies and computer simulations. It can be applied intuitively and experientially but also in a scientific and scholarly mode. It fits both theoretical and practical requirements.

My first encounter with *social network theory* came through *sociograms* in the 1960s.[4] They described how Laura related to John, how John related to Richard, and so on. Since the 1970s, interorganizational networks have been successfully applied in B2B marketing, as was explained in Box 6.4. These applications have stayed with me and kept pleading for attention. In the 1980s, I concluded that one of the big problems with relationship marketing, customer relationship management (CRM) and 1-to-1 marketing was their focus on the dyad. It limited the relationship to a single supplier and a single customer rather than addressing the whole context in which the dyad was embedded. I decided to write a book about networks in marketing. It first came out in Swedish under the title *Many-to-Many Marketing*, with the subtitle 'From one-to-one to many-to-many in the marketing of the network economy'.[5]

The study of network theory had become an eye-opener for me. I gradually realized that life is a network of relationships in which interaction takes place. This must of course show in each specific facet of life, including business and management. Network theory is both a theory of life and a methodology to explore the intricacies of life. Sometimes I hear that network thinking is a metaphor which can be enlightening. I take a contrary standpoint: *networks are the real thing*. Setting out on my network Odyssey, I had no clue that network theory had such a wide capacity to handle complexity.

Natural scientists promote visionary thinking by elevating theory to new heights. They even have the audacity to suggest 'a theory of everything'.[6] Greenwood and Levin say that 'Everyone is supposed to know by now that social research is different from the study of atoms, molecules, rocks, tigers, slime

---

[4]For a recent overview of social network analysis, see Scott & Carrington, 2011.

[5]Gummesson, 2004b.

[6]Barrow, 1992.

moulds, and other physical objects.[7] However, they have classic physics in mind, part of which still deserves a place in science, but modern physics adds new dimensions to visionary thinking.

How about medicine and psychology? Do they not clearly embrace both the physical, mental and social sides of life? But orthodox Western medicine likes to see itself as a natural science. Social medicine, psychiatry and other border sub-disciplines rank low in the pecking order of medical doctors; hardcore physically oriented doctors like surgeons reside at the top. Clinical cases are rejected as 'anecdotal' and science is narrowed down to evidence-based medicine and randomized experiments.

It gradually dawned on me that the narrative and network theory have a close affinity. Their unifying idea is to address real-world complexity characterized by masses of data, contextual dependency, dynamic situations, chaos and fuzzy variables. In the following, read what these two physicists have to say.

Buchanan[8] accentuates the connection between social networks and natural science networks. Their structures are almost identical, which also indicates the need to abandon the meaningless social/natural science categorization. He concludes: 'Physicists have entered into a new stage of their science and have come to realize that physics is not only about physics anymore, about liquids, gases, electromagnetic fields, and physical stuff in all its forms. *At a deeper level, physics is really about organization* – it is an exploration of the laws of pure form' (italics added). Barabási[9] underscores the application to the economic sciences: 'understanding network effects becomes the key to survival in a rapidly evolving new economy', and 'in reality, a market is nothing but a directed network'.

Table 7.1 lists specific concepts and properties that have emerged in network theory and they are further explained in the text. I have encountered them in both the social and natural sciences, but the contributions of the natural sciences are the more exciting. I want to inspire researchers in business and management, who most likely limit their search for methodology to the social sciences literature, to extend their search to the modern natural sciences.

Nodes, hubs (highly connected nodes), *links* and *interaction* are basic for all networks. The nodes can represent anything of importance for describing and explaining a phenomenon. A node is often a person or an organization, but it can just as well be a concept, an event or a machine; it is a matter of researcher discretion. For business and management which deals with both people and technology, especially IT that is now brought into every corner of society, it is essential that the human and technological elements can be shown in interaction.

---

[7]Greenwood & Levin, 2005, p. 53.

[8]Buchanan, 2003, quotation from p. 165.

[9]Barabási, 2002, quotations from pp. 200 and 208. See also Barabási, 2012.

Table 7.1 Network theory concepts in alphabetical order

Attraction	Fit-get-rich	Random networks
Cascading failure	Fitness	Rich-get-richer
Centralized networks	High tech/high touch	Robustness
Clusters	Holistic	Scale-free networks
Cluster coefficient	Hubs	Self-organizing
Connectors	Interaction	Six degrees of separation
Context	Iterative	Small world
Contingency	Links	Spreading rate
Critical states	Nodes	Strength of weak ties
Critical thresh hold	Non-linear networks	Structure
Decentralized networks	Parts	Systemic
Degree exponent	Phase transition	Tipping point
Distributed networks	Planned networks	Topology
Embeddedness	Power law	Winner-takes-all
Error tolerance	Preferential attachment	
	Process	

The network builds up the *parts and the whole* simultaneously, offering an explicit and orderly way of doing so. It is *systemic (holistic)* and thus caters for the basic property of *context*. It allows for the study of fragmented detail but offers techniques to put parts into context and not leave them hanging, as in most of mainstream research.

Each specific network applies the elements and properties in an individual way. Networks therefore come in many shapes and are shaped by many forces. Examples are *centralized networks* (1 hub), *decentralized networks* (many hubs) and *distributed networks* (no hub). The *topology* of networks refers to the network landscape, its size and the *structure* of nodes and links. Structured descriptions are usually linear, presenting events in steps like a chain (an example is the value chain in corporate strategy) or chronologically. Networks are independent of sequence; they are *non-linear* and *iterative*, jumping back and forth between the elements of a phenomenon.

Early network theory talked about *random networks*. Randomness in the mathematical sense exists in nature and social life as special cases but not as a general characteristic. Business networks can include random dimensions but they are primarily *planned networks*, influenced by the intentions and behaviour of numerous companies, consumers, governments and others. The structures and processes of networks have to be selective to be manageable. This becomes particularly obvious when a network grows. A dyad includes 2 people and 1 link. Double it to 4 people and the potential links grow to 6; double it to 8 people and the potential links will be 28, and so on, at an exponential rate. In principle, networks are *scale-free*, meaning that their size has no limit. In practice, they are limited by specific conditions and circumstances, such as a company owner's objectives, the size of the market, access to capital, and government regulations.

Clusters are dense groupings of nodes and links within which everyone can easily reach everyone else. The *cluster coefficient* is a measure of closeness. If the coefficient is 1.0, all members of the cluster are in contact with each other. It is zero when 1 member is related to all but the others only relate to this 1 member. If in a cluster of 4, which allows a maximum of 6 links, only 4 links exist then the coefficient becomes 0.66. Granovetter's[10] concept, the *strength of weak ties*, shows that society consists of highly connected clusters which are linked to each other by weak yet important ties; and his concept *embeddedness* that everything is embedded in networks and thus connected. These concepts support the notion of the *small world*, popularly expressed as *six degrees of separation*: no one is more than 6 steps away from anyone else in the world.

Hubs (or *connectors*) are organizations or people with a particular *attraction* to others and who build contacts with them. Becoming a hub is essential in business. For example, the more people visiting your webpage, the more visible you become and the more you can sell. The number of hits and orders a website receives is an indicator of hub status. Marketing management then could be described as nodes fighting for links. Studies of webpages show that they follow the mathematical *power law*. This states the same as the 80/20 rule. For example, 80 per cent of the links in a network go to 20 per cent of the nodes, that is, to the powerful hubs. This can be expressed mathematically by the *degree exponent*, which for most systems varies between 2 and 3. One study showed that the incoming links to webpages had a degree exponent close to 2, telling us how many highly popular links there were relative to the less popular.[11] It has been shown that the more links a hub has, the more likely it is that this hub will be preferred by newcomers; it is known as *preferential attachment*. It is an inherent growth factor – the bigger you are, the quicker you grow – expressed as the *rich-get-richer* syndrome. In business, large hubs kill small hubs through competition or swallow them through mergers and acquisitions. This is claimed to be an unavoidable consequence of the networked economy and growth strategies governed by natural laws.[12]

Not only size but also *fitness* may explain the attractiveness of a hub. A dominant hub with the most links can be overtaken by a new kid on the block with greater fitness. Very rapidly, Google passed established search engines such as Alta Vista; fitness compensated for the lack of hubs. At a slower rate and thanks

---

[10]Granovetter, 1973, 1985.

[11]Barabási, 2002, p. 68.

[12]Barabási, 2002, p. 200.

to fitness, the Linux open-code operative system became a threat to the Microsoft monopoly. The *fit-get-rich* network is scale-free with many hubs. A few big hubs co-exist with numerous links to a large number of small hubs with fewer links; it is an oligopoly. The *winner-takes-all* network leaves little to others and a single hub controls the bulk of the links; it is a monopoly. At one time, IBM practically had a monopoly on computer hardware and only anti-trust laws held them back. Airlines are obvious networks and in Europe the upstart Ryanair in 2007 passed the UK national airline of British Airways (founded in 1919) in size, measured as number of passengers. The reason was fitness, manifested in low prices and overall efficiency.

Phase transition is about the transfer from disorder to order. Power laws take over in phase transitions and the laws are general to behaviour in nature and society. For example, there are parallels between atoms and consumers. At a critical point, we have to stop viewing atoms as individuals as they group themselves in communities where the atoms act in unison. We recognize this in marketing: going from the individual to communities or segments that buy the same things for the same reasons. Free capitalist markets are *self-organizing* when millions of consumers make choices, not independently because they are influenced by the context of network belonging, but the variation is so huge that the choices can only be loosely and temporarily controlled. Companies try to exert control through individual relationship-building; para-social relationship-building through symbols such as brands and storytelling; availability and distribution networks; and even the creation of physical addiction (examples are medication and sugar). Progressively, the role of customer has become more powerful but is now recognized as an active resource in business, mainly because of Internet developments and social media. Companies are trapped between order and chaos and the dream is to reach the state of zero degrees Celsius when the rather disordered liquid water – customers – suddenly changes into a perfectly ordered and solid state – ice.

Nature's ecosystem has a greater topological *robustness* and *error tolerance* than human-made systems. It can sustain basic functions even if many nodes and links go bust. *Cascading failure* refers to a breakdown in one part of a network that builds up and spreads throughout the network. While sometimes a small node or link can make all the difference, sometimes the breakdown of a large number of nodes and links does not incapacitate a network. There is a *tipping point*, meaning that events accumulate and reach a point of sudden change. We may not note the signs of the gradual process because we understand too little of network behaviour. The breakdown of a large hub may cause instant failure. If the focus of business, government and the media is on big corporations, the gradual disappearance of small firms and the slowing down of start-ups and entrepreneurial activity will not be noted under way. Having reached the tipping point, the process may be irreversible and the effect can hit hard.

When an epidemic or an innovation spreads, we want to know the *spreading rate* – the likelihood that a person will adopt it – and the *critical threshold*, which is the quantity determined by the properties of the network in which it spreads. If the spreading rate is below the critical threshold, it will die out; if it is above, the number of adopters will grow exponentially. The thresholds of individuals vary widely, but a single person's behaviour can trigger collective behaviour and cause unexpected and sudden events.[13] No one foresaw the rapid development of mobile phones into a lifestyle and fashion product among consumers starting around 1990. In management, we rely on plausible explanations and storytelling about events and their links. New theory of *critical states* may in the future give other explanations, equally applicable to physical and social phenomena.[14]

Several of the general law-like findings that we have discussed are partly counterintuitive, among them the small world, the spreading rate and the tipping point. It is therefore essential that the outcome of studies in modern mathematics, physics and other sciences is also tried on social phenomena. Much to the surprise of natural scientists, certain network laws have been found to be universal and apply to such differing phenomena as the foodweb of an ecosystem ('who eats who'), the connected neurons in the human brain, the dissemination of innovation in consumer markets, the breakdown of financial markets, and the growth of Google. The World Wide Web is one of the largest human-made networks; it is an infrastructural network just like the roads, the electricity grid and the telecom system. They all display general structures and processes although the applications include specific features. There is obviously some organizing principle of the world on a deeper level that transcends the boundaries between the social and natural sciences.

For example, history is part of the humanities; it is the history of people and nations. Anything that is exposed to change has a history and therefore not only the social sciences but also the natural sciences are dependent on the past. Among them are archaeology, evolutionary biology, geology and astronomy, and the economic sciences economic history, management and economics. History, as we know from our school books, is based on narrative efforts to link events, find possible causes and come up with interpretations. The rationale for such storytelling is *contingency*; unique events occur in unpredictable ways. If life is networks and there are laws that control networks, sometimes mathematical laws can be found. As it is often claimed that history – at least in part – determines the present and the future, we need to be able to chart events and their links better than just as accidents and qualitative interpretations. It now seems as if the power laws and hubs of complex systems can help us. It has been demonstrated

[13]Granovetter, 1978.

[14]Buchanan, 2003, p. 106.

that dominant websites, mergers, globalization and financial breakdown obey the same laws as cells and fractals of self-similarity of river networks and tree branches. General laws apply to some extent, whether the object is people, corporations, cells, galaxies or the Internet.

If we deal with a fuzzy reality, we have to match it with research techniques that allow for fuzziness, and this is what modern physics and mathematics have been doing over the past 100 years. It has gone unnoticed in the quantitative social sciences.

It is only during recent decades that business and management have discovered what huge economic activity is going on in the organizing, financing and marketing of tourism, events, nations and cities. Box 7.2 offers an example of networks of tourist destinations.

Box 7.2   Using Network Theory to Structure a Fuzzy Industry

Tourism, travel, events, etc., are the epitome of a fuzzy category. This is something that picks from businesses and governments on international, national, regional and local level as well as NGOs and the commons, thus affecting all inhabitants of a certain destination and the way to get there. We may not yet have found a unifying concept, although we can use many attributes to describe each category. Hotels are primarily for temporary visitors but visitors also use the local streets, transportation and retailing. Their visits may be intertwined with the daily life of a place by relatives visiting relatives and businesspeople visiting buyers and participating in conferences. Cities and nations have their own unique history and culture which materialize in architecture, museums, restaurants, and so on. Places are dependent on travel agencies, airlines, the media and others outside their countries and their promotion of a certain destination and event.

In the effort to find a more general term, *destination marketing* has been suggested. It incorporates marketing and the destination but not other management disciplines such as finance and organization. An event takes place at a destination but even if thousands will travel to see it live, millions may watch it on television and not travel – they are, all the same, integrated with the business and management of the event. So it is definitely a complex service.

How then do we approach it in research and practice? We can write scientific narratives. They will become long but words and simple diagrams do not satisfy our need to define and condense the phenomenon under study. As we cannot overview it all at the current state of science, we need to pick out parts – but we then risk reducing instead of condensing. We can however take a step forward with network theory and its nodes and links or in systems theory terms with the system and its subsystems and components. Following the tenets of these theories, we can show how we extract the part we wish to focus on, still able to locate its place in the whole.

We need network and systems theory structures by means of graphs and even more sophisticated tools, like computer simulations. Many more complexity theories could certainly be applied, such as chaos theory and fractal geometry, but we have to try them out to find applications that suit business and management issues.

The idea was to show an example of a destination network but it would not be possible to read on a book page.[15] The destinations are competitors for visitors and events but they are also collaborators; there is obvious interdependence. Even this bird's eye view displays enormous complexity and the chart could include more nations, places and events. We can then go further into concrete detail and reach down to individuals and the substantive theory zone.

What do the graphic networks contribute? They can:

- lay bare interdependency and complexity on many levels

- be regularly updated to show ongoing changes

- give nations, cities, event organizers and other actors an idea of the context in which they are operating and a chance to identify potential competitors and collaborating partners

- make it possible to extract a piece of the network for special study without losing sight of the whole.

Systems Theory

In his seminal book *The Fifth Discipline*, Peter Senge pointed to the necessity of systems thinking that fuses techniques, ideas and visions into 'a coherent body of theory and practice', and noted that 'without systems thinking, the seed of vision falls on harsh soil'.[16] Smart service systems based on network theory and systems theory offer an attitude to business and management. By accepting the systems lenses and the specific concepts and properties, we can see business and management in a more productive light. Like network theory, it allows us to work at different levels of sophistication.

Systems theory is used in all types of science but not to its full potential. It does not align with positivism, but in its sophisticated applications it uses advanced mathematics in combination with computer simulations. But it is still complexity and holism that rules, not reductionism. We will deal with systems theory with applications in business and management.

---

[15]See the original source – Muñiz Martínez, 2012.

[16]Senge, 1990, p. 12.

The *Viable Systems Approach (VSA)* is a management application of systems theory.[17] It is within the same spirit of the complexity paradigm and network theory but with a somewhat different emphasis. It postulates that every business is a system, nested in a relational context where it is looking for competitive profiles – *viability* – through interaction with other stakeholders (A2A). In practice, it shows in the development and implementation of business models. Two key concepts are *consonance* and *resonance*. Consonance means that there is a potential compatibility between the systems components; resonance that there is harmonic and constructive interaction between the components so that results can be achieved. This determines the viability of the system, referring to its capacity to compete, collaborate and survive in a complex world, characterized by change, chaos and fuzziness.

The computer 'language' exerts a growing impact on service systems. In the 1960s when computer systems were primitive, the IBM salesman who negotiated with my then employer for the sale of a large system assured us that they would deliver a 'user-friendly' product. They did nothing of the kind. The first time I ever met something user-friendly was when I was introduced to the Apple Macintosh computer.

When you design software, you have to be precise and consistent. Software designers have always had a limited understanding of how users react; they were, and still are, mainly supplier and product focused. Websites have become an important contact point between suppliers and customers, but it often takes years, even decades, before a website has matured. They keep improving them, which will help users in the long run, and in the meantime new software versions are introduced. This takes up user time and causes irritation.

It shows how complex service systems can be. For example, for 20 years software companies have promised to rationalize the writing and keeping of patient records to gain several advantages: facilitate for doctors; store the records better; make records available for medical staff in other hospitals when they share a patient; and increase patient safety. So far they have not succeeded. It has led to more work for doctors and less time with patients, mistakes in records keep following the patient, and continuous changes in systems cause loss of information. Yes, it is complex and we do not have the ability to standardize and make all this smooth. To compensate for that, we need human interaction, pragmatic wisdom and openness to identify and correct problems.

The word *ecology* comes from the Greek *eco*, meaning 'house', and *logica* meaning 'study of'. It is the same eco as in *economy* which originally meant

---

[17]Barile & Polese, 2011; Badinelli et al., 2012.

'household management'. Ecology is mostly thought of as a branch of *biology* ('the study of life'), where it is the study of the relations between living *organisms* and their *natural environment*. It considers complexity and the interaction between the parts of a system as well as the whole. For most of us, ecology probably refers to environmental preservation and food grown in harmony with nature, without pesticides, artificial fertilizers and other chemicals, and free from genetic interference.

Ecosystems are complex adaptive systems where the interaction of life processes forms self-organizing patterns across different scales of time and space. The term is increasingly also used in management. One example is the food chain – a feeding hierarchy that moves from basal species to consumers. The pattern of food networks creates a complex food ecosystem.

The new mathematics challenges complexity and seeming chaos from a systemic and ecological perspective, just as case theory does. The old mathematics cannot deal with complexity. The new mathematics could be adapted to any kind of system, be it social or natural. It is not focused on describing reality in numbers but as patterns and relationships. Capra[18] summarizes the role of the new mathematics:

> We can still make very accurate predictions, but they concern the qualitative features of the system's behaviour rather than the precise values of its variables at a particular time. The new mathematics thus represents a shift from quantity to quality that is characteristic of systems thinking in general. Whereas conventional mathematics deals with quantities and formulas, dynamical systems theory deals with quality and pattern.

Ecosystems are hierarchical and organized in interacting and semi-independent parts that aggregate into higher orders of *complex* integrated wholes. They create *biophysical* feedback mechanisms between living and non-living components of the planet. An important concept in ecology is *feedback loops* that regulate and sustain systems like a thermostat. They correspond to interactive and iterative research. These feedback loops regulate and sustain local communities, *continental climate* systems and global *biogeochemical cycles*. Systems behaviour must be arrayed into levels of organization, *hierarchical ecology*. Changes in higher levels usually occur at slow rates, for example a change in infrastructure, while lower levels, such as day-to-day business decisions, exhibit continuous and rapid change.

Ecosystems are sustained by *biodiversity*, which is about life processes and the richness of species. It includes the variety of living organisms, the genetic differences among them, the communities and ecosystems in which they

---

[18]Capra, 1997, p. 134.

occur, and the ecological and evolutionary processes that keep them functioning, changing and adapting. Applied to the behaviour of individual consumers and consumer communities, it puts emphasis on the diversity in markets, its consumption patterns and the competition that offers numerous different types of service.

Predation is yet another aspect of community ecology that has a parallel in business and management. The word refers to those predators who kill, eat and plunder one another. We see it not least in the financial sector and in a professional inability to understand its mission in society. *Competition* is one aspect of this if it goes beyond the limit of what is good for the market. Healthy competition, giving everyone a chance to offer something better, is the positive side of competition. The other side is when a company cheats, overcharges, delivers faulty quality and makes promises that are systematically broken. In *The Predatory Society*, sociologist Paul Blumberg[19] explains how companies usually cheat their customers in some way, especially when it is difficult for the customer to note it or react to it. This negative side of competition is widespread.

Ecology is a human science as well. There are many practical applications of ecology in *conservation biology*, wetland management, *natural resource management (agriculture, forestry, fisheries)*, city planning (*urban ecology*), *community health, basic* and *applied science* and human social interaction (*human ecology*). In this sense, ecological thinking in business and management is both about our nature and about human interaction. It shows how biology and social life meet – quite obvious and trivial, isn't it?

Ecosystems sustain every life-supporting function on the planet, including *climate* regulation. They are regularly confronted with variations and disturbances over time and geographic space. It could be a forest fire, flood or drought. These disturbances create space for renewal just like entrepreneurship requires 'creative destruction'.

Ecological *resilience* is a cornerstone in ecosystem management. It is about the ability to adapt to new conditions and survive. Ecologists describe 4 critical aspects of resilience:

- *latitude* – the maximum amount a system can be changed before crossing the critical threshold where it breaks down

- *resistance* – how resistant a system is to change

- *precariousness* – how close the current state of the system is to its critical threshold

- *panarchy* – the degree to which a hierarchical level of an ecosystem is influenced by other levels.

---

[19]Blumberg, 1989; see also Box 9.7.

These ecosystem criteria can also be adapted to companies and other organizations.

Box 7.3 and Figure 7.1 show how healthcare can be described and analysed as networks of service systems. Figure 7.1 reflects fuzzy set theory and therefore the boxes and arrows are not straight; if they were not like this, they would deceive our minds and turn them back from complexity acceptance to the pseudo-orderly world of positivism.

Box 7.3   Healthcare as a Network of Service Systems

Medical service is traditionally described by the doctor/patient model, the 1-to-1. This is not a realistic description: healthcare requires many-to-many relationships. The linear notion of a one-way paved street to health with the knowledgeable doctor – the expert – telling the ignorant patient – the amateur – what to do and then the patient is cured, is not the general case but the exception. This expert/ amateur model builds on the assumption that the expert knows all and always knows best. Hospitals know a lot in absolute terms, but in relative terms they know remarkably little. The medical sector has managed to peddle an image of omnipotence and excellence, which is an extreme example of storytelling and brand management.

The outcome of healthcare emanates from:

- what medical staff does to a patient

- what alternative therapists do to a patient

- what both of the above do in interaction with a patient

- what the patient does as an individual

- what the patient's environment of family, friends and others do.

We can refer to S-D logic, stressing the co-creation of value and the integration of resources in a network of stakeholders. The importance of dialogue has been stressed for improving co-creation and doctors are increasingly trained in communication with patients. How this works is very individual, both on the doctor and patient side. In my experience, it is still too much of a one-sided encounter. The risk is that there is pseudo-interaction which is focused on being polite and friendly, but nothing beyond that.

In a management action research case, a Swedish hospital is compared to the Shouldice Hernia Clinic in Canada. The two hospitals are different. The Swedish hospital does several kinds of surgery, while Shouldice only does hernia surgery and is considered the world champion through a unique method. This description will emphasize one issue: the dyadic doctor/patient model does not show the complexity of healthcare. Network theory in graphical form can help us get a better view of reality.

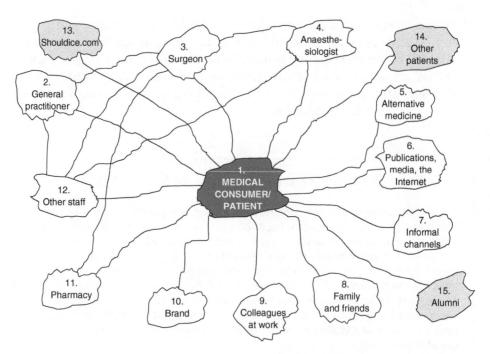

Figure 7.1 The hernia customer's position in a network of relationships. Nodes 1–12 are the same at both hospitals but nodes 13–15 are unique to the Shouldice hospital[20] (© the Author)

Box 7.4 offers an example of how machines can be seen as service systems rather than as manufactured products, all in line with S-D logic and Service Science.

Box 7.4   Machines as Service Systems: The Case of Airbus and Boeing

In new service theory – which defines service as value-in-use and not as the opposite of goods – an airplane is a coherent service system. Take the big passenger aircraft currently being built by the 2 major competitors, Airbus in Europe and Boeing in the USA. Their new aircraft are similar. They can pack in up to 850 passengers, they use lighter material and consume less fuel than earlier generations, and can consequently fly longer distances without refuelling. These machines are extremely complex. They cannot be described in simple equations or verbal narratives. They are complete systems. If you describe them in network theory terms, they consist of nodes and links. Nodes that are of special significance – hubs – are the engines which in turn consist of numerous nodes which link in complex patterns. Then you

---

[20]For more on the Shouldice Hospital case, see Heskett & Hallowell, 2013; Payne & Frow, 2014.

have the wings, the wheels, the passenger seats and the drinks that are served, just to mention a few; most of these are not visible to passengers. There are tens of thousands of nodes and considerably more links between them.

We can also say that they are complete implemented theories that have to consider real-world complexity. An economist can assume away a factor but an aircraft designer cannot. If the system is not complete, the airplane will not fly. Compare this with the global financial system. There are nodes and links but it is embarrassingly incomplete; it is a collection of fragments. The fragments may very well be rigorous, objective or whatever, but they do not stick together and therefore they lack validity.

The aircraft is a theory whose validity can be tested. The aircraft must be able to lift from the ground, stay in the air, move ahead, confront unexpected influences like bad weather, land and be controlled by the pilots. It must be able to interact with passengers, new airports, mists, darkness, etc. The 5 senses of the pilots are not enough; the support of instruments is also needed. Still, a skilled pilot with experience and pragmatic wisdom can handle an emergency situation beyond what the instruments may tell. In an effort to get at least a glimpse of what pilots do, I have spent time in the cockpit of the Concorde, Jumbo Jet and smaller planes, down to those that just take a single passenger. It is a light version of action research. By observing and discussing with the pilots, I have formed an impression of how they interact with their instruments (which are all over the cockpit), how they interact with the automatic pilot, how they use their experience and intuition, and how they relax by reading the newspaper and drinking coffee. I was even put in the fourth pilot's seat in a Qantas 747 (the Jumbo) when we landed one dark night at Singapore airport. I had earphones, I could hear the conversation, I could see the instruments. It left me with impressions that I could not have had as a passenger or by just interviewing pilots.

Stretching Systems beyond Their Critical Thresholds

Our society is based on complex networks of service systems that we are constantly dependent on. Some work well and can be trusted, others work most of the time, while others have frequent problems, and then there are systems that do not work at all but are still forced on us, defended by 'experts', politicians and bureaucrats.

Recall the resilience aspect of ecosystems called precariousness, referring to how close the current state of a system is to its critical threshold. My thesis is that we overrate the capacity of new technology and get caught up by its technicalities passing the critical thresholds without realizing it. So I would like to introduce 3 critical aspects that are counterproductive to resilience:

- *Technomania* – this literally means an obsession with technology. In its trail easily follows an illusion of power and relevance. For example, that through the application of quantitative methods and despite repeated failure for decades, the same search continues; that IT is hailed as the saviour of everything despite its many shortcomings; and that we are now entering the state of big data with even greater promises. We have put ourselves in a position where we are not primarily served by technology but are captive servants of technology.

- *Bureaucracymania* – bureaucracy literally means 'power from the office', usually an agency assigned to implement government decisions; it represents 'law and order'. Today, it mostly has the negative connotation of a 'control freak show', and the purpose of government – to serve citizens and add value to society – has become secondary or even gone completely. But the mania is also prevalent in private business. We let down those who have to use our systems, blaming the mistakes on users, and seldom improve them, or we even let them deteriorate. The processing time in public agencies can be endless; the 'culture' is too often to wear people out, not to serve them.

- *Legalomania* – the law and the courts offer a stack of loosely or non-related fragments of laws, regulations and practices; it is only partially a legal system. Its basic mission – to secure justice and safety – has been left behind. It has become a technical game, a lottery. It has also become a business to help its 'professionals' get power and boost their fees. The 'system' also undertakes to help organized crime, and the mob is dependent on cooperative lawyers and judges. The law is heavily nested in government and together they represent *legal-bureaucratic values*.

But optimism is a gateway to the impossible. We must explore our limits and sometimes it works, sometimes not. We have to carry out real-life tests to find out and we have to learn from them. And what should be high tech and what should be high touch? The reigning postulate is that technology is always better than people. It is not.

We also seem to have a desire to overwork our systems (for example, the tax system) so that they pass the critical threshold. Politicians make decisions that cannot be transformed into reality, such as promising healthcare to everyone but not providing adequate resources, and even if they put in unlimited funds the knowledge required to cure people is incomplete. It can result in waiting times of 2–10 hours in emergency clinics, which is not unusual in Sweden. I even saw an advertisement from the local government in a small town, saying that if you want to visit the emergency clinic you have to book at least a week before. So if you are going to have a car accident, let us know well in advance!

Service systems are sometimes driven by a desire to focus on productivity (cost reduction) instead of value for individuals and society. Therefore, we create hassle and discontent. If capacity is always used to 100% or more, we have no slack for contingencies. If we break through the capacity of the system, problems pile up and long waiting lines occur. We are in for constant fire-fighting. If train tracks are used to full capacity, which is common in metropolitan areas like London, and as train tracks are connected in a closed system, even a slight disturbance creates ripples through the whole system. The timetable cannot be kept and security is jeopardized. A solution would be to keep a buffer zone. An airplane has numerous electrical, hydraulic, mechanical and software systems. But each is doubled or tripled; if one breaks down, another takes its place. By having several independent systems, the probability that all will break down at the same time is close to zero. When you cannot design a zero-defects system, the solution is to multiply it and reduce the probability of breakdown. When a Jumbo Jet lands after 12 hours in the air, it should not just have 1 litre of fuel left, unless it is an emergency landing and the fuel has been emptied to reduce the risk of fire. A certain slack is not unproductive, even if a shallow short-term analysis may indicate so.

What is a complex system? Complex systems may be taken for granted when they work well and we find that unskilled employees can operate them. We may not realize that these 'simple' people tacitly get lots of activities and things together and that they are adaptable to the situation. Even the simplest systems, like getting a train ticket from a ticket machine, have elements of complexity; this is especially so for co-creating customers and before they have learnt how to use the system.

To boost its brand, a financial company speculates in a full page of a national newspaper under the heading: 'Where is the world going?' It starts by saying that human knowledge doubles every 4 years, meaning that we have learnt more in the past 4 years than during the past millennia. It then goes into urgent questions about the future of mankind. It stresses that in these times of uncertainty the financial company understands the value of knowledge. It says it lives on analysing and interpreting the future. The advertisement is eloquent and raises several crucial questions – but what is its *real* content? First, it is not knowledge that grows with the speed of light, it is stored data. Second, financial companies do not have a track record of forecasting the future correctly – rather the other way around. Third, they do not tell us that there is no coherent global financial system that can be overviewed; only certain bits and pieces are understood. The world economy and how it will affect us in the future is too complex; economists have a long way to go.

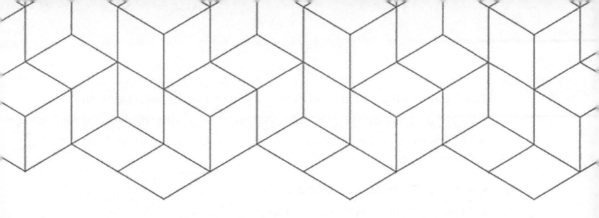

PART II

DO RIGHT

Think right, then do right. You need technical research skills to implement the right attitude. The philosophical and conceptual meets the technical and practical.

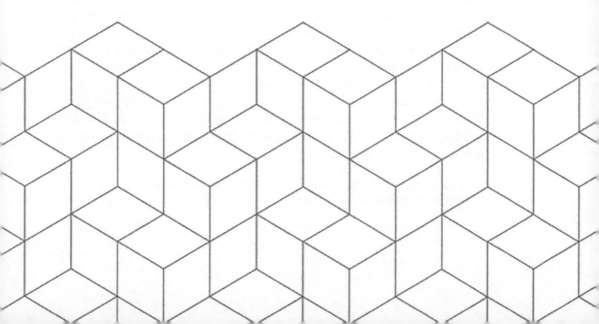

Part I and Part II are interdependent; they have a both/and relationship.

The following chapters are about the practice of research. Part II is a guide with checklists and examples for your research journey. It includes the following foci:

- *First Focus*: The research plan (Chapter 8)
- *Second Focus*: Access to case data (Chapter 9)
- *Third Focus*: Analysis and interpretation: linking data, theory and conclusions (Chapter 10)
- *Fourth Focus*: Research quality and productivity (Chapter 11)
- *Fifth Focus*: Report, communicate and defend (Chapter 12).

Within fuzzy set thinking, the term focus is used instead of step, stage or phase. The latter terms give the impression that you start at square 1, proceed sequentially and end up at the final square. We study complex phenomena and they are non-linear – and so is the research process. Figure 6.1 described the generation and conceptualization of data as an *iterative* process, moving from substantive theory through mid-range theory towards grand theory and then with a simplicity offspring to mid-range theory.

This means that the research plan is *dynamic* and *tentative*. You must be open to new data changing the conditions of your plan. New data may disturb what you have done so far and it is not unusual that researchers sweep such data under the carpet. But that is not in compliance with research ethics and transparency, and it is counterproductive to validity and relevance. Instead, you should welcome the new and use it to your advantage. It brings you forward as a scholar.

Case theory can be applied in numerous ways, depending on what you are studying and what resources you have. Learning what others have done is useful, and throughout the text you have met examples of case theory applications to make principles and recommendations easier to grasp. Read articles, theses and books based on cases and learn about the full applications. Some are excellent, others mediocre, and yet others may serve as failures to be avoided. You can learn both what to do and what not to do. Note: each case report has to be evaluated on its own grounds. The rank and brand of the journal, the authors or their affiliation has little pragmatic relevance. Now it is up to you.

> A really great talent finds its happiness in execution. (Goethe (1749–1832), German author, philosopher, diplomat and civil servant)

8

FIRST FOCUS: THE RESEARCH PLAN

The purpose of planning in case theory is to take control of a project and make an initial assessment of what needs to be done, how it should be done, and not least when it should be done.

The First Focus is your research plan. But within the iterative mode of the complexity paradigm a plan is always tentative. New data can require that the plan is revised. But the first plan provides a starting point and some direction which is valuable. As a researcher, you swing between the foci. You can, for example, start working with the First Focus, but to complete it you need to cast an eye on the Second and Third Foci and get an idea about what it is possible to plan, and then go back to the First Focus. You may start with the Second Focus if you run into an opportunity to do empirical research and then go to the First Focus to establish a plan. During the Second Focus – data generation – you often find that you have bitten off more than you can chew. Even if you want to do 10 cases studies of major companies on several continents and interview their CEOs, time and money may not suffice. You are then forced to go back to the First Focus to re-plan your study. Evaluating the quality and productivity of what you are doing (Fourth Focus) is an ongoing issue which may force you to make progress reports, not least to get feedback on what you are doing, and to prepare for the Fifth Focus, the final reporting. Most likely there is more to be done but there is life after death; the first research project may reincarnate in future projects.

The following headings are recommended for the research plan:

- the problem, research questions and purpose
- access to case data
- theory selection

- analysis, interpretation and conclusions
- reporting
- time plan.

Each of these will be addressed below.

Problem, Research Questions and Purpose

The first issue in research is to *define the problem* which you want to further understand or even solve. It could also be named *defining a research opportunity*.

Note this view on real and fictional problems: 'Truth is stranger than fiction, yet fictions rule the world as they are built into and a part of vested social structures. Thus socially structured vested fictions are a functional requirement of formal organization and social organization of life ... these fictions lead to pre-conceived professional problems to do research on and that do not exist.'[1]

Defining a problem means that the researcher has found something in society, organizations, the market, theory or wherever that he/she does not understand, or finds unclear or erroneous. The researcher may feel a desire to learn more about it and perhaps even set things right. If you define an irrelevant problem, ask the wrong research questions and set up a weak purpose, you may use elaborate research techniques but it will lead nowhere. A bad scenario is when extensive funds are allocated to the wrong problem and decision-makers apply the right solution to the wrong problem. This happens all the time in politics and university research.

Consider the expression *the privilege of defining the problem*. Who has this privilege? In the name of free science, it should be the researcher's own desire and curiosity that rule, or it should be a contribution to an ongoing research programme with researchers involved. The privilege often rests with senior professors with power over examinations, academic careers and research funds. At its best, the experience of these professors is a valuable resource that new generations of researchers can benefit from. At its worst, the mainstream has become so institutionalized that there is only scope for incremental contributions within the given paradigm. Governments in centrally controlled countries, such as in the former Soviet Union, decided what the right paradigm was, in this case a certain type of communism, and everything beyond this was a no-no in the social sciences. In such instances, research is quickly corrupted. Opportunism takes over and genuine curiosity has no place. We have similar tendencies in

---

[1] Glaser, 2005; quotation from p. 4.

freer countries as well when governments and politicians assume the definition privilege and encourage research and science for political or tactical purposes. As financing gradually becomes the controlling factor of research, private companies can also sponsor business schools and research projects that suit their purposes. As long as the research is registered as a consulting assignment, the funding organization can do what it wants, even demand a certain outcome, although this is unethical. Sometimes a power culture within a discipline exerts control over a researchscape and in practice you have to comply or leave.

Asking one or several *research questions* is of great help both to the researcher and the reader. It facilitates the evaluation of a study as you can compare the questions with the answers you come up with during and at the end of your study. The research questions should ideally be answered, but more often you have to settle for a compromise of partially answering them or just improving understanding of an issue and recommending further research. During the research, you may find that you have to rephrase your research questions. The reason can be that the questions are too demanding or that you find other questions of greater relevance. An iterative mode allows you to make changes but you are required to state them in your report.

Whichever scientific stance we advocate, all researchers should ask themselves:

- Do we address pivotal issues?
- Do bureaucratic restrictions or entrepreneurial initiative and curiosity control our choice of problems to study, the methodology we apply, and the analyses and interpretations we make?
- Can our research exert any impact and add value to people, organizations and society?
- Do we, on the whole, believe that what we are doing is the right thing for us to do?

In the same spirit, the *purpose*, which consists of one or a few short statements, tells us in brief what the research is driving at. A purpose of research is increased *understanding* and, from that, generating better theory. Within the positivist paradigm, the ideal is to establish causality. In addressing complexity, it is not enough to define an independent variable (the cause) and a dependent variable (the effect). Complex situations are fuzzy sets and lack linear simplicity.

Do something that matters, that enhances our understanding, develops theory or relates to better practice and action. Too much of research is more-of-the-same, me-too, research. Too much is stuck in methods rituals and the desire to please journal editors.

To prove how customers will react to a price increase, you may be forced to exclude a large chunk of reality and assume that the price increase is a truly independent variable, that the vast majority of customers are the same and react the same, and that the quality of all brands is the same. However, a price increase is not independent of what is happening in the market and in the general economy and it can suddenly become a dependent variable. Furthermore, there could be mutual interaction between two variables or no or little influence in either direction. And all these variants may occur simultaneously. Case theory insists that the researcher is striving for high realism in a complex world of fuzzy variables and relationships. Consequently, research will deal with increased understanding of mechanisms and multiple options and not with clear-cut causality. As part of understanding is to know about existing causality and to recognize it in a systemic and complex setting, we could talk about *causal networks*.

Often, both research questions and purpose are stated but it may sometimes suffice to state just one of them. The guiding principle should be to offer as much clarity as the problem allows. Examples are found in Box 8.1.

Box 8.1   Examples of Problem Definitions, Research Questions and Purpose

As all research is unique, these are examples and not role models. Use your pragmatic wisdom to establish relevance in each specific case.

- In her dissertation, the PhD student[2] describes the problem, purpose and research questions in the following way. Through work in business she had found that the processes of developing better services were difficult to pinpoint and that the models from literature did not concur with her practical experience. She writes: 'The purpose of the dissertation is to illuminate, analyse, interpret and discuss product development in service intensive businesses.' She asks the following research questions: '1. *How* are value-creating products being developed in service intensive companies? 2. *What* value-creating products and product dimensions are actually being developed? 3. With a focus on actors, knowledge and meaning: *Who* participates in the product development work?' The empirical base for this was 2 comprehensive cases.

- In a script that I reviewed for a 'top' journal, the authors said that their basic purpose was to study the interaction between bank managers and consumers. They perceived this interaction as a problem that needed to be improved. The overriding research question could, for example, be phrased as: 'What can be done to improve the supplier/customer interaction?' It could then be specified in a few sub-questions and detailed in an interview guide or a questionnaire. The authors applied an ambitious empirical research agenda to find answers but it was overkill in one sense and insufficient in another. The way they did the interviews and the survey seemed technically correct in the positivist sense, but they could have reached the same conclusions with fewer resources; productivity was low. The bigger mistake was that they claimed they had studied the interaction between the supplier and the customer but only had empirical data from the supplier. Interaction requires at least 2 parties and you cannot

---

[2]Dahlström, 2002; quotation from p. 252.

understand it by asking only one of the parties. Not until the end of the article do they point this out, saying that they did not have the resources to study customers and suggesting that others do this in future projects. As resources are always limited, their first priority should have been to find a reasonable trade-off of their resources between the 2 parties. Another issue was that the script was reviewed in 2011 and the empirical data was from 2007. In 2008 an international financial crisis broke out and changed the banking market drastically. The crisis was still not over in 2016. I rejected the script as I saw little possibility for the article to be revised based on their current empirical data.

- Defining the problem may require a longer discussion if a researcher observes something that is not recognized in the mainstream literature. Such was the case with service research in the 1970s. Grönroos[3] was one of the early students of service and addressed a research domain that had only been noted by a handful of academics in the world. Very few reports and articles existed. Making it credible to the reader that service was a substantial part of economic activity and was different from goods manufacturing thus deserved its own discourse. The purpose became to expose the problem through empirical cases and compare the outcome with extant marketing theory. It was pointed out that the study was limited to consumer services (B2C/C2B) and did not address the B2B market. If this limitation had not been made clear from the beginning, it may have misled readers into believing that the results were valid for services in general. The basic research question was how service companies carried out their marketing and the question was then detailed in a pilot survey and in personal interviews with 1–3 representatives in each of 15 service companies.

- One of my PhD students found that sponsorship was a significant and expanding way of financing sports and the arts. The problem was that the mechanisms of sponsorship were not efficient and many sponsorships failed. This, together with an ongoing change in the marketing paradigm, had to be explained before a purpose could be established. The purpose was then defined as 'to examine the process by which the partners in sponsorship relationships cocreate value'.[4]

Briefly defining the problem, setting research questions and giving a brief statement of the purpose is helpful to the reader. I sometimes get theses that start talking – endlessly I feel –about many things but not telling me in direct terms what they are about. They keep the readers guessing, but the readers are usually busy people and there is a risk that they will stop reading after a few pages. With practitioners, it is even more important to be clear – reports there start with a separate 'Management Summary' to give the stressed executive a chance to learn about the problem and the recommendations for a solution.

---

[3]Grönroos, 1979, pp. 249–252.

[4]Lund, 2011, p. 21.

For practical reasons, we have to cut out a piece of the perceived reality we are interested in. Our brains can only handle so much and there are time, money and other resource restraints. When complexity is in focus, a holistic rather than a reductionistic and fragmented approach to reality is called for. It has already been said that holistic means *seeing both the whole and the parts*. If we can only handle a part, we should make a conscious effort to see its place in the whole. This is inherent in the complexity paradigm and its scientific narratives. Even if our effort is incomplete, it is a way to be reminded of the fact that everything is contextual and dependent on numerous influences.

At the end of a research paper, there is often a section called 'Limitations'. It should be unnecessary if we have explained what our research is about at the beginning of the article when the problem definition, research questions and purpose are brought up; it is then understood that 'the rest is silence' (to quote Prince Hamlet's final words). If it is not explained until the end, there is an obvious risk that the reader is led to believe that the paper is addressing a broader field than it is.

It is hard to pinpoint complex, ambiguous problems and how you should address them. Problem definitions, research questions and purposes are partially fuzzy sets. In war, where the enemy is hard to locate, you close in on it from many directions. In the same way, you close in on the phenomenon you plan to study by first defining the problem and then establishing the research questions and purpose. It is a reasonable compromise that makes it easier for researchers and readers to grasp the essence of a project and move ahead.

Access to Case Data

In generating pertinent data, case theory has no inhibitions. All methods and techniques that appear in the literature, even self-invented ones, may be considered in creative combinations under a crucial condition: they should give satisfactory *access* to the data needed for your specific study. Do not begin by saying 'I'm going to do in-depth interviews'; rather, begin by asking 'How do I get the best possible access to important data in consideration of my time and other resources and my problem, research questions and purpose?'

Data can sometimes be accessed through documents and extant reports. As the fragmentation of knowledge is common in business and management, making syntheses in the direction of grand theory is called for. Case theory can begin inductively with new data where there is a lack of extant data and a suspicion that the mainstream theory is not adequate or is overgeneralized. Much of what is part of current paradigms are subjective or inter-subjective assumptions, badly supported conclusions and conventions that have become accepted in numerous references from a past context. This creates the image of eternal and rock-solid 'truths' – but they are not truths.

For example, goods have routinely been characterized as tangibles, and services as intangibles. There is some truth in the definition of services which I found in *The Economist* long ago: 'Services can be bought and sold but cannot be dropped on your foot.' The definition has an intuitive and humourous appeal but it is not helpful as the starting point for research. Despite that, the intangibility of services is repeated everywhere in statements like 'Services marketing is different from goods marketing because services are intangible and goods are tangible.' Intangibility is treated as an independent variable – a cause – which affects how service management should be done. An analysis shows that (1) goods and services always appear in combination; (2) the official statistics reporting from the 'manufacturing (goods) sector' and the 'service sector' are founded on inconsistent and overgeneralized categorizations and highly stylized data; and (3) the division does not open up for general goods versus service strategies. Tangibility/intangibility may be properties that can be relevant in special instances, but they are just one dichotomy among numerous others and certainly not overriding and general categories.

Theory Selection

Theory is a natural part of scientific research, but its role varies. Empirical data and theory are like a dancing couple interacting and holding each other, gliding apart and even stepping on each other's toes. You can start *deductively* by generating data related to extant theory. The researcher has found something in the literature which he/she wants to investigate, for instance a model that seems applicable to real situations or which should be exposed to a confrontation with reality in order to be confirmed, changed or abandoned. The result of a project can then be a modified or new model, or it shows how the existing model can be interpreted in one of several specific cases.

You can also start *inductively*, without received theory, and just 'let reality tell its story'. The most pure example is GT where researchers in the empirical part start afresh, not even reading up on the literature, and deliberately trying to be open and unbiased. The choice of theory can still be part of planning as it is desirable to later compare what we find in extant theory.[5]

It is up to the researcher to determine what may be relevant theory in a project. Sometimes it is necessary to list existing theories, explain them and then make a choice of one or several of these. It is a way for researchers to demonstrate that

---

[5]See further discussion on GT in Chapter 10.

they are well read on the theories and to enlighten their readers about available alternatives. I often see academic researchers go to the best-known 'top' journals and take it for granted that they will find the best theory there. They may or may not, but when I see such articles I stop reading them; the authors hide behind authority. You should decide for yourself what you find interesting and not be controlled by the past and the judgement of others; that will never make you a top independent researcher. It is one thing to listen to others, and quite another to do what you conclude is right. The number of citations of a theory or an author is no indication of their value to your research.

Case theory is not tied to any specific social science theory; all types of relevant theory can be used. It is most common to choose from one's own discipline and this choice usually falls on one of the most widely cited theories. Theories that have not established themselves in textbooks or have become trendy through recent events and the media can however be more original and relevant. The opportunities for innovation increase by the use of a cross-disciplinary and unorthodox choice of theory. For someone who studies business, such a choice could be to approach the marketing of a company with the help of a financial model, or to apply a theory from political science or education to organizational behaviour, or to be inspired by the natural sciences. For example, in my case study of hernia operations the patient's perceived quality of a service and value perspective is integrated with the expert's view of Western medicine.[6]

Analysis, Interpretation and Conclusions

At an early stage, the researcher should not only consider how to generate data and what theory to use but also what to do with the data. How do you find patterns in data from which you can derive concepts, categories, models and theories? Analyses and interpretations of data and theory lead to a number of considerations and conclusions. It actually starts during data generation and should be documented in memos. Authors end articles with a section called 'Discussion' and 'Theoretical and Practical Implications'. More often than not, I find the assumed implications exaggerated; it is a final effort to make their research stand out as important. Authors of articles often claim that they have designed a model that should be of great help to both researchers and practitioners, but they rarely explain how. I especially doubt the value of their contributions to practitioners.

It is natural that a section called 'Future Research' concludes a report; it opens up for follow-up research projects. However, it should be realistic and I see all

---

[6]Gummesson, 2000b.

the time that it is not. It can contain a statement like this: 'Being a single and exploratory case study it cannot be generalized. We now need to formulate hypotheses and propositions to be tested through a quantitative survey of a sample taken from many industries and countries.' This is positivism and does not comply with the complexity paradigm and case theory. A more constructive test of a theory is when you find something better; the old should then be dropped. Unfortunately, this is not easily done. As we have seen, the literature is full of references to old results, although improved research is available.

Both cases and surveys can sometimes be used for generalization. To increase the generalizability, validity and relevance of case theory, more cases can be added through purposeful sampling aimed at data saturation. However, it is easy to demand a lot of more research if you do not have to do it yourself. Therefore, any recommendation to carry out further research should be followed by a suggestion of how this could be done, what resources would be needed and when it may be ready. I made a rough estimate after having read one recommendation and found they would need 100 researchers for 10 years at the cost of £10 million. It is of course meaningless to make such suggestions. Use pragmatic wisdom!

Reporting

The planning should consider which target groups are to be reached by the research and how to reach them. You may have many target groups: your thesis supervisor, an examination committee, a client, the academic community, a conference audience, etc. The characteristics of the target groups should affect the research design and the way of reporting.

Time Plan

Professor Northcote Parkinson of the University of Singapore first published his famous *Parkinson's Law* in *The Economist* in 1955. Its best-known paragraph says: '*Work* expands so as to fill the *time* available for its completion.' The law was based on his experience from the British civil service but it was recognized by people all over the world. It is a single case transformed into grand theory. A practical conclusion: when you think you have a lot of time and hope you can just start and then reach the goal, you are in for an unpleasant surprise. The 'student syndrome' says that you start a task at the very last moment with no time to deal with unexpected obstacles – and those can be many in research.

Here is some practical advice to help you control your time plan:

- If it is difficult to overview a whole project, it is better to create a schedule for each separate part, for instance when each different case study shall begin and end, but do this within a *rough overall plan*.

- A *countdown* offers a more realistic timetable than if you start with day 1. It is not by chance that space programmes use countdowns. On a certain date, the rocket must be launched and this can only be postponed at considerable cost. Go through your calendar, take a look at how many days you can realistically work on the project and then start a countdown from your deadline.

- By working *iteratively*, you can improve your time keeping. It may sound odd but I recommend that you start writing the report on the first day, with title, tentative contents, foreword and those parts of method, theory, references and other areas which are already known. Then amend the report continuously, which is simple to do with today's computers. I warn against starting by reading all the literature, then doing the research plan and then collecting all the data. Eventually you sit there with an unmanageable stack of data and you may even discover that more data is needed. There will be little time left for proper analysis, interpretation, conclusions and reporting.

- It usually *takes longer* to do case studies than you foresee, often because you do not get immediate access to informants who will accept your invitation to be interviewed.

- However well you schedule, *the spurt at the end* will make working days long and night-time rest short. Such is life.

- Iterations between the foci are necessary and have to be done whenever the need arises. If you find in your Fifth Focus or before that the outcome of your research does not comply well with the initial plan, you can always change the plan as long as you alert the reader to this. In the final report, this should be done early so that the reader knows what is coming.

By failing to prepare, you are preparing to fail. (Benjamin Franklin (1706–1790), one of the founding fathers of the United States and inventor of the lightning rod)

9

SECOND FOCUS: ACCESS TO CASE THEORY DATA

Close access to high-quality data is crucial in case theory; it lays the ground for validity and relevance. This chapter presents the data-generating methods commonly recommended in the literature, merged with my personal experience, tacit knowledge and the tenets of the complexity paradigm.

Access and *data generation* are the key concepts of this chapter. The emphasis is on *data quality* – that data must closely represent the real world, and *data quantity* – that the number and size of cases should be satisficing – neither too little nor too much. The complexity paradigm requires contributions from interactive research where the researcher is involved and draws on both extrospection and introspection and on explicit and tacit knowledge.

Access in a business and management context means getting close to such things as customer behaviour to design a marketing plan for outsmarting the competition; a CEO and his/her strategic thinking about future developments; how the fast Asian industrialization will impact the West and how the West can react; and internal relations to find out how productivity and quality can be enhanced.

Case theory uses the term *data generation* instead of the conventional *data collection*. Being in fuzzy rather than crisp sets, data here is seldom there to be collected like you amass bottles for your wine cellar. Data is generated in the moment you observe something and *code* it, which means 'taking raw data and raising it to a conceptual level'.[1] It can further be elaborated as 'purposefully managing, locating, identifying, sifting, sorting, and querying data' and here 'coding is not a mechanistic data reduction process'.[2] It supports my claim that research should not reduce data but condense it.

---

[1]Corbin & Strauss, 2015, p. 66.

[2]Bazeley, 2013, p. 125

Improving Research Methods: Patching or Redesigning?

If weaknesses are found in research methods, scholars and other researchers should try to make improvements or replace them. A used car may be repaired and patched up to a point where it breaks down for good and a new car is needed. In a similar vein, it is necessary to rethink the basic design of a method, no matter how established it is in the past.

Patching seems to be the dominant strategy. When researchers discover that techniques are not perfect but keep claiming that their approach is extraordinarily scientific, which is common in quantitative research such as statistical surveys and microeconomics, they start laborious patching operations. For example, in presenting a survey they keep adding indexes and quantitative tests to their numbers tables and no one except a pure technician can understand them. Still, they claim that the results are useful theoretical contributions and recommend that practising managers use them.

Here is an example of methods patching. In one article – and it is no exception – I found 11 model fit indicators, all stated in 4 different columns of scores adding up into a 44-cell matrix. Most of the scores offered 3 decimals, thus claiming a high degree of precision. The article is deductive, taking extant research and models presented in articles and books as the vantage point. Some references were 30–40 years old and not valid anymore but written in top journals by renowned professors. The authors saw that as a guarantee and that there was accordingly no need for additional inductive research.

But the authors contradicted themselves. At the end of the article, there was a section called 'Limitations' with an apology that the research was not perfect and conclusive and a statement that the authors were aware of possible shortcomings. But why then did they do the survey in the first place? How are readers supposed to figure out how the shortcomings, together with the already hard-to-understand scores and indexes, affect the results presented in the article?

The next conclusion by the authors is that they offer a springboard for others to do future research. If anyone is interested in doing follow-up projects to improve their research, the question remains whether the same phenomenon that was studied a couple of years ago has not changed so much that previous research is irrelevant and it is better to start anew and do so inductively. The problem is that the emphasis is more on the reliability and rigour of the research process and its techniques than on the validity and relevance of the outcome.

Almost every report explains that the interviews lasted 1–2 hours and in a few instances the authors had scheduled a follow-up interview. Did the length increase quality or was the respondent just too talkative and went in all sorts of directions, or did his/her free speaking open the door to new information that had not been considered prior to the interview? The duration of an interview doesn't say anything about the quality of the data. It is obvious that personal and group interviews are interactive but the degree of interactivity depends both on the interviewer and the participants. Some interviewers create an open and relaxed atmosphere, while others restrain it.

The bulk of survey books deal with statistical technicalities and are barely, if at all, interested in the genuine validity and relevance of survey results and what lies behind the data. An exception is the book *Constructing Survey Data* which is a reflective approach to surveys.[3] It is a welcome contribution that essentially supports my complexity paradigm and its interactive, integrative, interpretive and pragmatic focus. The authors conclude: 'It is critically important to be aware that mistakes made in the research design and data collection steps cannot be eliminated through statistical artifice or mathematical manipulation.' The 368 pages are rich and well structured. It is recommended reading for quantitative research technicians and can be used as an encyclopaedia.[4]

Let us not forget the persona factor. As a researcher, you should not be *an impersonal research techniques administrator* but *a passionate entrepreneurial researcher*. Box 9.1 is an illustration of the persona of a researcher and his/her persistence in getting close access to data. It was passed on to me by Åke Ortmark, a leading Swedish investigative reporter and television anchor.[5] *True investigative reporters should not be mixed up with ordinary journalists*. They do not seek quick and unconfirmed sensation; they sometimes have a background in academic research and they have a strong drive to get close to their subject. Note that what is often hiding under the designation of investigative reporting and documentary is merely political propaganda – lobbyists often refer to statistics, research, etc. but are not interested in facts, only in expressing subjective opinion. These 'apparatchicks' are not only found in the former Soviet Union and today's Russia but also in countries that claim they represent the free world and democracy.

Getting close is a skill and an art but it is also the *privilege to access information*. True investigative reporters can also communicate to audiences in an engaging way. Their individual and workplace persona is more aggressive and daring than in the academic culture. In these respects, academic researchers can learn from genuine investigative reporters.

---

[3]Gobo & Mauceri, 2014, quotations from p. xviii.

[4]For a comprehensive overview of quantitative techniques, see Moutinho & Hutcheson, 2011.

[5]Ortmark, 1985, pp. 133–138.

Box 9.1   Getting Access to David Rockefeller

It is difficult to get access to the rich and the famous as they are surrounded by gatekeepers. Doing research for a book on influential financial families, Ortmark vividly described how he tried to get access to David Rockefeller, then head of the famous American Rockefeller family, after having interviewed other family members. The Rockefeller Foundation is omnipresent in research funding throughout the world and no one has been able to find out exactly how much it sets the agenda for university research and the choice of methodology.

David Rockefeller was a powerful political and financial celebrity in the USA. The reporter made use of introductions from influential people, made several personal visits to Rockefeller's office and frequently tried to contact him by phone. This went on for years. An army of assistants, public relations officers, secretaries and security people protected Rockefeller. The reporter was finally granted a 30-minute interview but Rockefeller revealed nothing new. Unfortunate as this may seem with regard to the amount of resources that were spent, the outcome is nevertheless interesting. Had the interview not taken place, the reporter would not have known what he might have missed.

How Many Cases, How Much Data and How Long the Projects?

Box 9.2 presents examples of cases studies where the mixed methods approach has been used. The size of an individual case – considering limits in resources – has to be established in each separate research project. There is also a connection between the size of a case and the number of cases. The most common is a single or a few cases but the examples below show a wide range of application of case theory.

Box 9.2   Multiple Cases and Mixed Methods

Example 1: Quality Management

The successful book *Managing Quality*[6] is based on cases and existing literature. Its theoretical and conceptual base is that of statistical and other approaches used in quality management. The empirical base is 9 US and 7 Japanese companies in the room air conditioning industry, constituting 90% of that industry in each country.

What actually was the study of, in terms of quality management? It could be any of the following: (1) quality management as a general phenomenon; (2) quality management in manufacturing industries in general; (3) quality management in

---

[6]Garvin, 1988.

the mechanical manufacturing industries; (4) quality management in the room air conditioning industry; (5) quality management in each specific company; (6) a comparison between quality management practices in companies in the same country; or (7) a comparison between quality management practices in the USA and Japan. The book presents a hierarchy of cases, all the way from multiple cases of quality management in specific air conditioning factories to an integrative, theory-generating case study of quality management on a general level.

The author expresses concern with the limitations of his research and the risk of basing general conclusions on 'anecdotal evidence', probably meaning too little data from too few companies in just 1 industry. He somehow feels it called for to apologize to the quantitative royalty. All the same, the book is advertised as a general book on quality management.

Example 2: Execution of Marketing Plans and Strategies[7]

This book is about the execution of marketing plans and strategies as opposed to the process of creating a plan. It embraces 38 cases from 22 companies, including operating units from AT&T, Frito-Lay and Hertz. The author labels the study 'an in-depth clinical examination'. Each case required 120–200 man-hours; the reports averaged 22 pages; interviews were done with 10–20 managers, plus an unpublished number of customers, distributors, competitors and industry experts. Some time was also spent travelling with salespeople and documents were collected.

The operating units were selected to represent different types of implementation problems – size, private vs public ownership, growth rate and competitive position. To the reader of the study, it is not obvious why these were chosen. B2C/C2B and B2B firms were over-represented, while services, governments and not-for-profit organizations were underrepresented.

'Though I have every confidence that the same rule of good marketing practice applies there [in industries that were not represented in the sample] as in more traditional settings, I cannot offer the empirical evidence to back up this faith.' So this book also ends with an apology for not doing mainstream quantitative research.

Example 3: A Holistic Case of Operations Management

A comprehensive and specific study of the world automobile industry was made by a team of researchers from Massachusetts Institute of Technology (MIT).[8] They spent 5 years and $5 million on investigating 80 car manufacturers. Some 60 researchers worldwide were involved, producing 116 research monographs. These formed the basis for a book, *The Machine that Changed the World*. It is fascinating reading for

(Continued)

---

[7]Bonoma, 1985.

[8]Womack, Jones & Roos, 1990.

(Continued)

anyone interested in corporate strategy, organization, quality, productivity, design, engineering and manufacturing.

It covered all the significant car manufacturers. Is this overkill? Apart from the ability to say something specific about each of the car factories, the relevant question is whether data from yet another factory adds anything to the understanding. When do we reach saturation? Can we really tell until we have studied them all? Would their conclusions be almost the same if we cut the number of cases down to a couple of factories? There is no general answer; judgement calls and pragmatic wisdom are required in each specific situation.

Example 4: Understanding Change and Stimulating Innovation and Entrepreneurship

This study has the purpose of gaining improved understanding of change processes and of how to stimulate innovation and entrepreneurship. These are highly dynamic and elusive phenomena and, in order to understand them in some depth, close access is crucial. This study is an instance of multiple cases and mixed methods and the researcher's preunderstanding was fully added: 'I do not rest my case for my analysis on any one study or any one way of examining American companies ... I drew on everything I knew, everything I saw ... from statistical data to personal observations and conversations.'[9]

The empirical work comprised the following: 5 years; 6 focused research studies; 100 companies (the author visiting 40 personally); 10 core companies examined in depth; 2 background studies of statistics on changes in labour force attitudes to work, and job content; content analysis of major summary sources of journals and speeches; 4 progressive company studies with views from 65 experts on human resources to nominate innovators in the human resource field; 4 research projects including 37 companies, out of which 10 were core companies for in-depth analysis; an innovation study with quantitative (coding information in 65 variables for statistical computer tests) and qualitative empirical comparisons (sorting data into categories, preparing case reports); a review of the previous literature; 264 interviews with managers (at 1–2.5 hours each); 6 cases of histories of change projects, 2 of which were 'arm's length' documentation (occasional snapshots and retrospective descriptions from informants) and the other 4 including direct observation, own field notes and those of colleagues, internal memos and minutes, surveys, formal interviews, informal conversations, and any documents and publications relating to the projects; 6 'whole' structure (culture and change strategies), highly qualitative and interpretive cases based on extensive contacts and detailed interviews; 1 study (General Motors) including 30 high-level corporate and workers' union informants, a review of statistics and reports, 50 interviews in 8 facilities involving field trips, a review of public documents, casual information, listening to presentations, reading books, articles and case studies, submitting the write-ups for

---

[9]Moss Kanter, 1983, quotations from pp. 384–385 and 371.

critique from informants, and finally gossip (which was not used, though); the remaining 'whole' cases included 20 informants, a minimum of 1 week on site, documents and clippings; and, finally, a study of changing personnel departments including 32 companies. The only data that is withheld is the number of people on the research teams; there must have been quite a few.

> I leaned toward rendering those dramas of life in the corporation which would make my conclusions come alive, which would cause readers to believe me not because of my numbers but because of the echoes of my ideas in their own experience ... I can be reasonably sure that my findings accurately reflect corporate America.

Example 5: Critical Incidents

The last example shows a different case approach based on a large number of mini cases. The *critical incident technique (CIT)* is an interview method for coming close to direct observation, yet avoiding some of its disadvantages. In a study, the authors investigated the 'service encounter', i.e. the occasion when a service is delivered in interaction with a customer.[10] In 3 service industries (hotel, restaurant and airline), 131 employees were interviewed, producing 355 usable incidents. The respondents were instructed to:

- think of examples when their or their fellow employees' interactions with customers were difficult or uncomfortable

- describe the circumstances of the incident

- provide details until the interviewer could visualize the incident.

The authors point out that CIT generates data with a level of detail and richness that give the researcher close access to the realities of the process being studied. The respondent could be asked to tell the tale in a more descriptive way but also in a more interpretative way, thus including emotions, conclusions, etc.

In a study of retail banking, customers were asked if they could recall incidents that had affected their relationship with the bank.[11] Here are summaries of 2 incidents:

- Incident 1. By mistake a bank had deposited the same amount twice in a young lady's account. She did not notice this and spent the money. When the bank found out about the mistake, it claimed the money back immediately. She did not have enough funds to pay and contacted the bank. The bank representative was most amiable and understanding. He said that it was the

(Continued)

---

[10]Bitner, Booms & Stanfield Tetreault, 1990.

[11]Olsen, 1992.

(Continued)

> bank's responsibility and that the error was caused by a mistake in transactions between 2 bank offices. The bank offered her an interest-free loan which she could pay back in instalments. Today, she is more critical of banks as she has discovered that they can make mistakes, but she is very satisfied with the way the bank handled the problem.
>
> - Incident 2. A bank customer did not know what interest rate the bank was giving on his account but happened to see in a list that he received the lowest rate on the market. He got upset and switched to another bank immediately, without contacting the first bank. The customer believed that the bank had tried to cheat him and that the bank managers had to blame themselves for losing him as a customer.
>
> CIT is an inductive method where no hypotheses are needed and the incidents, as they appear in the answers, are allowed to form patterns that the researcher can develop into concepts, categories, models and theories. The method allows more incidents to be collected than would be possible through direct observation; a single researcher can generate several hundred incidents. It gives plenty of room for the researcher's theoretical sensitivity and ability to interpret an event. However, it will not provide the researcher with the same intense feeling of an incident as they would get through direct involvement and observation, as it is still gaining access through intermediaries and understanding at second hand. The incidents have to be brief. CIT can generate important data concerning behaviour in well-defined situations.

Many lessons can be learnt from the examples in Box 9.2:

- The number of cases to be included in a study requires a judgement call; there is no objective rule to lean against. It is often routinely claimed that at least 5–10 cases are needed.[12] This not a well-founded recommendation as the number is always contingent on the situation. The notions of *theoretical (purposeful) sampling* and *saturation* offer the most reasonable guidelines. In theoretical sampling, you add cases that you believe may reveal additional data and you proceed until you see no new data emerge; you have then reached saturation. In practice, access possibilities and time can restrict the number of cases and force you to give up before saturation point is reached. You may then decide to do a follow-up project and interest others in doing so, and you may do a *meta-analysis* of published projects. You can also focus on some issues where you feel there is a need to go deeper and do some mini case studies, perhaps by asking some very specific questions by phone.

- How much data do we need? There is a feeling that the more data the better, but the more data the more work with analysis and interpretation, and the lower the productivity. Sometimes even a single or a few cases are adequate for generalization

---

[12]Eisenhardt, 1989.

and everything beyond that is just more of the same. Generating a lot of data may be an insurance policy against criticism. But it is non-productive to carry both a belt and suspenders to avoid being caught with your pants down. You may end up suffocated by a stack of data.

- There is a saying that 'fish and guests smell after 3 days'. Data may not smell after 3 days, but after 3 months it begins to smell, and after 3 years it definitely stinks. Depending on the research problem, at some point in time so much has changed that the data is historical. We are repeatedly told that business and society are changing faster and faster. Imagine, for example, data collected on Internet trade or the taste of music among teenagers a year ago. What is its validity today? Even if the data is of long-term interest and changes slowly, we get stressed by having it lying around, and the expectations on us to come up with something become pressing.

There is a risk when case studies are solely based on interviews that the researchers become limited to trivia or to mainstream research problems and theories. Research becomes more of the same and no progress takes place. Academic research in management is directed at analytical issues – figuring out intellectually what to do – rather than at hands-on execution – how things get done in real life. This may, at least to some extent, be ascribed to the research tradition of favouring statistical samples and formal questionnaire surveys which are not suitable for investigating comprehensive, complex and dynamic issues such as the implementation of a plan. The studies show a multiple case approach where interviewing is the core method supported by observation and the study of documents. You should learn from this that theory can be applied in numerous ways and you are free to use your knowledge and imagination to design these ways.

When Polonius asks Prince Hamlet 'What do you read, my lord?' and he replies 'Words, words, words',[13] I feel resignation in his voice. Academics swim in an ocean of spoken and written words and numbers and can easily drown in them. In a discussion, Glaser said: 'All is data!' It sounded simple. It stuck in my mind. Data is beyond words and numbers. And within case theory both explicit and tacit data have their place.

Words and numbers are nothing more than *images* – representations and symbols – and not the real thing. We become victims of reification when we mistake the representation for the real thing. We have had a series of revolutions in the way to communicate words and numbers beyond a limited physical setting: the printing technique, telecom, radio, television, rapid copying, the Internet and mobile communication. We have already noted that the volume of words and numbers is larger than ever and keeps growing at a speed beyond comprehension. Yet we spend so much time 'collecting' data and some data is difficult, even impossible, to get access to. We ask (words) people in interviews and they answer (words). But how do we know that we are asking the right questions and that we

---

[13]Hamlet, Act II, Scene ii.

are getting the right answers and understanding them correctly? The information we get may be wrong, slanted and incomplete.

In the 1960s, the Canadian media and communications philosopher Marshall McLuhan became famous for his statement *the medium is the message*.[14] He meant that the specific properties of a medium were more important than the actual content of the message. Transferred to the problem of getting access to research data, it means that if you get answers on a written questionnaire, by email, speak to a person on the phone, hold a personal interview or are present as an observer or an actor, these media communicate data in different ways. Data with the same content is perceived differently. Changing *message* to *massage* in his next book was McLuhan's way of saying that new media and new technologies are an 'extension of man' and each medium 'massages' our senses differently.[15]

Traditional data collection does not include *non-verbal language* ('body language'), *pictures* and *objects*. However, communications researchers point to non-verbal language as the dominant form of communication: gestures, body stature, facial expressions, looks, dress, office decor, and the elusive phenomena charm, charisma, vibes and chemistry. There used to be a saying that 'a picture is worth more than a thousand words'. Pictures can sometimes be very factual and reveal things that are difficult to communicate through words. But they are also easy to manipulate. We are surrounded by pictures through TV, the Internet, magazines, advertising on the streets and in store windows. Business and management research reports are conservative in this respect – with the exception of textbooks for undergraduates. Some of the most recent ones are poor in theory but richer in pictures than the tabloid and gossip press.

The term *artefact* is used for human-made objects. It has the same roots as artificial. It is mostly associated with objects of historical or cultural interest. These artefacts are carriers of data and therefore part of data generation. A *social artefact* is anything designed and used by people to meet their needs or to solve problems, or it is the outcome of their social behaviour. A document is an example of a social artefact used as a unit of analysis in social science research. Physical objects are absent in the economic sciences but in the natural sciences and the humanities they are common, like machines, archaeological findings and art. They want the real thing. How about in the economic sciences? Talking about poverty in statistical terms, seeing pictures of starving people in Africa or hearing about inhuman conditions in sweatshops only gives a vague idea about what it really is. Then we approach the ultimate stage in research – being there, doing interactive and involved research.

---

[14]McLuhan, 1964.

[15]McLuhan & Fiore, 1967.

The concepts of detached/involved research and extrospection/introspection were introduced earlier. Even if detachment and extrospection remain an ideal in the positivist paradigm, all methods have elements of involvement and introspection. This stood out in the research edifice in Figure 3.4. In the complexity paradigm, involvement and introspection are given equal status to detachment and extrospection. They all have their place in our search for knowledge; either/or becomes both/and. Dag Hammarskjöld, legendary Secretary-General of the United Nations who was killed in a plane crash in Africa in 1961, wrote in his posthumously published book *Markings*: 'The longest journey is the journey inward.' He assessed every situation based on external data to find pragmatic solutions and he was a man of action – but he also sought solutions inside himself. To the true scholar, the intellectual processing of data and experiences and the formation of conclusions are just as thrilling as the study of the external world.

Data-generation Methods

Data-generation methods used for getting access to business and management reality are listed in Table 9.1.

The methods will be discussed in the ensuing sections. Although each has a core of its own, there are no pure methods; they are all fuzzy sets. In the name of pragmatism, a mixed methods approach is often, but not always, preferable.

Table 9.1   Data-generation methods in case theory

- Existing material
- Interviews:
  - questionnaire surveys
  - personal interviews
  - group interviews
- Observation:
  - direct observation
  - participant observation
- Management action research:
  - real-time action research
  - retrospective action research
- Neuroscience
- Online research.

Methods should be combined to offer the best possible access. Only a lack of creativity, research funds, time and other resources can stop you.

The intention here is not to go too deeply into the technical details of each method. There is a large literature that deals with each of them and if you are going to use one I recommend you consult a book or two. Some literature is practical and short, guiding you through each step. You can also be guided by articles and books that report case research and explain how the projects were performed. In addition to your own practice, good mentors and role-model researchers are the most important aids to success.

I will compare the methods and stress the *interactive* content and the importance of getting *close access*. For a while, I thought I saw a scale from the least interactive to the most interactive data-generating techniques. The interactivity dimension is there but it does not follow a linear scale. There is also a plethora of special methods, such as the use of cameras to record families eating breakfast or watching TV, and garbage can searches to infer actual household consumption as compared to stated consumption. I will not go into these but they can be found in the literature and you may learn about them when working for a company or a commercial research institute.

A colleague at another university who has written several books on methodology emailed me that he went through 105 final MBA papers from 2013 and almost all were based on personal interviews or surveys. He concludes that 'our training in methodology is insufficient ... [and] ... our faculty needs new knowledge and new perspectives'.[16] To that we can add that students and even faculty are usually inexperienced interviewers and surveys are blunt research instruments. Access to data is limited and the outcome requires that the quality of sources is seriously evaluated.

The first data source to be discussed is *existing material*. I would have liked to classify it as an interview method in Table 9.1 but I was afraid it would confuse the reader. I would also like to classify it as interactive research but I thought that would be even more confusing. However, in the next section I will make this clear.

Existing Material

Existing material can be a rich source for cases. It comes in many forms and includes everything that is carried by media created by human beings – so-called *social artefacts*. It encompasses books, case reports, articles, archival records, notes, letters, mass media reports, audio recordings, videotapes, films, photos,

---

[16]Professor Lars-Torsten Eriksson, University of Gävle, Sweden.

statistics, organizational charts, internal memos, letters, brochures, memoirs, diaries, emails, Internet data, websites and social media.

Articles and books that report cases can be compared with your findings and help you reach saturation and thus increase the possibility for generalization. It may not always be possible for researchers to collect pertinent data on their own. The respondents may be dead, or live too far away; they may not grant an interview; or may not truthfully answer important and sensitive questions. On a macro level, there is data that we may not able to access ourselves, like changes in unemployment and the income gap. On the other hand, such data is highly stylized and full of errors. The numbers, percentages and rankings give the illusion of preciseness and control, but require technical skills and tacit knowledge to interpret.

A traditional term for the study of existing material is *desk research* as opposed to *field research*. Within the complexity paradigm, this distinction is misleading. Finding existing material can be very much of a field operation: travelling to libraries, stowed away archives in cellars, attics and offices. *Using existing material is seen as a form of interview; there is interactivity between a text and the reflective researcher.* For some, documents are just words, numbers and pictures. For others, the text comes alive and begins to speak and the researcher tries to find the actual meaning behind the material; compare this to the expression 'read between the lines'.

It a basic realization to have that a document is no truer because it is on paper. You interview the texts and the bookshelves. When reading answers from a questionnaire, you also interview a text although the questions were put by you and for your purpose. In this light, the traditional desk and field categories have no meaning.

Existing material is often referred to as *secondary data* as it was not created to answer your specific research questions. It may be too crude for your purpose. The available document may offer an account within a different paradigm or theory. For example, statistics that are compiled for macro use are too crude to fit a study on the micro level.

At this stage, it is urgent to point to the necessity of *evaluating sources* for credibility and relevance. In academic circles, the printed word usually has higher 'scientific' status than the spoken word, and lawyers and bureaucrats seem to automatically allocate higher credibility to the written word; it becomes an operational definition of evidence. This is most unfortunate and may lead to low validity of the research. But no source, however prestigious, can be taken for granted as reliable. You cannot, as is done in articles all the time, just refer to well-known professors and their articles in top journals as if they were the truth. If you use such references to support your conclusions, you are also responsible for their validity and relevance (see further the section 'Evaluation of Sources' at the end of this chapter).

A problem in using existing documents in studying what happened in an organization or a market is that decisions and events are not systematically and completely recorded. Important decisions like the acquisition of a competitor can be made over coffee and negotiated at an informal dinner. Certain events are not recorded for reasons of confidentiality. If they leak it may be detrimental; they may concern taboo areas or be tactics of a negotiation game. When documents are created, the real reasons for a decision may not be stated. To better understand while promising to be discreet about it, an interviewer may ask: 'Off the record, could you tell me how you felt about the decision?'

Documents for *internal marketing* – with the purpose of informing and influencing personnel with regard to various activities, events, strategies, new products, etc. – may include visions, policies, opinions and personal career ambitions which are not yet implemented and may never be. With the Internet and mobile phones, there are extensive possibilities to search for written and spoken messages. Even if they have been erased, they can be found. But for a researcher to use them requires permission or hacking skills. Ethical issues come up. We have also entered a new stage of data registration, as has been revealed by Wikileaks and others. Although the trigger for expanding data registration to practically all digital sources like mobile phones and personal computers was to discover terrorist activity, it can equally well by used for business purposes, especially where a state is involved.

A useful source of access to complex phenomena via existing material is offered by authors reporting their interpretation of events in which they participated. *Autobiographies* (memoirs) are written by business executives, economists, politicians, journalists and others involved in economic and management matters. *Biographies* of key actors and accounts about cases such as Absolut Vodka can provide valuable information. Even if the author's intention is to say what 'really' happened, the interpretations may be tainted by a wish to be remembered, take revenge on rivals, protect 'buddies' and nail 'creeps', hide taboos, etc. They have to be read with that in mind but they can open gates that researchers could never enter on their own at the same time as it can be hard to tell gossip, rumours and outright lies from solid information. That is a major reason for using two or more independent – meaning truly independent – sources that confirm the data.

One could expect the *annual report* of a public company to be a trustworthy document. It is an official statement of a company's situation and an assessment of its future. The balance sheet, the profit and loss statement, and key ratios are defined by law. This can be a valuable source in case theory. But an annual report can only be interpreted by someone with training and inside knowledge of an industry or company. You must understand the story behind the numbers: how they were compiled and evaluated, how their format is determined by legislation and tradition, and, if you are an investor, how to make predictions based on historical numbers. Financial journals present their own computations, and analysts make comments and draw judgemental conclusions, predicting the rise and fall of company stock. The ratio of accurate predictions is low and no better than a monkey selecting a portfolio of stock (yes, there have been such studies).

Even if an organization strives to make its annual report factual and objective, it has an element of promotion and a desire to stand out in a good light. If it is basically honest, we still have to understand that there may be some data that we do not access ('lying by omission') or that cannot be assessed for credibility. It is also constantly reported that companies provide homemade key ratios and sometimes conveniently suffer from amnesia in order to dress up their accounting.

The Enron Case (Box 9.3) shows that fraudulent behaviour and false data can impress the market for several years before detection. It is the epitome of what a business should not be.

Box 9.3   The Enron Case

Enron was an energy corporation headquartered in Houston, Texas. During the 1990s it grew at an exceptional rate, exploiting new opportunities offered by deregulation. It was hailed by *Fortune* magazine as 'America's Most Innovative Company' for 6 years in a row and its stock price soared.

Enron crashed in 2001. A public company has to submit an annual report and provide other information demanded by the authorities. It must have external auditors who analyse and evaluate the operations of the firm. Enron manipulated the price of its stock through a special department that artificially kept up the trade and applied 'creative accounting' by 'cooking the books'. It was audited and advised by one of the 'Big 5' and most prestigious auditing companies, Arthur Andersen. One of Enron's directors and the chair of its audit committee was Stanford University professor Robert K. Jaedicke. He was a most distinguished academic and served as president of the accrediting agency for US business schools. With his scientific background, why did he not see what was going on? He claims he did not and blamed it on others. In his position, he cannot just be excused as gullible. Google reports that he earned over $800,000 on Enron stock that he sold well in time before the fraud became public, and as director of a glamorous company he was highly paid. Media representatives have revealed that they were bribed to report false information to the public. Was this unknown to bankers, stockbrokers and financial advisors on Wall Street and in similar financial centres around the world? Not likely.

What can we learn from the Enron case? By applying case theory, we come close to the *whole* picture – not just bits and pieces – of what *really* happened in a very specific environment. Can the lessons be generalized from this single case and make us better understand organizational and corporate behaviour? Enron is a complex

(Continued)

object of study and the positivist paradigm will not suffice; we need the complexity paradigm. Let us just look at a few of the findings.

What happens in the daily work of a firm in a competitive market can only be found out if you are present, even if it may leave behind some documentation. And many things have to be kept confidential for competitive reasons. But other events are off limits and show a misuse of position. For example, it is rumoured that Enron executives hired secretaries at fancy salaries to be their mistresses and that they had long and lavish lunches at strip clubs paid for with Enron credit cards. This did not reach ordinary citizens who invested their savings in Enron stock to secure their pensions, and were recommended to do so by the media, financial analysts, banks and brokers.

An obvious observation is that we do not know the consequences of deregulation and that deregulation is no cure-all, as some politicians and others advocate. Another is that the scam remained undetected for so long despite the presence of a reputable auditing firm and a top accounting professor from a top university. How could that be? What should we expect from auditors, independent analysts and investigative reporters?

The Enron case shows how long it can take to detect corporate lies. It raises the question of whether you can use a single, specific case to generate mid-range and grand theory. My suspicion, however, is that most fraudulent and unintentionally erroneous information is never uncovered. Enron may seem extreme but because of that the case makes many of the weaknesses of data sources all the more obvious. In this sense, the single case serves as an eye-opener. However, Enron was followed by a long line of similar cases, definitely enough to generalize to a higher level. It was – and unfortunately still is – evidence of an epidemic, and no vaccine or antibiotics (more legislation, court trials and media coverage) have as yet managed to stop it. Enron and other cases have started a chain of events that keep popping up like weeds on a lawn.

Official statistics can be a rich source of easily accessible and inexpensive data that provides a quantitative supplement to case studies. They can be useful in describing a phenomenon and establishing connections between phenomena. But how high is the quality of the data? Just because it is released by a government institution does not mean it is reliable. It has been stylized to fit into a few established categories presented as crisp sets but which are in fact fuzzy sets. For example, the statistics of an economy consist of 3 overriding categories: the agricultural sector, the goods manufacturing or industrial sector, and the service sector. This is an example of how fuzzy statistical categorization can lose track of reality. The categories have emerged over several hundred years. First, the agricultural sector dominated, then the industrial sector and now the service sector. Unfortunately, these overriding sectors are so ill-defined that they do not reflect what is happening in business and markets. They may conceal reality rather than shed light on it and they may contain numerous uncontrollable errors. Statistical categories can be deliberate lies in order to mislead, for example when nations want to impress the world or to qualify as members of organizations like the EU.

Although statistics and numbers can be important sources in the economic sciences, they are obviously far from easy to use. Even if there is 'unlimited' access to data online, the offline physical meeting is not obsolete – and never will be. For academic researchers, it is indispensible to join associations and conferences in order to find out about state-of-the-art research. Newsletters, presentations and proceedings are also important sources. More importantly, you meet scholars from other universities and countries as well as practitioners. They can give you as yet unpublished references and scripts together with advice on current thinking and trends. Networking among researchers through personal contact and online is the most important way of monitoring current research. An online bibliometrics search may give some information but I have yet to see a bibliometrics study that impresses me as valid and informative.

We discussed understanding and preunderstanding in Chapter 3. General reports and statistics present knowledge via intermediaries, at second hand, third hand, or are even further removed from the original source. It is then difficult to evaluate source credibility. You do not interact with the phenomenon or its interpreters and are in the hands of other people's paradigms, preunderstanding and ability to generate, systematize, interpret and report data. It requires ingenuity not to get stuck in the ceremonial use of existing material, such as reproducing statistics because they have official status, without bothering about the validity of the statistical categories and the numbers they contain.

Existing material can be used for a wide variety of studies, but is rarely sufficient to represent a whole case; it is complementary to other data-generating approaches.

Interviews

This section compares 3 types of interviews: questionnaire surveys, personal interviews and group interviews. As surveys are by convention classified as quantitative research and case research as qualitative, they are usually not brought up in a book of this kind. But as I do not subscribe to the quantitative/qualitative divide, I bring them up. The major reason is to point out weaknesses which are rarely called to attention.

To distinguish what respondents claim they do from what they actually do, the concepts *espoused theory* and *theory-in-use* have been suggested.[17] There is often a big gap between the two and it does not stand out in interviews, especially not in highly structured and non-interactive surveys.

---

[17]Argyris & Schon, 1974, pp. 6–7.

Questionnaire Surveys

Research institutes sell standardized packages at competitive prices to companies and governments, promising that a survey will give them all the 'facts' they need to make decisions. This is appealing to practitioners who have to make quick decisions. Unfortunately, they are buying false security. They get more simplified and stylized *data* than *facts*. It is the same marketing tactic that guided Charles Revlon, one of the founders of Revlon cosmetics: 'We don't sell lipsticks. We sell dreams.'

Scholars should not fall into the same trap – but they do. An example: a colleague of mine visited a US business school to discuss possible cooperation in an international research programme. The chairman opened the meeting by saying: 'Let's have a look at your questionnaire!' When my colleague said he didn't have one, the answer was: 'Well, as soon as you have one we can start discussing our participation.' The answer was a robot-like positivist answer. There is not a single research technique so superior that it can be chosen by default. Never start by asking: What data collection method should I use? That is a technique-oriented approach. Start by asking: How can we get as close access as possible to the data we need? That is a results-oriented approach.

Questionnaire surveys aiming at quantification are probably the most frequently used data-generating tool in business and management studies. It is most unfortunate if they are perceived as identical with scientific research. Paraphrasing the service-dominant logic in Box 6.5, we could talk about a *survey-dominant logic* in research. Surveys can be used as input to case theory but only in select instances. Their contribution to understanding complexity and generating theory is severely constrained and they should by no means be a choice that is not reflected upon.

Long, long ago when I first learnt about surveys based on random statistical samples, the response rate was considered decisive for the quality of the data. It is not so anymore. Today's survey methodology has been characterized as 'a patchwork of practices backed by some theory'.[18] Even very low response rates are accepted. The need for a high response rate depends on the purpose of the survey, how it is designed and other factors. It is a reminder that even what is taught in higher education and claimed to be scientific may offer more face value, convention and intersubjective consensus than 'true truth'.

Questionnaires formalize and standardize interviews. The contact with respondents is either personal, semi-personal via the telephone, or less personal via ordinary post, email or the Internet. The questionnaire is structured with formal response alternatives on scales or with 'yes/no/don't know' reply alternatives.

---

[18]Quoted from Särndal, 2012.

These are sometimes supplemented with open-ended questions that allow free and verbal answers. Data is statistically treated and the more sophisticated are the techniques used, the more the method appeals to positivist researchers and the better they do in rankings.

Surveys claim to give statistically reliable answers to a series of questions by being rigorous and generalizable. It is a technique-oriented approach of asking many questions to many people and at least on the surface getting clear and straight answers. It is non-interactive research and as such it only qualifies for a marginal place in the complexity paradigm.

Most often, the researcher never meets the respondents. They are faceless, although you may have some data about them: gender, age, etc. In telephone interviews, there is some interaction but not much, especially if the interviewers are hired and targeted for a certain number of interviews per hour. They have little understanding of why the survey is structured the way it is and of the theme it is dealing with. They are therefore primarily interested in getting the interviews over with. If the interviews are carried out by those who are to analyse and interpret the outcome, the interview can become more interactive.

Questionnaires are sometimes placed where prospective respondents will come across them. Most of us have seen them in hotel rooms mixed with leaflets, hotel stationery, special weekend offers, instructions for the use of pay TV, and breakfast order forms. Do you ever fill out hotel room questionnaires?

Because of the excessive use of surveys in business and management, it should be mandatory to be aware of their strengths as well as their obvious deficiencies. We must remember that research institutes sell survey packages on the market and form a big industry with profit goals. Although surveys deal with numbers and utilize sophisticated statistical techniques, their design, interpretation and reporting of results are primarily subjective and qualitative.

Questionnaire surveys have some undisputed advantages; they can, if applied to the right problem and well implemented, answer questions of how much, how many and how often. The fact that a respondent's attitudes, opinions, tastes, etc. can be transformed into numbers on a scale gives the method a scientific flair.

Table 9.2 lists the sequential steps of a statistical survey. These steps are jam-packed with judgement calls, meaning that subjective and qualitative influences are legion even if the survey technique claims it is rigorous and objective (compare this with the research edifice in Figure 3.4).

That questionnaires can produce objective and rigorous research which can be tested for reliability is only true to some extent. Some of the items in Table 9.2 can be treated fairly objectively in accordance with recognized rules and rituals but they are surrounded by predominantly subjective items. The decisions taken on each item emanate out of the researchers' paradigm, preunderstanding and perception of the problem. Moreover, the answers are subjective, but they are

Table 9.2 Activities doing a statistical survey

1. *Decision on the purpose of the study* – a study needs a problem and a purpose. For example, if the relations between employees and managers are considered a problem in an organization, we might want to find out employee attitudes to managers.

2. *Selection of population to be studied* – what groups are we interested in: workers in factories, office staff, salespeople, customers or others?

3. *Design of the questionnaire* – what are the issues to be covered? How should questions be phrased and response alternatives be designed?

4. *Testing of the questionnaire* – a pilot test is made to prevent shortcomings such as easily misunderstood questions.

5. *Selection of sample* – suppose the number of employees is 50,000, located in 6 countries. We want to select a sample that is statistically correct so that we can base our computation on the representativeness of the results.

6. *Distribution of the questionnaire* – should it be sent on paper as ordinary mail to the respondent's home or workplace, or be sent by email?

7. *Reminders* – how, and how many times, should those who do not answer be reminded to secure an acceptable response rate?

8. *Receiving and processing of answers* – how should answers be recorded? Questions with given reply options are easy to tabulate, while open-ended questions are difficult. What statistical treatment should the numbers be exposed to?

9. *Analysis and interpretation of results* – who is the analyst and the interpreter? What is the preunderstanding and the paradigm of the researcher? What criteria for analysis and interpretation should be used?

10. *Presentation to the academic community* – should the results be presented in a strictly scholarly report or article, or in a popular book? Should there be oral presentations? Should the presentations differ depending on the various target groups?

11. *Presentation to practitioners* – what catches their interest in the report? What decisions do they expect to make from it? What can be transformed into action? Does the implementation provide feedback of the outcome to the researchers?

treated as facts in their context: 'It is a fact that the respondent said so!' As the answer is a black box – you ask a question (input) and get an answer (output) – from that you infer your ideas about the respondent. You can peep into the black box through some specific questions but it is hard to evaluate the factual content of the answer (see Figure 4.3).

In a corporate setting, studies are commissioned to form a basis for decisions and action, although they also serve the purpose of internal tactics and ceremonies. In a scholarly setting, results can be used to test a theory or just for general curiosity and a contribution to basic research. In both instances, persona factors can affect the official purpose of research.

In today's business and management researchscape, the strengths of statistical questionnaire surveys are taken for granted. When I hear surveys presented at academic conferences, the statistical technicalities take up the larger part of the speaker's time, along with questions and comments from the audience. I have sometimes raised the overriding problem of the survey technique versus other approaches, such as case research, but the answers usually show that the researcher is not familiar with the alternatives and even finds my question out of place.

Table 9.3 lists weak spots based on my own experience of answering surveys, making them, commissioning them for research institutes and using their results in decision-making and action in firms and government organizations. There are so many weak points and if many appear in the same survey, the synergy effects between them will have the survey nullified. Judgement calls and pragmatic wisdom are required on most of these items.

Table 9.3 Weak spots in statistical surveys

Instructions to respondents:

Instructions can be misunderstood.

Instructions are often not carefully read.

Questions:

Questions are too complex for respondents to answer.

It is difficult, even impossible, to answer hypothetical or retrospective questions, for example about innovations that are planned for the market.

Questions can be phrased to lead a respondent towards a desired answer.

Respondents lack knowledge but feel compelled to answer anyway.

Respondents say what they think the recipients want to hear.

The number of questions becomes too large and respondents feel pressed and just say something to get out of it.

The order in which the questions are asked may influence the result.

It is difficult to ask sensitive and taboo questions and get honest answers.

Respondents have answers to important questions that are never asked and the interviewer will never know.

(Continued)

Table 9.3 (Continued)

Reply alternatives:

The alternatives can be leading.

Respondents state attitudes even if they lack them.

The alternatives are not complete.

The alternatives are overlapping.

Respondents have alternatives that are not offered.

Response rate:

A low response rate can bias the outcome, although its size is contingent on what the survey is about, how the sample is designed, etc.

Administration of a survey:

The interviews are done by temporary staff who have a target of, say, 4 interviews per hour and are paid accordingly.

If the interviewer has a question that the respondent cannot answer, the interviewer may get impatient, making the respondent choose one of the listed alternatives as swiftly as possible.

Interpretation of answers:

Respondents may give a generalized answer instead of answering a specific question.

Researchers impose biased preunderstanding on the material.

Reporting the results:

Aggregating replies conceals important data and variations.

There can be percentage illusions, for instance 1 answer can be listed as 50% if you only have 2 answers in a sub-category.

The format and medium for reporting affect the audience's perception and interpretation.

Validity and reliability:

A preoccupation with reliability may also mean that the same errors are replicated in subsequent studies.

Validity is seldom properly established.

Errors and deliberate lies during an interview can give rise to low quality answers.

In some literature, you can find these and similar weaknesses listed. Yet the results of a survey are often interpreted and presented without communicating how serious the weaknesses are. This becomes particularly disturbing when reporting to audiences who do not understand the limitations, such as decision-makers in an organization, politicians or the news media. The research can easily regresses to rigorous ignorance and noledge.

One example of false security in data generation and analysis is offered by surveys in which questions are sent to businesses (usually with structured response alternatives) to find out, for instance, how marketing planning is done in a B2B setting, how the key account managers operate, or what technology can offer in the future. A lower and lower response rate of 10 per cent or even less is currently considered adequate – but only intersubjectively, not objectively. The explanation I have received is that businesses are reluctant to respond for lack of time, supported by a feeling that the questionnaires are of little import. My experience from working in business is that surveys are rarely, if ever, completed by executives. They are handed down the organization to someone who happens to have the time – but not the necessary knowledge to reply. The quality of the data of the returned questionnaires then is uncertain and cannot be accepted at face value. The numbers that come out of it are incomplete and often distorted, even if checks on the non-responses are done. The survey does not penetrate complex and ambiguous issues; it touches some spots on the tip of the iceberg. If a mixed methods approach is used, other sources and techniques can add completeness, but the survey may also be a costly detour with little real value added.

Questionnaires are useful for clearly defined problems. They do not work for complex problems with a set of intertwined variables and fuzzy phenomena. Consequently, they do not reveal much about complex dynamic processes such as decision-making and implementation in a company. They offer limited access to the phenomenon to be researched. The interaction with the respondent is formal and restricted.

Personal Interviews

This section deals with personal interviews with individuals. Interviews are, by convention, categorized as *formal (structured)* and *informal (unstructured)*. This is unfortunate terminology. The formal ones are the hard structured and standardized questionnaire surveys that were just covered. When we talk about *personal interviews*, it means that they are interactive and sensitive to the respondent.

Personal interviews are usually carried out with an *interview guide*, a checklist that includes the topics to be covered. Questions are formulated in the course of the interview and can be asked in any order that the interviewer judges beneficial. The answers are usually open-ended and are registered by means of notes or tape recordings. A personal face-to-face interview is more similar to a conversation and dialogue than to a question-and-answer ritual.

The selection of questions is governed by the actual situation confronting the interviewer. It is sometimes called *probing* but I prefer the term interactive. The interviewer listens attentively and registers the reactions of the respondents. Attention is paid to what the respondents consider important, even if this was not included in the original interview guide. This inductive aspect is important to allow sensitivity and avoid forcing. The researchers have total freedom to change the form of the interview during a study and to exclude or add to areas of interactive inquiry. During the interview, they could ask for copies of documents that seem to be of special interest.

Personal interviews strive to go beyond the obvious and become *in-depth interviews*. Although the verbal statements are the main focus, attention should be paid to whatever observation can add relevant data.

Documentation of interviews, *field notes*, can be made in 3 ways. Using the first way, the intention is to preserve the interview in its original form without editing or comments. The interviewers make notes and/or record the interview. Audio recordings only preserve the verbal part of the interview, but a video camera allows the researcher to preserve other cues as well.

The second way is to write down facts. In an interview with a manager, these could be frequency of customer calls, quantity of goods sold, or profit margin, followed by supplementing them with reference to available documents. The third way is to write *memos*, noting impressions, ideas and tentative conclusions. Hence, a 2-hour interview can result in anything from a few lines of notes to several pages.

The first strategy allows researchers to return to the verbal part of the interview as often as they want, even though this is time-consuming. It also provides an opportunity for others to evaluate a researcher's conclusions in relation to the empirical material. However, the material will not shed light on the following items:

- whether or not the researcher has spoken to the right people
- whether or not the researcher has obtained all the available and relevant written material
- informal interaction between the interviews
- non-verbal communication between the researcher and the respondents.

Using the third way, the researchers draw conclusions during the interview meaning that a re-examination of the topic may require a new interview at a new point of time. It is quick, which is particularly essential if the interviews are part of an action programme, or if the interview time with the respondent is limited. Hence, it will not be possible for an outsider to follow the interview stage by stage, and the chance to assess reliability is reduced. But even the first way allows only a limited opportunity for others to examine the interpretation of a change process. A huge pile of paper and tapes may create a solid impression, but because of its volume it may be practically impenetrable. A PhD student recently told me she had done 230 interviews which resulted in transcripts of 8,000 pages. This is more material than anyone can handle and research productivity is reduced. On the other hand, it may provide the researcher with valuable substantive data. However, it has to be tried against the principles of purposeful sampling and saturation.

Interactive interviews are more demanding of the interviewers. The interviewers' paradigm and preunderstanding play an active role throughout the study. If the same researchers who interpret and report the studies conduct the interviews, they get close access to the studied phenomenon, or at least its carriers – the respondents. The interaction is direct. It becomes an understanding at first hand if it is about the respondents and their personal experiences; an understanding at second, third, etc. hand if the respondent is an intermediary between the researchers and the actual phenomenon.

Validity is improved by the ability to let questions evolve in the course of a research project. Questions can be asked to check understanding. Data is generated in a process where impressions and interpretation occur simultaneously. Data will arise in a context which is not necessarily very clear in the beginning; in fact, it should not be clear. Since one purpose of case theory is to improve understanding and stimulate discovery, the generation of concepts, properties, categories, models and eventually theories should not be determined beforehand. Interviews should be inductive first, its data arranged through a deductive process next, and then inductive again. Thus, a spiral is created that lifts understanding from the basement of the research edifice to the first floor and further upwards. In doing interviews, you should use your judgement to assess whether you gain new data from the next interview or whether you have emptied the well of its contents. Researcher persona is an instrument here; the more sensitivity and open-mindedness you can offer, the more aspects of reality you can perceive. A skilled interviewer can improve data quality by establishing a trusting relationship, while an abrasive or dispassionate personality can easily kill the many-to-many interaction.

With unstructured responses and an openness to new issues, ambiguity is likely to arise; if it does not, it may be a sign of your perception being too selective. The words you use in the interview have fuzzy definitions as they represent fuzzy phenomena.

An interview can be systematic despite all the flexibility that is needed. It is probably better to say that it should be professional. Only people with the right personality, who have studied interviewing techniques and the theory of scientific inquiry behind the techniques, and have conducted interviews themselves, can make good interviewers.

Box 9.4 shows how the selection of respondents is dependent on the researcher's ability to find the way in a tightly knit network of personal contacts, as in the classic Chinese guanxi.

Box 9.4   Interviewing in Chinese Guanxies[19]

Guanxi is the term for the special type of network that has dominated business in China for thousands of years. It has a correspondence in the West to *relationship marketing*, a phenomenon that exists in various forms in all countries but was not part of marketing theory until the 1990s. At one extreme, you only do business within a network of relationships where you can trust people; they are either your family, friends or friends of friends. At the other extreme, business is less personal like the supermarket.

When you want to do market research in China, you have to cultivate a tree of relationships – *guanxishu*. This means that you cannot follow the Western marketing research manual, even if China, through its increasing globalization, is opening up to traditional Western methods. To do interviews, you need an introduction to a person and if you manage to establish trust the person will introduce you to the next respondents. This is often referred to as a *snowballing* strategy. It is a variant of purposeful sampling where your next source should be where you think you can get added data on your way to saturation. In this case, the continued sampling is relational and you will be offered access within a network.

The network in an empirical study in China with 44 respondents is shown in Figure 9.1. The use of a *guanxishu* with face-to-face interviews and Chinese style snowballing proved beneficial. It is a good example of interactive research.

The authors end with a comment of general concern for data generation: 'Essentially, Western and Chinese researchers are learning a common lesson; it is becoming increasingly harder to obtain data where businesses and people are over-surveyed and over-interviewed. In such environments a connection is becoming crucial irrespective of whether the target is identified through guanxi or some form of more basic Western relationship-orientation.'

Interviewing several stakeholders in a business deal is not common. But if you take a network view this is necessary; all nodes and links in a network influence each other and keep changing. A network quickly becomes complex which traditional positivism cannot handle, although gradually more sophisticated

---

[19]Based on Kriz, Gummesson & Quazi, 2014; Figure 9.1 from p. 37, quotation from p. 43.

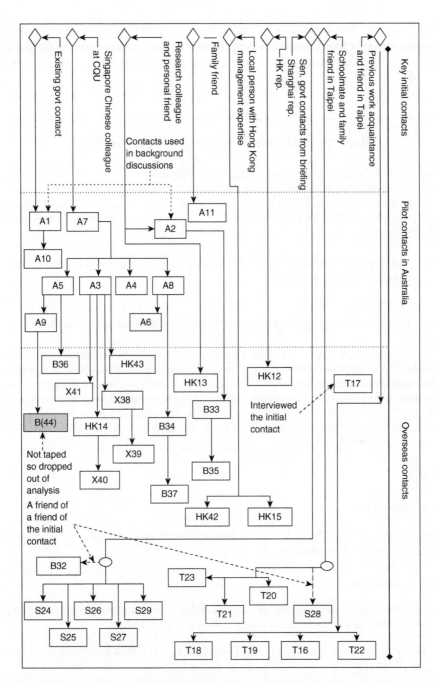

Figure 9.1 The researcher's *guanxishu*. The letters represent the following designations: A: Mainland and Hong Kong Chinese now residing in Australia; X: Mainland Chinese from Xiamen; T: Chinese from Taipei; B: Mainland Chinese from Beijing; S: Mainland Chinese from Shanghai; and HK: Chinese from Hong Kong

quantifications and computer simulations may open up doors. In business and management disciplines, there is no tradition to attack this complexity but case theory can help us build it over the long term. Box 9.5 is a modest effort but even that shows its importance.

Box 9.5   Interviewing Several Stakeholders[20]

In my PhD dissertation on the marketing and buying of professional B2B service, I interviewed, among others, lawyers, architects, advertising agencies, management consultants and software consultants. I also made 4 cases based on specific buying and selling situations and the interaction between the stakeholders. In the cases I interviewed:

- several people in the consulting organization that were somehow involved in or affected by the specific case

- several of those involved on the client side

- people in other consulting firms who were competing for the same contract.

I had expected people to say different things, but I had not expected them to be that different. The perception of what had happened was truly divergent and sometimes contradictory. It made the complexity of human interaction stand out. By analysing and interpreting the data, I deepened my understanding to a new level and got much more credible and realistic cases. The project is from the 1970s but I do not find that much has happened since, although the context for professional service has partially changed.

Group Interviews

Most interviews are individual, but sometimes group interviews can be more efficient. They can be of different kinds:

- Interviews with a small group of, say, 2 or 3.

- Interviews with a larger group like a board of directors, a management team or representatives of different departments, perhaps 10 or 20 people.

- Focus groups, which follow a formal procedure which will be described in the following paragraphs.

- Delphi studies and scenario writing.

---

[20]Gummesson, 1978.

The advantage of having several people in a group is that you can get answers to more things than if only one or two are present. It may feel more efficient for the researcher as individual and personal interviews are time-consuming. It raises productivity but it is hard to know how it affects quality.

Focus groups are group interviews focused on a specific issue such as a problem in a company or consumer perceptions of a new product.[21] The method has grown in popularity. It is interactive research where the interaction has broadened from the dyad of the interviewer and the respondent to the interaction between the interviewer and a whole group and between the participants. The group members can stimulate each other, but the situation can also be perceived as inhibiting; you may be willing to reveal something on a 1-to-1 basis, but not in front of a whole group. The focus group is led by a moderator with expertise in group dynamics. It can be observed by other researchers as well as by decision-makers in organizations, usually through a window or a TV monitor.

A focus group meets once, usually in a 2-hour session. The recruitment of the members is crucial. They should be knowledgeable on the focused subject and willing to participate. They must not regularly participate in focus groups and become 'professionals'; that affects their group behaviour.

It is sometimes useful to have a group, for example users of a certain brand, meet regularly over a longer period to discuss changing patterns of behaviour, tastes, etc. These groups are referred to as *panels*.

The demand in positivism that theory must be *predictive* to be called theory is not part of the complexity paradigm. Even if prediction will always remain uncertain, two methods are used to do more systematic and reflective guesswork and to prepare for change.

One is *Delphi studies*.[22] A select group, usually of specialists in a certain field, individually and anonymously answer questions of each other and make comments. After each round, the coordinator edits the outcome and you are asked new questions and whether you want to change your initial answers. Usually, after 3 rounds the coordinator produces a document of the concerted outcome. This occurs at a distance and is suitable for online research.

In *scenario-writing*, you produce alternatives futures – scenarios – based on different assumptions. It is pragmatic as it can also include plans on what action to take if a certain scenario occurs and what effect it might have on your company or its markets. In that way, a company is prepared and can be quicker in reacting to changes. Scenarios usually involve several participants from suppliers, customers and consultants.

---

[21] For practical advice on focus groups, see Kueger, 2009.

[22] They are named after the Greek Oracle of Delphi. From 1400 BC to 400 AC, Delphi was considered by the Greeks as the centre of the world. It became a meeting point for intellectual discussion between scholars, just like conferences are today.

Observation

This section reviews *observation* methods from *ethnography* and *anthropology*. It is a way of studying cultural phenomena such as customs, beliefs, behaviour and the social organization of man in a natural context. Its traditional domain was primitive societies but it is increasingly applied to markets and corporate life. Observations are multiple stimuli situations and with an open and creative mind you can make new discoveries.

In observation, you need all your senses to listen, ask and watch. As our capacity goes beyond the 5 senses and includes tacit knowledge, extrospection and introspection are supportive of each other. Everyone active in business is aware that non-verbal language constitutes a major source of information. Surveys, however, are limited to the verbal.

Observation requires intensive fieldwork in which the researcher gets personally involved in a cultural context. It is used in the study of organizations to lay bare a decision process; in consumer research to better understand how consumers relate to a product; to try out new business models; etc. The *corporate anthropologist* has entered business firms to do scholarly work as well as consulting assignments.

Direct observation is *interactive* but unobtrusive not to disturb the object of study. An anthropologist told me that he would like to be 'a little fly on the wall', thus being inconspicuous but able to move freely around without intervening in the situation. Even in the natural sciences, emphasis is placed on the neutrality of the observer. According to quantum physics, an electron cannot be observed without the observation method changing its behaviour. So even when it is meant to be unobtrusive and without intervention by the researcher, the object of study can be affected.

Participant observation is interactive by intention. The observers are part of the studied environment and take part in their work and social life. They even live with them but do not try to change anything, just learn.

The long period over which a culture is studied – months or years – was characteristic of the anthropological method when applied in foreign cultures where the researcher did not speak the language and had little preunderstanding of the values and behaviour. This should be contrasted to the 1–2-hour interviews which are usual in case studies. It takes time to become an accepted member of an organization and to be able to understand what is happening. The length of time also depends on researcher preunderstanding and professionalism, and help from *informants* and *gatekeepers* who can give or refuse access. A few hours or days in a setting is not observation in this sense; it is far too superficial. You need to get beyond observations that you may find odd or unfamiliar. First impressions have value and should be carefully recorded as they can never be repeated. However, they may also turn out to be erroneous and you fail to see the specific and salient characteristics of a certain situation. *Shadowing* is a variant of the ethnographic method for studying organizations and 'implies following and recording organizational actors during their everyday activities and interactions by using video/audio recording and/or taking field notes'.[23]

Sensitivity and openness combined with preunderstanding is a productive vantage point. It requires researchers to develop their persona to balance preunderstanding with new information that conflicts with it. It is a both/and strategy.

Box 9.6 accounts for impressions from a long consulting assignment where I was deeply engaged. Understanding the organizational culture was a must for me to do my job. I had to give initial priority to open, inductive observation.

Box 9.6   Combining Preunderstanding, Theoretical Sensitivity and Presence

My client was a large global B2B company with some 60 subsidiaries and several more offices and factories and allied parties forming a huge network both inside its formal organizational structure and outside.

Before I started to work for them, both academic researchers and consultants told me that the company was rigidly bureaucratic and old-fashioned. It had never let consultants or scholars from the management area inside, but there were close academic relationships on the technological side. Despite the fact that it was a household name, I did not know much about the company. When I first entered the premises, I got a feeling of dullness. Walls were painted grey or some undecided colour typical of an old school, a hospital or a government institution. The employees were dressed in subdued colours and there was not much laughter around. When you walked down a corridor you did not see any life; the employees were locked up in their cells with closed doors. There was an obvious risk that my observations would be tainted by these initial but superficial images of the company.

Something rang in disharmony though. The company was 100 years old and had survived all the ups and downs in its world markets. It was profitable, although it had not particularly excited the stock market. I attempted to keep my mind as open as I could to fresh observations and let the empirical data float freely before I started to put it into a pattern. In the beginning everything was hush-hush; even the most harmless piece of information was withheld. I was dependent on interviews to begin to understand the company. Early on, I asked to visit subsidiaries abroad, as I knew from other studies that the gospel of corporate headquarters (HQ) is not necessarily the truth in the field. The management of subsidiaries – in Europe, Africa, Asia, Australasia and the Americas – turned out to be more open. I tested ideas on them by showing them simple and incomplete models, asking them to fill in the missing pieces or change the structure. Being a visitor I became socially acquainted with the

(Continued)

---

[23]Vásquez, Brummans & Groleau, 2012, p. 145.

(Continued)

local top management and employees, as most of them entertained me at lunches and in the evenings; that did not happen at home. The informal interaction in relaxed conditions was an extremely valuable source of information.

Underneath the rigid and bureaucratic surface, I found impressive energy and commitment. For example, when tenders were being submitted people worked around the clock to meet deadlines. With few and big customers, complex technology, long negotiations and delivery times over several years, winning big contracts was a necessity for survival. Tenders were huge; the biggest I saw consisted of 30 binders to be submitted in 20 copies. It filled a whole container. Hundreds of engineers and others were involved and dependent on each other.

Where and when does such a network organization exist? It officially existed from 9 to 5, though some factories worked 2 or 3 shifts and flexitime was introduced in many of the subsidiaries. But 9 to 5 is dependent on location. When it was noon at HQ in Europe, it was 5am in the Mexico City factory and 6pm in the Bangkok office. In the early morning, HQ people could interact with colleagues in Asia from their homes; in the late afternoon and the evening they could connect with offices in the Americas. They travelled extensively, often as a pair or in a small group. While travelling, in hotels and restaurants, work was being done and contacts were being made. Where should I be physically present?

One thing at HQ caught my imagination. Perhaps I drifted away but when something intrigues you it may very well be something important. I am referring to the executive lunch room. Those who had access were identified by a napkin envelope with their name on it. As a management consultant in a strategic change process and retained for a long period, I was allowed into this watering hole, the purpose being to facilitate my access to executives. The room became an information centre where I could talk to people who were protected by gatekeepers and therefore usually difficult to have contact with. I could catch subsidiary managers on a short visit from oversees; I could speak informally about issues that concerned me, pick up the latest gossip and get new clues for my research. My presence in the lunch room also facilitated my work by reminding others of my existence and that I was empowered by top management.

My mission was neither to figure out the lunch room culture nor to be a change agent of its system. But the lunch room was in itself an intriguing sub-culture and I assumed that it reflected the corporate culture and held clues to the more significant events to which I was trying to contribute. It took some time to understand the pecking order that had informally developed. There were 3 time slots for lunch: 11.30, 12.15 and 13.00. Each executive was assigned to one of these but was allowed to deviate occasionally. I learnt that 12.15 was the most prestigious time as the president and the senior vice-presidents came then. The other 2 slots were equal in status. In theory, you could sit anywhere – each table seated 4 people – but the table in the far left corner was informally assigned to the top executives at the 12.15 seating and was free at the other times. There were other tacit contracts which I never quite grasped.

An executive could bring business visitors to the lunch room if it was announced beforehand. Coffee was served in an executive lounge where only employees were allowed, while visitors and their hosts went to a guest lounge. In the first lounge, it was said, any member of staff could talk freely without the risk of being overheard by an outsider. My identity and position as consultant created uncertainty among some executives. Was I one of them or an outsider and could I be trusted to sit in their lounge or should I be exiled to the guest lounge? I usually went to the executive lounge, but sometimes the person I lunched with automatically took me to the guest lounge. As far as I could make out, I was the only person ever to have a napkin of my own who was not a regular executive.

Observation mostly takes place in a natural context and not – as in focus groups – in a lab-like context. Observation can also take place in a lab experiment which has been designed to resemble a real situation – but it is a stylized environment, where a complex reality is reduced to a few operationalized constructs. Psychologists seem to like this and assume they are in control. I am sure it works in select situations but it is hardly ever used in business and management. The true natural context is superior. Anthropological studies are traditionally focused on societies and cultures represented by a physical setting. Companies are not so easily defined and observation often requires resources not available to the researcher. It can be difficult in the sense that you cannot physically be at an event because you do not know where and when it will occur. Even if you can figure out that an incident is likely to occur, it may be infrequent. The incident may also occur frequently and continuously in many locations (e.g. decision-making processes) but you cannot be physically present everywhere.

When and where are you supposed to make observations? Whatever slice you cut out of a company – its investment decision-making processes, personnel policy, product design, quality management, sales negotiations, and so on – the researcher's dilemma is where to be present. Is it simpler in a local store or a little factory? Not necessarily, as companies are networks and small companies export, import and increasingly operate globally online. So organizations are hybrid and pulsating societies which, in some respects, change every minute, and in others are quite stable; they are fuzzy sets. They consist of an internal core which is part of a larger network within which interaction takes place. Presence thus constitutes a challenge.

Access is improved through increased involvement and presence; the researcher is offered opportunities to get closer to reality than in interviews. This adds to the potential validity of the research but makes reliability a difficult issue. By observing a process that is not repeated or, if repeated, is difficult to access by others, and using one's personality as the most important scientific instrument, the researcher makes it hard for someone else to replicate the study.

Observation over long periods of time means that only very few cases can be studied by the same researcher. The importance of working with a team or in close relationship with other researchers, as well as using existing material, grows. This adds to the validity and generalizability of the research.

Observation requires presence but not action. Action research, presented in the next section, integrates presence and action.

Management Action Research

Action research[24] is the most demanding and far-reaching data-generating method. I was tipped off by a consultant colleague who had found an enlightening book by Peter Clark (1972). Clark stressed the opportunity for *privileged access* to data and events not only by being present but also by taking action. From that and other influences, I developed *management action research* which is a business and management adaptation of the original method. It responds to all the criteria of the complexity paradigm, including interactive research, extrospection and introspection, recognition of the persona factor and good subjectivity – all within the idea of pragmatic wisdom. I have since been engaged in several management action research projects.

Originally, action research was proposed by psychologist Kurt Lewin and stood for research done together with those who were at a disadvantage, like workers in a plant that was threatened with closure. The workers did not have expertise enough to come up with possible solutions and to defend their rights. The researcher's role was to encourage them to help themselves by asking the right questions and working out a strategy together with them. This was done in interaction where both the researcher and the workers were experts, the researcher being able to analyse, interpret and formulate and the workers knowing how their factory functioned. I refer to this as *societal action research*. Later action research is described in many forms and sometimes stands out as almost anything.[25]

Management action research gives unique first-hand access to data in an organization. The action researcher represents the dual, both/and role of independent researcher and either employee or external consultant. Researchers can also use action research with themselves as the object, for example as consumer, employee or investor. With yourself as the object, you can hardly get closer access, can you?

Here are the characteristics of management action research based on the literature and my own research projects:

- *Action researchers take action.* Management action research goes a step further than participant observation by demanding that researchers actively influence the events they are studying by working in an organization, taking part in decision-making and implementation, or studying something self-lived as a citizen or consumer.

---

[24]Other terms are action science and participatory research.

[25]See a special issue of the *European Journal of Marketing*, Perry, ed., 2004.

- *Action research has dual goals.* One is to contribute to the solution of a particular problem; the other is to contribute to science. It is the same as the goals of case theory: to particularize and to generalize. With dual goals it is easy for mainstream researchers to say that there is a role conflict. Yes, there is, as always, when both/and is part of your paradigm. But when is life absent of goal conflicts? We have them in organizations as well as in our private lives. To dismiss them is to fall into the linearity trap. But it is not so within the complexity paradigm where the guiding star is both/and, not either/or. This requires you to position your findings in relation to previous research and literature and to distribute them through publications and presentations. If you use extant theory, you may contribute by testing the theory. You may keep your mind open and put received theory aside and generate new theory. Management action researchers, when taking action, must prioritize their practice even if they feel uneasy from a scientific perspective. The real situation comes first and the task of science – to understand reality in a more general way – comes second. According to Argyris et al.:[26] 'Becoming an action scientist involves learning to reflect on reflection-in-action, making explicit the theories-in-use that inform it, and learning to design and produce new theories-in-use for reflection and action.' This requires sensitivity and the ability to further develop extant theory and in the process test it, but also to generate new and better theory.

- *Action research addresses complexity in a holistic mode.* Case theory is used to getting access to complex realities or realities that are hidden and difficult to come across with traditional methods. The action researcher must focus on the totality of a problem, but make it simple enough to be understood by those involved so that decisions can be made and action take place. Decision-making and action usually take place under time pressures and imperfect knowledge. The action researcher must therefore also be able to work with heuristics and checklists and apply pragmatic wisdom to be 'optimally incomplete'.

- *Action research is interactive but each party can also act on its own.* Interaction is applicable to the understanding, planning and implementation of change in business firms and other organizations. The researchers interact closely with the people and the environment they are studying. Action research requires co-creation between the researchers and the client personnel and other stakeholders, feedback to the parties involved and continuous adjustment to new information and events. It is resource integration between the parties involved. For the practitioner, this is a natural way of working. According to Clark, it becomes an 'uneasy partnership' for the mainstream positivist. For example, in redefining the business model of a company, new information is needed about the market, financial solutions and technology. The analysis and interpretation lead to conclusions and decisions which should lead to action and results. It is an iterative process and the adjustments interfere with the original research design. It does not mean that those involved are constantly interacting. Some tasks are better performed by a single person or a small group but the outcome of this will affect the whole project. In the extended view of interaction, a person reading a document is also seen as interaction. Reading is not a passive exercise but is interaction with a text. It is obvious that the demands of the positivist paradigm are not applicable to action research and if researchers try to apply them, they will become bad advisers as well as bad scholars.

---

[26]1985, p. 82.

- *Preunderstanding of the organizational context and the conditions of business and management is essential.* Graduates of business schools, as well as their professors, are often accused of being too theoretical and too quantitative. Although they state that they are midwives rather than pregnant mothers and only assist in the process of birth, preunderstanding of the operations of a firm is necessary. This preunderstanding can be based both on understanding at first hand through personal experience and understanding at second hand through books and other intermediaries. Note: having preunderstanding is not the same as being biased and firmly rooted in past experience. To avoid bias, the researcher must engage in reflection as well as in interaction with others.

- *Management action research can engage all types of data-generating methods.* Interviews, observation, statistical surveys, archival data, and so on, can be used as long as the added dimensions – interaction and involvement – are in the core of the research, and explicit and tacit knowledge, extrospection and introspection are part of it.

- *Action research can be limited to real time but retrospective action research is also an option.* Action researchers should make field notes and memos and summarize observations and conclusions at the end of the day. I have had PhD students with experience of business and government who had participated in interesting processes and took time out to reflect and learn more. Their insights are valuable and should be exploited. They have had privileged access to events that no outsider can acquire. They can do *retrospective action research* and, if necessary, supplement it with data from other sources. This is not the same as writing memoirs where authors sometimes have other purposes as well, for example to show how clever they were.

- *Management action research requires its own quality criteria.* It does not fit the positivist paradigm but it fits the complexity paradigm and should be evaluated accordingly. Consideration has to be given to explicit and tacit knowledge as well as to practical consequences.

- *You do not choose an action research project, the project chooses you.* You must be observant and grab the opportunity when it pops up. To do fully-fledged action research, you need to have a task and be able to influence, make decisions and take part in the implementation. It is no simple matter to find assignments that are suitable for action research. A researcher can rarely state: 'I have chosen my subject and I intend to engage in an action research project.' It is not enough that the researcher has obtained funding for the project. An organization must also have a problem which gives the researcher scope to go in and act. One can also follow the opposite approach: a consultancy assignment is available and seems to offer the opportunity for action research. As an employee, you can do action research and probably more easily spot opportunities.[27] You can also do action research on yourself and your household.

- Action research also requires detached *reflection* where researchers analyse and interpret the data within a more general, long-term framework and develop theory through concepts, properties, categories and models. This reflection takes place within a single case but could also be extended over a longer period with several

[27]See Coghlan & Brannick, 2010.

cases. This *hermeneutic spiral* of preunderstanding–understanding–preunderstanding and so on, as well as the journey from substantive theory through mid-range theory to grand theory, was explained earlier. As far as reflection is concerned, the action researcher is governed by the 'rules' of the scientific game, whereas in dialogue and action the demands of the 'real world' problem are uppermost.

- Finally, although these requisites are mandatory, it is hard for researchers to score top points on all of them. The reason is not least that the situations they have lived through have required action for practical reasons in the first place. It will be a matter of weighting the criteria and assessing whether the project could pass as satisfactory action research.

Box 6.7 offered an example of action research where the main theme was testing the validity and relevance of a strategic planning model. It was a single case of real-time action research. Box 9.7 is an example of retrospective action research for the generation of grand theory.

Box 9.7 Retrospective Action Research for Theory Generation[28]

Sociologist Paul Blumberg has studied 'shady practices' in competitive markets and generated grand theory for understanding them better. He aligns with case theory in the following ways. First, his starting point is the real world; it is an inductive, empirical approach. Second, he has not been satisfied with descriptions and mid-range theory but strived towards grand theory. Third, his cases are about the lack of ethics and the ubiquitous corruption in market economies.

The prime issue in the study of shady practices is how to access reliable data and really get to know how companies cheat. One way is to study consumer experiences and from them infer the underlying business strategies. Another is to ask the firms. But they would not give you the true picture, rather let you meet their PR manager who will lecture you on their high level of CSR – or more likely not receive you at all.

Blumberg found a simple way of getting access to the desired information. He asked his students to tell him what kind of bad practice they had met in companies where they worked or had worked. In this way, it became retrospective management action research because the students had not set up an action research programme with their employers and made real-time notes and interpretations. It can create an ethics problem if you are still working in a firm – should you be loyal to your employer or to society? But if you had worked there casually during your studies and keep the company anonymous, it should not pose a problem.

(Continued)

---

[28]Based on Blumberg, 1989.

Blumberg had misgivings about the ability of the students to produce useful reports but found that the quality was surprisingly high. Based on over 600 cases, his book ends with a chapter on the morality of the marketplace and the paradox of capitalism. Integrating his findings with extant theory of markets, he has contributed a grand theory of how markets work. It is not a book advocating that the planned economy is better but a book where anyone – marketing people, consumers, legislators – can learn about how markets work in reality.

Blumberg's book should be required reading for every student of marketing and economics, but I have never seen the book quoted in textbooks. In March 2016, 37 years after publication, it has only been cited 67 times which means that the book has not reached out to those who really should read it.

When access is refused, or when the researcher's presence is considered a disturbance or even a threat, *covert inquiry* can be used. Academic researchers are generally too frightened to embark on such ventures, which is a pity. For example, how do you investigate the increasing problem of corruption and organized crime which has dramatic effects on working life, finance, the functioning of markets, pricing and quality? Researchers in business and management simply ignore it, believing that it is handled by criminologists. A possible strategy is to attend court trials and interview police officers, lawyers, judges and ordinary citizens who have been exposed to a crime. You have difficulties in meeting criminals unless you have an introduction from someone they trust – and that is not so easy to get. They do not want their operations to be understood by outsiders. Therefore, infiltration may be the only action research option. Researchers, however, are expected to follow some ethical code. Research should be overt, i.e. those who are studied should know what is going on. This code of ethics unfortunately rules out research in taboo areas, such as tax evasion, the narcotics trade and other illegal activities.

In some cases, a covert approach – where the researcher infiltrates an organization – is the only option. It is done by investigative reporters and the police as a last resort when information is covered up and hard to access. It is demanding and could be used more in business and management. You have to make clear what ethical complications this strategy might lead to and not misuse it. For example, when someone is trying to find data that is withheld for legitimate reasons, such as a tender in the competition for a contract, then it becomes industrial espionage.

Box 9.8 is about covert research through infiltration.

Box 9.8 Wallraffing: Covert Action Research

German investigative reporter Günter Wallraff[29] has become famous for his inside stories from companies and other organizations. He has given his name to his method: 'wallraffing'. In one of his books, he reports on his life as a poor Turkish immigrant. By impersonating a Turk, he gets first-hand understanding of the actual treatment of immigrants. He is employed in a hamburger restaurant and later in a factory where harmful asbestos is used in manufacturing. He also approaches churches in order to become a member and a funeral parlour to prepare for his death. He can himself experience the inhuman and illegal treatment of immigrants. How can you uncover such practices using conventional methods and sticking to a traditional ethical code? His fellow workers also confide in him things they would only tell their peers.

In a conscious but yet modest way, he provokes his employers and others. It is meant to uncover hypocrisy and create a dialogue on working conditions and the treatment of unskilled labour. The empirical content becomes unique. His data could be used in scholarly research if it had been connected to theory and the empirical studies of others. Wallraff's covert research was necessary to study shady organizations that were hiding behind false fronts; I therefore consider it ethical. It should not be confused with the scandals of reporters from the Murdoch media empire tapping private phones and computers and paying paparazzi to intrude on privacy.

The overreliance in industry and government on 'professionals' with academic training, but not being present where the real action is, has backfired. The Japanese seem to have been more successful in realizing the power of the employee, their tacit knowledge and presence.

Access to the reality of complex processes can never be better than in action research. Being part of an event, with a stake in its outcome, activates researchers and force them to take on responsibility. Getting close to reality paves the road to validity. The researcher as an instrument and the development of their persona – openness, creativity, a multi-perspective outlook on life, etc. – become an important part of research. No research is as demanding on the researcher's persona as action research. Knowledge and understanding do not exist without a medium to carry them. The 3 elements of knowledge – the knower, the process of knowing and the known – particularly stand out in action research.

---

[29]Wallraff, 1985.

Neuroscience

There is a need not just to establish input–output relationships around what happens in the minds of customers, employees, shareholders and others, but also to peek inside the black box. In marketing research, psychologists and psychiatrists are used to interpreting market and organizational behaviour. The two belong both to the social and natural sciences but make limited use of technology. *Motivational research* in marketing attempts to uncover the deep and hidden motives for consumer behaviour through tacit knowledge and observations, interviews and participation. Ernest Dichter (1979) was a pioneer and described himself as a 'people watcher', constantly asking why. Why do gentlemen wear ties, which he described as coloured pieces of cloth without any practical function? And why did the world's most researched car model, Ford Edsel, become a flop?

Dichter labels his research as *cultural anthropology* applied to the peculiar customs of American consumers. His data-generation procedures are a combination of creative observation and lengthy interviews, which he describes as 'mini psychoanalysis'. These procedures easily lead into taboo areas and both the tie and Ford Edsel were interpreted in Freudian terms relating to the male libido. Motivational research is at the opposite extreme to the statistical survey. It has been highly influential in consumer product development and advertising by highlighting the goings-on in the consumer black box. It has also been heavily criticized for being speculative, even being referred to as 'psycho-babble'.

To explore the universe of the human mind and individual and group personas, there is little cooperation with natural scientists and little use of advanced technology. It would still require both explicit and tacit knowledge as well as extrospection and introspection. The mental iron curtain between sciences and their different traditions and methodologies prevents genuine innovation.

The accelerator at CERN to find the Higgs particle, mentioned earlier, is an extreme example of investment in technology for basic research purposes. Social scientists have difficulty in securing resources for such research but are increasingly in need of it. A prominent example of high-tech-based research is Martin Lindstrom's study of how our brains react to advertising. This was not a research programme started by an academic institution but by a prolific consultant. Due to his positive relations with industry, he managed to raise US$7 million to engage brain researchers with advanced laboratories.

Neuroscience is literally picking your brain. This is an example of the interdependency between the natural sciences, the social sciences and the humanities. Mainstream empirical studies in the social sciences are restricted to hearing and seeing. This is detached research, whereas I recommend involved and interactive research. Neuroscience gives us access to data direct from our nervous system without the interference of interpretation and selective perception.

Neuroscience is not really used in the business and management disciplines, not in theory and education anyway. How much it is used in practice we do not know but I suspect it is a lot in certain industries. It is costly, and major corporations can afford it while academic institutions cannot. Traditionally, funds are given in large amounts to the natural sciences, but expect the social sciences to need only pencil and paper and, lately, a computer!

Industries that have been subject to heavy regulation to restrict the consumption of unhealthy products like tobacco and alcohol, use sophisticated techniques to circumvent regulations. Lindstrom's experiments, accounted for in his bestsellers *Buyology* (2008) and *Brandwashed* (2011), show how neuroscience has been applied to reach beyond interviews, observations and introspection. He found that traditional market research methods did not find out what consumers really think because 'our irrational minds, flooded with cultural biases rooted in our tradition, upbringing, and a whole lot of other subconscious factors, assert a powerful but hidden influence over the choices we make'.[30]

Considering these conclusions, there is reason to add neuroscience to the business and management methodologies. It is an opportunity to eradicate the boundary between the social and natural sciences. It requires cross-disciplinary and international projects but these are also recommended by many research funds, for example in the EU.

The next case exposes you to an application of neuroscience (Box 9.9).

Box 9.9 Understanding Cigarette Consumption by Uncovering the Brain's Deepest Secrets

In order to curb the harmful use of tobacco, governments have escalated their restrictions on cigarette advertising. In the 1950s, the then movie actor and later US President Ronald Reagan appeared in an advertisement smoking a Chesterfield cigarette, saying that he was sending Chesterfields to all his friends: 'the merriest Christmas any smoker can have'. At that time, cigarette companies could claim whatever they wanted. Later advertisements were allowed to expose a brand but with no teasing text or pictures to make smoking appealing, such as the 'healthy' cowboy with a Marlboro in his mouth (the model who played the cowboy got free cigarettes and died of cancer!) Today, dead skulls and scary texts appear on the packaging and in the ads: 'Cigarette smoking can harm your health' and 'Smoking causes fatal lung cancer'. This all sounds perfectly sensible, but does it have the intended effect?

(Continued)

---

[30]Lindstrom, 2008, p. 18.

(Continued)

Here is the big surprise: Lindstrom's research showed that the scary messages triggered a reflex in consumers' nerves that *made them eager to have a cigarette* – totally contrary to reason and verbal communication. Governments unknowingly acted against their own intentions and helped tobacco companies promote their products. As the marketing of cigarettes was curbed, companies looked for innovative ways to understand the cause of consumer behaviour. As governments and research are slow, conservative and short of money, they made cigarette companies look for novel research methods like brain research. This helped Philip Morris, for example, to redesign motels and British pubs where the lounges are furnished with red sofas designed in shapes from the Marlboro logo and the TV screens show cowboys and horses to evoke the image of the Marlboro Man.

Lindstrom concludes that marketers:[31]

are still doing the same old stuff: quantitative research, which involves surveying lots and lots of volunteers about an idea, a concept, a product or even kind of packaging – followed by qualitative research, which turns a more intense spotlight on smaller focus groups handpicked from the same population ... What we know now ... is that what people say on surveys and in focus groups does not reliably affect how they behave – far from it.

There is no doubt that advanced brain research could give us new knowledge and do away with several of the current types of studies used to explore consumer behaviour. If you are lucky enough to get to practise it, you should of course also reflect on this openly.

Online Research

Online research is a recent methodology made possible by the Internet. One type is the traditional survey transformed for the Internet, which gives productivity advantages. Another is ethnography performed on the Internet – *netnography* – where you explore the social behaviour and data available on blogs, social networking sites, fan forums, etc. It is a type of documented reality that allows us to do studies from the desk.

Traditional research methods were developed for physical settings, the telephone and letters, but online research has its own peculiar characteristics. I have limited experience of online research, except for having been exposed to it in a number of cases. Following my own conclusion that you do not understand a

---

[31]Lindstrom, 2008, p. 2.

method properly if you have not used it and reflected on it, I only want to draw your attention to it. There is an emerging methods literature on online research and applications.[32]

I will be brief and only mention a few things that have a specific bearing on case theory. Everyone has some familiarity of online interaction today and some are deeply into it. New generations grow up with it; it is a big part of their social life almost from babyhood. It is in interaction with hosts like Google and within a much more active role of citizens and customers (C2C interaction) that customers co-create systems. And this is expanding and changing continuously. McLuhan foresaw the World Wide Web and other modern media 30 years before they became reality, but did not live to see the explosion of email, the Internet, smartphones, text messaging, blogs, and their development into social media and increasingly also into commercial media. This way of communicating and the volume and velocity of data, along with the hopes put on big data, will affect our research methods.

Online research opens things up for creative variety, but I also see that the cheaper and faster applications like surveys and interviews may have the same basic shortcomings as before. They can be very productive, with rapid access to existing data instead of only from archives and traditional publications. The online option is recent and will not make physical presence and offline research redundant. It is a both/and future within the spirit of high tech/high touch. Sometimes high tech even supports high touch, for example through Skype and podcasts. Note that it is not just a matter of organized analysis; it is equally a matter of interpretation and combined explicit and tacit knowledge.

Online living creates a novel society. The Internet is a social network with billions of users worldwide. The users are the nodes and no one is President of the Internet. Some nodes become hubs and have a special appeal, for example the website or blog of a sports star, a fan club or a TV network.

> Keep on asking, and you will receive what you ask for. Keep on seeking, and you will find. Keep on knocking, and the door will be opened to you. (The Bible, Gospel of Matthew 7:7)

A difficult problem is the evaluation of sources and it is becoming even more difficult. What in the blogs, tweets, etc. is genuine and what is fake, planted for a specific purpose or just plain babble? And who do these texts represent? Crimes are committed by irresponsible users and by criminal organizations. The number of specialists on 'interpreting' the truth for us is steadily growing, and as ordinary citizens we do not know how to uncover their tricks though researchers are largely victims as well. We must always ask ourselves: What is the quality of the data? This is what the next section is about.

---

[32]See e.g. Edberg, 2013; Sörman-Nilsson, 2013; Charan, 2015 (on consumer research).

Evaluation of Sources

It is absolutely vital to evaluate the credibility and contribution of our sources. The term *source criticism* is unfortunate as it is negative and directs your mind to fault-finding, incompleteness and other limitations. Instead, you should be *constructively critical* of your sources. I recommend the term *evaluation of sources* as it has a positive connotation in the sense that we should search for sources that seem credible and that, at the same time, offer useful data for a specific study. In some areas of business and management research, what is not liked by people is often just left in silence – this is the most effective way of killing something. This is unfortunate; the persona factor takes over when a 'respected' researcher must always be referenced and cannot be argued with, without the researcher risking repercussions in their career.

Excellence in case theory requires skills to access data and to analyse and interpret documents, interviews, observations, experiences and other data sources. In the original and positive sense of the word trivial – from the Latin *trivialis* meaning 'common and accessible to anyone' – I consider science trivial. This is far from the derived and negative meaning of trivial: insignificant, petty and trifling. I mention this because science is about the basics of life, and the basics can never be trifling, basics like forecasting the weather, nutritious or dangerous food, strained relationships in society, the heating of houses, and how leadership is best exerted to create an efficient working organization. So everyone has a most personal stake in science. Consequently, science should be accessible to anyone.

Science is also about technicalities, which require skills that folk in general do not have. But even the most humble job develops tacit knowledge that can be much more valid than the knowledge generated by science. Just as much as socially accepted knowledge can be wrong, scientific knowledge can be wrong. A respondent's answers and comments are always slanted, unknowingly and without malice or deliberately, or with various motives and power behind it. Increasingly – which should be obvious to those in accounting, corporate strategy or marketing, and to economists and political scientists – politicians, reporters, public relations people, lobbyists and spin doctors manipulate our perception of what is going on. Politicians are considered liars, it seems, by a majority of people; salespeople are known to overpromise and lie by omission; and accountants help 'cook the books'. The phenomenon is not new but today's 'spinning' of information has become a profession. Consultants are hired to promote certain 'facts' and suppress others, and their only loyalty is to those who pay their fees. The distortion of fact can be skilfully disguised as a documentary on television or a scientific column in a journal; 'truth' in the classic sense is for the weak and gullible. A majority of professionals probably do not even know what the truth is, or that they are lying and distorting fact.

We instinctively know that the tabloid press and gossip can be unreliable sources that need to be double or triple checked. It seems to be less understood that official statistics can be a pack of lies, defined for a specific political or business purpose and compiled under a series of assumptions that are not known to the user of the statistics. Interviews with CEOs, consultants and politicians are often misleading, as the interviewees are speaking for their own sake. Annual reports and accounts, as well as statements from financial analysts, can be outright deception, not just in such spectacular cases as those of Enron, Arthur Andersen and many other companies throughout the world. The dazzling elegance of statistics and the equally dazzling eloquence of words written by advertising agency copywriters can communicate almost anything that has been asked for by a political party or a company. Without sound judgement and ethics, the rigour and systematic modus operandi of researchers does not produce knowledge. Evaluation of the credibility of a source has to be made: is it too journalistic; is it there to enhance the image of a company or to boost the ego of the presenter? Usually there is an element of this – which is human and acceptable to a degree.

Company cases presented at conferences are usually success stories. I sometimes ask the speaker if this is what they *have done* or what they *plan to do*. Mostly it turns out to be plans or the early stages of implementation. There can be a gorge between the neat plans and the ensuing reality. Therefore, we have no evidence of the actual functioning of the activities and strategies of the case. They could exist only in a boardroom dreamland but they could also be profit-making innovations.

The use of references has been mentioned on several occasions in previous chapters. The celebrity and name-dropping method – when the reference list becomes a Who's Who in the discipline and when only top-ranked journals are cited – has been chastised. Unfortunately, by following this reference strategy you increase the likelihood of getting an article accepted. No one can really accuse you of anything – except of being a mainstream traditionalist. Such references should not be used just because they are historical; business and management are not about history. The fast pace with which Internet companies start up, grow or disappear, the volatility of financial markets, the continuously changing ownership of firms and the difficulty for an outsider in understanding network organizations, make much of the approved scholarly research methods obsolete. Scholars of business and management disciplines have to learn methods that allow them to generate data, analyse, interpret and report much, much faster and to act faster. Glaser often points to the scholar being too slow: 'A grounded theory project should not take more than 6 months; 2 years is far too long.'[33] Whether 6 months or 2 years is too little or too long has to be decided

---

[33]From a discussion with Glaser in 1999.

Table 9.4 Data deficiencies

Deficiencies	Examples
Mainstream methods	Understanding of interviewing methods insufficient
Low quality data	Common in macro statistics and surveys
Inadequate categories	Common in macro statistics and surveys
Obsolete data	Too old to be of relevance except as history
Planned deception	Using doctored data to confirm a conclusion
Lying by omission	Leaving out data when selling an investment fund
Presenting covariation as causality	The general PIMS results
False documentaries	A dishonest narrative disguised in scientific jargon
Subtle smear campaign	Calling case study research 'anecdotal evidence'
Irresponsible lobbying and PR	Hiding the true purpose when raising research funds
Subtly misleading the reader	Company annual reports

for each individual case, but the general message is indisputable. Although the speed of change in society has proliferated, the speed of research is often embarrassingly slow and the speed of knowledge entering education and implementation is still slower.

Table 9.4 shows examples of the quality deficiencies of sources. The examples mean that the deficiency frequently occurs in the area but not necessarily; being observant and reflective are always important.

For example, a headline in a newspaper is not written by the author of the article and may very poorly reflect its content. TV news is full of one-liners and complex events are reported in a few minutes. It means that they can be reduced, or even if well condensed it may be difficult to see the point in a reasonably correct way. There is a lot of context-less nonsense. The headline is mainly there to sell the paper and to make people agitated, but often only reflects some odd detail in the article. It rarely reflects the true content – and how could it in just a few words? Although I have argued for well over 20 years now that academe should listen to what business, government and NGOs have learnt about quality, it seems to be a cry in the desert.[34] As we are addressing quality in business and management research, we may profit from its practice. Judging from the references in articles, books and student and PhD theses, business schools only turn to statistics, mathematics, sociology and ethnography to learn about research and science; rarely do they look to the natural sciences.

---

[34]Gummesson, 2000a.

It is increasingly common to let bibliometrics evaluate sources, meaning that an article published in a top international journal or written by a well-known professor is automatically of high quality. A source from a lower ranked publication, from an unknown author or written in a language other than English, is equally automatically classified as being of less quality. My evaluation of bibliometrics is discussed in the Fourth Focus in Chapter 11 which is about the quality and productivity of research.

The Journey in Methodologyland Continues

In this chapter, the journey in Methodologyland has taken us to detached archives (written words and numbers), to standardized data in surveys (written and spoken words), to interactive interviews (words, observation), to direct observation (seeing, hearing, physical artefacts), to participation (but not intervention), to action research (making decisions, taking action), to introspection, to the scientific high-tech measurement of human brain cell activity, and to the Internet as a research instrument.

The first 5 methods are mainstream. The next method, action research, especially in the pragmatic sense of management action research that I have introduced, is used too infrequently for the following reasons: (1) it is not found in the standard methods manuals; (2) its strengths are not properly explained and understood; (3) researchers may find it too demanding; and (4) there is a fear of getting involved and being accused of not being objective. Neuroscience is an example of the necessity to dissolve the barriers between the natural sciences, the social sciences and the humanities. Its results clearly point out that interviews and observations can be grossly misleading. Neuroscience is a type of introspection, although it is so in a natural science mode. Online research is made possible through IT. It can be used both for doing fast and far-reaching surveys at low cost, and for studying material on the Internet, such as websites and social media. In this capacity, it is a survey technique and ethnography in a new context.

Some of these data-generation options are overused (written material, surveys and other interviews), some are underused (observation, management action research, neuroscience) and online research is at an early stage of development.

Considering the advantages of action research, I find it grossly underused in business and management. It is often performed in 'light' versions where the involvement of the researcher is more as an observer. I am sorry to say but I often find academic researchers non-scholarly, driven more by convenience than by genuine curiosity and risk-taking. This is part of the individual researcher's persona but maybe even more of the persona of the academic environment – the researchscape – and the dependency on pleasing examiners and superficial bibliometrics that can support or block a career. Action research may also be scary for many researchers as you cannot strictly follow steps in an approved procedure, like you can more easily do with a survey (even if a survey includes judgement calls). It is easy to be criticized for being too involved and becoming too subjective, even corrupted by the object of study. Such criticism does not consider the loss of access and the loss in both the quantity and quality of data that is typical of detached research.

10

THIRD FOCUS: ANALYSIS AND INTERPRETATION – LINKING DATA TO THEORY AND CONCLUSIONS

In case theory, analysis is reserved for the explicit and step-wise process of extracting information and knowledge from data through extrospection. Interpretation is about giving meaning to data and extrospection joins forces with introspection and tacit knowledge. In this process, data is generating theory and conclusions.

In Chapter 1, it was mentioned that analysis and interpretation start early. If you have chosen a theme for your research and defined a problem worth investigating, detailed it in research questions and a purpose, you need to analyse, interpret and conceptualize it to generate some kind of theory.

In analysing and interpreting both numerical and non-numerical data, you are fighting for your life in a stormy sea. Terms, concepts and advice are all over you, sometimes knocking you on the head, sometimes giving you a mouthful of cold water, sometimes making you feel like you are drowning. If you do numerical analysis, you may think you are on safe ground on a warm and still beach. That is what the tourists in Thailand thought when the tsunami hit and killed thousands of people.

Doing scientific research, with the purpose of acquiring knowledge and understanding, then making decisions, taking action and reaching positive results, is more like being in the stormy sea. Through the more rigorous numerical criteria and indexes, it may seem easier to analyse the data but it is not easy to interpret the meaning of it and its consequences. If you just settle for the mainstream criteria of quantitative research and accept them at face value, you make it easy for yourself, you even act irresponsibly.

By convention, case research is considered qualitative and primarily interpretivist. It is inspired by *hermeneutics* which was originally a method for interpreting the text of the Bible, and *phenomenology* which is the study of phenomena as we subjectively perceive them. The *hermeneutic spiral* is an expression for iterative research, where you go from one stage of preunderstanding to another of more advanced understanding in a never-ending process. The iterative spiral, embracing substantive, mid-range and grand theory, was shown in Figure 6.1.

Although both Yin and Eisenhardt, in presenting case study research, accept qualitative and interpretivist approaches, Yin exposes a positivist undertone and Eisenhardt says outright that quantitative hypothesis testing is the next natural step. This is often so that those well versed in a certain methodology, such as quantitative techniques, and then apply another method, can let the old paradigm infringe on the new paradigm, even when this is not intellectually justified.

In Chapter 9, the focus was on access to data and data generation. Linking empirical data, applying theory and drawing conclusions are also part of this process. Because of their inherent non-linearity, it feels inappropriate to treat these phenomena sequentially – but the book format does not leave us much choice. You have to try and alleviate the effect as best you can by both treating them separately and together, even if this requires certain repetitions. Bazeley[1] even presents the whole case research process under the rubric of data analysis, thus accepting the simultaneity and non-linearity. To me, the actual writing is an analytic and interpretative process, starting with memo writing during data generation. When I see a text in front of me, preferably a few days later, gaps and inconsistencies stand out. I have even found myself in the position of saying 'I wonder who wrote this?', then realizing I did! The text speaks back to me; it becomes an interactive process.

The theme of this chapter is strategies, techniques and advice for analysis and interpretation. In theory generation, an overarching strategy is to condense, generalize and simplify. If you do so too hurriedly you come out wrong. But when is the right moment? This requires judgement calls and draws on your pragmatic wisdom. There is further the need to see every detail as part of the whole context to which it belongs. Persona factors must also be considered. For want of grand theory, you have to accept mid-range theory simplifications as currently the best option.

Analysing and interpreting data, both new data through your own empirical research and what is available in existing theory and publications, is a difficult area which held me back from writing this book for many years. I have gradually learnt that I share this feeling of inadequacy with other social scientists. But is it inadequacy or just that it laid bare that the process from data to conclusions and recommendations is messy? If you use mathematics and statistics, the process is more well-ordered and technique-oriented than if you use words and

---

[1]Bazeley, 2013.

non-verbal language. But the research edifice in Figure 3.4 showed that whichever approach you use, the explicit/tacit, objective/subjective, quantitative/qualitative and sequential/iterative concepts are present. Part of research is to make tacit knowledge more explicit, only to find that there is residual insecurity, ambiguity and ignorance.[2]

The heading of this chapter includes analysis and interpretation whereas usually only analysis is stressed. What are they, how do they differ and how do they interact? They are part and parcel of the same issue: how to make sense of data. The term *analysis* is primarily associated with techniques and research designs that are explicit and rigorous and can be replicated by others, meaning quantitative research. But what do we actually do when we analyse? In quantitative research, a series of statistical and mathematical techniques and procedures are used. If you follow these, you may feel inoculated against criticism; the scientific community will accept your research, on the grounds of technique application and procedures more than on your contribution to valid and relevant knowledge. You deconstruct and categorize a complex problem in its detail but have limited idea about how to set it into useful theory. The expression 'paralysis by analysis' holds a lot of truth.

Statistical research also requires the less controlled *interpretation*. In non-quantitative research, the procedures are more varied and less easy to describe. They are not bound by rules and regulations in the same way. In case theory, tacit knowledge exerts an influence. The idea of calling the case narrative scientific is to encourage conscious efforts to avoid distortion. It is a demanding task and you can only arrive there through an open attitude and lifelong practice. Personally, I have not given up hope yet. Some of your failure or success can be rooted in your genetic persona but some can be learnt.

A reminder: tacit knowledge and introspection require both a lenient and a disciplined mindset; it is both/and, not either/or.

Analysis is allegedly solely linked to objective and rigorous statistical procedure. Interpretation is sometimes called 'mushy and woolly' in a derogatory sense; I will stick to 'fuzzy' from set theory. Analysis and interpretation have a unique core, but the overlap is considerable. Interpretation is not as explicit, transparent and orderly as analysis, and replication is more difficult but often irrelevant in a dynamic environment. Noting that researchers have difficulties in interpreting data, I have chosen to list a series of strategies that can be helpful in research practice. These are inspired by literature on sociology, education,

---

[2]In an insightful book edited by Bryman & Burgess (1994: 21), social scientists define hurdles to pinpoint the truth and offer ways of getting around them. Some of this is useful for us but none of the authors come from business and management and they do not directly connect to our research context.

psychology and ethnography. More books are also appearing that apply non-quantitative methods specifically to research in management.[3]

We sometimes hear people say that data speaks for itself. This is seldom so; data has to be analysed and interpreted. I once talked to our Minister of Agriculture who told me that according to official statistics, the US consumer ate twice as much chicken as the Swedish consumer. His conclusion was clear: 'There is great potential for increasing chicken sales in Sweden.' So he let the state (meaning the taxpayers) invest in a new chicken factory in an area of Sweden where there was high unemployment. He made sure this reached the news and he was hailed for his contribution to employment.

The factory never made it. First, the Swedes did not want to quickly double their chicken consumption; second, the factory was wrongly located from a distribution point of view; third, it was probably not well managed; and fourth, there were privately owned chicken farms to compete with. Politicians rarely use research or have the ability to analyse and interpret. They claim they know, mainly driven by securing more votes in the short term, and they are therefore seldom reliable. A next step should have been to test whether consumers were interested in eating more chicken and also to look into the consumer black box, interview supermarkets, etc. The state should have made sure that the factory was properly designed, located and staffed and its products skilfully marketed. Then the business should have been constantly monitored and the implementation quickly revised if things changed. A business model can be right – but very often the problem is poor implementation and slow adaptation to changed conditions. An analogy with another market may inspire a search, but the analogy does not provide evidence of success.

When research is primarily based on verbal language and even if extended to network, systems, fuzzy set and chaos theory, we find that we land in a pile of data. We may feel frustrated: How should we sort it out and find patterns? Today's software can help us structure data and find patterns, which saves time but does not relieve us of the tasks of analysis and interpretation. By writing memos rather than long descriptive field notes, we also save time.

Those solely devoted to quantification try to translate everything into numbers, indices, probabilities, etc. If they had studied fuzzy set theory – which comes from modern mathematics – and thus accepted that reality cannot be stylized and forced into square boxes but rather consists of fuzzy sets that can vary in density and be overlapping, they could search for ways of making the fuzziness mathematical. Those who represent word- and observation-based research urge you to go through your field notes and memos meticulously, make comparisons and check for consistency. Methods books offer long lists of what to think of and still you may feel you did not really get the final answer.

---

[3]See e.g. Remenyi et al., 1998; Easterby-Smith et al., 2015; and in marketing Carson et al., 2001.

Recommendations from the Methods Literature

Analysis and interpretation are interdependent and in this section the two will be discussed. Traditional mathematical and statistical techniques will not be accounted for. It would take too much space and there are numerous textbooks on them. My interest is in the missing aspects of science, namely how the complexity paradigm and a combination of explicit/tacit knowledge and extrospection/introspection can help us understand the world better.

Because of the complexity that non-numerical analysis and interpretation pose, it is no wonder that many have tried to find simplified strategies and techniques together with straightforward advice for the researcher. This is commendable as long as it does not try short cuts that put a blind eye to complexity. I wish I could give you a single and clear checklist for the analysis and interpretation of case theory. But I cannot; it is too complex. I therefore give you the best I have found in the methods literature supplemented by my own experience. It is then up to you to decide what to do. If you have read the book so far and combined it with your common sense, you will find a pragmatic solution.

Analysis and interpretation are discussed in numerous publications on case-based research and on other methodologies. I stick to what I am most familiar with and so far see as being of interest for case theory, either as useful or non-useful.

To structure a problem and present conclusions, graphic design based on matrices and boxes-and-arrows models seem to be the most common. These models have visual advantages, but by being drawn as a collection of crisp sets they are also visually misleading. They seem so conclusive and it is hard to include variety and diversity. Adding numbers and indexes to them, like the structural equation models, is an effort to add further value to them. But if it is statistical, it has all the weaknesses of reductions, averages, randomness, approximations, etc. offered by statistical language. In the course of research, they may help to structure your memos but they are not sufficient as the result of a case study. However, articles on business and management often end up with boxes-and-arrows models and textbooks are full of them. Network and systems theory offer such models but also allow for advanced complexity.

Yin offers a whole set of 'logic models'.[4] The book by Miles, Huberman and Saldana (2013) offers structures for handling non-numerical data. In a chapter called 'Relational analyses', Bazeley presents a large number of examples of boxes-and-arrows models, including network theory applications.[5] Consult them.

---

[4]Yin, 2014, pp. 155–168.

[5]Bazeley, 2013, pp. 282–324.

Case theory adds network, systems, fuzzy set and chaos theory to the dominating qualitative and verbal language of traditional case study research. They have been treated in the previous chapters and if you intend to use them in more depth, go to the specialized literature on them.

This chapter offers a review of a selection of these, together with my personal experiences and comments. As Yin is the best-known author on case study research, his recommendations will be considered first.

Yin

Yin offers strategies for analysis, analytic techniques and quality principles. Some of his techniques may very well be useful within the complexity paradigm but some may not. Here I will point to areas where case theory differs from Yin's view. If you want to penetrate Yin further, the best thing is to take a look at his book. You can start by comparing the tenets of the complexity paradigm with Yin.

Among the major differences are that case theory acknowledges the interplay between explicit and tacit knowledge and sees action research as the best method to get proper access. Yin is not specifically dealing with business and management or other economic sciences, and, as said before, I do not consider a research method universally applicable. A method may have a generally valid core, but each application has to be adapted to the context in which it is used.

Yin suggests that theoretical propositions or hypotheses should lead your case study. This is a deductive and positivist approach. You may use case theory to test extant theory but it is done differently, though you could also start inductively and not feel committed to extant theory and its preconceived ideas. Initially, your preunderstanding has to be set aside and sometimes also the paradigmatic conditions. It is common to say that this cannot be done. However, it is a matter of training, experience and discipline. All research requires a balancing act even if we do not explicitly recognize it. It is about both/and. I recommend that your perceived problem, research questions and purpose take the lead, even if these change under way when you know more about your object of study.

You should look for core variables – those that seem to have a major influence and density; they can also include many sub-variables.

Yin[6] proposes 4 general strategies and within those 5 analytic techniques and they are extensively described in his book. Further, 'you must do everything to make sure that your analysis is of the highest quality. At least 4 principles underlie all good social science research.'[7] Here they are interspersed with my comments:

---

[6]Yin, 2014, pp. 136–168.

[7]Yin, 2014, p. 168.

1. You must seek to attend to *all the evidence* and leave no loose ends or you will be vulnerable to alternative interpretations. You must exhaustively cover your research questions, which requires that they are *sharp and not vague*. However, if the world consists of fuzzy sets not everything will be sharp.

2. You must, if possible, address *all plausible rival interpretations*. If others present rival interpretations, you could assess whether there is any evidence to support them and, if so, include them in your research. However, Yin's 'interpretation' has a lower status than in the complexity paradigm and is more geared to positivist 'causal explanations'.

3. You must address *the most significant aspect* of your case and demonstrate *your best analytic skills*. You must *avoid detours* to less important issues. But small factors can also interfere, which chaos theory and tipping points show.

4. You should use your own *prior, expert knowledge* and demonstrate awareness of the topic through your own research or the current thinking. Current thinking within your research field may be what you confront, however, because you consider it irrelevant and obsolete.

Among the words used that require judgement calls and the application of your explicit/tacit knowledge and pragmatic wisdom are: at least (?) 4 principles; do everything (?) to make sure (?); the highest quality (?); good (?); all (?) the evidence; sharp (?); if possible (?); all (?) plausible (?) rival interpretations; and your best (?) analytic skills. Sometimes it is useful to turn around guiding principles to make sure they do not just offer truisms and banalities. Here are some examples connected to the above requirements: make sure you do not make a bad analysis; be vague; go for the lowest quality; just do a few things to make sure; use your worst analytic skills; and focus on the most insignificant issues. Is it helpful to learn that this is *not* what you do?

Yin recommends the following analytic techniques:[8]

- pattern matching – this is his favourite but it is also a positivist approach: you compare your empirical data with 1 or several predictions; if the new data matches an extant pattern, it is an indication of internal validity when you try to establish causal relationships
- explanation building
- time-series analysis
- logic models – extended ways of establishing cause and effect with boxes and arrows
- cross-case synthesis.

Take a look at them and see if you find them useful in your specific case theory project. The next section puts the focus on interpretation.

---

[8]Yin, 2014, pp. 142–148.

Hermeneutics and Interpretive Research

As mentioned before, *hermeneutics*, today mostly referred to as *interpretive research*, stems from the interpretation of the Bible. Using it in business and management is perhaps not so far from the original context, considering that the modern market economy is a materialist religion where money, shopping and consumption are worshipped. And the concept got its name from the Greek god Hermes, who among other things was the patron of invention and trade. His equivalent in Roman mythology was Mercury, whose name lives in the word 'merchant' and who is considered the god of business. Hermes and Mercury were also the gods of thieves, however that should be interpreted. Referring to the shortcomings of today's business – corruption, lack of CSR and organized crime – it holds true to some extent. But the government sector and politics are no better.

Interpretive research does not follow a set of strict rules; it is rather the name for a conscious search for meaning and understanding. Within a pragmatic spirit, the following optional strategies and guidelines for research practice have been formulated:[9]

- Interpretive research can be applied to all types of data. In the flow of spoken and written words and numbers, symbols, observations, feelings and thoughts, interpretation becomes an integral part of daily life. It gives meaning and understanding to what we do. It goes beyond numbers and words to all expressions of human life, including tacit knowledge.

- To increase credibility, the researcher should offer possible alternative interpretations and argue for or against them.

- All research builds in part on assumptions and restrictions that established researchers share – intersubjectively, subjectively and, more rarely, objectively – through tradition or agreement. Interpretive research is also based on the researcher's paradigm, preunderstanding and understanding.

- The hermeneutic helix is an extension of the hermeneutic circle that introduces advancement, moving upwards and downwards to advance theory, as Figure 6.1 showed. We move from preunderstanding to understanding on a higher level; from parts towards the whole; and from a substantive, specific theory zone to abstract and general zones. There is thus interaction between what we know and what we have just learnt, between slices of data and a systemic whole, and between the concrete and the abstract. We can only give meaning to parts if we put them in a context, a theory.

- We interpret and re-interpret data in an iterative trial-and-error process of both theory generation and theory testing. Through this process, case theory is not just left to generate theory; it also tests theory to improve its validity and relevance.

---

[9]On the use of hermenutics/interpretivist approaches, I am indebted to the work of Per-Johan Ödman (especially Ödman, 1985 and 2007). I do not use his conclusions and recommendations literally but have merged them with the complexity paradigm and interactive research.

- Three privileges influence our interpretation. One is the *privilege to define the problem to be researched* and *to ask the research questions*. It was mentioned in Chapter 8 that in an ideal, free academy this should be the privilege of anyone, but in reality a PhD candidate is dependent on the preferences of the supervising professor and the researchscape of a university department. The professor in turn is dependent on the preferences of committees, companies and governments that control the money. *Privilege to access information* was noted in Chapter 9. And finally, the *privilege is to interpret the research*. Who draws the conclusions and who has the credibility or power to endorse a certain interpretation and publish it?[10]

- The positivist paradigm claims that quantitative research can offer explanations by establishing *causality* between an independent and a dependent variable, while other research can enhance the more mushy *understanding*. In interpretive research where complexity is addressed, this type of causality is not sufficient, and understanding, including wisdom through tacit knowledge, is more realistic.

- It is obvious that interpretive research requires a context in which to position knowledge. We have already dealt with context as part of the complexity paradigm and seen that there is no methodology that is generally applicable to every topic or discipline but rather has to be adapted to the context, like business and management, and make it credible that it can make a contribution.

There is a series of possibilities for assessing the validity and relevance of interpretations. These will be commented on below within the context of the complexity paradigm and business and management disciplines. When I write this, it stands out in such bright lights how many detailed instructions researchers are given. These will never be complete and even so be too many to comply with. My recommendation, put forth in Chapter 1, is to practise, reflect and learn the hard way:

- *Skilful use of texts* – the text could be verbal and mathematical with tables and diagrams, be written by someone, but also be a transcribed interview. It may sound safe to record interviews but those of us who have transcribed them know that we are faced with time-consuming work. When you see a verbatim transcription of an informal interview, the language is very different from the usual written language. There are more words, repetitions, sighs, laughter, pausing, people speaking at the same time, and background sounds than you notice during the interview. During an interview, you also make non-verbal observations. Some of this may appear on a video recording. If you are in an interactive interview, you automatically interpret and edit impressions simultaneously and you are not explicitly aware of this; there is a tacitly ongoing interpretive process. A general recommendation is to write memos, and if possible make an audio recording which you can fall back on for verbatim quotations, and make the scientific narrative more authentic for the reader. At the end, it is a matter of interpreting the text but also of relating it to other data, for example comparing interviews.

---

[10]Attention to these privileges was drawn to me by the Swedish novelist and philospher Lars Gustafsson.

- *Argumentation* – Ödman says that interpretation is qualitative in itself and that the method of testing corresponding to statistical testing is linguistic. This deviates from the complexity paradigm where statistical tests also have to be interpreted and cannot just be 'objectively' analysed. We have to ask what they mean for decision-making, action and outcome (recall the research edifice in Figure 3.3). Ways to do this are dialogue, extrospection through interaction with others who can question our conclusions and suggest others, and introspection. It is an outer and inner dialogue. This is done with an open mind and is different from one-sided advocacy.

- *Source evaluation*, sometimes referred to as *source criticism* – I prefer evaluation of source quality, as discussed in Chapter 9. The word criticism is easily taken in a destructive mode to find faults rather than as a constructive search for improvements.

- *Data representation* – according to convention, case narratives should be 'thick and rich'. As told in Chapter 3, the scientific narrative is different from the verbal and descriptive narrative and is primarily conceptual, drawing on network theory and others. Articles have limited space while books and reports do not have such limitations. We have to adjust to this limitation, just as the predominant linearity of a text is a limitation. Therefore, we cannot say that one way of writing is right and one is wrong. We can envy quantitative presentations which can show tables packed with numbers and indices and a language that is denser than the verbal, but this is primarily because much of the richness and variety of the real case have been removed. And it is not easy even for those trained in statistics to read these tables – and do they take the time to really do it and to check if the technique has been used correctly? There is no simple rule, only this: Develop your empathy and get into the clothes of the reader. Write for the reader!

- *Akribeia* (or *akribia*) – the term comes from the Orthodox Church, meaning strict adherence to the *letter* of the law as distinguished from adherence to the *spirit* of the law. It is an important distinction as the letter cannot cover all possible instances; instead, pragmatic wisdom allows us to *interpret the spirit* of the word. In the social sciences, akribeia is also used to emphasize the importance of striving for *correctness* with data and fact; we can often find errors or carelessness in the detail of scientific reports. Here content and form go together. If the content of research is basically good but it is presented in an article that does not read well, it may not reach out; the reader gets irritated and gives up. There is also the opposite, that a seductive, well-written article may get attention despite the fact its content is poor. It should go without saying that you should not only pay attention to the message of an article but also to details such as correct references. Those who are not living in English-speaking countries are clearly at a disadvantage as scientific articles today must be published in English to get cited and be added to your impact factor. If your English is good but is not your native language, your vocabulary is limited and you may miss the subtle meaning of words. There are translators, yes, but they are at an extra cost and unless they understand your topic they may not be able to express the actual message of what you write. My recommendation is that if you can, write in English and then let a friend whose mother tongue is English look at it and, if necessary, get the help of a translator, but finally you must make sure that the revision does not distort the message. Make sure that figures and diagrams are easy to read and well related to in the text. And it may sound trivial but check your spelling. If you make a presentation to an audience, speak clearly and not too fast. Especially at an international conference, most of the listeners have English as their second or third language.

- *Application of criteria for interpretation* – case theory puts emphasis on the validity and relevance of interpretations. We should use all our data and not leave any unattended to or unexplained. If we cannot get it into our conclusions and theory, perhaps we have to start again or at least point out that there are leftovers. We have to decide what seems reasonable and this is a judgement call. If we train ourselves to see alternative interpretations and not just 'promote our darlings', we can get far. The same goes for the persona factor and the conclusion is that *the researcher is the most important research instrument*. With a metaphor from music: the violin is dead without a violinist who keeps practising and improving his/her skills.

Many have pointed out that you risk ending up with a huge pile of data that you do not know what to do with. That is typically so if within the positivist paradigm you divide your research into linear steps: read the literature, make a plan, collect data, analyse the data, draw conclusions and, finally, write a report.

Grounded Theory (GT)

Barney Glaser and Anselm Strauss published their seminal book *The Discovery of Grounded Theory* in 1967. The *American Sociological Review* wrote: 'The authors successfully transmit the sense of adventure, the air of excitement and of positive apprehension over what is discovered as one tracks down clues and sorts among attractive alternatives.' Note the words *sense of adventure, air of excitement, positive apprehension* and *attractive alternatives*. They are all expressions of *passion*.

Here are some basic characteristics of GT, but as the continued text explains it takes effort to become a fully fledged GT researcher:

- GT is *inductive first* and *deductive second*. Contrary to positivist methods, the advice to the researcher is *not* to read up on extant literature. Instead, let reality tell its story by assuming 'a disciplined blank'. As with everything, we seldom manage 100% but awareness and training take us a long way. At a later step, new data can be compared with extant theory. Through *constant comparison*, a *snowballing learning effect* is achieved.

- GT is not about description but about *conceptualization,* the same as the scientific narrative. Descriptive generalization, common in quantitative research and most of qualitative research, leaves you with a perennial struggle, as can be seen in mainstream methods books. In qualitative research, the explicit goal is *description* characterized by such terms and concepts as accuracy, truth, trustworthiness and objectivity. Bazeley[11] lists sequences of them and all have a mission in analysis and interpretation. They are interrelated and overlap, thus showing the complexity and fuzziness of the world. They may all be relevant but their mass makes them difficult to get together: describe, compare, contrast, relate, extract, explain, contend, extend, defend, read, reflect, connect, evolve, theorize, scribble, doodle, and so on.

---

[11]Bazeley, 2013.

- *All is data* and data can be generated by using all conventional techniques and in whatever way you find meaningful. Sampling is *purposeful* and stops when *saturation* is reached; there is no random sampling.

- GT is an expression of pragmatic wisdom, using both explicit and tacit data. Data is organized in categories connected by a *core category*.

- Documentation of data is mainly done through continuous *memoing*. Memos are *theorizing write-ups* produced in a 'stream of consciousness' fashion.

- The phases of *coding* data strictly follow certain *rules and procedures*.

- *Sorting* leads to theory generation showing the relationships between concepts.

One of my first impressions of GT was not that of just another research method but I also saw it as a way of life. It had relevance for practice, 'tremendous grab' as Glaser expressed it. When I complained to him that I did not quite understand how to do a GT study and felt frustrated, he said, 'Evert, you understand more of GT than you think.' It was encouraging but I did not take it too literally. By introducing the complexity paradigm, merging explicit and tacit knowledge into pragmatic wisdom, applying it to the context of business and management and including the persona factor, I feel more confident. Knowledge does not only come from an academic ivory tower where professors open a window once in a while and announce to an admiring mass that they have seen the light and we had better do as they say. Scientific research must be accepted as an integral part of our lives, a merger of specialist knowledge and everyday life.

References to GT have already been made in this book and there are more to come. I consider GT the most complete and balanced research methodology available; demanding – but rewarding. It is probably the most cited methodology in the social sciences. Today, half a century after the first book and with all the follow-up books, articles, seminars and PhD theses, GT is more alive than ever. The first book accounted for the discovery of GT in an intellectual sense. It could have stopped there – but it did not. GT would not be complete before researchers started to use it more extensively.[12]

My first encounter with GT was in the 1970s when writing a PhD dissertation. I asked senior professors what they thought about GT – and they were lukewarm. One said: 'It was popular for a while but we seldom talk about it anymore.' GT was sticky and I decided to go direct to the source. But I could not find the authors. Imagine: there was no Google or other search engine at that time. I called the US Embassy in Stockholm and they were helpful. Within 15 minutes,

---

[12]An essay on my personal and professional relationship with Glaser, 'Grounded Glaser', is found in Martin & Gynnild, 2012, pp. 223–233.

they called back and gave me Glaser's private phone number in the San Francisco area. When going to the USA for a conference in 1984, I phoned him and asked for an appointment. He was reluctant and sounded quite grumpy. But I insisted and after a while he gave in and invited me to his home on a Saturday at 10am. We spent 6 hours together. He quickly loosened up and engaged himself in my problems and questions. Tired of teaching and the economic prospects it offered, he had left his chair at the University of California, San Francisco. He was also tired of the criticism of GT and the slowness of its adoption. The only discipline where GT was widely spread was nursing. Many cherry-picked GT strategies and merged them with qualitative research, claiming they had done GT. They had not. This shows how difficult it can be to use a research methodology.

Glaser impressed me by using GT in his personal life. He had built a house on the slope of a hill using GT and wrote a book about the experience – *Experts versus Laymen* (1972). He started a small and successful financial company and a real estate company that made him wealthy. He also started his own publishing company, but for other reasons. He got dissatisfied with conventional publishers and felt he had to follow their regulations and decisions instead of his own mind. He started Sociology Press in 1970 to control the situation and has since written and edited 36 books which can be ordered on the Internet. He deals with every order personally and finds it a way to keep track of who buys his books and frequently enters into contact with them on GT issues. He is also the publisher of the peer-reviewed online journal *Grounded Theory Review*. When we parted he was going to go wind-surfing. He was 54 years old and learning. 'I just apply GT', he explained. GT is created to be usable, to be validated in action: walk your talk.

How difficult it can be even for seasoned senior scientists to handle methodology is illustrated by the following episode. In 1991 Strauss and Corbin published a book called *Basics of Qualitative Research* with the subtitle *Techniques and procedures for developing grounded theory*.[13] Glaser's reaction was aggressive. He considered that the book violated the idea of GT by categorizing GT as one among many qualitative methods – what he refers to as *qualitative data analysis* (QDA). Classic GT is not just a qualitative method, and in line with case theory considers the conventional quantitative/qualitative categorization irrelevant.[14]

He first demanded that his former co-author withdraw the book, which Strauss refused. Glaser then wrote a short book, *Basics of Grounded Theory*, with

---

[13]A 4th revised edition, by Corbin & Strauss, was published in 2015. After Strauss' death, Corbin appears as first author.

[14]Quantitative aspects of GT are explained in Glaser, 2008.

the subtitle *Emergence vs. forcing.*[15] Page by page, he explained the difference between GT and the methodology presented in Strauss and Corbin. The persona factor was highly involved in this controversy, which explains part of the dispute, but I cannot go into that here. We all thought that Glaser and Strauss had become personal enemies but they had not; they stayed close friends until Strauss died in 1997.

Glaser resumed our contact by sending me his book about the controversy. I then decided to invite him to Stockholm University to give some seminars on GT. Glaser said yes and told me that this was the first time since he had left the university world that he had been invited overseas. In retrospect, I feel I did something important without realizing it. Later, when Glaser gave me one of his new books, he had written by hand: 'For Evert, who started me on the worldwide trek to this book. Thanks for waking me up 20 years ago. Barney.'

In his book dealing with the controversy with Strauss, he outlined what is now called *classic* or *orthodox* GT. The Corbin and Strauss book is pedagogical and easier for researchers to use but this makes it thick (at 456pp). Glaser has since written a series of short books on specific GT themes to explain each in more detail and compiled *Readers* where you can meet GT applied in practice. When I talk about GT, I stick to the Glaser version and then we can talk about books on QDA where GT has been inspirational. Glaser does not condemn this and says that QDA methods are quite worthy, respectable and acceptable – but they are not GT. He reminds us that the goal of GT is to generate theory that accounts for a pattern of behaviour which is relevant and problematic for those involved in research and practice.

Classic GT is defined in the following way:

> GT is a straightforward methodology. It is a comprehensive, integrated and highly structured, yet eminently flexible process that takes the researcher from the first day in the field to a finished written theory. Following the full suite of GT procedure based on the constant comparison method, results in a smooth uninterrupted emergent analysis and the generation of substantive or formal theory.[16]

GT concepts and guidelines are underused in business and management. GT studies come up with concepts and categories that do not easily become part of business and management textbooks or reference lists in articles. The conventional business and management terms, concepts and categories stay put. Box 10.1 gives some examples developed for business and management by GT researchers.

---

[15]Glaser, 1992.

[16]Glaser with Holton, 2004, p. 3.

Box 10.1   Business and Management Concepts
Developed in GT Studies

A favourite study of mine from the 1960s is Simmons' 'The Milkman and His Customer: A cultivated relationship'.[17] The researcher studied sociology and had not taken courses in marketing but had practical experience as a milkman. By using GT he developed a theory of relationship marketing (RM) based on the core concept of *cultivated relationship*. Simmons' case was told 20 years before researchers in marketing claimed they had invented RM. This single case still represents the core of RM; it makes grand theory. Home delivery of milk is a small industry today but it has had its offsprings. Stew Leonard started out as a milkman, then built a dairy product store and now operates 4 huge fresh food stores in Connecticut and New York. Despite its thousands of customers each day, it is known for personal service and for cultivating relationships. It practices RM.

In his GT study of *Folkoperan*, an opera in Stockholm, Sweden, the researcher used interactive research through presence, observation, personal interviews and focus group data generation.[18] He followed the production of an opera performance from the first meeting of those involved, through rehearsals and other meetings, and he was there at the opening night and the discussions that followed after that. He spent the day and often evenings and weekends with the opera team and they had their meals together. He did not understand Swedish but turned this handicap into a strength; he was forced to sharpen his perception of non-verbal data. His observations were later discussed and checked with the opera staff. The outcome of the study of the process was the concepts of *ambiguity*, *transformation* and *reflexivity*. This is substantive theory, emanating from a particular case, which could probably be generalized to higher theory zones.

Another example is the case of B2B selling, which, as the author explains, is a complex area that is not sufficiently conceptualized.[19] He found the core category to be *business manoeuvring* with the sub-categories of *business standardization, business fraternization, personalization* and *probationary business rationalization*. It is substantive theory which could also climb the higher theory zones, as well as provide mid-range theory simplification to be used by practitioners.

Finally, an economist disappointed with mainstream methodology and its output, decided to try out classic GT.[20] By studying 12 businesses he came up with *opportunizing* as the core variable. It explains how companies create, seize and exploit situations to secure survival and growth. Opportunizing is what businesspeople do all the time. It can be further explained through 3 primary sub-core variables: *perpetual opportunizing, triggering opportunizing* and *spasmodic opportunizing*. Then there are further sub-core variables which are also dependent on each other.

To understand the meaning of this, I suggest you read their reports. Reading the full story of how someone did a GT study makes the methodology and the results more tangible. Look up articles in the *Grounded Theory Review* (free online access), and Glaser has edited several *Readers* with examples of GT applications.

---

[17]Simmons, 1993.

[18]Lowe, 1995.

[19]Åge, 2009.

[20]Christiansen, 2006.

It would take too much space here to try to explain GT, its systematic approach to analysis and interpretation and the practical activities it embraces. Glaser has created a 'supportive empire' around classic GT. You can become part of it and get GT advice straight from the horse's mouth. Here are my recommendations:

- You are best off with a personal mentor who can guide you and follow your progress while you are working on a GT project. The mentor must have practical GT experience; having read up on GT is not sufficient. And after everyone had talked about the difficulties of grasping all the subtleties of GT, Glaser got tired and said: 'Just do it!' You have to practise a method to fully understand it.

- If you do not have a mentor in your researchscape, contact others using classic GT by looking up the Grounded Theory Institute. You can become a member and actively communicate with others on GT matters. Under 'Home', its website presents useful checklists, one showing the main differences between classic GT and GT variants, and the other the classic GT process. A brief but easy-to-read article is Glaser with Holton (2004): 'Remodeling grounded theory' (which can be downloaded via Google).

- A book by Holton and Walsh (2017) is a practical 'how to' guide to classic GT.

- GT fans have put together a book, *Grounded Theory: The Philosophy, Method, and Work of Barney Glaser.*[21] Chapter 3 by Guthrie and Lowe, 'Getting through the PhD process using GT: A supervisor-researcher perspective', is useful for anyone, not just for PhD students.

Mulling and Muddling Through

Mulling and *mull things over*[22] mean to think about something deeply and at length. That this is a big issue in our lives is shown by the large number of synonyms there are for mull: ponder, reflect, consider the pros and cons, brood on, evaluate and examine, to mention a few. It is trial and error.

Also in quantitative research there is considerable muddling and mulling which materialize in tsunamis of indexes, scales, decimals, etc. Analysis is breaking down reality into smaller and smaller categories and concepts, 'boxes'. It should include putting the parts together in useful patterns and building something up to more general and grander theory. This requires interpretation and the absence of the glue of tacit knowledge and a systemic, holistic mind prohibits this. The breaking down has taken over and the building up at the end of a quantitative article often stands out as an embarrassment to science – this is especially so in sections where they talk about how useful their results are for managers.

---

[21]Martin & Gynnild, 2012.

[22]Wolcott, 1994.

Political scientist Charles Lindblom became famous for his article 'The science of muddling through'.[23] (1959). Political scientists muddle through – although they do not really know how, they keep on and at best learn in the process. Can it really be called science, as in the article title? It can if you accept complexity. The alternative rejects complexity and with that also applied research and pragmatism. In quantitative research, you have already dismissed the disturbing data, made facilitating assumptions and adjusted the research to fit a mathematical and statistical language. Microeconomics, a sort of pure theory, has already been given as an example.

But muddling through is everywhere when you make simplifying assumptions about reality, even sweeping assumptions that the 'normal person'or the 'majority of scientists agree'. Muddling through is what you have to do when you attack a problem or theme that has no theory, or if you don't trust the received theory.

The administrative man is the myth of the rational decision-maker, starting with the ranking of values and objectives, then the analysis of alternatives and their consequences, and eventually choosing the 'best' alternative. The reality is bounded rationality: imperfect data, limited analysis, little or no explicit theory, and quick decisions to meet a deadline. This is of course so. There are difficult trade-offs to make between alternatives and a lack of time and other resources. My personal observation is that government bureaucracies are breaking laws, that there is considerable corruption and that those officials who realize this are afraid of blowing the whistle. But most have been so programmed by the 'system' that they do not see that they are working in a pseudo-world. Those with formal or informal power have taken control of their lives and this in turn trickles into our lives as a sticky syrup. Government organizations, both politicians and employees follow an incremental muddling-through model and just build on the existing behaviour. The system is hostile to reform and innovation and it is inefficient for us citizens.

Software for Analysis and Interpretation

A US professor once triumphantly told me that 'we are now turning qualitative stuff quantitative to make it truly scientific'. He did not ask for my reaction. He was confident that his 'discovery' impressed me, so I found it meaningless to argue and said nothing. Later, I was told that 'we can now analyse words, observations and other qualitative data rigorously with the help of computer programs – gone are the days of anecdotal and subjective interpretations'.

Those who said so were trapped by one-sided training in positivist thinking and its research techniques. The truth about software is that it 'will not do the

---

[23]Lindblom, 1959, 1979.

analysis for you, nor can it think for you. Rather, its data management and querying capacity support you to carry out *your* analysis by removing the limitations imposed by paper processing and human memory.'[24]

Changing language from words to numbers and to computer logic will not do the trick, but simultaneously using many languages can increase the validity and relevance of our research. We have met the mixed methods approach. I find it only natural to apply this in whichever way you think beneficial for enhancing knowledge. I have also explained that explicit knowledge and tacit knowledge are equally necessary to achieve scientific results. Useful outcomes always take precedence over research techniques.

Qualitative data analysis programmes keep developing, along with digital communication and social media. From having been primarily a coding tool, the software has broadened to facilitate thinking, linking data, writing and doing graphics. It has become increasingly flexible and able to address complexity. It is important to note that software is not doing the analysis and interpretation for you but rather facilitating it in many ways, for example the retrieval of data and combinations and relieving you of time-consuming sorting jobs. Today, software for analysing words and text can store data in an orderly way, provide structures and hierarchies of data, perform certain analytical tasks and respond to questions that the researcher puts to the data. This can support the life of the researcher and increase research productivity. Software assists, but it is not the boss. It does not take over the human researcher's role as analyst/interpreter and the need to continuously fine-tune analytical and interpretive skills:

> computers cannot perform the creative and intellectual task of devising which categories or types of data are relevant to the process being investigated, or what is a meaningful comparison, or of generating appropriate research questions and propositions with which to interrogate the data, and so on.[25]

Many software programs for *computer-assisted qualitative data analysis software* (with the pompous acronym CAQDAS) now exist and keep developing. Among them are Atlas.ti, HyperRESEARCH, MAXODA, NVivo and The Ethnograph. I have limited experience of using them so I will not give specific recommendations. They are also continuously being updated and improved. To make them useful, you have to read about them, but, above all, practise them with a reflective mind.[26]

Recall that in case theory quantitative and qualitative are just two of many properties of research and not overriding categories, and it is about addressing complexity with whatever tools there are.

---

[24]Bazeley & Jackson, 2013.

[25]Mason, 1994, p. 108.

[26]Bazeley & Jackson, 2013.

Many witness how time-consuming, intellectually difficult and emotionally frustrating the analysis and interpretation of piles of qualitative data can be. Lyn and Tom Richards have described the situation of a 5-year project at the end of year 1:[27]

> [The project] had already amassed a vast quantity of very rich, very unstructured material: informal interviews, field notes and taped discussions ... As the material built up, the task of controlling it became paramount. The choice appeared to be between reducing most of the data to statistical format and creating innovative methods. The project was not hostile to statistical reducing ... But it aimed at questions whose answers could not be quantitative ... two surveys later, we had accrued a substantial body of superficial responses to questions about interaction.

This is how the Richards got started on developing the NVivo software for analysis of qualitative data.

Constant Comparison

A key to qualitative research analysis is comparison. Data is compared with data, with existing theory and with the results of previous research. This continuous comparison is part of a sense-making process where patterns are formed and turned into concepts, categories and eventually theories.

Meta-analysis is the name given to statistical methods that combine evidence from several studies, preferably randomized experiments that in evidence-based research are declared as the Gold Standard of science. It does not include other aspects such as results from qualitative research or case studies and it does not accept tacit knowledge. So a meta-analysis is not the same as a synthesis of all available knowledge. A criticism is that it only relies on published studies and can be driven by political and other agendas. The risk is, however, that there is a hard push for a limited slice of research as the sole truth.

I should like to draw special attention to the key issues of *conceptualization* and *contextualization*. They are interwoven and stress different aspects of theory generation. Concepts are needed, and in times of major changes new concepts – *reconceptualization* – are urgently required. The common mix-up between the term, which is a label, and a concept, which is an idea, and the content behind the facade provided by the label is referred to as *reification* – mistaking the representation of an object for the object itself. *Relabelling* is not the same as reconceptualization, although branding and re-branding are used in marketing to create perceptions among customers about the content of a product or service, sometimes linked to improvements, but sometimes without altering

---

[27]Richards & Richards, 1994, pp. 146–147.

the content. A postmodern marketer, though, may claim that the customer's perception of the brand is the reality and that the real reality is unreal.

Contextualization refers to the need to place single data in a broader context, that is, to generate theory. Theory orders data in a context. A theory is a roadmap and a good roadmap makes it possible for travellers to navigate in a territory that is unknown to them. When conceptualization has taken place but not been extended enough to provide a context, bits and pieces of knowledge risk being misunderstood and misused. Customers do not live isolated lives and consume a single service at a time as if it was a standalone. They live in a context and consume a service mix in all sorts of combinations. If I am treated well in a store, I am likely to go back. If the driver of my taxi to the hotel is unpleasant, I will be in a bad mood entering the hotel which will affect my behaviour and my perception of the hotel.

Theory generation, moving from raw data to conceptualization and contextualization, may be the most valuable contribution a scholar can offer. As researchers, we are rarely if ever innovators; we rather start out as observers and messengers. However, it is not enough to be reporters of events. We have to add value to the phenomena we present; that is what scholarship is about.[28]

If you start on an abstract level, you have no lifeline to the empirical ground; you hover in thin air. When theories are not well grounded, going back and testing them is not enough. Because of preconceived hypotheses, concepts and categories, the test may just become a self-fulfilling prophecy. For example, service and B2B marketing used to be (and still is, in student textbooks) forced theory, thus missing the substance of these areas. When service marketing and B2B marketing, through research based on real-world data, extracted relationships, networks and interaction as core variables, these areas were marked as special cases, despite the fact that they constitute the bulk of marketing. Later, relationship marketing and CRM were labelled a special case, whereas in reality they offer a paradigm shift.[29]

By continuous theory generation and following the format of the hermeneutic helix, there is no strict distinction between generating and testing theory. If the researcher is guided by a desire to understand more and improve theory continuously, the never-ending journey becomes a continuous test of ever-tentative theory.

I offer here an invitation to *scientific pluralism*. We are in an eternal dilemma, constantly having to ask the questions: What do we really know? What is it worth? How do we get to know more? This ongoing journey is a fascinating treasure hunt for many but for others it is the avoidance of assassination – a scary monster. We probably would all like law and order and simplicity and security. To get that, however, we would have to do away with the magic of life

---

[28]Glaser, 2001, specifically deals with the move from description to conceptualization.

[29]Gummesson, 2017.

and convert science into a set of regulations and institutions, which is increasingly being done by the bibliometrics system. We then restrict the scientist – the discoverer, innovator and entrepreneur – to being a controlled and manageable bureaucrat heeding pre-set routines. But new knowledge should not be a threat, even if it temporarily might shatter our careers, received theories and beliefs.

With a pluralistic strategy, we will develop a diverse community of individual 'knowers', offering a medley of 'processes of knowing' and consequently a variety in what is 'known'. In my view, pluralism is the only way to keep science alert, innovative and entrepreneurial.Compose your own methodological symphony. Like searching for a fugitive, using helicopter lights and police patrol cars, surround a phenomenon from many directions and at a point in time you may catch it.

Conclusion – or confusion?

If you have read the chapter and feel confused it is all right – but there is no reason to feel frustrated. You have only been confronted with the scientific research reality which too many shun. To design true simplification is legitimate but too much in research is not simple – it is simplistic in the derogatory sense of simple. Case theory analysis and interpretation still have many miles to travel before we can feel reasonably satisfied – but this is so too in positivist and quantitative research.

This very much leaves you with an unsolved problem, but it also opens up for your contributions. In the pragmatic sense, you have to do something in the meantime even if there is no final answer. Do that, listen to advice from others – but not from omnipresent and compulsive fault-finders. They may say you have done wrong or that you must improve your study.

A shot of Absolut Vodka could make you more innovative, although you may lose in rigour. Let us take the risk with Box 10.2.

Box 10.2   An Absolut Shot[30]

In an early effort to establish whether there was a market for Absolut Vodka, the concept was tested. The USA and Canada would be the first markets; they constituted 70% of the world market of vodkas. A market research institute was assigned by the future importer to study the potential market and assess the chances for Absolut. The conclusion was that Absolut would be an absolute loser:

(Continued)

---

[30]Hamilton, 2000; quotations from pp. 258, 260 and 272.

(Continued)

- Vodka was not associated with Sweden but with Russia.

- The name was wrongly spelt – Absolut – but the correct 'absolute' was a common word and could not be protected as a brand.

- The see-through bottle would not be seen when it stood on a shelf in a store.

- The ergonomics of the bottle were not bartender-friendly; it was easy to drop because of the short neck which gave a bad grip and the pieces of the bottle would forever be lost on the floor.

Everything in the study had face value. It sounded right but represented just a portion of the truth. It was not put in the context of the network of people, events and perceptions that would together make up the outcome. It was a huge simplification, still following the format of mainstream market research. As luck would have it, the decision-makers did not buy the results. The market study teaches us several lessons about research, science and finding the real truth.

Absolut Vodka became a commercial hit. Vodka is a generic product that used to be the cheapest way for a Swedish worker to get drunk on a Saturday afternoon. In the 1970s the producer asked: How can we export Swedish vodka? There were already well-known brands like Smirnoff. Today, 50 years later, Swedish vodka is one of the top global liquor brands. Research question: How did it happen? Purpose: Describe, analyse and interpret the process and come up with credible conclusions.

Even in retrospect, it is hard to know which combination of brand, bottle design, product quality, premium pricing, relationship marketing, advertising, distribution network, C2C interaction and public relations made Absolut a smashing hit. Or was it the timing? Or skilled implementation? For some unknown reason, tastes were changing from brown whisky and rum to colourless gin and vodka.

Success factors cannot be broken down into individual activities and strategies, such as pricing or advertising, and then ranked according to importance. They form a unity where the parts interact. In line with chaos theory and the tipping-point concept, supported by the old adage 'the straw that broke the camel's back', even a small factor can determine the final outcome. Therefore, the success of Absolut cannot be explained by statistical, deductive and reductionist analysis techniques. You cannot just ask customers what is most important and whether or not they would drink Absolut. You cannot know if you are asking the right questions and consumers may not know the answers to your questions – but answer anyway. The launch of a product is not influenced by one single, independent strategy at a time. It is influenced by the whole – a network of products, places, people, locations, emotions, experiences, and so on.

As a businessperson, you should read the case. It gives a taste of the many relationships and networks that contributed to the successful outcome. There are networks that could only be partially controlled by someone and where the spontaneous interaction of individual actors made things happen. The networks had many chauffeurs and hubs, which, in some divine and self-organizing manner, made Absolut a winner.

11

FOURTH FOCUS: RESEARCH QUALITY AND PRODUCTIVITY

Quality and productivity will be used as overriding concepts for the evaluation of both the research process and its outcome. Quality is about what is good or bad research, and productivity is the ratio between the output and the input of research resources. In publishing, the evaluation is affected by the explicit and tacit knowledge of editors and reviewers and increasingly by the systems for international standardization of research and education.

Quality and productivity aspects have appeared on and off in the previous chapters, especially in Chapter 10 where the focus was on analysis and interpretation. In case theory, quality and productivity are used as key terms but evaluation and review are more common in the methodology literature. All these terms represent fuzzy concepts and we have to treat them accordingly. I draw on my own experience; the methods literature; the review process of article and book scripts and conference papers; the use of bibliometrics; the selection of winners of the Nobel Prize in Economic Sciences; how business and government organizations handle quality/productivity; and how stakeholders, first of all customers and citizens, perceive quality. Researchers can learn good and bad lessons from all of these.

We are confronting complex issues that require contingent solutions and reflection. Quality and productivity can sometimes be precisely defined and operationalized but they also have to be combined with judgement calls and pragmatic wisdom. 'I know it when I see it' is a way of defining quality that does not sound scientific in the classic sense; it is based on pragmatic wisdom. It is sometimes the best and quickest way. It is also used by hard-nosed quantitative researchers whose favourite expression is 'rigorous research' at the same time as they use expressions like 'it is reasonable to conclude that' or, in a derogatory sense, 'case study research is anecdotal'.

Objectivity cannot do without subjectivity and intersubjectivity, and explicit knowledge cannot do without tacit knowledge. For example, the decision to release a wine onto the market is taken by a single person or a small group of connoisseurs with superior noses, tongues and eyes. They sniff and taste and look at the wine. No better method has been found. *The Wine Bible*[1] lists over 80 quality dimensions of wine and several more can be added. Many of us have been to wine tasting and listened to the fancy lingo of the experts and noted their facial expressions and rituals. So there are explicit quality dimensions and tacit ones, and it ends up in the condensed conclusion of most of us: I like the wine, or it is all right but no more, or it is not good.

This frustrates positivism and technology freaks: Let us make an instrument that does it rigorously with quantitative indicators! Such indicators can be used for easily identifiable quality dimensions like the content of alcohol but not for the subtle dimensions that form the consumer's experience of a wine.

The overall assessment of a research contribution is also a nose-tongue-and-eye exercise. This is especially true for innovative research that challenges the existing paradigm and mainstream 'truths'.

The standard definition of productivity is 'the ratio between output and input': the higher the output in relation to the input, the higher the productivity. It is also expressed as low cost per unit and productivity improvement is often the same as cost-cutting. A measure of the productivity of an individual researcher or a research group is their number of publications. The cost of research is a constant headache as research projects need extensive funding and frequently take longer than foreseen.

Note: There is no general trade-off between quality and productivity. It has to be established in each specific situation. The idea that higher quality costs more seems to be cut in stone but is mere mythology. Higher quality can cost more, cost less or cost the same as before; it is contingent on the situation. So too in scientific research.

The term *efficiency* is used for a combination of quality and productivity. It simply means *doing things right*. It is distinguished from *effectiveness* which refers to *doing the right things*, for example asking important research questions.[2] In academic research, this is not self-evident. A PhD student told me once that she wanted to study the co-creation of value. Her professor said that this was not a good idea 'because co-creation is difficult to define and measure'. His preoccupation was the research process – doing things right (here meaning quantitative, positivistic research) – but not doing the right things. Doing the right things in science are addressing issues of relevance and using a methodology that fits the topic. In innovation research, when we are travelling unexplored roads, it may turn out that we did the wrong thing but that is also

---

[1]MacNeil, 2001.

[2]I avoid the terms efficiency and effectiveness as they are easily mixed up and cause misunderstandings.

a result to be learnt from. The project cannot be accepted as right, but all the same it contributes to our understanding.

Productivity was introduced in the 1920s in the manufacturing processes of standard components coming out of a factory assembly line. Input then was the cost of manufacturing and both output and input could be well defined, especially as the margin of error in industrial components sometimes has to be miniscule. By developing and automating processes and monitoring electronic chips to the minute detail, manufacturers managed to reduce the number of defect chips from 80% to almost nil. It required investment in systems, equipment and people but this cost was trifling per component. Motorola became known for its *zero-defects strategy* which meant just 2–3 defect electronic chips in a million. This was a dramatic increase in quality and productivity and the price of components could be reduced to a tiny fraction of what it used to be.

Is the same approach applicable to research? In answering this question, it is necessary to understand that *the productivity ratio works for known and repetitive processes under complete control with unambiguously defined indicators. The ratio does not work for new findings and new research approaches, i.e. discontinuities, paradigm shifts, innovation and entrepreneurship.* As these are hailed as the keys to the development of a nation's welfare, we should take the consequences and support research where individuals and researchscapes are given the freedom to follow their own minds and take risks.

Sometimes an abundance of data that has required extensive archival research, large surveys, numerous interviews, audio recordings and transcripts during a lengthy period of time is mistaken for high quality. Quality will not forever go up; after a while it enters a state of diminishing returns. Rich descriptions can become filthy rich and thick ones can become obese, all leading to a reduction in both productivity and quality. We have to strive for bounded rationality with a satisficing outcome, all within our pragmatic wisdom.

Extant theory as well as conventional research techniques can both enhance and impede the quality and productivity of research. A lot of theory and methodology in business and management are inadequate but are applied anyway. Rational explanations for abandoning them often do not reach out. One reason is the persona factor – the originator is a respected academic with a high profile. In contrast, unknown researchers can produce excellent research that is never taken notice of.

Quality evaluation in the social sciences is mainly tied to the reliability and rigour of the research process and less – sometimes not at all – to the value and usefulness of the research results. In business and management, the validity and relevance of both the research methodology of producing and delivering something, and the ensuing action and its results must be in focus.

Assessing research processes and scientific contributions is obviously a challenge. One of the dilemmas is to use the right criteria. There is a big difference between law-and-order-based science, such as deductively testing hypotheses, and innovation where free-wheeling creativity and unconventional behaviour are the hallmark.

Quality/productivity approaches in business and management practice have been the object of intense research and improvements since the 1980s, but I do not find that scientific research has developed in the same constructive way. Conducting an open dialogue will increase awareness and help us improve the assessment of research. The problem is hidden behind conventions, unwarranted claims, rituals, images and academic, political and administrative efforts to monopolize research quality and productivity. It has become a forceful system and the individual academic can do very little about it. So the old saying 'If you can't beat them, join them' becomes a reality, at least for the time being. Fortunately, there is considerable discontentment with the current systems.

In summary, there are several problems with quality/productivity in research and education (Table 11.1):

Table 11.1   Quality/productivity problems in research

- Research is often driven by other than scientific purposes: financial interests, fads and fashion, media hype, political values, administrative issues and new technology. IT is the most obvious technology that currently controls our private lives and jobs; we frequently become its servants instead of being served by it.

- Despite valuable contributions from numerous thinkers and authors of books and articles, today's research and education in the social sciences is primarily driven by positivism from the Classic Scientific Revolution of the 1600s, and not by the developments of the past 100 years, simply put from Einstein onwards. Quantitative research is by default treated as the gold standard of science.

- There is a preoccupation with the accuracy of fragmented data, not considering its context, interdependency and the need for theory generation.

- Although innovation and entrepreneurship are held up as top priorities, innovators and entrepreneurs are met with suspicion.

- The careless categorization of phenomena is starting civil wars in science, blocking our vision and leading us to issues of no import.

- Methodological ritual is getting most of the attention in research and the value of the outcome is often treated lightly or not at all.

The following sections present criteria that can be used in case theory when studying business and management issues. They represent a pragmatic view based on a balance between criteria that catch the essence of research, those that are understandable for researchers and those that can realistically be implemented.

Quality Criteria in the Methods Literature

I was recently asked to evaluate research proposals for certain EU-sponsored programmes. I declined for lack of time, but primarily for the feeling of uncertainty that the evaluation criteria gave me. Among them were: 'scientific quality of the proposal is the prime selection criteria'; the proposal should have 'high scientific relevance for the research field'; and it should be 'sound' and 'rigorous'. These criteria all seem reasonable but none can be objectively established. They are fuzzy and can only be assessed by combining explicit and tacit knowledge with the persona of the examiners. And also I knew nothing about those who would evaluate my evaluation.

This section presents examples of recommendations from the methods literature. It feels natural to start with Yin who recommends 4 basic criteria:[3] *construct validity* (identifying operational measures), *internal validity* (when looking for causality), *external validity* (another term for generalizability) and *reliability* (the results can be replicated by others). Yin claims that these 'are common to all social science methods'. As you have learnt already, I disagree with this conclusion – all methods must be adapted to the context in which they are applied. Furthermore, Yin's criteria are derived from the positivist and quantitative paradigm. I agree with Lee (2006) that we need 'contingent criteria' to evaluate qualitative research in management, but that there are institutionalized biases in favour of quantitative research. Thomas & Magilvy (2011) go further and considers reliability and even validity irrelevant in case study research.

From Yin's criteria, I will connect to the general social sciences methods literature. Its 3 most frequently mentioned quality criteria are *reliability*, *validity* and *generalizability*. Here are my comments on them.

Reliability (replicability) refers to the extent to which research can be replicated by others who will arrive at similar results. It is held up as the gold test of scientific results. I have often pointed out that reliability is not a reliable way of evaluating case theory.[4] Replication may not be attainable when you study complexity; it may not even be desirable. As the complexity paradigm includes ongoing change, reliability cannot merely be about control and replication. Reliability in theory generation must encompass evolution and open up to continuous improvements through reflection, dialogue and more profound interpretation.

If several researchers present the same findings, these seem likely to be 'true'. It may however be no more than a self-fulfilling prophecy. If the researchers were educated by professors who read the same literature, belong to the same professional

---

[3]Yin, 2014, pp. 45–49.

[4]Gummesson, 2000a, pp. 91, 190.

associations, write in the same journals and present papers at the same conferences, it would be highly surprising if they came up with different results.

A single researcher or a team will reach a point where their resources – knowledge, money, time, access – are consumed. This may occur long before saturation has been reached. The results can be seen as tentative, but most knowledge is tentative especially in periods of change. Mid-range theory is tentative but can be accepted as the best we have at a certain point in time and as therefore useful. Good checklists are helpful and requested by practitioners.

Reliability can perform a few important jobs in case theory:

- *discover mistakes* – anyone can make mistakes and others can help find and correct them
- *expose incompetence* – is the researcher knowledgeable enough?
- *uncover fraud* – a police function, to curb dishonest research and nail the villain.

Validity in its generic sense is of cardinal importance in case theory. The first decision in terms of validity concerns what research to prioritize, what research questions to ask and what the purpose of the study is. Have the researchers been able to capture the essence of the phenomenon they are chasing or have they studied something else? Did the researcher shoot a deer during the hunting season or was the victim a cow grazing in the field? My experience is that reliability is used as a substitute for validity when validity seems beyond reach. It then plays the part of a 'validity crutch'; the researcher establishes reliability and assumes validity.

Generalizability was treated in Chapter 6 in the discussion on theory generation. Here are a few more aspects relating to quality. A routine argument by positivist research for rejecting cases is that the outcome cannot be generalized; it is not representative of the phenomenon we are studying. Figure 6.1 showed my view of the iterative trajectory from generating substantive theory valid only for a very specific domain, through mid-range theory to grand and universally valid theory.

When generalizability is brought up, it is usually in a statistical and descriptive sense. It is taken for granted that numbers are important and can be generalized, as long as they were contrived according to an approved quantitative procedure, but in my view the outcome is 'rigorous noledge' characterized by 'precise approximation', 'precisely perhaps' and non-existent people defined as 'averages with distributions' and 'percentages'. Probabilities, distributions, etc. can only be meaningful in specific instances; they are not generally valid and they create a blurred image of real people.

'Highest quality' is not something absolute; quality is always relative to its context. Quality can be a technically well-defined concept in manufacturing, such as delivering no parts that malfunction or break down, but it can also be *customer perceived quality* and *value-in-use* which are the subjective experiences of those who buy and use a product, such as a car. If you buy a cheap second-hand car, you know that it may break down and not run forever. In relation to your needs and wallet, this car can be experienced as high quality as it makes transportation more comfortable than before. If you can afford a new Toyota Lexus or a Lamborghini, high quality means something different.

Guba and Lincoln (1994) argue that qualitative research should not be evaluated by means of reliability and validity alone – those criteria were designed for positivistic research. They suggest *trustworthiness*, summarizing the *credibility*, *transferability*, *dependability*, *conformability* and *authenticity* of a study and its results. Credibility is about the links between your data and your findings and how reasonable you perceive them to be; transferability is generalizability, if you can transfer knowledge from one case to another; dependability, how careful the researcher has been in data generation, conceptualization, analysis and interpretation; conformability, how well your results are supported by those who are involved in what you study and what other researchers have found; and authenticity, how genuine or real the research stands out.

All these guidelines show that we need pragmatic wisdom to do scientific research; explicit, objective, rigorous, rational and the like are neither sufficient nor realistic.

Through constant comparison, which is held up as a major strategy in qualitative research but could be used in all types of research, others could bring research forward without feeling obliged to build on it in a strictly cumulative sense. You do, for example, 3 case studies and then compare them with cases carried out by others. As a case includes multiple nodes and links, the comparison can seldom be direct but it can still add useful knowledge. This is well in line with my own thinking.

Seale (1999) lists several detailed efforts to establish general quality criteria but advocates that such *criteriology* is non-productive. He sees qualitative research as a craft skill, and researcher experience and persona as the most valuable instruments. He wants to erase the borders between philosophical, political and theoretical positions; research could benefit from whatever there is: conventional positivism, interpretivism, constructivism, postmodernism, and so on. But he is not as eclectic as I am here when claiming that we should include approaches from the natural sciences and the humanities as well.

Quality/Productivity of Published Material

This section draws on my experience of publishing articles in scientific journals and sometimes in practitioner journals and news media; writing books, contributing with book chapters and editing books; speaking at international conferences, starting conference series, chairing conferences and publishing in conference proceedings. In addition, I have continuously reviewed journal, book and conference scripts, been a member of some 25 editorial and review boards, and guest editor on several occasions.[5]

The next and last chapter (12) is focused on aspects of reporting case theory, but these aspects are also quality/productivity concerns. It is an example of how the Fourth and Fifth Foci are fuzzy sets and thus overlapping.

The reasons for scientists to publish continuously are to disseminate new research for others to learn from, to encourage others to replicate your studies or build on them, and to make sure you can advance in academia or at least keep your current meal ticket. Publishing is the most important part of reporting academic research, while in consulting oral presentations together with management summaries are most valuable.

In doing research you need to consider the state of the art of your subject and to select references from extant literature. When you write articles or books, you also need to decide where to publish them. Therefore, the following sections will cover references and publications.

References

By reading the literature you learn what has been done and you can avoid reinventing the wheel. Remember, however, that if you start your empirical work with a truly inductive approach, you should keep an open mind and put the reading of the literature on hold until later.

Today's overwhelming amount of published material is both an asset and a nuisance. Most of it is in English but a lot is published in both well-known and lesser known tongues. For example, German, Spanish and French are widespread languages in which business and management literature is published. It is difficult to be well read even if you limit your literature search to English and your own native tongue.

The US literature has dominated, and still does. The Americans hard sell their publications and the content is somehow perceived as being international, although it may only reflect specific US thinking and conditions. The USA has 5% of the world population and sometimes I even see in articles that 'the world is now one global community'. English-language journals can increasingly be read globally as English takes over in science and there is a tendency to devalue what is written in other languages. Considering the millions of different environments

---

[5]For the experience of others and research on the subject of writing and publishing, see e.g. Firat, 2010; Tadajewski, 2016.

in which business and management take place – nations, industries, cities, companies, government organizations, etc. – it is essential to recognize diversity and variety. There are commonalities to consider but people and cultures are not 'averages' or 'majorities versus minorities' in the positivist, statistical sense. Persona and researchscape properties have to be taken into account; they cannot be standardized as 'global'. Global is taking on a new meaning through high tech, but until we are replaced by robots we are still human beings with high-touch needs. Increasingly, US journals are accepting more international submissions, but is this because those authors have adopted a US research and writing style?

Using keywords to search for references is technically possible but gives a lot of noise as well as missing vital references. Such short cuts can turn into detours or even lead you totally astray. You only find the acknowledged literature which has been widely communicated. I could list articles that are highly cited but were misleading even when first published and those that were once relevant but are today hopelessly obsolete – and still appear as standard references. Note that the more you are cited, the more you are cited. It is a self-generating process that does not guarantee the value of the reference. The reference list partially becomes a name-dropping list. Feyerabend (1975) pointed out that the *consistency criterion* from the positivist paradigm – that new theories should be consistent with established ones – will only make defunct theory and cherished prejudices live on.

Long ago I found that the best way to keep up with goings-on was to participate in conferences and accept invitations to give guest lectures at universities and other organizations. It meant high-touch interaction with people during sessions but also being there at coffee breaks, lunches, dinners, cultural events, and sometimes being invited to their homes. I got to know about their projects and thoughts straight from the horse's mouth and long before they were published. I made friends and built a supportive international network far beyond mechanical and electronic systems. High tech facilitates personal contact but does not replace it; it is both/and.

In conclusion, search for references that make sense to you wherever you can find them. Just searching for references in top journals will severely limit your possibilities and you may easily be trapped in a limited selection as well as a host of outdated ones. References from conferences and new journals will not be there. Top journals are not prominent in fulfilling case theory requirements.

Where to Publish and Journal Rankings

I respect those who undertake to be editors as the work is hard, especially as the number of submissions keeps growing at the same pace as the 2-article-per-year demand for promotion is implemented. At conferences, I hear journal editors praise their system of certifying the quality of the articles accepted for publication. They praise the review process and thank their excellent reviewers for their dedicated work. They proceed by telling us how the number of submissions increases, how many are desk rejected and how many are accepted after a review process. This is all very well but I recommend journal editors apply pragmatic wisdom and also lay bare the weak sides of the evaluation process.

It is recommended that everyone publish in 'top journals'. Top journal can mean that the quality of the journal content is outstanding; the journal has a premium image/brand; or both.

Ideally, a high score on content should lead to a high image/brand. But we know from marketing that this is not automatically so and that is the reason why *brand management* has become one of the hottest topics in business. Suppliers should make sure you are correctly *perceived* in the market. If this is based on genuine quality it is legitimate, but to a large extent branding means exaggerating good sides and holding back weak sides. Remember, the image of a product is not the product per se, and the image of a scientific journal is not the journal proper. A top journal may be the top one within a certain paradigm or school of thought and this has been erroneously generalized. For example, a journal on methodology may be considered the top one by strictly adhering to quantitative research without understanding the basics of case theory.

Top journals are often suspected of favouring the mainstream and deterring entrepreneurial, innovative research where paradigm shifts are involved. I have many personal experiences of this but it is not always true. A minority of the articles are theory generating in an effort to reach higher levels of abstraction and generalization. When listing the types of articles the top journal would consider publishing, the top journal editor-in-chief quoted in Chapter 3 concluded that theory-based articles can be published 'but these are not easy'. Is this a warning not to submit theory-generating articles? Or is he saying that they will be judged harder than other scripts (which I have heard editors say)?

In some countries and universities, only articles in the 2 highest tiers of their ranking system count for promotion. This is not supportive of research, and it is especially counterproductive to innovation and new research areas and new specialized journals. When a new field of research starts up, it has no established publication outlet. To start a new journal takes several years and to get highly ranked takes 10 years and up. I was recently shown a journal ranking from Australia where the bottom group was called 'Low quality and new journals'. The statement equates low quality with new! In this way, new approaches are held back and obsolete references can live on for decades. How about the speed of dissemination of new research results? Where is the wisdom?

A question is how sustainable the journal system will be. One of the top journals in management got 300 submissions annually 10 years ago and now gets 800. This puts a heavy burden on the editor. A former top journal editor told me that editors used to look for strengths in articles in order to publish them, but now they look for a weakness to justify the quick desk rejection of as many articles as possible. If a journal can only publish 10% of the submissions, it means that very few academics can get a script accepted in a top journal, even over a lifetime.

Further, there is a backlog of several years, so from starting to write a script, going through a review process to getting it published can take years. That period may include many rounds of reviews and revisions with a string of judges involved. Sometimes this process can improve the article but there is also the risk that the many changes will kill the novelty and core message. Film star Clint Eastwood, best known as the uncompromising cop Dirty Harry, is also a celebrated director and winner of 4 Academy Awards (Oscars). He usually settles for just 1 take of a film scene. In an interview, he said that there is the risk of 'killing with improvements'. It intuitively appealed to me; 'improvements' often just mean 'changes' and they can dampen a researcher's passion and originality.

In more and more universities today, career academics are almost solely evaluated on their international articles. These authors have then followed the guidelines for the journals they have targeted. An article is usually between 5,000 and 12,000 words and starts with an abstract of 200–300 words to give a quick overview of its purpose, empirical data and its processing, links to theory, references, methodology, analysis, interpretation, conclusions and recommendations. Journals have different goals and you need to read their mission statement first. While the mission often sounds great, the preferences of the editor and the reviewers may differ when it comes to it. For example, they say that they direct themselves both at science and practice but in reality they give credit to quantitative techniques and little weight to efforts to offer practical recommendations. So you should read some articles from the journal you have selected to submit to and analyse the structure and content of its articles. Top journals may contribute to a certain law and order, but they only represent part of the quality/productivity issue.

Journals provide 'Instructions for Authors', and be careful to follow them to avoid rejection due to formalities. Even if not openly expressed, make sure that you reference previous articles from the journals you submit to, as editors are anxious to get citations that give their journal a higher ranking. Sometimes the instructions are negotiable, for example the length of an article. In the 1980s, I submitted a script to a top US marketing journal. It addressed marketing as relationships, networks and interaction. The reviewers arrogantly said that it had nothing to it and it was rejected. I could not understand their reaction but I felt they would not listen to me. Instead, I sent the script to a British high-ranking journal that had 8,000 words as the limit when my article was almost 12,000. I did not see how I could shorten it without losing its message, so I asked the editor to take a look and if he liked it give me some idea of how I could reduce it. He replied that he did not want to reduce it. It was published in 1987 and the article is still continuously cited with a total of 1,500 citations (2016). It was further developed into many other articles and conference papers and a book published in 8 languages, of which the 4th revised English edition is in progress.[6] Altogether, the theme of the first rejected article has now reached some 10,000 citations. This and other examples show that my most cited publications that have introduced new thinking have all been rejected at first as being of no interest.

Research that generates new theory and is grounded in substantive data and guided by pragmatic wisdom could have an impact on academic research as well as on practice. The following rejection account is worth thinking about. It took 5 years for Vargo and Lusch to get their article introducing S-D logic published in the *Journal of Marketing* (*JM*) (classified as a top journal) after revisions, rejections and negotiations.[7] Had it not been for the fact that one of the authors was a former editor-in-chief of *JM* and had insider knowledge, it may not have been published at all. In the 80-year history of *JM*, it is now its most cited article. At the end of 2016, it had passed 10,000 citations while the runner-up had only half as many. It is theoretical and striving to go beyond mid-range theory and into the grand theory zone but also to give back to mid-range theory and facilitate action. It is still work in progress and numerous articles to develop S-D logic have followed. As the Service Science programme of IBM found S-D logic a usable theory, IBM works to design better service systems in interaction with its clients. When some say that S-D logic is 'only theory', it is a misunderstanding and a demand to force their tentative theory to be prematurely implemented and not therefore have the desired impact.

Real inferior scripts are probably weeded out in top journals but the bad news is that the innovative ones are as well. Breakthrough innovation requires disturbing the reigning paradigm. The fear of an editor-in-chief of publishing something that later turns out to be a mistake must not make a journal abstain from risk-taking. The opposite risk is that only the mainstream and mediocre will be published. There are seminal contributions that are rarely cited because they were not published in an English-language 'top journal'.

When you begin to publish, do it wherever you have a chance. You learn each time to do it better. In the beginning, you'd be best taking advice from an experienced author who may help you improve the script and even become your co-author. Co-authors used to be limited to 2 or 3 but now there can be 4, 5, 6 or even more. If an article is the outcome of group research, this may be all right but there is also the risk that people who have hardly done anything will be listed as authors, such as well-known professors whose brand may add some credibility.

---

[6]Gummesson, 2017.

[7]S-D logic was briefly explained in Box 6.5.

The publishing landscape used to consist of scientific and professional journals, books (monographs, chapters, professional books and textbooks), conference proceedings and reports. The landscape is rapidly changing its character. With e-journals and e-books, you do not need the mediation of publishing companies and publication can occur without delay. Add to this the wild flora of social media like Twitter, Facebook and YouTube and professionally focused sites like LinkedIn and Researchscape. The best thing about the new media is that they open up an unregulated market with numerous, decentralized decision-makers guided by different paradigms. To me the printed article and the book will remain attractive but new generations using e-pads as toddlers may grow up and think differently.

When writing this book, I asked a prominent Swedish economics professor how he and his colleagues establish the quality of PhD theses. These are less written as traditional monographs today and increasingly consist of a collection of articles or conference papers. 'The articles should have been published in highly ranked international journals or be in the process of being published', he said. During the PhD process, the candidates write up their research in articles that are submitted to journals. Hopefully 4 or 5 of them are accepted for publication and can be edited into a thesis together with an introduction. 'So the quality is determined by journal editors and anonymous reviewers, not by the university and its professors', I said. 'You are right', he replied. 'But is this satisfactory?' I continued. His answer: 'Of course not. But this is the way it has become.'

Peer Reviews

Peer reviews are usually done by 2 or 3 researchers who have reached a certain level in their discipline. *Single blind review* means that the reviewers are anonymous to the authors and *double blind* that both reviewers and authors stay anonymous to each other, the names being known only to the editors. The idea is that reviewers should only be influenced by the text and not by persona factors. The peer review system has face validity; on the surface it looks rational and straightforward. But it is not that simple. Although mature and constructive reviewers can be very helpful both to editors and authors, there are numerous hurdles. The Committee on Publication Ethics (COPE) has set up ethical guidelines for reviewers.[8] The fact that these include 55 points to consider is a reminder that we are facing complexity. It is not obvious how this quality system could be implemented except that several judgement calls are required to make sense of it; single numbers or scales do not.

---

[8]Can be found via Google.

Table 11.2 summarizes some of the things that authors should watch out for:

Table 11.2 Problems with blind peer reviews

- Reviewers are sometimes not knowledgeable – for instance, quantitative researchers cannot evaluate case theory.

- Reviewers may be locked in their paradigm and do not accept or understand other paradigms.

- Reviewers should point out both the strengths and weaknesses of a script.

- Some reviewers exert repressive control – censorship – which is the hallmark of dictatorships.

- Reviewers are consultants and not decision-makers, but rushed or weak editors often just do as the reviewers say.

- It is sometimes easy for reviewers to identify the authors. It is a dilemma for authors building on their previous research which they want to refer to but cannot without revealing their identity.

- Hiding behind anonymity, reviewers are not forced to take responsibility, which can bring out the dark sides of their persona such as arrogance.

- The time period from review to publication can be 2–5 years, although efforts are made to speed it up and there can also be pre-publication on the Internet.

- Reviewers are not paid. For me a review takes 4–8 hours which means that if I have a full workload already, it can be difficult to squeeze it in.

Handling revisions and rejections can be demanding of authors. Table 11.3 lists points to consider:

Table 11.3 Points to ponder for authors

- Read the editor's letter and the reviewer comments and give each serious consideration. Doing minor revisions is usually not a problem, just do them.

- If asked to do a major revision, stay cool and do not feel discouraged; rewrite and resubmit in a constructive mode.

- If you believe in your message, you should not tolerate demands to change or dilute it. It is especially risky when you go beyond the mainstream and offer innovation. It is however better to be a diplomat and be civil and avoid confrontation.

- Do not approach a journal which is biased against case research; the editor will never understand your text. A widespread rumour claims that you must include a quantitative part to get articles published and that only a single or a few cases that generate theory are insufficient. This is partially true but my hope is that things will change in favour of theory generation and case theory.

- As the author, you may find that reviewer comments make sense, but sometimes they do not and you feel unjustly criticized. If you do, say so and take a stance.

- If the script is desk rejected by the editor without submitting it to reviewers and with no invitation to resubmit, it is important that the grounds are serious and reasonable. The most obvious is that a script has several shortcomings or that the theme of an article does not fit a journal's mission and priorities. If you find that the reviews are outright incorrect, showing that the editors or reviewers do not understand the topic or are not up to date on its current developments, you should point this out.

- Some of the best articles need very few references, especially if they are introducing innovative thinking. To 'round up the usual suspects' is not productive even if these are academic celebs. All the same, to increase the chances of getting published, it is smart to include the sticky references even if they they are not needed for rational reasons.

- Editors like it when articles from their own journal are cited as the number of citations are considered when journals are ranked.

- The text should not constantly be intercepted by author names and years; it impairs the reading. Articles should of course lean on still viable past results but they should have their prime focus on the present and the future.

- Reviews should be specific and, if possible, also constructive to help authors improve a script. Authors may have been working for months or years on the script and are dependent on getting it published. If they write 'the purpose is not clear', 'the constructs are not precise' or 'important references are missing', the reviewers have to support what they say and set the authors in the right direction. Too often I meet critics who just throw general statements around without justification.

- When submitting case research and the editor or the reviewers are strict mainstreamists confessing to a positivist hypothetico-deductive procedure as the only way of doing research, you had better submit to another journal. Table 3.1 showed such an example from a 'top journal'.

- If reviewers are arrogant and/or ignorant, do not hesitate to make a protest to the editor. There is the possibility that you can resubmit the script after some revision and get new reviewers.

- To be invited to write a paper is a great privilege. Even if it will go through a review process, it is usually a 'friendly review'; the real review had already taken place when you were invited and considered to be an authority that they would like to have among their authors.

- Sometimes reviewers take refuge in methodological technicalities and lose the focus of the content and contribution.

- You should know that even for an experienced author it is unusual to get an article accepted without some revision.

Editors send a letter to the authors based on their conclusions together with reviewer comments. As a reviewer, you often get the other reviewers' comments as well and can compare them with your own.

Being a reviewer is demanding. It is a complex undertaking and there is no simple formula. So, as a reviewer, stay humble! Box 11.1 offers some examples.

Box 11.1   Rotten Rejections[9]

Assessing scientific scripts has the same issues as assessing novel or film scripts. In world literature, we can find authors who were rejected for decades. When George Bernard Shaw submitted his first scripts to publishers, a reviewer said: 'will never be popular ... and perhaps scarcely remunerative'. Part of his rich body of work is *Pygmalion* which later became *My Fair Lady* ('the perfect musical') and he won the Nobel Prize in Literature in 1925. J.K. Rowling's *Harry Potter* was rejected 7 times and has sold 450 million copies. Irving Stone's biography of Van Gogh was rejected 17 times, then sold tens of millions of copies in over 70 languages. These examples are no exceptions, rather the rule. The rejections probably weed out the worst scripts but we do not know how many masterpieces meet the same destiny.

The academic world suffers from the same problems. Fred Smith barely passed at Yale University with his final paper (C–), outlining the concept that built FedEx, one of the world's most successful courier operations. Michel Foucault did not get his PhD thesis accepted at Uppsala University, Sweden. He was later to become one of the most influential contemporary social philosophers and his rejected thesis became a philosophical bestseller.

Here is an example from business and management. There are several laws and principles suggested in a humorous way but with a serious and dense message qualifying them for the grand theory zone. Among the best known that have stood the test of time are *Parkinson's Law* and *Murphy's Law*. Another is *The Peter Principle* launched by Laurence J. Peter and stating that 'In a hierarchy every employee tends to rise to his level of incompetence.' The script was first submitted in 1964 to McGraw-Hill. The reply: 'I can foresee no commercial possibilities for such a book and consequently can offer no encouragement.' After turndowns from 30 publishers, it was finally accepted 6 years later. It sold 200,000 copies in its first year, staying on The New York Times Best Seller list through 1970, and was translated into 38 languages.

One indicator of quality is the number of buyers of a book, another is the value of its contents, and in bibliometrics it is the number of citations by other academics. High sales do not mean great content but a book that appeals to a large audience, though its content can be great as well; and great content does not mean high sales but could be a great contribution to a discipline and to society. Both types and all variations in between can justify publication. This only shows that there is no bibliometric or other procedure emanating from the positivist quantification paradigm that can certify the quality of a publication.

---

[9]*Rotten Rejections* is the title of a thought-provoking and amusing book edited by André Bernard, 1991; see also Henderson & Bernard, 1998.

Bibliometrics, Scientometrics and Altmetrics

The expression *publish or perish* has been around in science for ages. Its basic meaning is that you should share your research through articles, books, reports and oral presentations. It opens up for interaction with wider audiences, and your research can be tried by others and further developed. From having been a common-sense guideline, the expression has now been broadened and today is replaced by increasingly elaborate control procedures. Formal evaluation systems try to standardize scientific research and higher education on an international basis. *Bibliometrics* is the most common designation but it is sometimes replaced by *scientometrics*. My experience of marketing tells me that the latter term was just invented to make the metrics sound more scientific. *Altmetrics* is critical of much in the established bibliometric systems and goes further, for example by considering the impact of material published in the new electronic media: e-books, e-journals, social networking sites, blogs, tweets, etc. The current bibliometric quality/productivity management of research relies on reductionism, premature simplification and illusory preciseness through a few terms like 'impact factor' and 'top journal', without properly recognizing complexity and variety, diversity and persona factors. Science has also become a business and is being marketed using the same strategies as those for shampoo and cookies.

The demand to 'publish or perish' also requires good bedside manners of the researcher. There has emerged an international convention that articles in peer-reviewed academic journals are the one and only way to academic promotion and recognition. In some countries, books do not count, much less internal research reports written in languages other than English. Universities and business schools are the object of assessment by ranking committees. Although this was meant to make quality certain, it is resource-intensive and the outcome is doubtful.

Before we go further into these metrics, let us recall the core tasks of academic research and education:

- to make a discovery to enhance knowledge and find the 'truth'
- to help us understand reality on a deeper level
- to assist people to manage their lives and societies better
- to teach students the state of the art of a discipline
- to encourage students to reflect on and find their personal approach to their discipline.

The Humboldt University of Berlin, Germany, became a role model for European universities.[10] It considered the union between teaching and research, government

---

[10]See further Anderson, 2010.

funding and freedom of study for the individual scholar. This remains to a limited extent today but teaching and research are now often separated; research is financed through applications to funding bodies, companies and government organizations; and students can be driven hard on certain course programmes without having much time for reflection.

Enormous resources are today put into systems of measuring the quality/ productivity of research and education. These systems can be characterized as being standardized, centralized, political, financial, administrative and bureaucratic in the first place. The systems leave out persona factors, variety, diversity and risk-taking, and thus exclude innovation and entrepreneurship. They force their way through academia by controlling money, employment and promotions. They stimulate quantity which is through some wizardry transformed into quality: a girl kisses a frog who turns into a prince, they marry and live happily ever after! These systems may have some advantages but they also take energy away from the core tasks of academia, and they are incomplete and often contradictory. Apart from some elements, such systems do not qualify for entry into the complexity paradigm.

With the Internet, international conferences and exchange programmes between universities, your network changes. Where you take your exam or have a position is a hub but those people who are physically present there are of less import to your research than your personally designed international network. The quality/productivity of research and education emerge out of a network of interdependent factors and interaction between people, and these can be recommended but not secured through regulations from above. Local professors used to be the decision-makers within their researchscapes and the culture and norms within these. The advantage was the physical presence of the professors and their expertise in a discipline. They could get to know their people. A mature professor could interact in a constructive way with students and researchers and get the best out of them and the collective researchscape. This also had disadvantages. It was dependent on the persona of the professors who sometimes became too dominant, hindered innovation or just supported their favourite subjects, methodologies and people; some were even passive and lazy.

To do a good job, the professor could use both explicit and tacit knowledge; the current control procedures are left to what can be expressed in a number or index. The new metrics is a favourite of the positivist creed. Consequently, 'the application of mathematics and statistical methods to books and other media of communication' should be applied.[11] I wonder if Freud could explain it. Instead of dealing with 'the real reality', we hide behind 'an image of reality', in this case what statistics can show. It becomes truth-by-appointment. It was started by governments and others who wanted to ensure that research money was well

---

[11] Pritchard, 1969.

spent. So bibliometrics is based on the positivist paradigm, claiming it is rigorous, objective and rational, and thus conflicts with the complexity paradigm and the reality of the economic sciences. Despite its claims, the process includes subjective, intersubjective and arbitrary assumptions being made, all based on convenience and judgement calls. Unfortunately, the impact factor and its index system do not produce the desired result.

Measurement is useful only when its indicators can be used for practical action. It must not require too many resources in business or government agencies and take away resources from core tasks. I have continuously met situations where the measurement becomes the core task. For many years, I worked in a large international management consultancy where we had to fill in forms every fortnight stating what we had done. The survival imperative was 'being on the clock', i.e. how much of your time had been invoiced to clients during the past period and with an estimate for the next period. These were simple indicators; they were easy to follow and they could be acted on. But the consulting company also wanted to know what we did when we were 'off the clock': idling, personal development, developing a new service, and so on. This was meaningless and forced consultants to manipulate the data and lie. Some general time was necessary, though, to inform consultants about changes, to offer them a certain amount of education and to develop new consulting services, but that had to be defined as special projects.

> Assess work for its contributions and not for its shortcomings. (Bengt Lidner (1757–1793), Swedish poet)

In its 2015 White Paper, 'Using bibliometrics in evaluating research',[12] Thomson Reuters (TR) hard sells its measuring procedure and takes its stance in Lord Kelvin's statement that 'To measure is to know. If you cannot measure it, you cannot improve it.' A White Paper was originally a factual document used in politics and government to support a solution to a problem by informing and persuading. Today, it is also used in marketing to promote new products and new technology. Lord Kelvin was a British natural scientist who made contributions in numerous areas and was highly regarded. As is often the case with innovative geniuses, they both succeed and fail. For example, Kelvin claimed: 'There is nothing new to be discovered in physics now. All that remains is more and more precise measurement.' A few years after Kelvin's death in 1907, Einstein published the general theory of relativity, to be suceeded by quantum theory and a series of theories that constitute the modern natural sciences. Kelvin also said that 'Radio has no future' and 'Wireless [telegraphy] is all very well but I'd rather send a message by a boy on a pony'. He could, however, adapt to new knowledge

---

[12]Pendlebury, 2015.

and after a visit to the USA he changed his mind and gave full support to the radio, telegraph and telephone. He also said something that complies with the complexity paradigm, its holistic view and use of systems and network theory: 'All the properties of matter are so connected that we can scarcely imagine one *thoroughly explained*, without our seeing its relation to all the others; without, in fact, having the explanation of all.' This reminds us not just to look at the fame of scientists – their *brands* – but also to make our personal evaluation of the *content* behind the brands.

I mostly look up the Publish or Perish site[13] if I want to get a quick look at the citations and impact factors of researchers and journals. It uses the Google Scholar database, is straightforward and continuously updated. For authors, I primarily look at their number of publications and citations,[14] summed up in the h-index impact factor. I avoid the evaluation of academics as educators, especially when it is based on surveys among students.[15]

Note that this is solely about the *impact on academics* who are in the same situation as the author, namely looking to get their scripts published. It does not at all measure *impact on practitioners*. In the applied sciences, you should demand to know the impact on those who may use your research as well.

When you have an academic career today, you are forced to chase your impact factor. We implicitly assume that those who stress the impact factor mean 'good impact', but the number of citations does not show that. It is an unscientific assumption that those who cite an article can tell good from bad. It becomes a shallow and mechanistic quality indicator. Altmetrics goes further and tries to handle problems that bibliometrics neglect. But the big question is: Can it be handled by the use of positivism and numbers? No! The impact factor is not the condensation of what it claims; it dwells in the mid-range theory zone and therefore cannot be used without extensive interpretation in each specific case. It requires the combined use of explicit and tacit knowledge, judgement calls and the application of pragmatic wisdom.

The critique against bibliometrics is massive. The way it tries to solve its task is to include more indicators, indexes, decimals, statistical conjecture and fuzzy categories, ending up in 'precise approximations' and 'rigorous perhaps' based on averages, randomness and probabilities. Wharton School professor Scott Armstrong (2004) states that an article should provide useful knowledge but only 3% of articles in academic journals do so; that a high ranking of the journal helps the authors speed up their academic careers but does not necessarily

---

[13]See www.harzing.com/resources/publish-or-perish

[14]For advice on how to get cited, see Judge et al., 2007.

[15]For a critical review of the use of bibliometrics to measure the quality of educators, see Díaz-Méndez & Gummesson, 2012.

advance knowledge; that the reliance on reviewers reduces the chance of publishing innovative research; that the current procedures to promote faculty based on bibliometrics inhibit scientific progress; and that the real work starts after publication when authors can arouse interest in their articles by making them available on websites and social media, publish follow-up articles and hit the speakers' circuit. It has also been concluded that 'business schools that adhere most slavishly to evaluations based on quality of journals tend to be those that are making few scientific contributions'.[16] In a later study, Armstrong[17] says that papers published in leading academic journals speak an arcane language that is inaccessible to most people.

Peter Lawrence, biology professor at the University of Cambridge, UK, is another outspoken critic. In a conversation with a journal editor – 'The heart of research is sick' – he explains what is wrong and how it should be set right.[18] Pragmatic wisdom is called for. He says everything there is to say and I recommend that you read the text; it is only 6 pages long. Mixed with my own experiences, I like to highlight these items:

- It should be research first, administration second.

- Much of the academic literature is unreadable.

- The article storyline is first and foremost orchestrated to the need to get published and cited.

- Building large research groups is in vogue; there is something suspicious about people working alone. We need both.

- Bibliometricians often score people incorrectly, not properly understanding the academic context.

- Everything is focused on volume but it is impossible to get a high volume of citations if your research field is small or if you work in a new area.

- Academics may be spending 30–40% of their time using up intellectual and emotional energy on concocting grant applications.

- Quality techniques have moved from business and management to universities and public research agencies and spawned an enormous bureaucracy: form filling, targeting, assessment, evaluations, reporting. The core idea of quality/productivity has largely got lost.

- Research results are ordered by special interest groups, all the way from private companies to political parties and governments. When adverse results come out, the report is shredded.

---

[16]Van Fleet, McWilliams & Siegel, 2000.

[17]Armstrong, 2011, as quoted by Baker, 2012, p. 4.

[18]Lawrence, 2011. For an in-depth analysis of the current use of bibliometrics and its pros and cons, see Adler & Harzing, 2009.

- There is also fashion in research; those who are 'politically correct' may be favoured.

- Research should, first of all, be discovery but grant applicants are often supposed to present a definitive plan and the expected outcome before the research is done.

- When you write a grant application, do not tell the truth about what you are really going to do. If you get the funds, do what you really intended to.

- People feel under pressure, get defensive and will not reveal what they are doing as it may be plagiarized by others; enormous resources have been put into codes of ethics but there is nothing about enforcement.

- There is no evidence that competition leads to higher creativity and more innovation.

- It is tempting to fall into the trap of 'measuring what can be measured' even if the measure has little significance. The bibliometrics may preserve the outdated and you become cited because you have been cited in a self-perpetuating mode.

My verdict is therefore: You can use some version of bibliometrics and its explicit information as advisory, but do not take its impact factor and other indexes as the sole motive for decisions, for example about the promotion of an academic and the distribution of research funds. You have to add tacit knowledge, judgement calls, the acquaintance of persona factors and pragmatic wisdom to evaluate a researcher or an educator.

Nobel Prize Quality

In 2011 the new CEO of the Nobel Foundation executing his first award ceremony, said: 'This represents the most superb in science.' It sounds appealing. The selection of Nobel laureates is an elaborate process with numerous people involved. Could its criteria be used to evaluate the quality of findings based on case theory? My thought was that being perhaps the most prestigious scientific award in the world, the Nobel Prize should have found a superior procedure for establishing the quality of science. The idea was not as brilliant as I first thought. Again, this pointed out to me how demanding and uncertain it is to evaluate science.

At his death in 1896, its founder, the Swede Alfred Nobel, was one of the richest men in the world. He was an inventor with over 350 patents, the commercially most successful being dynamite. He was also an entrepreneur who exploited his inventions through numerous companies. In his will he gave enough money to his family to live comfortably but the bulk of his fortune was given to prizes for 'those who, during the preceding year, shall have conferred the greatest benefit to mankind'. Five prizes were established: in Physics, Chemistry, Physiology or Medicine, and, as Nobel took a great interest in the humanities, in Literature and Peace. When Sweden's central bank celebrated its 300th anniversary in 1968, it donated to the Nobel Foundation an additional Prize in Economic Sciences to be included among the other Nobel Prizes under the same conditions.

Giving the Nobel Prize to a person should require an elaborate evaluation process. But the process is the epitome of non-transparency. The Prize in Economic Sciences receives some 300 nominations each year, and the criteria used to evaluate the contribution to science should be of the greatest interest to the academic community. Unfortunately, we are deprived of this; the documents are only made public after 50 years. As the Prize in Economic Sciences was first handed out in 1969, we do not, as yet, have access to any of these documents and the former members of the Awards Committee, if still alive, cannot speak freely. When there is access it will mainly be of historical interest. Furthermore, how much is documented? My conclusions are based on my experience as 1 of approximately 3,000 official international nominators for the Prize in Economic Sciences. I have also studied the winners, been to a large number of the official prize lectures and had discussions with some of the winners. In addition, I have interviewed members of the Prize Committee, the former CEO of the Nobel Foundation and the former head of the Nobel Family Association. Some have told me stories that are probably not meant for the public but have added an extra dimension to my understanding of the selection of winners.

How do you select 1–3 people out of a few hundred nominees as the winners? Science is not the Olympics Games with elaborate technology to establish that the winner was 4 hundredths of a second ahead of the next runner. Those who do not win the Nobel Prize are not losers in this sense.

According to Nobel's will, the Prize is for a *specific contribution*, meaning a discovery, an innovation or improvement; it is not an award for lifetime contributions. The Prize 'is to go to the most worthy'. Each year a Committee for the Prize in Economic Sciences is elected, consisting of 5 members and some adjunct members. The Committee also consults others for special evaluations. Its choice of winner(s) is reported to the 9th Class of the Royal Swedish Academy of Sciences. The 9th Class has about 50 members, half of them Swedes and the rest from around the world. More than 20 are economists, only 2 are from business and management, and the remaining half of the seats are shared between all the other social sciences including law.

There should be an enormous wealth of scientific and methodological knowledge hidden in the extensive investigations for the Prize in Economic Sciences. Contrary to the claim that science should be open, it is closed to scientists, students and everyone outside of the Academy of Sciences. The prize winners present their contributions at public lectures but why theirs are better than anybody else's is kept confidential.

I should like to see a book on scientific methodology based on decisions to award the Prize in Economic Sciences. Why keep scientific research in the dark?

Academic writing is characterized by dullness. Of course, the content of articles and books can be very exciting per se but it is often concealed by the detached and impersonal way of writing. A text does not become serious and scientific just because it is dull. When did you ever laugh or smile when reading an article in a top journal? I do not mean funny jokes but a sense of humour and exciting stories that have a message consistent with the message of the article, book or oral presentation. The Vodka case in Box 2.2 is an exception.

It is sometimes helpful to poke fun at something and see it in a relaxed and humorous light, but can we do that with such a serious thing as research and science? (Box 11.2).

Box 11.2   Poking Fun at Science

Nonsense articles disguised in academic jargon are sometimes published to test academics and make them see what they are doing in a more humble light and with a sense of humour. During 2016 my article 'Lip service: A neglected area in services marketing' passed 100 citations since its publication in 1987. I wrote it as a reaction to pompous and irrelevant articles and conference presentations that I was exposed to in service research. It was meant as satire and only to be distributed to some close friends. The editor of the *Journal of Services Marketing* heard of it and asked for a copy. Then he wanted to publish it! I had to make sure that he understood that it was a satire – and he did. The article 'Salt passage research: The state of the art'[19] followed the format of a scientific sociology article and is a meticulous analysis of the expression 'pass the salt, please', with method, empirical data, theory connection, hypothesis testing, footnotes and references.

The Ig Noble Prize is an American parody of the Nobel Prize. The name is a play on the word 'ignoble', meaning 'not noble'. It 'honors achievements that first make people laugh and then make them think'. It is 'an award for achievements that cannot or should not be reproduced'. Among its winners are Michael Milken, the father of the junk bond 'to whom the world is indebted'; the executives, directors and auditors of Enron, WorldCom, Xerox and Arthur Andersen 'for adapting the mathematical concept of imaginary numbers for use in the business world'; the directors, executives and auditors of the 4 Icelandic banks 'for demonstrating that tiny banks can be rapidly transformed into huge banks, and vice versa and for demonstrating that similar things can be done to an entire national economy'; and the executives and directors of Goldman Sachs, AIG, Lehman Brothers, Bear Stearns, Merrill Lynch and Magnetar 'for creating and promoting new ways to invest money – ways that maximize financial gain and minimize financial risk for the world economy, or for a portion thereof'.

Quality/Productivity Lessons from Organizations and their Customers

In the 1920s, the manufacturing industry began to use more systematic approaches to mass production, especially to control quality on the assembly

---

[19]First published by M. Pacanowsky in 1978 and reprinted under the pseudonym M. Pencil in the *Journal of Communication*, 2006.

line. Since then quality has gone through a series of ups and downs. During the Second World War, it became imperative that explosives, weapons, ships, aircraft and other equipment were reliable but also that productivity in manufacturing and logistics was improved. How many defects caused severe injury and death we do not know. In the aftermath of the war, the world was crying out for cars, television sets, household equipment and other consumer products, and industry for machinery, trucks, and so on. Systematic quality and productivity management was underdeveloped. Cars broke down constantly, needing continuous service, and radios and TV sets had to be taken to the dealer for repair. Today, the quality of computers and software is questioned, given hard-disk breakdowns and the possibility of hackers breaking into systems, even the most elaborate ones used by defence and government agencies.

Since the 1980s, efforts to improve quality/productivity management have been intense in business and government organizations and research can learn from them.

I have expanded on the most frequent criteria from the methods literature by also looking at total quality management (TQM); widespread quality awards, such as the Malcolm Baldrige National Quality Award in the USA and the European Quality Award; and the internationally accepted procedure for becoming a certified supplier – the ISO 9000 standard. These emanate from manufacturing and later also from service production, originally in a commercial context but today also adapted for not-for-profit organizations. What these add to conventional scientific quality criteria is a focus on the customer and user, and a recognition that quality is partly a matter of perceived quality relative to needs and price. Furthermore, the awards, as well as ISO 9000, offer an approach to improving quality by deploying a checklist of a large number of criteria and guidelines. Through their systems of examiners and judges, the awards offer an elaborate objective and intersubjective procedure for assessing both quantitative and qualitative criteria.

Belatedly, in the 1980s, it was realized in the Western world that quality and productivity cannot be upheld without the concerted effort of every detail in an organization and its network: its manufacturing, leadership, human resource management, distribution system, suppliers, and so on. The awards provide extensive lists of criteria, questions and comments – 40–50 pages – which have to be considered by those who seek to improve and maintain quality and productivity. They increasingly stress the outcome while initially the emphasis was on following procedures and installing enablers, i.e. on methodology. Compared to this variety and richness, mainstream scientific quality criteria stand out as meagre.

Japanese companies have managed to elicit suggestions for improvements from their personnel at a rate unheard of in American and European companies. The importance of engaging every employee in making both major and minor improvements was expressed by J.M. Juran as 'the vital few and the trivial many', which he later changed to 'the vital few and useful many'.

The most noted example is Toyota, where, in 1990, its employees contributed with an average of 48 suggestions – 1 per week per employee – as compared to 1 suggestion per employee every 12 years in a US car factory. Moreover, suggestions were taken seriously and were implemented at short notice. The work of academic researchers, consultants and internal experts has actually been taken over by the people on the job. Their daily work offers the best access, and gradually they create ideas and solutions that an outsider could never present. *Continuous improvements*, a Toyota strategy stemming from the 1930s and doggedly implemented ever since, is the best strategy for both developing and testing quality and stimulating innovation.

Initially, it was *lean production* – to get a high output with a low input, i.e. to enhance productivity, and *just in time* – neither doing things too early nor too late. These are not the same as cost-cutting in the conventional sense, where lower cost often means lower quality and the quality problem is loaded onto customers and society. It is a holistic concept and a systematic technique. Its goal is to enhance customer value through, for instance, eliminating all sources of time-wasting.

In businesses and other organizations, the word quality has gradually been replaced by *excellence* which is wider, with quality, productivity and the financial outcome as key elements. In scientific research, there is a desire to be excellent, meaning that you get recognition in your discipline through awards, publications, citations, a prominent position at a renowned university, and earn money from books and consulting and speaking assignments. Excellence does not necessarily mean all of this. Some of those who are most visible are skilled at self-promotion and creating an image of being the leader in their field. Some are much more humble and do not get all the accolades but may very well make better contributions. Sometimes the match is fair but sometimes it is highly unfair. We are again reminded that the image is not the real thing.

Comparison with Quality Assessment in the Natural Sciences

The effort to establish quality of science through a journal review system is seriously meant but is also misused. The problem is not limited to business and management research. Although the natural sciences are constantly held up as the benchmark for superior science, the problems are similar. Here are some examples.

Hannes Alfvén, Professor of Physics at the Royal Institute of Technology, Stockholm, Sweden, was hailed as a genius and won the Nobel Prize in physics in 1970. Still, he had trouble with the peer review system and rarely got an article accepted in scientific journals. When he submitted an article on the theory of magnetic storms and auroras to the American journal *Terrestrial Magnetism and Atmospheric Electricity*, his paper was rejected. The reason for this was that his findings did not agree with the theoretical calculations of mainstream physics. Of course they did not; it was an innovation! Said Alfvén: 'When I describe the [plasma phenomena] ... most referees do not understand what I say and turn down my papers ... With the referee system which rules US science today, this means that my papers are rarely accepted by the leading US journals.' He was often forced to publish in what the mainstreamists condescendingly call 'obscure journals'.

Many of his theories about the solar system were verified as late as the 1980s through external measurements of planetary magnetospheres. One was the 'plasma phenomena' but Alfvén noted that astrophysical textbooks poorly presented them. The same pattern can be discerned in today's textbooks on business and management which list more outdated theory than discoveries of the past decade.

American chemist Linus Pauling made seminal contributions but also stepped outside the conventionally defined disciplines. He became the premier chemist of his time, was awarded the Nobel Prize in 1954 and is included in a list of the 20 greatest scientists of all time by the magazine *New Scientist*. Four decades of research led him to new ways of discovering the molecular structures of complex substances, and how structures of simple molecules could be used to predict structures of more complex ones and to predict chemical behaviour. His book on this is one of the most-cited texts in the history of science. He further took his chemical knowledge to medicine and public health, claiming that vitamin C had a preventive effect on colds and could help heal cancer. This was highly disputed and he was accused of scientific misconduct.

Inspired by his wife's pacifism, Pauling became a peace activist. He joined Albert Einstein, Bertrand Russell and several other leading scientists and intellectuals and signed the Russell–Einstein Manifesto. He was awarded his second Nobel Prize, this time for Peace, for his work against the use of nuclear weapons. The US government responded by putting him under FBI surveillance, cancelling his research grants, refusing him a passport, stripping him of his security clearance and accusing him of being a communist. Political power was used to interfere with creative scientific work. He presented evidence that the seemingly trivial increases in background radiation caused by fallout could cause birth defects and cancer worldwide. His book *No More War!* contributed significantly to the development of the first nuclear test ban treaty of the Cold War period.

Each challenged the mainstream by presenting a more useful paradigm. This is risky in itself but they then went further and linked their results to the effect on man by protesting against the testing and use of nuclear weapons. They based their protests on solid research but went against the political and military establishments. They merged the natural sciences with the social sciences and the humanities; in today's terminology they should be called life scientists and give a genuine content to the expression. Today, companies are accused of a one-sided focus on profits – 'shareholder value' – thus neglecting their role as *corporate citizens*. Corporate social responsibility (CSR) has become a concept and a sub-discipline in business and management. We could equally well talk about *scientific social responsibility* (SSR). Just as companies cannot be allowed to be free-wheeling standalones in society, scientists must show concern when they see their findings misused, putting the world at jeopardy. We also need *scientific citizens*.

In medicine, planned manipulation to get published has gone far. I read on Google that since the 1970s it is established practice for pharmaceutical companies to give research on a new pill to professional ghost writers. They write several articles based on material which, mind you, cannot be checked from the outside. No transparency – and transparency is one of the hallmarks of science! They then offer a Key Opinion Leader (KOL) from the academic world to pose as the lead author. The articles are well-written but emphasize the superiority of the new pill as compared to similar medication offered by competitors, while risks and side-effects are held back. This is unobtrusive marketing – but at the same time it is sophisticated scientific fraud.

A Quality/Productivity Checklist

Inspired by the pragmatic approach of the quality awards, a case theory quality/productivity checklist is given in Table 11.4. It is further an effort to combine lessons from the evaluation of quality/productivity in academe, business and other organizations. As case theory addresses complexity, it is natural that the assessment of quality/productivity is complex, too. Do not be put off by the many points in the checklist; still, it is only 2 pages as compared to the 50 pages for quality awards. Bazeley[20] explores the dimensions and criteria of research quality in a 20-page chapter which clearly shows the complexity as soon as you leave the positivist format of a reduced and primarily linear reality.

The checklist can be used for 3 purposes:

- *guidance* during the selection of a topic, research questions, research techniques and other elements of the research process

- *prevention*, i.e. under way detection of weaknesses of the research process and early revision

- evaluation of the *final outcome*.

---

[20]Bazeley, 2013, pp. 401–421.

In business, the focus has gone from checking the quality of the final product to stopping errors under way – prevention – following the imperative: 'Do it right the first time.' In this way industry has largely eliminated the quality checks that were made before a product was transported to customers, and customers can abandon arrival control. This is productive in B2B where the product goes into a new production or selling process and in B2C/C2B where consumers do not have to complain and demand compensation.

However, note that quality management in industry is primarily focused on the systematic assessment of continuous and controlled activities and not on innovation. One of the most innovative companies for decades is 3M. It boasted a creative culture and proved that it gives results. When a Six Sigma quality programme was implemented, profitability and shareholder value rose, mainly because productivity was improved through short-term cost reduction. After a couple of years, long-term effects began to surface. The creative environment had lost its zest to a state where it became critical to re-establish its vitality.[21] If innovation is restricted to rules and regulations, it dies by definition, although at later stages elements of discipline and standard procedure are necessary to reach implementable results.

In academe, there is a similar development albeit not as clear, especially if the project only contains a limited amount of repetitive behaviour and a larger element of developmental work. But research should never be the object of a last-minute verdict from some smart alec coming in from the outside. What is required is a delicate balance between checking quality under way without interfering with unorthodox and innovative thinking. We must keep alive the iterative aspect of the research process when we move between the different foci, as what we learn later may inspire revisions of earlier foci. In universities, seminars and progress report presentations are held with supervisors and other researchers during the course of a faculty project. Senior researchers and project leaders are there as mentors and coaches and younger researchers are there to learn for their own projects.

No one can score high on each point in the checklist. Such a demand would inhibit discovery and dynamism, and it is actually not feasible as some of the items are trade-offs; if one goes up another goes down. The goal should be to reach a satisficing level with regard to the type of research and the imperfections that exist in any research practice. Procedural adherence – 'I went by the book and followed the rules' – is not a sufficient defence; it promotes ritual over results.

The list is a revision of earlier efforts and is hopefully more complete but still kept short. I tried to structure the answers but think it better that you feel free to answer them in your own words, as is mainly done in quality award applications

---

[21]Hindo, 2007.

in industry. There is an addition which I do not particularly like but felt forced to include. With less free research money and more dependence on commercial and politically influenced funding, it is necessary to start by asking questions about the possible dependency on financiers.

The outcome of the quality/productivity assessment is a weighted conclusion through reflection and dialogue. For example, a precise statement of the researcher's paradigm (point 2 in Table 11.4) may be premature if the researcher is experimenting with a new paradigm. It may not be clear what premises guided the researcher; this may require further study in a new project. If the demand is initially too strict, it will mentally impede the researcher's efforts. They will feel

Table 11.4 Case theory checklist for quality/productivity assurance and assessment

0. To establish initial credibility:

- Who financed the research?
- Did the financiers put pressure on the way you designed your research?
- Did they indicate that they expect you to arrive at certain results?
- What will they do with your report if the results are negative to their business or political interests?
- Do any of the researchers have a special connection with any interest groups and have an incentive to slant the research in a certain direction?

1. Through research reports, readers or listeners should be given a chance to follow the research process and how conclusions were drawn, and also be able to draw conclusions of their own.
A report should include:

- a statement of a problem and research topic, research questions and purpose of the study
- a description of methods of data generation, analysis and interpretation
- a well-documented scientific narrative
- an account of the research process
- motives for the selection of cases
- limits of the research project
- a report that reads well and/or oral presentations
- the presentation of results and conclusions, either for academic or practical use or both, which should be as clear as possible, bearing in mind the influence of fuzzy sets and tacit knowledge
- information for the reader if taboo information has been discovered but is anonymized or disregarded for ethical or other reasons.

2. As far as is realistically feasible, researchers should present their paradigm and preunderstanding:

- compliance – does the research comply with the complexity paradigm and case theory? If not, state and support your deviations
- the researcher's preunderstanding, prior experience and other pertinent persona information
- philosophies, ideologies or specific theories and concepts that underpin the project
- personal and professional values and whether these have changed in the course of the research.

3. The research should possess credibility, including:

- correct data, including a correct rendering of statements and views from the data sources
- awareness of data quality evaluation
- analysis and interpretation supported by data
- confidence demonstrated in the theory, concepts and conclusions that are used or generated in the research
- honest presentation of alternative interpretations and contradictory data
- avoidance of deliberate or unintentional deception
- conclusions that accord with one another as far as possible, considering that data and its links can be fuzzy
- actors in the cases able to recognize what is presented in the report, though as cases are often perceived differently by different actors the divergences should be accounted for
- a selected methodology and its techniques appropriate to the problem, purpose and research questions.

4. The researcher should have had adequate access, so consider the following:

- data-generating methods and techniques should give adequate access to pertinent data, not too much, not to little
- difficulties in deploying desired access methods
- problems and limitations which arose through denied access
- problems and limitations in access which arose through time and money constraints
- have access limitations impaired the quality of the research?
- did the generation of data reach a saturation point?
- if saturation was not achieved: why, what effect could it have had on the outcome, what have you done to minimize possible bad effects, and could future research add to saturation?

(Continued)

Table 11.4   (Continued)

5. An assessment on the generality and validity of the research: substantive, mid-range, grand theory:

- To what theory zones do the results apply?
- How closely does the research represent the phenomenon which the researcher aimed to study?
- Does other research confirm or disconfirm the findings?
- Do the results bear out or disagree with extant theories and concepts?

6. Relevance; the research should make a contribution, for instance:

- theory generation: generate theory that confirms, rejects or improves current theory and knowledge
- generate checklists, heuristics and models that simplify complexity so that it can be used in practice
- have relevance by dealing with interesting and meaningful issues
- a satisficing trade-off between methods, techniques and results
- be of value to the scientific community, a client and/or society in general
- actively be made available to the scientific community, the client and society
- are the recommendations for future research realistic?

7. The research process should be dynamic, in terms of:

- the extent to which the researcher has continuously learnt through inner reflection and dialogue with others
- a demonstration of creativity and an openness to new information and interpretations
- the ability to switch between deep involvement and distance
- a demonstrated ability to improve the research design if called for during the research process.

8. The persona of the researchers and their researchscape should include:

- commitment to the task of research
- integrity and honesty, being able to voice convictions
- flexibility and openness, being able to adjust to changed conditions and new – even disturbing – information.

9. Productivity; how well the resources are used:

- Were the 'manpower' resources adequate?
- Was the funding sufficient?
- Was the time frame adequate?
- Other resources?
- Would you have done better with more resources? Which?

10. How is the research presented?

- Which were your target groups: academia, practitioners, the general public?
- Was it reported in journal articles, books or other media?
- Did you make oral presentations?

11. Finally, make these 'quick and dirty' tests:

- Use your pragmatic wisdom and apply the *Schoolmaster's Test*, asking and answering the question: Do the research and its results make sense?
- When you have come up with some results in the mid-range and grand theory zones, try them on some events or cases that you are familiar with and see if there is a reasonable fit.

forced to play safe and avoid risk-taking. Another example is the demand for adequate access (point 4). Access can fail if you were denied interviews with key sources or you had to cut down on some activities because you ran out of time. It becomes a quality/productivity trade-off. An awareness of access limitations helps when assessing validity (point 5).

Researchers should use their pragmatic wisdom to make quality certain during the process of research. As there are no simple and unambiguous rules for the assessment of case theory, it is tempting to be critical of whatever is presented if one is in that mood. It is required that the examiner of a report or thesis based on case theory deploys appropriate criteria. It is not unusual for ignorant reviewers to lean on criteria from statistics and hypothesis testing, in the conviction that these represent general criteria for scientific evaluation. Furthermore, quality must be set in relation to productivity, i.e. what time and other resources were available to the researcher.

It is possible to establish simplistic demands like '2 articles per year in blind-reviewed scientific journals' and 'only international – i.e. English-speaking journals – count'. Such statements may encourage quality/productivity but they also tie the hands of scientists. They encourage risk avoidance, 'more-of-the-same' and 'me-too' research, robot-like testing of received theory, and impose constraints on what is amenable to research – all because this is convenient to measure. It encourages ritual over results. The ritual should be a supportive enabler, it should facilitate the researcher's survival in a messy world, but the enabler is just a means, not the end. Strict ritualism discourages true search which includes risk-taking that may result in discovery and enhanced knowledge. At the end of the day – even with convenient simplifications – the overall assessment rests on judgement calls. Objective criteria are preferable (if they exist in a truly objective form) and intersubjective, peer-approved criteria can facilitate research over a period of time – but not forever. Researchers must also be trusted with the ability to understand and do what is right, as was pointed out in Chapter 3. Life becomes easier and productivity goes up.

In TQM great weight is given to the target group (customer, client, user) and to the fact that quality is a combination of subjective perceived quality and quality-in-fact. Transferred to research, this means that target groups should be considered. It is not enough that a project be technically perfect; it should also add something of interest to others. However, students participate in education and their papers are, first of all, vehicles for personal learning. The students should demonstrate that they have learnt theory and methodology and can communicate in a report. The demand for an addition to knowledge is there anyway but to a lower extent than if the project is carried out by a senior researcher or a consultant.

The main purpose of the comprehensive checklists that go with quality awards is not to help win an award but to encourage organizations to take a systematic approach to quality and productivity and make continuous improvements. The award checklists do not use scales. As scales are popular in academic research, it could be tempting to use them and have numbers that can be added up. In comparing different research projects, it could be tempting just to have to compare a single number for each project in the futile belief that everything is condensed into this number. In agreement with what has been found in business practice, such a number cannot hold a collected quality/productivity conclusion as each checklist item is complex and the items are not necessarily additive. For example, a research project that is strictly quantitative and hypothesis-testing, including only a few operationally defined constructs and links, cannot easily be compared with a highly innovative project that addresses complexity and recognizes the ambiguity and fuzziness of numerous factors and their links. Instead, each item requires some words or paragraphs of explanation around liking or disliking what the researchers do. It will be less precise but it will be of higher validity and relevance. So I stand by the lesson from business practice that numbers and scales are too blunt as arbitrators.

If you do academic research, the results must be accessible to anyone. If you have a consulting assignment, it is proprietary information and the client is free to decide what to do with it.

There is a desire for completeness and transparency in science. In their article 'The absent, the hidden and the obscured: reflections on "dark matter" in qualitative research', Weiner-Levy and Popper-Giveon (2013) use the 'dark matter' metaphor from astrophysics for what has been left out of qualitative research. 'Dark energy' and 'dark matter' account for 95% of the universe; what we can observe (stars, galaxies), called 'normal matter', is only 5%! This is still a mystery in modern physics. Is it also a mystery in business and management research?

There can be many reasons for omissions, legitimate ones like the information being proprietary or too sensitive to be published, even with the risk of getting sued. The existence of taboos should be mentioned in the report and the reasons for omission explained. As has been pointed out already, it is not only qualitative research that may not use data properly. Stylized and operationalized quantitative research has not even picked up the missing data. It has been excluded from the very beginning, for example in a survey or by forcing received concepts and models on the respondents. In GT, data is analysed and interpreted during the collection phase, meaning that data is generated and the result is written down in memos.

Make sure that you really introduce the book right, check terms and concepts for consistency, keep down the terminology and don't pour unnecessary terms and concepts on the reader. It is helpful to do the index as a writer because it will show you how and where you have explained something, avoid duplication and ensure that terms and concepts are consistent and explained the first time they appear, even if more elaborate explanation will follow later in the text. My very last activity is to read every sentence and see if it can be shortened without losing in legibility. The structure of the book will be changed under way. You start with an outline of a chapter but then you find that it could be improved; and you fill each chapter with sections but later you may, for example, find that a section first put in Chapter 7 fits more naturally into Chapter 6.

In her comprehensive book *Qualitative Data Analysis* (2013), Pat Bazeley's ground is analysis; it is omnipresent in research. From there she extends to data collection methods, conclusions, presentations, and so on. She sees qualitative research primarily as dealing with cases, acknowledges mixed methods approaches and does not just focus on conventional reliability/validity assessments. There is close affinity between our ways of thinking but our backgrounds and interests are different. It shows that in research we have to address complexity as well as simplicity, that contextual and persona factors are imperative and that every effort to lay bare what scientific research is requires both explicit and tacit knowledge. Her advice is overwhelming, and her checklists are comprehensive and embrace the social sciences in general; mine are focused on business and management. Reading her book reminds me that practising research and being reflective is the highway to understanding science.

Having said before that the quantitative/qualitative divide creates unnecessary methodological controversies, I prefer to say that her focus is non-numerical analysis, not treating statistical and mathematical methods. At the same time, she is open to mixed methods studies and the use of graphics in the form of diagrams and social network analysis but does not refer to general network theory or systems theory. One of her strengths is her familiarity with software for analysis and how she integrates this with the traditional paper-and-pen and scribble-and-doodle methods. To cover all this, it is inevitable that her book would be big (443pp). But it is well structured and indexed so you can easily find the parts you are most interested in.

This was said for qualitative research. But there may even be more dark matter, 'dark figures', in quantitative research. Operational definitions may have excluded difficult-to-find data and the excuse is lack of resources or difficulty in access. An example is fraud in organizations, where some is known but is too sensitive to be reported, and the firm is afraid of making it public ('It would be bad for our image'). More often than not, those who reveal ongoing fraud in companies or government, whistleblowers, get fired and then scandalized while the villains often go free, sometimes even to continue their scams. It is hard to understand; there is no rationality behind it, just dark persona factors, and it is certainly unethical. Unfortunately, academic researchers are not so brave and dodge these issues. They are left to investigative reporters, some of whom are excellent scholars and detectives, while others get stuck on a path of seeking out sensationalism – of far less import, but good for making headlines.

12

FIFTH FOCUS: REPORT, COMMUNICATE AND DEFEND

Case theory can be reported, communicated and perceived in many ways. You should actively make your work known to potential users or it is doomed to oblivion. However, it is a matter of co-creation, and all parties – producers as well as users – carry a responsibility, though as producer you have to take the initiative. Conventional case study research is often perceived as second-rate so you can also take it as your mission to promote case theory. The chapter ends with advice on how to defend the use of case theory.

The previous chapters include aspects that are pertinent to the final reporting but in this chapter reporting is in focus and additional aspects are brought up.

Communication models used to define two opposite parties – *sender* and *receiver* – and treated them as crisp sets. That is yet another either/or approach to abandon in favour of fuzzy set theory. The old approach puts the entire burden on the originator of a message and sees the others as passive recipients without responsibility. Instead, we have talked about interactive research, co-creation, resource integration and networks of involved stakeholders – all with an operant role.

Reporting case theory in written form has its problems because of the linear structure of an article or book text. Chapter 3 brought up the issue of making a text more non-linear and still readable. The story of how a company grows and becomes successful can become a thrilling novel like the book on Absolut Vodka, and still be a scientific narrative. We can take inspiration from fiction writers and high-class reporters on how to write in an engaging way without spoiling the seriousness of the content.

There is an anecdote about two students meeting on campus. One says: 'I missed the lecture today. What did the professor talk about?' Fellow student: 'He didn't say.' The professor's rhetoric must have been inadequate or the student had been too passive. Making oral presentations gives you the freedom to be non-linear, even if some linearity is necessary to avoid the audience getting lost. When people say 'this is just rhetoric', they usually mean empty talk, window-dressing or outright lies presented in smart disguise to cover something up, all character- istics of the manipulative demagogue. It is used in politics, marketing and not least in finance. But consider the original denotation of *rhetoric*: 'the ability to speak or write effectively'. According to Aristotle, rhetoric has these dimensions:

- *logos* – mostly associated with scientific researchers; presentations of their work should be consistent and constructive

- *ethos* – the credibility, character and reputation of the author/speaker and the trust this instils in the audience

- *pathos* – the emotional and passionate side, the one that positivists exclude from research as they see all subjectivity as non-scientific.

Branding has been mentioned as an increasingly popular strategy for acquiring credibility. It is used to establish a favourable image of products and suppliers but also of political parties, government agencies, NGOs and universities, and in the creation of celebrities, including film stars and scientists (Hawkins, Nobel Prize winners), and medical research programmes. *Story-telling* is used in marketing to make a brand stand out in a desired light, in a way that is easy to understand and even funny. The problem is: Is the story true or false? Even if CSR is in vogue, the ethos is often lacking. CSR frequently becomes window-dressing, delegated to a public relations department and outside consultants without real power and little top management commitment.

It is easy to fall into the trap that *content* means everything in a research report and *form* is cosmetic. Marshall McLuhan's thesis that 'the medium is the mes- sage' is worth considering for case theorists. Content in scientific research must of course be no. 1 but content and form should 'go together like a horse and carriage', to quote one of Frank Sinatra's greatest hits. In the song it was not content and form but 'love and marriage'. It is the same thing in science. An article with a great message in a 'top journal' will reach a large academic audi- ence, while the same article published in a lower ranked journal may be noted only by a few or not noted at all. However, if the content is of little value, it is unfortunate that the brand of the journal can spread a halo effect on an article.

Reputation is an idle and most false imposition; oft got without merit, and lost without deserving. (Shakespeare, Iago in Othello, Act II, Scene iii)

'How to Give a Killer Presentation'

The heading is taken from a *Harvard Business Review (HBR)* article that gives hands-on advice about presentations. It is written by Chris Anderson, curator of TED.[1] He says that 'presentations rise or fall on the *quality of the idea*, the *narrative*, and the *passion* of the speaker' (italics added). The article offers live examples of presentations as well as a list of 10 ways to ruin a presentation. But Anderson also says that there is no single best way of doing a presentation: 'So do not ... try to emulate every piece of advice I've offered here. Take the bulk on board, sure ... [but] play to your strengths.' So even if the article is full of advice, just as methods books are, the author urges you to do it your way. One thing he clearly points out is that you must spend time practising your presentations.

Having listened to so many lectures and conference presentations, both by academics and practitioners as keynote speakers or speakers to small groups in parallel sessions, I could not agree more. Too many presentations are simply lousy and the speakers do not seem to understand that – and no one wants to be rude and tell them! I had been taught to give lectures, but gradually I began to see my oral presentations as *performances* and as requiring a balance between *show* and *content*. Read the 'killer article' and use the advice as a checklist before you make your next presentation.

Target Groups

For one who is trained in marketing, it is striking how production-oriented research reports are. A central question in research is who I want to reach: Which are my *target groups*? It has already been said that all those involved in a discipline carry responsibility to share their resources for the co-creation of value. Target group refers to those who you believe to have a stake in your research, and you should do your best to capture their attention and make your research available to them. Consider this:

- The prime goal for any scholar should be to contribute to knowledge and understanding, being free from undue influences. You can become a mainstream, well-behaved 'me-too' researcher and follow the crowd; this is the easiest way out. You can also follow your own beliefs and take risks. The academic community has an obligation to advance science to the benefit of society. Consultants are too often controlled by the need to get more assignments and therefore say what they think the client wants to hear, like politicians say things to gain votes, even if they know they are not sticking to the truth. It is understandable – but unprofessional.

---

[1]Anderson, 2013; a pdf of the article is available via Google. TED is a non-profit organization spreading powerful ideas mainly through short talks – see www.TED.com Other helpful checklists for academic publishing in business and management are found in Gilmore, Carson & Perry, 2006.

- For papers by undergraduate and masters students, the target is the examiner in the first place; you need to get your grade. It is education for you and you should learn something during the process. If on top of this you learn something which could be important to the research community or to practitioners, do try to communicate it.

- For the PhD student, it is the supervisor and the examiners who constitute the prime target group. Getting a PhD is an education; it is getting a driver's licence that allows you to drive your research more independently in the future. Most PhD theses go unnoticed both in research and practice and this is unfortunate. It is a great bonus if your thesis can contribute with specific or generalizable knowledge.

- In submitting to a journal or conference, your first target is the editor or conference chair and the reviewers. In most established journals (but not all), editors and reviewers have limited knowledge of case theory and the complexity paradigm. Too many stay put in positivistic and quantitative research and consider case theory second rate and at best an overture to the 'real thing', statistical hypothesis testing.

The biggest problem with communication is the illusion that it has been accomplished. (George Bernard Shaw)

PowerPoint Presentations (PPT)

Connecting to Shaw, PPT can be an efficient means of turning a lecture or presentation into a performance, sometimes combined with video clips. With PPT you can structure and condense your thoughts, illustrate them and make your message come alive. However, I am constantly disturbed by the way both academics and practitioners misuse PPT and videos; most of them just do not communicate. Worst of course is if there is no obvious message but just piles of boxes-and-arrows models, statistics, diagrams and text. The speaker may have a great message which never reaches out because they do not consider their target group. This can easily be changed but it requires preparation. Here are some dos and don'ts:

- Show the title, your name and affiliation on the first slide. Do not keep repeating logos, dates, etc. on every slide.

- The presenter puts on a fully loaded image of text, numbers, curves, etc. and then starts speaking. There is no clear connection between what the presenter is saying and what is on the screen. Should the audience listen or read? It cannot do both.

- Build up a slide gradually as you speak by using simple animations.

- Do not use fancy colour background designs that disturb your text or pictures. The contrast is often bad, like putting blue text on a green background.

- Ensure that your text is not too small to read from a distance.

- Some presentations are best done without pictures. For example, when you talk about an airline you do not need to show an animated aircraft crossing the slide.

- An oral presentation consists of what the presenter says and the slides they show. The spoken word leads, while the slides are a sidekick to jack up communication.

- If the audience is international and you speak English, speak slowly and distinctly. The majority may have English as a second or third language, and many won't be familiar with acronyms and names of local institutions, dialect and slang.

- Video clips are often technically bad, and the sound is too loud, not loud enough or missing. Some look like commercials for yet another revolutionary shampoo.

- If you use symbolic pictures, the symbolism must be clear and not a riddle to be deciphered.

- If the presenter stands in front of the picture, your audience will only see half of it.

- Wear a microphone headset. If you hold a microphone, you must hold it close to your mouth (and not in front of your belly) and it occupies one of your hands if you want to use gestures. You can stay still or move on stage but do not run around in the room.

Unfortunately, architects rarely understand what a room is meant for. Like most 'professionals', they seem to want to show off to other architects rather than support the users. For example, they may introduce artistic design and overloaded technology without proper instructions for the users.

Written Presentations of Case Theory

Chapter 11 brought up publishing as a quality/productivity issue but also showed the connection to getting your research known. References, journal rankings, peer reviews, citations and bibliometrics were discussed.

Most research results in business and management never reach beyond the author's desk. Even if an article is published, access to it may be difficult or just random. It needs to be read and then cited by others in articles, books and conference papers. There is no natural selection process in this; it is influenced by the researcher's ability to market themselves – but they also need a bit of luck, one thing they cannot really control. The more 'branded' the researcher becomes, the more attention will be given to them. Or the researcher has a branded professor and they write together and the junior researcher can become a brand as well. The old saying that 'a good product sells itself' is rarely true. If an author is cited by well-known researchers, it becomes legitimate and safe to quote them.

Traditionally, publishers do basic marketing through catalogues and sales visits. Adapting to the new media context, publishers make efforts to increase co-creation and add life to articles and books beyond the point of publication. Universities are connected to e-libraries and academics can download articles for free or they are found on the authors' websites. Some social media are specialized in science like LinkedIn and Researchscape and offer platforms for authors as well as for readers. Increasingly, e-books and e-journals are published that speed up the publication process and presentations are available on YouTube. But most of the marketing has to be done by the author in order to get cited to enhance their impact factor and sales.[2]

Reporting should be well organized and coherent. It should be as dense, clear and simple as possible without losing its message. It should not be embedded in long lists of references that cut up the sentences and it should avoid ornamentation with fancy terms and unnecessary words. The only remedy is rewriting and rewriting again and again; when you create something novel you cannot do it right the first time. If you try to, your innovative thinking will be disturbed. Let if flow. For example, I estimate that the chapters in this book have been rewritten up to 30 times. Gradually, the improvements become fewer and fewer but you have to put a stop to it at some point. Still, doing it a 31st time I am sure I could find things to improve.

The abstract is important for guiding the reader into an article. For a book, a short introduction is needed. Do not start with a funny story or a lengthy historical background. Be direct! *Emerald* is the publisher of over 200 journals in management, information science and engineering. They require an abstract that follows a certain format, still giving authors freedom to adapt it to their specific article (Box 12.1). It is not the only way of writing abstracts but it is a useful checklist for anyone. For complete author guidelines, go to the journal you plan to submit to and stick to their instructions.

Box 12.1   Structured Abstracts for Emerald Journal Articles: A Checklist

An article must have a structured abstract with 4–7 sub-headings, the number depending on the type of article, and it is limited to 250 words. There should further be up to 6 keywords and 1 of 7 possible definitions of article type. As an example, this is the abstract for the article 'The collective consumption network':[3]

Purpose: The purpose of the article is to introduce a network perspective to the study of collective consumption. We examine the characteristics of heterogeneous consumption collectives formed around a Finnish footwear brand. The case is both theoretically and practically relevant. It differs from previous research by featuring consumer grassroots activities, face-to-face interaction and strong pre-existing social relationships.

---

[2]For a recent article on how to get cited, see Baron & Russell-Bennett, 2016.

[3]Närvänen, Gummesson & Kuusela, *Managing Service Quality*, 2014, p. 545.

Design/methodology/approach: Qualitative case study research was conducted with different methods of data generation, including interviews, participant observation and cultural materials such as newspaper articles and photos.

Findings: A new concept of collective consumption network is introduced. Five kinds of consumption collectives are identified: place focused, brand focused, activity focused, idea focused and social relations focused. The strength of ties as well as the role of the brand vary within the collectives.

Practical implications: Suppliers should find an appropriate network position, where they can enable and support shared value creation. Developing skills to identify and cultivate weak links as well as mobilize resources is important.

Originality/value: The findings illustrate the heterogeneity and complexity of collective consumption. In particular, the article discusses the way self-organizing and emergent consumption collectives and the supplier interact and integrate resources within the network.

Keywords: C2C, collective consumption, interaction, resource integration, network, brand.

Paper type: Research paper.

The abstract is also a useful checklist for the authors to make sure they have not missed anything. I usually start by sketching a possible abstract, and then revise it gradually. When you feel that your text is complete and coherent, go back to the abstract and check whether it is consistent with the final text. The final version may not look like the first sketch but it got me under way.

Avoid the most common flaws in books and longer reports:

- *Make it quick and easy to find notes and references* – it is easiest if they are at the bottom of each page. They should not be too long. The worst thing, but common also in published books, is having endnotes of each chapter or collected somewhere later in the book. One example in a recent book: the chapters are numbered 1, 2, 3...; the corresponding endnote section is numbered I, II, III... When you see a superscript for a note you first have to look up which is the number of the chapter, then to find the pages where the endnotes are collected. Further, the full reference is given in the first note where it appeared, not in a reference list, meaning that finding an author requires you to search for the first time it appears.

- *Make an index* – it requires some work, but the work serves good purposes. First, for yourself as the author, it helps you discover inconsistencies in terminology and in the spelling of names and terms. Second, a reader can easily look up where and how you have used a certain term, concept or reference throughout the report. If you use an indexing computer program, you still need to go through it manually and make corrections and clarifications. You will never be entirely satisfied with the index – it requires a series of judgement calls which may satisfy one logic but violate another – but by being careful you increase readability and limit deficiencies. Take a look at an index of one of your books and test its usefulness for you as a reader. Always think in terms of what readers need to find and make them happy. Examiners of PhD dissertations, who have difficulty in finding things, will develop adverse attitudes to the text, not least because they are pressed for time. An index adds a hypertext quality to your text, allowing the reader to search for themes and enter the text at their discretion. If it is an e-publication, readers can find words, names, etc. themselves and no index is needed.

- *Avoid appendices* – these are common practice among scholars and should only be used in exceptional circumstances. If there are many appendices, readability goes down.

- *Include author bios* – a really detached scholar who believes in the purity of objectivity and that the 'text should speak for itself' might find this unwarranted. However, scientific readers are also human. Your affiliation, highlights of your career, previous publications and current research interests, all add to human interest and help to build your brand identity. You may even add a photo and some words about your family and hobbies.

- Book editors are very useful and you need them, even if you are experienced in editing. As all professionals, they are sometimes victims of fad and fashion and then become more production-oriented than reader-oriented. It is important that the roles of author and editor are reasonably clear.

[Writing is] largely a matter of application and hard work, or writing and rewriting endlessly until you are satisfied that you have said what you want to say as clearly and simply as possible. For me that usually means many, many revisions. (Rachel Carson (1907–1964), author of *Silent Spring*, the book that started environmentalism and ecological awareness)

Most research in business and management is fragmented, adding a tiny piece to a knowledge domain. Therefore, a journal article usually ends with sections called 'Implications for theory and research', 'Implications for practitioners', 'Limitations' and 'Future research'. Here is a brief example of how such recommendations are frequently presented:

Our study suffers several limitations, some of which suggest promising directions for future research. Longitudinal studies are needed to gain better understanding of the causality between the variables. Another limitation is that we only studied 1 industry in 1 country. In order to generalize the results, data is needed from the contexts of other industries and cultures. The limited scope of the study meant excluding several pertinent variables. Future studies must ... etc., etc.

I do not endorse such recommendations; they are not realistic. As a reader, you could ask yourself several questions. In what way are the 'directions for future research' promising? Longitudinal studies are costly to undertake. Longitudinal can mean a shorter or longer time span depending on the research questions but is mostly a matter of several years. Can it be done? And who is motivated to do it? And even if it is done, would it lead to findings of relevance to companies, customers or the economy in general? A single journal issue contains several articles on different topics and all demand resources for future research. New journals are founded continuously and the submissions to existing journals grow every year. In reviewing articles, I sometimes ask authors to draw up a tentative future research plan where they estimate the funds and number of researchers needed to follow their recommendations and expand on the original research, how long it would take and what the potential contribution to knowledge might be. I have made estimates and found it to be a matter of hundreds of thousands of pounds, engaging hundreds of researchers over several years. If your research raises interest, keep an open code and support those who want to contribute to its further development.

Research is not inherently cumulative or additive. Studies are made differently, at different points in time and may be hard to compare and merge into a model or theory. Meta-analysis has been mentioned as a recommendation in methods books but it can be difficult with cases, especially when markets and societies keep changing. One solution is to have a long-term research programme involving several researchers who do a large number of cases chosen through theoretical sampling. They can uncover variety and eventually be analysed to show commonalities and differences and lay the ground for grand theory.

There are journals with a clear and unabashed bias against case study research, mainly due to too much inbreeding within the editorial and review boards, where there is a lack of knowledge of case theory. Their reasons for being more careful when accepting cases, qualitative studies and new theory are not convincing. Statistical studies are often deficient, hiding essential flaws intentionally or out of ignorance, as you have read in earlier chapters.

If you are a young researcher and want to pursue an academic career, you have to publish in journals which are ranked in your country's or university's evaluation system.[4] But I advise young researchers to practise by publishing first in less recognized journals and submitting abstracts and papers to conferences. This is easier, but the most important thing is that you train yourself to write and present. With that training in the background, you stand a much better chance of later publishing in higher ranking journals.

Addressing Practitioners

Practitioners have other needs and interests than academic researchers; the academic/practitioner gap is still a problem. Academic journals in business and management are hardly read by practitioners, as has been pointed out earlier. You may find exceptions in countries where there are still business and

---

[4]See Billig, 2013, on the writing style of today's academics and the necessity to adapt to political and bureaucratic 'correctness'.

management journals in which both academics and practitioners write; in English *HBR* is the great example.

New research can reach practitioners through special conferences, executive training programmes and management consultants. If your research is consultancy, your target group is the client organization. Within that there can be several target subgroups who see your results differently. Some may like your recommendations, but for others they may stand out as wrong or a threat to their current position. Clients can also be of different kinds: businesses, other organizations such as NGOs, political parties, and society in general.

When you get an assignment, secure access to the people who have the ability and power to make decisions. A frequent problem for consultants is that the top decision-makers – CEOs, vice presidents, board directors – are hard to keep in touch with. They often feel they have not got time and send others to summarize the results for them. Then you have no control over what is communicated. In other instances, when you have made a consulting agreement with managers at lower levels, access is easier.

If you find that a company is badly managed in some respect, you can explain it in different ways:

- At the final reporting stage, start with a *Management Summary*. Practitioners want to hear your conclusions and recommendations first. Methodology, theory, analysis and interpretation approaches can be explained later when you defend your recommendations and if specifically asked for.

- If you tell them all the mistakes they have made and how badly the company is managed, you may create in them a negative and defensive attitude.

- If instead you tell them that there is a great potential for improvement and recommend where they should start, you may be able to help with certain things and this is a great opportunity to get extended assignments.

- Sometimes consultants do their job independently and do not write progress reports; rather they just make a final presentation with a written report to be read by the client. However, much of consultancy is interactive co-creation between the consulting firm and the client and therefore the persona factor is important, as are interim checks. If you do management action research, you are in close interaction with the client personnel, making them part of the assignment.

Case Theory Ethics

Ethics is a big and difficult issue and it has been touched on in the previous chapters. There is no simple solution; it is essentially about honesty and pragmatic wisdom. Here are a few things to think about:

- Consider the ethical framework within which research is used in your particular project. For example, action research will give you close access to sensitive data which you would not get through interviews. How should you use that data?

- The term scientific misconduct refers to situations where researchers have invented data to fit their theory or give credit for a discovery to the wrong person. Sometimes they do it to themselves: plagiarism. This has always been around but has become more common with the Internet. Software to reveal when a text has been copied from someone else is used in business schools to check student papers and PhD theses. Plagiarism can also be unintentional and may simply be due to a mistake or a lack of knowledge.

- Doing market research on children and teenagers by adding addictive flavours to food and forcing brand awareness on them is done by psychologists working for major companies. To me, this sort of thing is morally objectionable.[5]

- There is no way to guarantee absolute anonymity and protection of sources.

- The best thing is to build on trust – but who can you trust?

- Lies are omnipresent; small ones by a respondent to dodge an interviewer's questions, and big ones in national statistics and company annual reports. Researchers are obliged to lay bare such frauds.

- Countries and industries have different laws and regulations. There are sometimes voluntary agreements among, for example, market researchers.

- How about infiltration or walraffing? In some cases, it is the only way to find the truth.

- How should you handle taboo information, such as non-public scandals or the personal shortcomings of executives? Such information can exert a decisive influence on the course of events. Should scientists be whistleblowers?

- There is a trade-off between being specific and perhaps causing commotion and having to anonymize the material. If the purpose of a case study is not to look at a single case but to learn a more general lesson, anonymity may be possible. Readers will have to lift themselves to a conceptual level where they are spared substantive detail. But you cannot anonymize the Absolut case, so you may be forced to censor the description and the conclusions. Should scientists be censors?

- Reporters and paparazzi are known to intrude on the privacy of unwilling respondents, often causing turmoil and conflict – but sometimes breaking the ice. Many reporters are known to go too far but many scholars are too timid and considerate. Science is a matter of balancing ethics against potential benefits.

- If you object to someone's research results and methodology, the meanest way to abuse this person is by calling them non-scientific and a representative of junk science. The next meanest way is to pretend that the research does not exist and let it die a silent death.

---

[5]See Lindstrom, 2004, 2008, and his e-books.

Defending Case Theory

What should you answer to those who question the value of case theory and its applications? The best way seems to be that you learn to become your own successful case theory defence lawyer. I hope answers have been provided in the book, but here are additional comments and advice.

The senior Swedish TV anchor and author on economic and political issues Åke Ortmark uses a rule of thumb (sorry, heuristic sounds more scientific!) in addressing an audience. He defines 3 target groups:

- *like-minded people who are already with you* – they will listen and learn and enter into constructive *dialogue*; it is a *win-win* situation

- *those with an open mind* but who have not considered the issue before or have not made up their mind – they constitute your number 1 target group; you may win them or you may lose them

- *opponents who dislike your approach or your persona* – sometimes it is meaningless to try to explain what you mean. They enter into a *win-lose debate*; you only get objections back and there will be no *win-win dialogue*; leave them alone.

As case theory is not properly understood by mainstream researchers, you have to count on being attacked from time to time. Flyvbjerg lists and explains 5 misunderstandings of case study research. They are:[6]

1. General, theoretical (context-independent) knowledge is more valuable than concrete, practical (context-dependent) knowledge.

2. One cannot generalize on the basis of an individual case; therefore, the case study cannot contribute to scientific development.

3. The case study is most useful for generating hypotheses – that is, in the first stage of a total research process – whereas other methods are more suitable for hypothesis testing and theory building.

4. The case study contains a bias toward verification, that is, a tendency to confirm the researcher's preconceived notions.

5. It is often difficult to summarize and develop general propositions and theories on the basis of specific case studies.

Read Flyvbjerg's article and how he responds to the misunderstandings. The following are some of the more common criticisms and suggested responses:

- *Be prepared*; when the attack comes it is too late to find the arguments.

- *Do not apologize, challenge!* Defend yourself and do not pose as the underdog. A common trick of those who consider themselves superior is to put the burden of proof on

---

[6]Flyvbjerg, 2006. The article can be downloaded via Google.

your shoulders. Turn it around and put it on theirs. They are usually not prepared for this and easily get lost in clichés and slogans. They may even become arrogant and unpleasant, like Bunge, Dawkins and Marx. Human, yes, but should it not be beyond the dignity of a true scholar?

- Paradigmatic differences are the most difficult to solve. But it can happen, as when Lord Kelvin changed his mind about the radio and telecom. Ólavur Christansen is one of the very few economists I have met who felt dissatisfied with the mainstream economics paradigm and searched for something better. He found GT and did a seminal project on business and management.[7] He went from being a mainstream time-series analyst and econometrician to becoming a skilled user of classic GT.

- When generalizability is brought up, it is usually in the statistical and descriptive sense. It is taken for granted that numbers are important and can be generalized, as long as they were contrived according to an approved quantitative procedure and the outcome is 'precise approximation' and 'precisely perhaps'. Probabilities and distributions can be meaningful in specific instances but they are not generally valid. Ask for examples (and references) of where statistical research has developed the discipline concerned and provided general and mid-range theory.

- 'This has not been scientifically proven.' It could mean that studies have not been able to prove this, or that no studies have been done. If studies have not proven it, it could of course be that there is no connection. But it could also be that it was studied using inadequate methodology providing inadequate data and obviously ending up with erroneous inferences. This is typical of today's Western medicine, where they now claim that evidence-based medicine is the gold standard approach to knowledge without mentioning its narrow scope.

- 'This is pseudoscience.' Let them prove it.

- 'It is widely accepted in science that...' The mainstream, the intersubjective agreement, is just a temporary platform for getting things done.

- Comments that I have heard in research seminars are usually of limited value. To some extent, they are part of a learning experience, meaning that you have the right to say something less clever and get constructive comments on it. But too often they are better understood as part of individual persona and researchscape factors. Academics often feel frustrated and conflicts are common.

- I often get both lecturers and students who come up to me and say: 'I wish we could go about things in the way that you outline but we live in a system that doesn't allow it.' You may have to comply because you are forced to, but you can also try and persuade your professors or examiners to change their minds.

- 'I had expected you to use the well-established model of Professor X!' Then they say that given their 'expectations' the paper is bad. If they substitute expectations for 'prejudice', it may make more sense.

- 'Your reference list is incomplete!' You can always say that; it puts no demand on you. 'Incomplete' could simply mean that some highly cited celebrity writers and 'top journal' articles are left out because they are outdated; beware of name-dropping.

---

[7]Christiansen, 2006.

Research is not linearly cumulative, and a paper in business or management is rarely just an historical account; it should be directed at what is currently valid and what might be valid in the future.

- 'I am sceptical!' Anyone can say that at any time.

- 'This is not problem free!' Nothing new is problem-free. The remark is that of a typical 'critical academic', the fault-finder who is not looking for future improvements.

- 'Section B could be considerably shortened while the conclusions in section C need to be expanded.' This is easy to say but ask the person to explain in more detail what should be reduced and what expanded. The person will probably not reply and you'll end up with the Bunge syndrome of derogatory and abusive language.

- They say: 'Research shows that...' Ask what research, and do not forget to ask what methodology was used.

- 'There is no scientific evidence that...' This should be answered with questions like 'Have any studies been done?' If no, there is of course no 'scientific' evidence in either direction.

- Watch out for those who hard sell theories, models and results from empirical studies. There must be an open code.

The Book Ends but Your Journey in Methodologyland Continues

The text has been rich in short narratives to add flesh to the skeleton of principle guidelines, methods, techniques, categories, concepts and theories. They include all the foci, but with varying emphasis. The examples have been fragmented and have only shown summaries or excerpts, however. They do not give a complete picture of case theory in management and business, but they are complete within themselves. By reading how others have done it, you can calibrate yourself as a research instrument. I recommend that you read full cases in articles and books.

This book has been an invitation to dialogue rather than an effort to tell the reader how things are or should be. Put in Internet lingo, there is an open-source code like the Linux operative system which invited computer geeks to develop an initially crude concept and has continued to do so since 1991, and Wikipedia presents itself as 'the free encyclopaedia that anyone can edit'. S-D logic supports the customers' role as co-creators of our economies viewed as networks, and the IBM Service Science development programme perceives society as a bundle of service systems. The same supplier–customer role duality applies to scholars as they swing between being producers of science and consumers of science. 'Dialogical orientation'[8] should outrank the hard sell, win-lose debates and defence of established but often outdated concepts, theories and methods.

Relax in front of science. You cannot do good science if you are tense. Be intense with good intentions, yes, but tense, no!

---

[8]Ballantyne & Varey, 2006.

REFERENCES

Adler, Nancy J. & Harzing, Anne-Wil (2009). When knowledge wins: Transcending the sense and nonsense of academic rankings. *Academy of Management Learning & Education*, 8 (1), 72–95.

Åge, Lars-Johan (2009). *Business Manoeuvering*. Stockholm: Stockholm School of Economics.

Aiden, Erez & Michel, Jean-Baptiste (2013). *Unchartered: Big data as a lens on human culture*. New York: Riverhead.

Alvesson, Mats & Sköldberg, Kaj (2009). *Reflexive methodology*. London: Sage (2nd edn).

Anderson, Robert (2010). The idea of a university today. *History and Policy*, Policy Papers, March.

Anderson, Chris (2013). How to give a killer presentation. *Harvard Business Review*, June.

Argyris, Chris & Schon, Donald (1974). *Theory in Practice: Increasing professional effectiveness*. San Francisco, CA: Jossey-Bass.

Argyris, Chris, Putnam, Robert & McLain Smith, Diana (1985). *Action Science*. San Francisco, CA: Jossey-Bass.

Armstrong, J. Scott (2004). Does an academic paper contain useful knowledge? *Australasian Marketing Journal*, 12 (2), 62–63.

Armstrong, J. Scott (2011). Evidence-based advertising: An application to persuasion. *International Journal of Advertising*, 30 (5), 743–767.

Badinelli, Ralph, Barile, Sergio, Ng, Irene, Polese, Francesco, Saviano, Mariluisa & DiNauta, Primiano (2012). Viable service systems and decision making in service management. *Journal of Service Management*, 23 (4), 498–526.

Bagelius, Nils & Gummesson, Evert (2013). Criminal marketing: The inhuman side of business. In Richard Varey & Michael Pirson (eds), *Humanistic Marketing*. Palgrave Macmillan.

Baker, Michael J. (2012). Editorial. *Social Business*, 2 (1), 1–10.

Baker, Michael J. (2015). Editorial. *Journal of Customer Behaviour*, 14 (4), 271–273.

Baker, Michael J. & Foy, Anne (2012). *Business and Management Research*. Argyll, UK: Westburn Publishers (3rd edn).

Bakir, A. & Bakir, V. (2006). Unpacking complexity: Pinning down the 'elusiveness' of strategy. *Qualitative Research in Organizations and Management*, 1 (3), 152–172.

Ballantyne, David & Varey, Richard J. (2006). Introducing dialogical orientation to the service-dominant logic of marketing. In Robert L. Lusch & Stephen L. Vargo (eds), *The Service-dominant Logic of Marketing: Dialog, debate, and directions*. Armonk, NY: M.E. Sharpe.

Barabási, Albert-László (2002). *Linked: The new science of networks*. Cambridge, MA: Perseus.

Barabási, Albert-László (2012). *Network Science*. Available at http://barabasi.com/networksciencebook/

Barile, Sergio & Polese, Francesco (2011). The viable systems approach and its potential contribution to marketing theory. In Barile, Sergio et al. (eds), *Contributions to Theoretical and Practical Advances in Management: A viable systems approach (VSA)*. Avellino, Italy: Interational Printing Srl, EDITORE.

Baron, Steve & Russell-Bennett, Rebekah (2016). Editorial: Beyond publish or perish – the importance of citations and how to get them. *Journal of Services Marketing*, 30 (3), 257–260.

Barrow, John D. (1992). *Theories of Everything*. London: Vintage.

Bazeley, Pat (2013). *Qualitative Data Analysis: Practical strategies*. London: Sage.

Bazeley, Pat & Jackson, Kristi (2013). *Qualitative Data Analysis with NVivo*. London: Sage (2nd edn).

Bejou, David (2011). Compassion as the new philosophy of business. *Journal of Relationship Marketing*, 10 (1), 1–6.

Berger, Peter L. & Luckmann, Thomas (1966) *The Social Construction of Reality*. New York: Anchor Books.

Bernard, André (ed.) (1991). *Rotten Rejections*. Harmondsworth: Penguin Books.

Billig, Michael (2013). *Learn to Write Badly: How to succeed in the social sciences*. Cambridge: Cambridge University Press.

Bitner, M. J., Booms, H.B. & Tetreault, M.S. (1990). The service encounter: Diagnosing favorable and unfavorable incidents. *Journal of Marketing*, 54 (1), 71–84.

Blumberg, Paul (1989). *The Predatory Society*. New York: Oxford University Press.

Bohlin, Ingemar & Sager, Morten (eds) (2011). *Evidensens många ansikten (The many faces of evidence)*. Lund, Sweden: Arkiv förlag.

Bonoma, Thomas V. (1985). *The Marketing Edge*. New York: Free Press.

Brodie, Roderick J., Coviello, Nicole E. & Winklhofer, Heidi (2008). Investigating contemporary marketing practices: A review of the first decade of the CMP Research Program. *Journal of Business and Industrial Marketing*, 23 (2), 84–94.

Brodie, Roderick J., Saren, Michael & Pels, Jaqueline (2011). Theorizing about service dominant logic: The bridging role of middle range theory. *Marketing Theory*, 11 (1), 75–91.

Brown, Ellen Hodgson (2007). *Web of Debt*. Baton Rouge, LA: Third Millenium Press.

Brown, Ellen Hodgson (2013). *The Public Bank Solution*. Baton Rouge, LA: Third Millenium Press.

Brown, Stephen (1993). Postmodern marketing. *European Journal of Marketing*, 27 (4), 19–34.

Bryman, Alan & Burgess, Robert E. (eds) (1994). *Analyzing Qualitative Data*. London: Routledge.

Buchanan, M. (2003). *Small World*. London: Phoenix.

Bunge, Mario (1996). In praise of intolerance to charlatanism in academia. In Paul Gross, Norman Levitt & Martin W. Lewis (eds), *The Flight from Science and Reason*, 98–115. New York/Baltimore, MD: New York Academy of Sciences/The John Hopkins University Press.

Burell, Gibson & Morgan, Gareth (1985). *Sociological Paradigms and Organizational Analysis*. Aldershot: Gower.

Capra, Fritjof (1997). *The Web of Life*. London: Flamingo/HarperCollins.

Carson, David, Gilmore, Audrey, Perry, Chad & Gronhaug, Kjell (2001). *Qualitative Marketing Research*. London: Sage.

Cassell, Catherine, Symon, Gillian, Buering, Anna & Johnson, Phil (2006). The role and status of qualitative methods in management research: An empirical account. *Management Decision*, 44 (2), 290–303.

Cave, Tamasin & Rowell, Andy (2014). The truth about lobbying: 10 ways big business control government. *The Guardian*, 12 March.

Charan, Ashok (2015). *Marketing analytics: A practitioner's guide to marketing analytics and research methods*. Singapore: World Scientific.

Christiansen, Ólavur (2006). Opportunizing: A classic grounded theory study on business and management. *Grounded Theory Review*, 6 (1), 1–23.

Christopher, Martin, Payne, Adrian & Ballantyne, David (2002). *Relationship Marketing*. Oxford: Butterworth-Heinemann (2nd edn).

Cicero, Marcus Tullius (1971). *On the Good Life*. London: Penguin Classics.

Clark, Peter (1972). *Action Research and Organizational Change*. London: Harper & Row.

Coase, Ronald (1937). The nature of the firm. *Economica*, 4 (16), 386–405.

Coase, Ronald (1960). The problem of social cost. *Journal of Law and Economics*, 3 (1), 1–44.

Coase, Ronald H. & Wang, Ning (2011). The industrial structure of production: A research agenda for innovation in an entrepreneurial economy. *Entrepreurship Research Journal*, 1 (2), 1–11.

Coffey, Amanda & Atkinson, Paul (1996). *Making Sense of Qualitative Data*. Thousand Oaks, CA: Sage.

Coghlan, David & Brannick, Teresa (2010). *Doing Action Research in Your Own Organization*. London: Sage (3rd edn).

Cohen, Don (1998). Toward a knowledge context: Report on the first annual UC Berkeley forum on knowledge and the firm. *California Management Review*, 41 (3), 22–39.

Convergence (1988). Special issue with focus on participatory research, XXI, 2–3.

Corbin, Juliet & Strauss, Anselm (2015). *Basics of Qualitative Research*. Thousand Oaks, CA: Sage (4th edn).

Coviello, Nicole, E. (2005). Integrating qualitative and quantitative techniques in network analysis. *Qualitative Market Research*, 8 (1), 39–60.

Coviello, Nicole E., Brodie, Roderick. J. & Munro, Hugh J. (1997). Understanding contemporary marketing: Development of a classification scheme. *Journal of Marketing Management*, 13 (6), 501–522.

Crossen, Cynthia (1994). *Tainted truth: The manipulation of fact in America*. New York: Simon & Schuster.

Czarniawska, Barbara (2004). *Narratives in Social Science Research*. London: Sage.

Czarniawska, Barbara (2008). *A Theory of Organizing*. Cheltenham: Edward Elgar.

Dahlström, Karin (2002). *Värdeskapande produktuveckling i tjänsteintensiva företag (Value-creating product development in service incentive businesses)*. With summary in English. Stockholm University, Sweden.

Dawkins, Richard (2011). *The Magic of Reality: How we know what's really true*. New York: Free Press.

Dawkins, Richard (2015). Is it a theory? Is it a law? No, it's a fact. Available at https://richarddawkins.net/2015/11/is-it-a-theory-is-it-a-law-no-its-a-fact/

Dennett, Daniel C. (1995) *Darwin's Dangerous Idea: Evolution and the meanings of life*. London: Penguin.

Denzin, Norman K. (1989). *Interpretive Biography*. Newbury Park, CA: Sage.

Díaz-Méndez, Montserrat & Gummesson, Evert (2012). Value co-creation and university teaching quality: Consequences for the European Higher Education Area (EHEA). *Journal of Service Management*, 23 (4), 571–592.

Dichter, Ernest (1979). *Getting Motivated*. New York: Pergamon Press.

Easterby-Smith, Mark, Thorpe, Richard & Jackson, Paul R. (2015). *Management and Business Research*. London: Sage (5th edn).

ECCH (1997). What makes a good case? *The Newsletter of the European Case Clearing House*, autumn/fall, ref. no. 397-119-6. Available at www2.econ.iastate.edu/classes/econ362/hallam/CaseStudies/WhatMakesAGoodCase.pdf

Eckstein, Harry H. (1975). Case study and theory in political science. In Fred J. Greenstein & Nelson W. Polsby (eds), *Handbook of Political Science*, 7, 79–137. Reading, MA: Addison-Wesley.

Edberg, Birgitta (2013). *Social affärsutveckling i nätverksekonomin: sociala medier, ny affärslogik* (Social business development in the network economy: Social media, new business logic). Solna, Sweden: Liber.

EdChoice (2009) Milton Friedman on Donahue – 1979. [Online] Available at: https://www.youtube.com/watch?v=1EwaLys3Zak (Accessed 13 December 2016).

Edvardsson, Bo, Enquist, Bo & Hay, Michael (2006). Value-based service brands: Narratives from IKEA. *Managing Service Quality*, 16 (3), 230–246.

Eisenhardt, Kathleen M. (1989). Building theories from case study research. *Academy of Management Review*, 14 (4), 532–550.

Eisenhardt, Kathleen M. & Graebner, Melissa E. (2007). Theory building from cases: Opportunities and challenges. *Academy of Management Journal*, 50 (1), 25–32.

Fendt, Jacqueline, Kaminska-Labbé, Renata & Sachs, Wladimir M. (2008). Producing and socializing relevant management knowledge: Return to pragmatism. *European Business Review*, 20 (6), 471–491.

Feyerabend, Paul (1975). *Against Method*. London: Verso.

Firat, A. Fuat (ed.) (2010). Commentaries on the state of journals in marketing. *Marketing Theory*, 10 (4), 437–455.

Flanegan, John C. (1954). The critical incident technique. *Psychological Bulletin*, 51, 4, 327–358.

Flyvbjerg, Bent (2001). *Making Social Science Matter: Why social inquiry fails and how it can succeed again*. Cambridge: Cambridge University Press.

Flyvbjerg, Bent (2006). Five misunderstandings about case-study research. *Qualitative Inquiry*, 12 (2), 219–245.

Flyvbjerg, Bent (2011). Case study. In Norman K. Denzin & Yvonna Lincoln (eds), *The Sage Handbook of Qualitative Research*. Thousand Oaks, CA: Sage (4th edn).

Ford, Henry (1922/2008). *My Life and Work*. CruGuru.com.

Foroohar, Rana (2016a). *Makers and Takers: The rise of finance and the fall of American business*. New York: Crown Business.

Foroohar, Rana (2016b). American capitalism's great crisis. *Time*, 23 May.

Friedman, Milton & Friedman, Rose (1980). *Free to Choose: A personal statement*. San Diego, CA: Houghton Mifflin Harcourt.

Fukuyama, Francis (1995). *Trust*. New York: Free Press.

Game, Ann & Metcalf, Andrew (1996). *Passionate Sociology*. London: Sage.

Garvin, David (1988). *Managing Quality*. New York: Free Press.

Geertz, C. (1973). *The Interpretation of Cultures*. New York: Basic Books.

George, Alexander L. & Bennett, Andrew (2005). *Case Studies and Theory Development in the Social Sciences*. Cambridge, MA: MIT Press.

Gilmore, Audrey, Carson, David & Perry, Chad (2006). Academic publishing. *European Business Review*, 18 (6), 468–478.

Gladwell, Malcolm (2000). *The Tipping Point*. London: Abacus.

Glaser, Barney G. (1972). *Experts Versus Laymen: A study of the patsy and the subcontractor*. Mill Valley, CA: Sociology Press.

Glaser, Barney G. (1978). *Theoretical Sensitivity: Advances in the methodology of grounded theory*. Mill Valley, CA: Sociology Press.

Glaser, Barney G. (1992). *Basics of Grounded Theory*. Mill Valley, CA: Sociology Press.

Glaser, Barney G. (2001) *The Grounded Theory Perspective: Conceptualization contrasted with description*. Mill Valley, CA: Sociology Press.

Glaser, Barney G., with the assistance of Judith Holton (2004). Remodeling grounded theory. *Forum Qulitative Socialforschhung/Forum Qualitative Research*, 5(2). Available at www.qualitative-research.net/index.php/fqs/article/view/607/1315

Glaser, Barney G. (2005). The roots of grounded theory. Keynote presentation given at the 3rd International Qualitative Research Convention, Johor Bahru, Malaysia, 23 August.

Glaser, Barney G. (2008). *Doing Quantitative Grounded Theory*. Mill Valley, CA: Sociology Press.

Glaser, Barney G. & Strauss, Anselm L. (1967). *The Discovery of Grounded Theory*. Chicago, IL: Aldine.

Glasser, William (1965). *Reality Therapy*. New York: Harper & Row.

Gobo, Giampietro & Mauceri, Sergio (2014). *Constructing Survey Data*. London: Sage.

Goldacre, Ben (2009). *Bad Science*. London: Harper Perennial.

Granovetter, Mark S. (1973). The strength of weak ties. *American Journal of Sociology*, 78, 3–30.

Granovetter, Mark S. (1978). Threshold models of collective behavior. *American Journal of Sociology*, 83, 1420–1443.

Granovetter, Mark S. (1985). Economic action and social structure: The problem of embeddedness. *American Journal of Sociology*, 91, 481–510.

Greenwood, Davydd J. & Levin, Morten (2005). Reform of the social sciences and of universities through action research. In Norman K. Denzin and Yvonna S. Lincoln (eds), *The Sage Handbook of Qualitative Research*. Thousand Oaks, CA: Sage.

Grönroos, Christian (1979). *Marknadsföring av tjänster (Marketing of services)*. With summary in English. Stockholm, Sweden and Helsinki, Finland: Akademilitteratur, Marknadstekniskt Centrum and Hanken.

Gross, Matthias (2012). 'Objective culture' and the development of nonknowledge: Georg Simmel and the reverse side of knowing. *Cultural Sociology*, 6 (4), 422–437.

Guba, Egon G. and Lincoln, Yvonna S. (1994). Competing paradigms in qualitative research. In Norman K. Denzin & Yvonna S. Lincoln (eds), *The Sage Handbook of Qualitative Research*. Thousand Oaks, CA: Sage.

Guba, Egon G. and Lincoln, Yvonna S. (2005). Paradigmatic controversies, contradictions, and emerging confluences. In Norman K. Denzin & Yvonna S. Lincoln (eds), *The Sage Handbook of Qualitative Research*. Thousand Oaks, CA: Sage (3rd edn).

Gummerus, Johanna & von Koskull, Catharina (eds) (2015). *The Nordic School: Service marketing and management for the future*. Helsinki, Finland: Hanken School of Economics. E-book available at www.hanken.fi/en/about-hanken/organisation/departments-and-subjects/department-marketing/cers/nordic-school-book

Gummesson, Evert (1978). Toward a theory of professional service marketing. *Industrial Marketing Management*, 7, 89–95.

Gummesson, Evert (1982). *Att använda företags- och marknadstrategiska beslutsmodeller* (Using corporate and marketing strategy decision models). Stockholm, Sweden: Marketing Technology Center.

Gummesson, Evert (1987). Lip service: A neglected area in services marketing. *The Journal of Services Marketing*, 1 (1), 19–23.

Gummesson, Evert (2000a). *Qualitative Methods in Management Research*. Thousand Oaks, CA: Sage (2nd edn).

Gummesson, Evert (2000b). Sustainable service strategies: Lessons from health care. In Edvardsson, Bo, Brown, Stephen W., Johnston, Robert & Scheuing, Eberhard E. (eds), *Service Quality in the New Economy: Interdisciplinary and international dimensions*. Proceedings from QUIS7. New York: ISQA.

Gummesson, Evert (2001). Are current research approaches in marketing leading us astray? *Marketing Theory*, 1 (1), 27–48.

Gummesson, Evert (2002a). Relationship marketing and the new economy: It's time for deprogramming. *Journal of Services Marketing*, 16 (7), 585–589.

Gummesson, Evert (2002b). Practical value of adequate marketing management theory. *European Journal of Marketing*, 36 (3), 325–349.

Gummesson, Evert (2003). All research is interpretive! *Journal of Business and Industrial Marketing*, 18 (6/7), 482–492.

Gummesson, Evert (2004a). Return on relationships (ROR): The value of relationship marketing and CRM in business-to-business contexts. *Journal of Business & Industrial Marketing*, 19 (2), 136–148.

Gummesson, Evert (2004b). *Many-to-many Marketing*. Malmö, Sweden: Liber.

Gummesson. Evert (2005). Qualitative research in marketing: Road-map for a wilderness of complexity and unpredictability. *European Journal of Marketing*, 39 (3/4), 309–327.

Gummesson, Evert (2006). Qualitative research in management: Addressing complexity, context and persona. *Management Decision*, 44 (2), 167–179.

Gummesson, Evert (2007). Case study research and network theory: Birds of a feather. *Qualitative Research in Organizations and Management*, 2 (3), 226–248.

Gummesson, Evert (2012). The three service marketing paradigms: Which one are you guided by? *Mercati e Competitività*, 1, 5-13.

Gummesson, Evert (2017). *Total Relationship Marketing Renewed*. Abingdon: Routledge (4th edn).

Gummesson, Evert & Grönroos, Christian (2012). The emergence of the new service marketing: Nordic School perspectives. *Journal of Service Management*, 23 (4), 479–497.

Gummesson, Evert & Polese, Francesco (2009). B2B is not an island! *The Journal of Business & Industrial Marketing*, 24 (5–6), 337–350.

Gummesson, Evert, Kuusela, Hannu & Närvänen, Elina (2014). Reinventing marketing strategy by recasting supplier/customer roles. *Journal of Service Management*, 25 (2), 228–240.

Gustavsson, Bengt (2003). The nature and understanding of organization from a Samhita perspective. In Dasgupta, Aruna (ed.), *Human Values of Indian Management: A journey from practice to theory*. Dehli: Macmillan.

Guthrie, Wendy & Lowe, Andy (2012). Getting through the PhD process using GT: A supervisor-researcher perspective. In Vivian B. Martin & Astrid Gynnild (eds), *Grounded Theory: The philosophy, method, and work of Barney Glaser*. Boca Raton, FL: BrownWalker Press.

Haas Edersheim, Elizabeth (2007). *The Definitive Drucker*. New York: McGraw-Hill.

Hagelin, John (1998). *Perfect Government*. Fairfield, IO: Maharishi University of Management Press.

Häggström, Olle (2016). *Here Be Dragons: Science, technology and the future of humanity*. Oxford: Oxford University Press.

Håkansson, Håkan, Ford, David, Gadde, Lars-Erik, Snehota, Ivan & Waluszewski, Alexandra (2009). *Business in Networks*. Chichester: Wiley.

Hamilton, Carl (2000). *Absolut: Biography of a bottle*. New York: Texere.

Hastings, Gerard (2013). *The Marketing Matrix*. Abingdon: Routledge.

Hawking, Stephen (1996). *A Brief History of Time*. London: Bantam Books (2nd edn).

Hawking, Stephen (2013). *My Brief History*. New York: Bantam Books.

Hawking, Stephen & Mlodinow, Leonard (2010). *The Grand Design*. London: Bantam Books.

Heller, Robert (1984). *The Supermanagers: Managing for success, the movers and the doers, the reasons why*. New York: E.P. Dutton.

Henderson, Bill & Bernard, André (eds) (1998). *Rotten Reviews and Rejections*. Wainscott, NY: Pushcart Press.

Heskett, James & Hallowell, Roger (2013). Shouldice Hospital Limited. *Harvard Business School Supplement*, 913-405 (February).

Hindo, Brian (2007). At 3M, a struggle between efficiency and creativity. *Business Week*, 11 June, 8–12.

Holbrook, Morris B. (2003). Adventures in complexity: An essay on dynamic open complex adaptive systems, butterfly effects, self-organizing order, coevolution, the ecological perspective, fitness landscapes, market spaces, emergent beauty at the edge of chaos, and all that jazz. *Academy of Marketing Science Review*, 6. Available at www.amsreview.org/articles/holbrook06-2003.pdf

Holton, Judith H. & Walsh, Isabelle (2017). *Classic Grounded Theory: Applications with qualitative and quantitative data*. London: Sage.

Hunt Shelby & Madhavaram, Streedhar (2012). Managerial action and resource-advantage theory: Conceptual frameworks emanating from positive theory of competition. *Journal of Business & Industrial Marketing*, 27 (7), 582–591.

Hunt, Shelby D. & Morgan, Robert M. (1997). Resource-advantage theory: A snake swallowing its tail or a general theory of competition? *Journal of Marketing*, 61, 74–82.

Johnson, Phil, Buering, Anna, Cassell, Catherine & Symon, Gillian (2007). Defining qualitative management research: An empirical investigation. *Qualitative Research in Organizations and Management*, 2 (1), 23–42.

Judge, Timothy A., Cable, Daniel M., Colbert, Amy E. & Rynes, Sara L. (2007). What causes a management article to be cited: Article, author or journal? *The Academy of Management Journal*, 50 (3), 491–508.

Kahneman, Daniel (2011). *Thinking, Fast and Slow*. London: Penguin Books.

Kaldor, Nicholas (1957). A model of economic growth. *The Economic Journal*, 67 (268), 591–624.

Karabell, Zachary (2014). *The Leading Indicators: A short history of the numbers that rule our world*. New York: Simon & Schuster.

Kotler, Philip (2015). *Confronting Capitalism*. New York: Amacom.

Kotler, Philip (2016). Why behavioral economics is really marketing science. *Evonomics*, 1-3.

Kozintets, Robert V. (2010). *Netnography: Doing ethnographic research online*. London: Sage.

Kriz, Anton, Gummesson, Evert & Quazi, Ali (2014). Methodology meets culture: Guanxi-oriented research in China. *International Journal of Cross Cultural Management*, 14 (1), 27–46.

Krueger, Richard A. (2009). *Focus Groups: A practical guide for applied research*. Newbury Park, CA: Sage.

Krugman, Paul (2012). *End this Depression Now!* New York: W.W. Norton.

Kuhn, Thomas (1962/1970). *The Structure of Scientific Revolutions*. Chicago, IL: University of Chicago (2nd edn).

Lasagna, Louis (1964). A discussion on the need for a new declaration of medical ethics. *The New York Times*, 28 June.

Lawrence, Peter (2011). The heart of research is sick. *Lab Times*, 2, 24–31.

Lee, B. (2006). The qualitative inquiry in the business and management field: Symposium at the Second International Congress of Qualitative Inquiry. *Qualitative Research in Organization and Management*, 1 (2), 141–145.

Lee, Nick & Lings, Ian (2008). *Doing Business Research*. London: Sage.

Lindblom, Charles E. (1959). The science of 'muddling through'. *Public Administration Review*, 19 (2), 79–88.

Lindblom, Charles E. (1979). Still muddling, not yet through. *Public Administration Review*, 39, 517–526.

Lindstrom, Martin (2004). Branding is no longer child's play. *Journal of Consumer Marketing*, 21 (3), 175–182.

Lindstrom, Martin (2008). *Buyology*. New York: Crown Business.

Lindstrom, Martin (2011). *Brandwashed*. New York: Crown Business.

Lindstrom, Martin (2016). *Small Data: The tiny clues that uncover huge trends*. New York: St. Martin's Press.

Linestone, H.A. & Zhu, Z. (2000). Towards synergy in multiperspective management: An American-Chinese case. *Human Systems Management*, 19, 25–37.

Löbler, Helge (2013). Service-dominant networks: An evolution from the service-dominant logic perspective. *Journal of Service Management*, 24 (4), 420–434.

Lovelock, Christopher H. & Gummesson, E. (2004). Whither services marketing? *Journal of Service Research*, 7 (1), 20–41.

Lowe, Andy (1995). The basic social processes of entrepreneurial innovation. *International Journal of Entrepreneurial Behavior & Research*, 1 (2), 54–76.

Lund, Ragnar (2011). *Leveraging Cooperative Strategy: Cases of sports and arts sponsorship*. Stockholm, Sweden: Stockholm University School of Business.

Lusch, Robert F. & Vargo, Stephen L. (2014). *Service-dominant Logic*. Cambridge: Cambridge University Press.

McLuhan, Marshall (1964). *Understanding Media: The extensions of man*. New York: Mentor.

McLuhan, Marshall & Fiore, Quentin (1967). *The Medium Is the Massage: An inventroy of effects*. London: Penguin.

Machiavelli, Nicolo (1513/2012). *The Prince*. Available at www.gutenberg.org/ebooks/1232

MacNeil, Karen (2001). *The Wine Bible*. New York: Workman Publishing.

Maglio, Paul P. (2011). Modeling complex service systems. *Service Science*, 3, 4, i–ii.

Maglio, Paul P. & Spohrer, James C. (2008). Fundamentals of Service Science. *Journal of the Academy of Marketing Science*, 36 (1), 8–20.

Marcus, Gary & Davis, Ernest (2014). Eight (No, nine!) problems with big data. *The New York Times*, 7 April, p. 23.

Martin, Vivian B. & Gynnild, Astrid (eds) (2012). *Grounded Theory: The philosophy, method, and work of Barney Glaser*. Boca Raton, FL: BrownWalker Press.

Mason, Jennifer (1994). Linking qualitative and quantitative data analysis. In Alan Bryman and Robert G. Burgess (eds), *Analyzing Qualitative Data*. London: Routledge.

Mayer-Schönberger, Viktor & Cukier, Kenneth (2013). *Big Data: A revolution that will transform how we live, work and think*. New York: Houghton Mifflin Harcourt.

Meehl, Paul (1986). Causes and effects of my disturbing little book. *Journal of Personality Assessment*, 50, 370–375.

Mele, Cristina & Polese, Francesco (2011). Key dimensions of service systems in value-creating networks. In Haluk Demirkan, James C. Spohrer & Vikas Krishna (eds), *The Science of Service Systems*. New York: Springer.

Merton, Robert Sr. (1979). *The Sociology of Science: Theoretical and empirical investigations*. Chicago, IL: University of Chicago Press.

Miles, Matthew B., Huberman, Michael A. & Saldana, Johnny M. (2013). *Qualitative Data Analysis*. Newbury Park, CA: Sage.

Mintzberg, Henry (1979). *The Structuring of Organizations*. Englewood Cliffs, NJ: Prentice Hall.

Mintzberg, Henry (1983). *Structures in Five*. Englewood Cliffs, NJ: Prentice Hall.

Mintzberg, Henry (2007). *Tracking Strategies … toward a General Theory*. Oxford: Oxford University Press.

Moss Kanter, Rosabeth (1983). *The Change Masters*. New York: Simon & Schuster.

Moutinho, Luiz & Hutcheson, Graeme (eds) (2011). *The Sage Dictionary of Quantitative Management Research*. London: Sage.

Muñiz Martínez, Norberto (2012). City marketing and place branding: A critical review of practice and academic research. *Journal of Town & City Management*, 2 (4), 369–394.

Naisbitt, John (1982). *Megatrends*. New York: Warner Books.

Naisbitt, John (1999). *High Tech/High Touch*. London: Nicholas Brealey.

Närvänen, Elina, Gummesson, Evert & Kuusela, Hannu (2014). The collective consumption network. *Managing Service Quality*, 24 (6), 545–564.

Nonaka, Ikujiro & Takeuchi, Hirotaka (1995). *The Knowledge Creating Company*. New York: Oxford University Press.

Ödman, Per-Johan (1985). Hermeneutics in research practice. In Torsten Husén and Neville T. Postlethwaite (eds), *The International Encyclopedia of Education*. Oxford: Pergamon.

Ödman, Per-Johan (2007). Hermeneutics. In Bengt Gustavsson (ed.), *The Principles of Knowledge Creation Methods*. Cheltenham: Edward Elgar.

Olsen, Morten (1992). *Kvalitet i banktjänster* (Quality of bank services). With summary in English. Stockholm/Karlstad: Stockholm University and the Service Research Center (CTF).

Ortmark, Åke (1985). *Maktens människor* (The people of power). Malmö, Sweden: Wahlström & Widstrand.

Pacanowsky, Michael (1978). Salt Passage research: The state of the art. *Change*, 10, 8, 41–43; reprinted under the pseudonym M. Pencil (2006) in the *Journal of Communication*, 26, 4, 31–36.

Packer, Martin (2011). *The Science of Qualitative Research*. New York: Cambridge University Press.

Parkinson, C. Northcote (1958). *Parkinson's Law: The pursuit of progress*. London: John Murray.

Patton, Michael Quinn (1990). *Qualitative Evaluation and Research Methods*. Newbury Park, CA: Sage (2nd edn).

Payne, Adrian & Frow, Pennie (2013). *Strategic Customer Management*. Cambridge: Cambridge University Press.

Payne, Adrian & Frow, Pennie (2014). Deconstructing the value proposition of an innovation exemplar. *European Journal of Marketing*, 48 (1–2), 237–270.

Pendlebury, David A. (2015). *White Paper: Using bibliometrics in evaluating research.* Philadelphia, PA: Thomson Reuters.

Perkins, John (2004). *Confessions of an Economic Hit Man.* San Francisco, CA: Berrett-Koehler.

Perry, Chad (ed.) (2004). Action research in marketing. Special issue of the *European Journal of Marketing,* 38 (3/4).

Peters, Tom & Waterman, Robert J., Jr. (1982). *In Search of Excellence.* New York: HarperBusiness.

Pfeffer, Jeffrey & Sutton, Robert I. (2006). *Hard Facts, Dangerous Half-truths and Total Non-sense.* Cambridge, MA: Harvard Business Review Press.

Polanyi, Michael (1966). *The Tacit Dimension.* Chicago, IL: University of Chicago Press.

Pritchard, Alan (1969). Statistical bibliography or bibliometrics? *Journal of Documentation,* 25 (4), 348–349.

Reindhart, Andy (1998). *Steve Jobs on Apple's Resurgence: Not a one-man show.* Bloomberg Businessweek, 12 May.

Remenyi, Dan, Williams, Brian, Money, Arthur & Swartz, Ethné (1998). *Doing Research in Business and Management.* London: Sage.

Richards, Lyn & Richards, Tom (1994). From filing cabinet to computer. In Alan Bryman & Robert G. Burgess (eds), *Analyzing Qualitative Data.* London: Routledge, pp. 146–172.

Russell, Bertrand (1914/1993). *Our knowledge of the External World.* New York: Routledge.

Saren, Michael & Pels, Jacqueline (2008). A comment on paradox and middle-range theory: Universality, synthesis and supplement. *Journal of Business & Industrial Marketing,* 23 (2), 105–107.

Särndal, Carl-Erik (2012). Tore Dalenius insatser och inflytande i surveyvetenskap och praktik (The contributions and influence of Tore Dalenius in survey science and practice). *2012 års Dalenius-föredrag,* Surveyföreningens årsmöte (in Swedish).

Saunders, Mark (1999). Quantitative methods in marketing. In Baker, Michael J. (ed.), *The IEBM Encyclopedia of Marketing.* London: Thomson.

Saunders, Mark, Lewis, Philip & Thornhill, Adrian (2012). *Research Methods for Business Students.* Harlow: Pearson (6th edn).

Saviano, Roberto (2006). *Gomorrah.* New York: Picador.

Saviano, Roberto (2015). *ZeroZeroZero.* New York: Penguin Random House.

Schildt, Göran (1995). *Lånade vingar (Borrowed wings).* Helsinki, Finland: Söderström.

Schön, Donald (1984). *The Reflective Practitioner.* New York: Basic Books.

Schumacher, E.F. (1973). *Small Is Beautiful: A study of economics as if people mattered.* London: Blond & Briggs.

Schumpeter, Joseph A. (1950). *Capitalism, Socialism and Democracy.* New York: Harper & Row (4th edn).

Scott, John & Carrington, Peter J. (2011). *The Sage Handbook of Social Network Analysis.* London: Sage.

Seale, Clive (1999). Quality in qualitative research. *Qualitative Inquiry,* 5 (4), 465–478.

Senge, Peter M. (1990). *The Fifth Discipline.* New York: Doubleday Currency.

Shah, Shvetank, Horne, Andrew & Capellá, Jaime (2012). Good data won't guarantee good decisions. *Harvard Business Review,* 90 (4), 23–25.

Simmons, Odis (1993). The milkman and his customer: A cultivated relationship. In Barney G. Glaser (ed.), *Examples of Grounded Theory: A reader.* Mill Valley, CA: Sociology Press.

Simon, Herbert (1957). A behavioral model of rational choice. In *Models of Man, Social and Rational: Mathematical essays on rational human behavior in a social setting*. New York: Wiley.

Sokal, Alan (1996). Transgressing the boundaries: Towards a transformative hermeneutics of quantum gravity. *Social Text*, 'Science Wars' issue, 46/47, 217–252.

Sörman-Nilsson, Anders (2013). *Digilogue*. Milton, Qld, Australia: Wiley.

Staal, P.C. & Ligtenberg, G. (2007). *Assessment of established medical science and medical practice*. College voor Zorgversekering, Diemen, the Netherlands (www.cvz.nl).

Stacey, Ralph D. (2009). *Complexity and Organizational Reality*. Abingdon: Routledge (2nd edn).

Stacey, Ralph D. (2010). *Strategic Management and Organisational Dynamics: The challenge of complexity*. London: Financial Times/Prentice Hall (5th edn).

Stacey, Ralph D., Griffin, Douglas & Shaw, Patricia (2002). Complexity and management. *Journal of Macromarketing*, 22 (December), 198–201.

Stebbing, L. Susan (1939/1961). *Thinking to Some Purpose*. Harmondsworth: Penguin Books.

Sternberg, Robert J. (1985). *Beyond IQ: A triarchic theory of human intelligence*. New York: Cambridge University Press.

Stewart, Matthew (2009). *The management Myth: Debunking modern business philosophy*. New York: W.W. Norton.

Strauss, Anselm & Corbin, Juliet (1991). *Basics of Qualitative Research*. Thousand Oaks, CA: Sage.

Tadajewski, Mark (2016). Academic labour, journal ranking lists and the politics of knowledge production in marketing. *Journal of Marketing Management*, 32 (1–2), 1–18.

Taleb, Nassim Nicholas (2007). *The Black Swan*. London: Penguin Books.

Tapp, Alan (2005). Why practitioners don't read our articles and what we should do about it. *The Marketing Review*, 5 (1), 3–12.

Tarkovsky, Andrey (1986). *Sculpting in Time: Reflections of the cinema*. London: The Bodley Head.

Taylor, Frederick W. (1911). *The Principles of Scientific Management*. New York: Harper & Brothers.

Tegmark, Max (2014). *Our Mathematical Universe: My quest for the ultimate nature of reality*. London: Allen Lane/Penguin Books.

Thomas, Eileen & Magilvy, Joan K. (2011). Qualitative rigor or research validity in qualitative research. *Journal for Specialists in Pediatric Nursing*, 16 (2), 151-155.

Timmermans, Stefan & Berg, Marc (2003). *The Gold Standard: The challenge of evidence-based medicine and standardization in health care*. Philadelphia, PA: Temple University Press.

Van Fleet, D.D., McWilliams, A. & Siegel, D.S. (2000). A theoretical and empirical analysis of journal ratings: The case of formal lists. *Journal of Management*, 26, 839–861.

Van Maanen, John (2000). Foreword, in Gummesson, Evert, *Qualitative Methods in Management Research*. Thousand Oaks, CA: Sage (2nd edn).

Van Maanen, John (2011). *Tales of the Field: On writing ethnography*. Chicago, IL: University of Chicago Press (2nd edn).

Vargo, Stephen L. & Lusch, Robert F. (2008a). Service-dominant logic: Continuing the evolution. *Journal of the Academy of Marketing Science*, 36 (1), 1–10.

Vargo, Stephen L. & Lusch, Robert F. (2008b). Why service? *Journal of the Academy of Marketing Science*, 36 (1), 25–38.

Vásquez, Consuelo, Brummans, Boris H.J.M. & Groleau, Carole (2012). Notes from the field on organizational shadowing as framing. *Qualitative Research in Organizations and Management*, 7 (2), 144–165.

Vigen, Tyler (2014). *Spurious Correlations*. New York: Hachette Books.

von Wright, Georg Henrik (1971). *Explanation and Understanding*. London: Routledge & Kegan Paul.

Waddock, S.A. & Spangler, E. (2000). Action learning in leadership for change. In Sherman, F. & Torbert, W. (eds), *Transforming Social Inquiry, Transforming Social Action: New paradigms for crossing the theory/practice divide in universities and communities*. Boston, MA: Kluwer.

Wallraff, Günter (1985). *Ganz unten* (At the very bottom). Cologne, Germany: Verlag Kiepenheuer & Witsch.

Walton, John (1992). What is a case? In Ragin, Charles C. & Becker, Howard S. (eds), *Exploring the Foundations of Social Inquiry*. New York: Cambridge University Press.

Weiner-Levy, Naomi & Popper-Giveon, Ariela (2013). The absent, the hidden and the obscured: Reflections on 'dark matter' in qualitative research. *Quality & Quantity*, 47 (4), 2177–2190.

Wolcott, Harry F. (1994). *Transforming Qualitative Data: Description, analysis and interpretation*. Thousand Oaks, CA: Sage.

Womack, James P., Jones, Daniel T. & Roos, Daniel (1990). *The Machine that Changed the World*. New York: Rawson.

Woodside, Arch G. (2010). *Case Study Research: Theory, methods and practice*. Bingley, UK: Emerald.

Yin, Robert K. (2014). *Case Study Research: Design and methods*. Thousand Oaks, CA: Sage (5th edn).

Zetterberg, Hans L. (2013). *The Pursuit of Knowledge: The many-splendoured society*, 4. Charleston, SC: CreateSpace.

Zuckerman, Myron, Silberman, Jordan & Hall, Judith A. (2013). The relation between intelligence and religiosity: A meta-analysis and some proposed explanations. *Personality and Social Psychology Review*, 17 (4), 325–354.

INDEX